SPORT AND PE

a complete guide to

AS LEVEL STUDY

KEVIN WESSON • NESTA WIGGINS

GRAHAM THOMPSON • SUE HARTIGAN

Hodder & Stoughton

A MEMBER OF THE HODDER HEADLINE GROUP

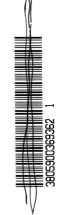

A catalogue record for this title is available from The British Library

ISBN 0 340 804 947

First published 2002
Impression number   10   9   8   7   6   5   4   3   2   1
Year   2005   2004   2003   2002

Cover photographs courtesy of Action Plus

Page layout by Hardlines, Charlbury, Oxford.
Printed in Great Britain for Hodder & Stoughton Educational, a division of Hodder Headline Plc, 338 Euston Road, London NW1 by The Bath Press, Bath.

Contents

Acknowledgements

The au ors would lik to thank their families for all their support during the writing of this book. Nesta Wiggins would also like to thank Gwyneth Goodchild, Librarian of the Sixth Form College Colchester, for her assistance in compiling references for this book.

The publishers would like to thank the following picture libraries and photographers for permission to reproduce their images:

Action Images

    10.10

Action Plus

Steve Bardens:	7.17
Ann Bolton:	20.10
Richard Francis:	5.1
Tony Henshaw:	15.2
Glen Kirk:	5.2, 5.5, 6.5, 7.7, 9.10, 13.3, 15.3, 18.9, 20.4, 20.5, 20.7
Peter Tarry:	15.5

Allsport

Clive Brunskill:	9.8
David Cannon:	16.8

James Davis Travel Photography

    10.7, 10.8

Empics

Jon Buckle:	13.4
Tony Marshall:	P.15, 13.1
Mike Egerton:	13.2, 16.4
Ross Setford:	14.1
Simpson:	14.4

Eye Ubiquitous

    P.91, 10.9, 10.11

BJ Fearnley

    10.6

PA Photos

    15.5

Introduction

When examining the performer in action, an understanding of anatomical and physiological concepts within a sporting context is required. For example, a distance run involves the interaction and coordination of many of the body's systems to enable successful performance; the cardiovascular and respiratory systems work together as a delivery service, delivering oxygen and nutrients to fuel the working muscles, while simultaneously ridding the body of any undesired waste products of metabolism such as carbon dioxide. Meanwhile the skeletal and muscular systems are interacting; the bones acting as levers to provide movement, while the muscles (the engines of movement) provide the power to drive the levers. The nervous and hormonal systems direct and control the body's actions to enhance performance. The body is therefore a complex machine with the components or systems working together to enable effective participation in sport.

Training however, can develop the body's system to improve and enhance performance.

What is exercise physiology?

Exercise or sports physiology (to ease confusion these terms have been used interchangeably in this book) is a branch of the much broader area of anatomy and physiology:

- Anatomy is the study of the body's **structure**:
- Physiology seeks to discover how the body works and **functions**.

Sports physiology then puts these findings into a sporting context and specifically examines how the body adapts and develops in response to exercise.

Training has a significant part to play in the body's development and as such is vital to the study of sports physiology. Training implications have therefore been highlighted throughout this section – do look out for them!

The terminology used when studying anatomy and physiology can sometimes be a little complex, particularly if you are new to the subject. The following section may ease your understanding, by explaining some of the terms that are regularly featured throughout the text.

Terms of direction

When describing regions of the body, positions relative to the 'anatomical position' are used. The anatomical position refers to a person standing upright, facing forwards, with arms positioned downwards and the palms of the hand facing forwards.

The table below provides a list of common terms of direction central to the study of anatomy and physiology. Relate these to the position of parts of your body.

superior	a structure higher or closer to the head than another
inferior	a structure lower or closer to the foot than another
medial	towards the midline of the body
lateral	away from the midline of the body
anterior/ventral	towards the front of the body
posterior/dorsal	towards the back of the body
superficial	towards the surface of the body
deep	internal or below the surface of the body
proximal	a structure or body part closer to the point of attachment than another
distal	a structure or body part further away from the point of attachment than another
left	towards the left side of the body
right	towards the right side of the body

Fig. A

Using sticky labels place the following labels on the appropriate region of a partner's body:

The *lateral* aspect of the knee joint.
The *medial* aspect of the ankle joint.
The *proximal* region of the index finger.
The *distal* region of the big toe.
The *posterior* aspect of the upper leg.
The *anterior* aspect of the lower leg.
The *most* superior point of the body.
The *most* inferior point of the body.

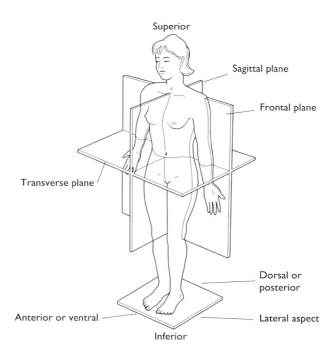

Fig. B BODY PLANES

Planes of the body

In order to explain the body's movements, it is often useful to view the body as having a series of imaginary lines running through it. These are known as the **planes of movement** or the planes section. The imaginary lines divide the body up in three ways (see fig B). Firstly, the median or sagittal plane splits the body vertically into the left and right sides, the horizontal or transverse plane divides the body into superior and inferior sections and runs horizontally, while the frontal or coronal plane runs vertically and divides the body into anterior and posterior sections.

The body or body parts can move in these planes and a knowledge of them will certainly be of benefit to the coach and athlete. In gymnastics, for example, movement in all planes may occur in the performance of full twisting somersaults. What other sporting situations can you think of where a knowledge of planes of movement may be of use? The diagram above summarises the movement patterns which occur in each of the body's planes.

For further investigation into this, and other factors concerning the body's movement, refer to Chapter 11.

Anatomical Language

Sometimes it is possible to work out an anatomical term through basic understanding of more general terms. Words are often prefixed or suffixed to give greater meaning. For example, any word suffixed by '**itis**' means inflammation; any word prefixed by '**arthr**' relates to a joint. Therefore the condition '**arthritis**' is an inflammation of the joints. The table on p 4 gives common prefixes and suffixes together with their meanings.

PREFIX/SUFFIX	DEFINITION	PREFIX/SUFFIX	DEFINITION
a-	without	-itis	inflammation
ab-	away from	lip-	fat
ad-	towards	-lysis	breaking up
-algia	pain	macro-	large
an-	without	mono-	one
arthr-	joint	-morph	shape/form
brady-	slow	myo-	muscle
cardio-	heart	neuro-	nerve
cerebro-	brain	osteo-	bone
chondr-	cartilage	peri-	surrounding
-cyte	cell	pneumo-	air/gas/lungs
derm-	skin	poly-	many
ergo-	work	somato-	body
glyco-	sugar	syn-	together
haem-	blood	tachy-	fast
hepato-	liver	therm-	heat
hypo-	deficient	-trophy	nourishment
hyper-	excessive	-vascular	blood vessel

Using this table, define the following terms:

- **bradycardia**
- **osteocyte**
- **pericardium**
- **glycolysis**
- **hepatitis**
- **cardiac hypertrophy**
- **periosteum**
- **myofilament**
- **somatotype**
- **cardiovascular**

chapter 1

Skeletal Considerations

This chapter examines the structure and function of the skeletal system. The principal focus is on the functional aspects of the system, with particular reference to human movement during physical activity.

The chapter will take the student through an examination of the labelling and classification of **bones** and the structure of skeletal tissues, including the identification of bony landmarks.

Central to the study of movement is **arthrology** – the study of joints. This stage of the chapter will classify joints, giving practical examples from sporting action. A discussion of the types of movement occurring at the articulations follows, which forges specific links with the kinesiology unit of the muscular system (Chapter 2).

Finally, there is a discussion of the beneficial effects of exercise and training on the skeletal system, with reference made to other chapters of the book.

The skeletal system

The 206 bones that make up the human skeleton are specifically designed to provide several basic functions, which are essential for participation in physical activity. In conjunction with other components of the skeletal system (including the periosteum, ligaments and joints), the skeleton can perform the following functions.

Functions

Support

The skeleton provides a rigid framework to the body, giving it shape and providing suitable sites for attachment of skeletal muscle.

Protection

The skeleton provides protection for the internal organs. For example: the vertebral column protects the spinal cord; the cranium protects the brain; and the rib cage principally protects the heart and lungs.

Movement

The bones of the skeleton provide a large surface area for the attachment of muscles – the engines of movement. The long bones in particular provide a system of levers against which the muscles can pull.

Blood production

Within the bones, bone marrow produces both red and white blood cells. Red blood cells are generally produced at the ends of long bones such as the humerus (arm) and the femur (thigh), and in some flat bones such as the pelvis and sternum (breastbone). White blood cells are usually produced in the shafts of long bones.

Mineral storage

The bones of the skeleton have storage capabilities for vital minerals such as calcium and phosphorus, which can be distributed to other parts of the body when required.

The structure of the skeleton

The bones of the skeleton can be divided into two distinct categories; the axial and the appendicular skeleton:

- the **axial** skeleton provides the main area of support for the body, and includes the cranium (skull), the vertebral column (spine) and the rib cage.
- the **appendicular** skeleton consists of the appendages or the bones of the limbs, together with the girdles that join onto the axial skeleton.

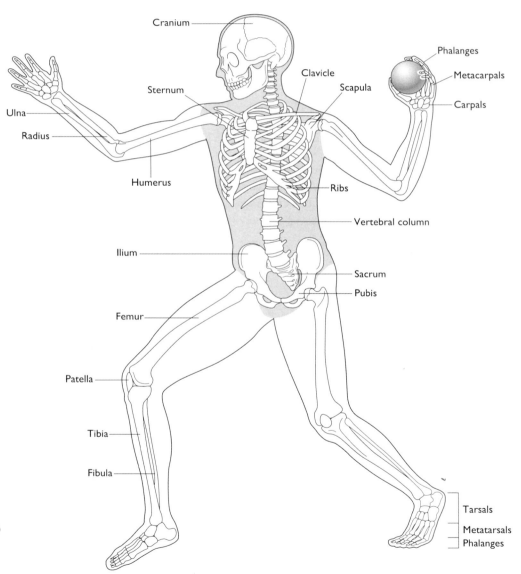

Fig. 1.1 BONES OF THE AXIAL AND
APPENDICULAR SKELETON
Source: Davis, Kimmet and Auty (1986)

 **Using sticky labels, label the bones on a partner's body.**

List the bones in the axial and appendicular skeletons in fig 1.1.

The structure of the vertebral column

The vertebral column consists of 33 bones; 24 bones are individual and unfused, while the remaining nine are fused together. There are five principal areas of the vertebral column.

The cervical vertebrae (7 unfused bones)

The cervical vertebrae are essentially the bones of the neck, and support the weight of the head by enabling muscle attachment through the transverse and spinous processes. The top two vertebrae, the atlas and the axis (fig 1.2(c)), enable the head to move up and down and side to side respectively.

The thoracic vertebrae (12 unfused bones)

The 12 thoracic vertebrae allow the attachment of the ribs via the transverse processes. These bones, together with the ribs, form the rib cage which protects the heart and lungs.

The lumbar vertebrae (5 unfused bones)

The 5 lumbar vertebrae are the largest of all the individual vertebrae. Their large centrum or body offers a great deal of weight-bearing capacity, while their large processes secure the attachment of the muscles. This muscle attachment, together with the intervertebral discs of cartilage, forms cartilaginous joints, which enable flexion and extension (forward and backward movement) and lateral flexion (side to side movement) of the trunk.

The sacral vertebrae (5 fused bones)

The 5 fused sacral vertebrae form the sacrum which fuses to the pelvis at the sacroiliac joint. The sacrum and the pelvis bear and distribute the weight of the upper body.

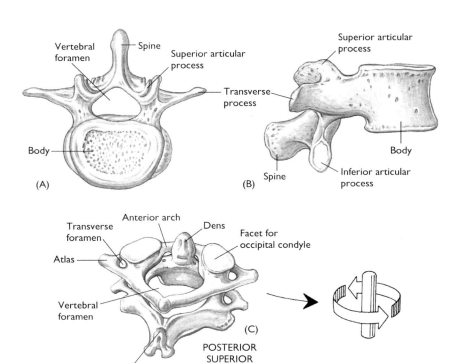

Fig. 1.2 STRUCTURE OF A TYPICAL VERTEBRA (A) THIRD LUMBAR VERTEBRA VIEWED FROM ABOVE (B) THIRD LUMBAR VERTEBRA VIEWED FROM THE SIDE (C) THE AXIS AND ATLAS

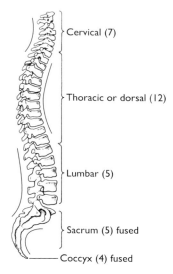

Fig. 1.3 Structure of the vertebral column

The coccyx (4 fused bones)

The coccyx forms the very base of the vertebral column, and acts as a process for muscle attachment.

Each vertebra consists of two parts:

1 a vertebral body (centrum)
2 a neural arch.

The size of each vertebral body increases from the cervical vertebrae to the lumbar vertebrae, in order to support the weight of the body. The neural arch enables muscles to attach via the transverse and the spinous processes, while the articular processes link to adjacent vertebrae.

In between each vertebra exists a disc of fibro-cartilage – a tough, resilient tissue which helps to absorb shock and allows a small amount of movement between the vertebral bodies. The vertebral column also exhibits four curves as shown in fig 1.3. The cervical and lumbar curves are **convex** in shape; the thoracic and sacral curves are **concave**. These curves of the vertebral column increase the strength of the structure as well as absorbing shock from jumping or walking, and thus reducing the risk of injury.

State how the structure of each region of the vertebral column is suited to its function, taking examples from a range of sporting activities.

Structure of the rib cage

The rib cage is composed of 12 pairs of ribs which form the walls of the thoracic cavity:

- The first seven pairs of ribs attach directly onto the front of the sternum via costal cartilage.
- The next three pairs are attached to the seventh rib, also via costal cartilages. These are known as 'false' ribs.
- The remaining two pairs of ribs do not attach to anything other than the thoracic vertebrae, and are called 'floating' ribs.

The rib cage offers protection to vital organs such as the heart and lungs, and also enables the lungs to inflate by moving upwards and outwards during inspiration. The ribs are also attached to each other via intercostal muscles which help the rib cage carry out its respiratory function. During exercise for example, the internal intercostal muscles contract and help pull the rib cage downwards. In this way the athlete can increase his/her breathing rate and increase the amount of oxygen and carbon dioxide that can be exchanged in the lungs, and therefore ensure adequate delivery of oxygen to the working muscles and removal of carbon dioxide and other metabolites.

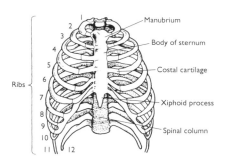

Fig. 1.4 Structure of the rib cage

Bones

Types of bones

Bones are designed to carry out a variety of specific functions, and fall into one of five categories, largely according to their shape:

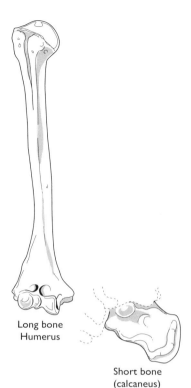

Long bone
Humerus

Short bone
(calcaneus)

Flat bone(scapula)

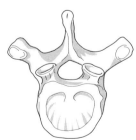

Irregular bone
(vertebra)

Sesamoid bone
(patella)

Long bones

Long bones are cylindrical in shape and are found in the limbs of the body. Examples of long bones include:

- femur
- tibia
- humerus
- phalanges (although not great in length, these possess the cylindrical shape and so also fall into this category).

The primary function of long bones is to act as levers, and they are therefore essential in movement. When running for example, the psoas, iliacus, and rectus femoris muscles pull on the femur to cause flexion of the hip, effectively lifting the leg off the ground. The rest of the quadricep group (the vasti muscles as well as the rectus femoris) then pull on the tibia causing extension to take place at the knee joint, enabling the lower leg to 'snap' through. This is the first stage of a running action. Their other vital function is the production of blood cells which occurs deep inside the bone.

Short bones

Short bones are small and compact in nature, often equal in length and width. They are designed for strength and weightbearing, for example when performing a handstand, and include:

- the bones of the wrist (carpals)
- the ankle (tarsals) and calcaneum.

Flat bones

Flat bones offer protection to the internal organs of the body. Examples include:

- the sternum
- the bones of the cranium
- the bones of the pelvis
- upon close inspection, it can be seen that the ribs are also flat.

Flat bones also provide suitable sites for muscle attachment, with the origins of muscles often attaching to them. In this way the muscle contracting has a firm, immovable base against which to pull, and can therefore carry out its function effectively. For example, a major function of the quadricep muscle group is to pull on the tibia, causing extension at the knee. In order to raise the tibia, the muscle must have a stable base against which it can pull, in this case, the ilium. The bone can now act as a lever and cause movement to occur as outlined earlier. The pelvis, sternum and cranium also produce blood cells.

Irregular bones

Irregular bones are so named due to their complex, individual shapes and the difficulty in classifying them. They have a variety of functions which include protection. Examples include:

- the vertebrae (protect the spinal cord and help to absorb shock when running and jumping)
- the bones of the face.

Sesamoid bones

Sesamoid bones have a specialised function: they ease joint movements and resist friction and compression. They are usually developed in tendons and are covered with a layer of articular cartilage as they exist where bones articulate. Although generally small in appearance, sesamoid bones do vary in size, the largest and most obvious being the patella which is situated in the quadriceps femoris tendon and aids the smooth articulation and movement between the femur and the tibia. The patella also prevents the knee from hyperextending.

Bone landmarks and bony features

Upon close inspection of bones it can be seen that they are not smooth as depicted in many diagrams, but in fact possess an enormous landscape of their own. The surface of bones contain bumps and protrusions and indentations or depressions, each having a specific role and function.

Table 1.1   FEATURES AND ANATOMIC LANDMARKS OF BONES

ANATOMIC	DEFINITION STRUCTURE	EXAMPLE	FUNCTION
condyle	a rounded projection of bone – forming part of a joint	tibial condyle	aids the smooth articulation with the femur at the knee joint
crest/ridge	a ridge on the surface of a bone	tibial crest	aids the attachment of the tibialis anterior muscle at the front of the lower leg
epicondyle	a bony bulge adjacent to a condyle	epicondyle of the humerus	enables the attachment of the muscles of the forearm
fissure	cleft or groove on the surface of a bone	bicipital groove	where the tendon of the bicep brachii muscle sits, enabling smooth contraction
fossa	a depression in the bone	olecranon fossa	enables smooth articulation between the humerus and ulna
process	a bony projection	acromion process	provides an attachment point for the clavicle and shoulder muscles
spine	sharp pointed process	iliac spine	enables the attachment of the hip muscles
tubercle	a small surface nodule of a bone	iliac crest	
tuberosity	a large surface nodule of a bone	tibial tuberosity	the point of attachment of the quadricep femoris on the tibia
trochanter	large knob at the top of the femur	great trochanter	provides attachment sites of muscles of the hip and thigh

Using a selection of bones, inspect and identify some of the structures and landmarks outlined in table 1.1.

Name the bone or bony landmark described:
1 **the tip of the shoulder**
2 **the bump on the anterior of the lower leg just below the kneecap**
3 **the projection found on the medial side of the upper arm at the elbow joint**
4 **the bony projections found in the pelvic area on which we sit**
5 **the bony ridge felt when we place our hands on our hips**
6 **the bony projection found at the very tip of the elbow.**

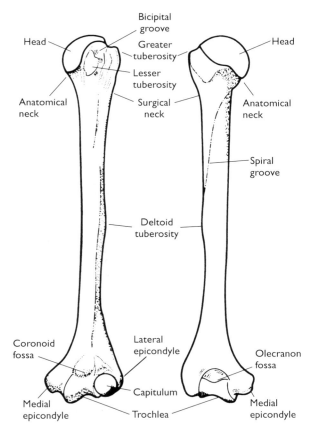

Fig. 1.5 THE HUMERUS (BONE OF THE UPPER ARM)

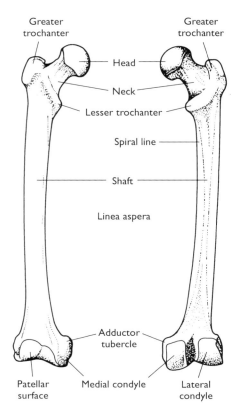

Fig. 1.6 THE FEMUR (UPPER LEG BONE)

The structure and development of skeletal tissues

The tissues making up the skeletal system consist of cartilage and bone.

Cartilage

Cartilage is a soft, slightly elastic tissue, consisting of cells (chondrocytes) which exist in small spaces called lacunae. Cartilage is avascular, meaning that it does not possess a blood supply and receives nutrition via diffusion from the capillary network outside the tissue.

All bones start out as cartilage in the developing foetus, until it is gradually replaced by bone. There are three basic types of cartilage found in the body:

1 **Hyaline or articular cartilage** is a fairly resilient tissue and is found on the articulating surfaces of bones that form joints. It is bluish in colour and is composed of a fine network of collagen fibres. The cartilage protects the bone tissue from wear and reduces friction between articulating bones. Joint movement improves the nutrition supplied to this tissue and can encourage growth. Hyaline cartilage therefore often thickens as a result of exercise which further protects the joints. During the exercise period, articular cartilage will soak up synovial fluid released from the synovial membrane, thus improving mobility at the joint.

2 **White fibrocartilage** is a much denser tissue. It is tough, and its shock absorption properties mean that it is often found in areas of the body where high amounts of stress are imposed. For example, the semi-lunar cartilages of the knee joint resist the huge amount of stress often incurred as a result of performing activities such as the triple jump. Other examples are the intervertebral discs and in the socket of the hip joint.

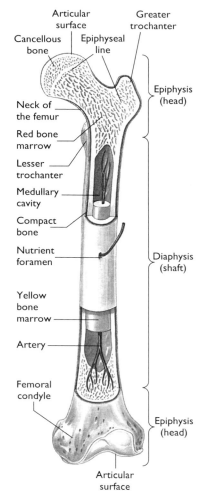

ANTERIOR VIEW
(left femur)

Coronal section through proximal
epiphysis and dissection
of medullary cavity

Fig. 1.7 STRUCTURE OF A LONG BONE
VIEWED IN CROSS SECTION
Source: Kapit & Elson (1993)

The growth and development of bones

3 Yellow elastic cartilage is a much more pliant and flexible tissue giving support and also flexibility. The external ear and the epiglottis are examples.

Bone

Bone differs from cartilage in that it is a rigid, non-elastic tissue and is composed approximately of 65% mineral components (including calcium phosphate and magnesium salts) and 35% organic tissue such as collagen, a protein which gives the bone some resilience and prevents the bones from breaking on the slightest of impacts. Viewed under a microscope, it can be seen that mature bone consists of cells called **osteocytes** which exist in spaces known as **lacunae**. These bone cells are supported by thick collagen fibres which exist in a matrix composed of minerals.

Bone tissue can be categorised into either compact or cancellous, and is best illustrated by viewing a longitudinal cross-section of a long bone.

Compact bone or hard bone forms the surface layers of all bones and the whole of the cylindrical shaft of long bones. It goes some way towards protecting bones from external forces or impacts and has great weight-bearing properties. Surrounding the compact bone is the **periosteum**, which is a fibrous and extremely vascular tissue. In addition to its vital role in bone development, the periosteum enables tendons to attach to bones, which transmit the muscular 'pull', and therefore allows movement to take place.

Cancellous or spongy bone lies beneath and alongside compact bone, and has a honeycomb or **trabecular** appearance. This criss-cross matrix of bony plates is developed along lines of stress on the bones and is constantly reorganised in response to the altering orientation of stress. For example: the stress alters when an infant starts to walk as opposed to crawl.

The trabecular matrix has proved to be the most effective way of combining strength with the minimum of weight, so that bones can take much stress, yet are light and easily moved. In addition to this function, the spaces of the cancellate bone are filled with red bone marrow, since the bony plates offer some protection to the manufacture of red blood cells here.

With the important function of blood production, the bony tissue is extremely vascularised, enabling nutrients to reach the bone and blood produced within the bone to enter the body's circulatory system. **Vascularisation** is aided by Haversian and Volkmanns canals which conduct blood vessels to and from the bone. The nourishment by Haversian canals lead to the bone cells lying circuitously around the canal. This concentric pattern of bone cells is known as the Haversian system and occurs as a result of the vascularity of the bony tissue.

Bone is formed via the process of **ossification**.

1 Some bones, such as the flat bones of the skull, form directly in membranes. This development is known as **direct** or **intramembranous ossification**.
2 The short and long bones are formed by the gradual replacement of hyaline cartilage, from the foetal stage of development until full maturation in our late teenage years. This is known as **indirect and endochondral ossification**.

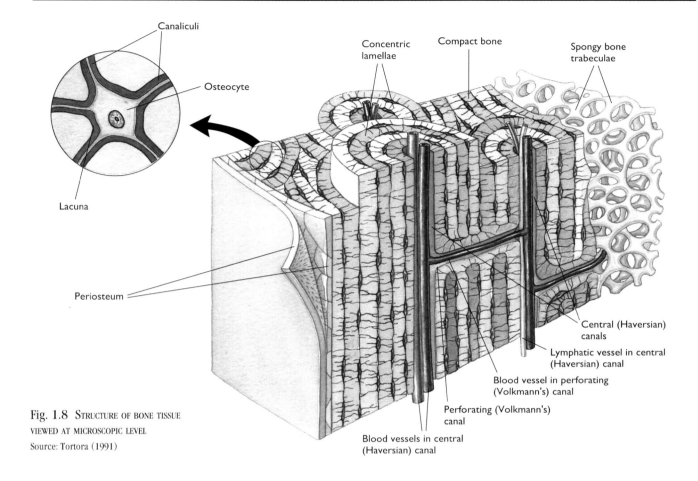

Fig. 1.8 STRUCTURE OF BONE TISSUE
VIEWED AT MICROSCOPIC LEVEL
Source: Tortora (1991)

Joints and articulations

So far we have seen that some bones of the skeleton act as levers, which move when muscles contract and pull on them. Where two or more bones meet, an articulation or joint exists. However, movement does not always occur at these sites, and joints are typically classified according to the degree of movement permitted.

Types of joint

Fixed or fibrous joints

These are very stable and allow no observable movement. Bones are often joined by strong fibres called sutures; eg, the sutures of the cranium.

Cartilaginous or slightly movable joints

These are joined by a tough, fibrous cartilage which provides stability and possesses shock absorption properties. However, a small amount of movement usually exists: for example, the articulations between the lumbar bones due to the intervertebral discs of cartilage.

Synovial or freely movable joints

These are the most common type of joint in the body, and the most important in terms of physical activity, since they allow a wide range of movement.

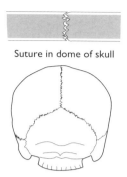

Suture in dome of skull

The joint is enclosed in a fibrous joint capsule which is lined with a synovial membrane. Lubrication is provided by synovial fluid which is secreted into the joint by the synovial membrane. In addition, where the bones come into contact with each other, they are lined with smooth yet hard wearing hyaline or articular cartilage.

Synovial joint stability is provided by the strength of the muscles crossing the joint, which are supported by ligaments which may be inside or outside the capsule. Ligaments are very elastic and lose effectiveness to some degree when torn or stretched.

Some synovial joints possess sacs of synovial fluid known as bursae which are sited in areas of increased pressure or stress and help reduce friction as tissues and structures move past each other. Pads of fat help to absorb shock and improve the 'fit' of the articulating bones. This is particularly true in the knee joint to help the articulation of the femur and tibia.

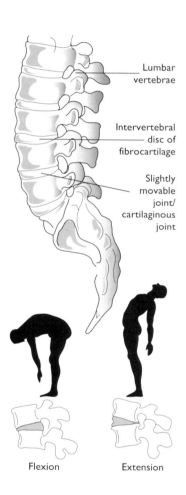

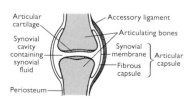

Flexion   Extension

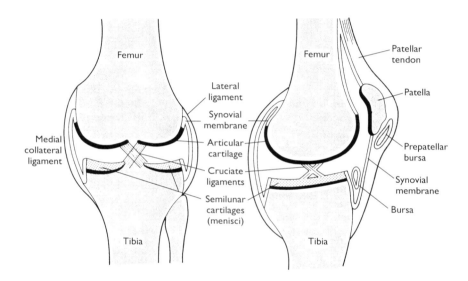

Fig. 1.9 The knee joint

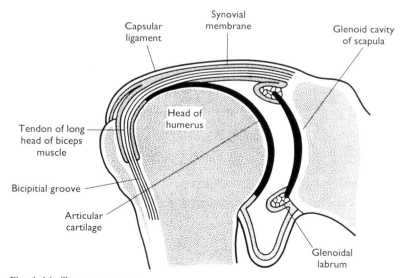

Fig. 1.11 The shoulder joint

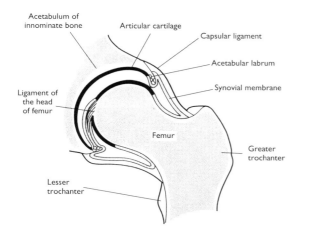

Fig. 1.12 THE HIP JOINT

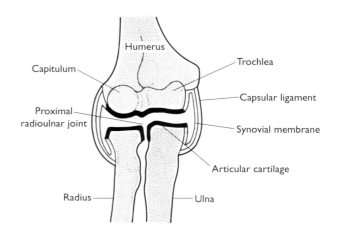

Fig. 1.13 THE ELBOW JOINT

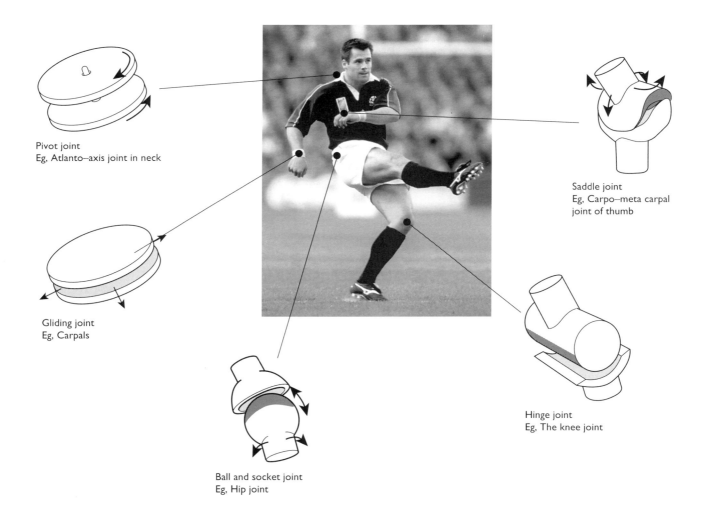

Pivot joint
Eg, Atlanto—axis joint in neck

Gliding joint
Eg, Carpals

Ball and socket joint
Eg, Hip joint

Saddle joint
Eg, Carpo—meta carpal
joint of thumb

Hinge joint
Eg, The knee joint

Explain how the knee joint is structured and how this suits its function in relation to sporting activity.

Types of synovial joint

Synovial joints can be further subdivided into six basic types.

1 A **hinge joint** is a uniaxial joint which only allows movement in one plane. For example: the knee joint only allows movement back and forth. Strong ligaments exist in order to prevent any sideways movement.
2 A **pivot joint** is also uniaxial, which allows rotation only. For example: the cervical vertebrae where the axis rotates on the atlas.
3 An **ellipsoid joint** is biaxial, allowing movement in two planes. For example: the radio-carpal joint of the wrist allows back and forth as well as side to side movement.
4 A **gliding joint** is formed where flat surfaces glide past one another. Although mainly biaxial they may permit movement in all directions. For example: in the wrist, where the small carpal bones move against each other.
5 A **saddle joint** is biaxial and generally occurs where concave and convex surfaces meet. For example: the carpo-metacarpal joint of the thumb.
6 The **ball and socket joint** allows the widest range of movement and occurs where a rounded head of a bone fits into a cup-shaped cavity. For example: in the hip and shoulder.

ACTIVITY 7 — **Try to explain, where possible, how each type of synovial joint has a role to play in sporting activity.**

Movement patterns occurring at synovial joints

The movements that occur at joints can be classified according to the action that is occurring between the articulating bones. These are called movement patterns. A movement of a limb or body part will always have a starting point (point A) and a finishing point (point **B**). Through analysing the position of the finishing point relative to the starting point, we can form a classification of movement. You may also recall the discussion in the introduction on body planes, this also can aid our understanding and classification of joint actions.

Flexion

Flexion occurs when the angle between the articulating bones is decreased. For example: by raising the lower arm up to touch the shoulder, the angle between the radius and the humerus at the elbow has decreased. Flexion of the elbow has thus occurred. Flexion occurs in the median plane about the horizontal axis. A muscle that causes flexion is known as a 'flexor'. In the instance at the elbow, the bicep brachii is the flexor muscle.

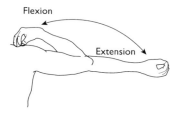

Extension

Extension of a joint occurs when the angle of the articulating bones is increased. For example: when standing up from a seated position, the angle between the femur and tibia increases, thus causing extension at the knee joint. Extreme extension, usually at an angle of greater than 180° is known as **hyper extension**. Extension occurs in the median plane about the horizontal axis. A muscle that causes extension is known as an 'extensor'. In the example of the knee joint, the quadricep femoris group is the extensor.

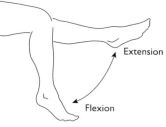

Abduction

This is movement of a body part away from the midline of the body or other body part. For example:

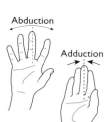

- if arms are placed by the sides of the body and then raised laterally, abduction has occurred at the shoulder joint

- if fingers are spread out, movement has occurred away from the midline of the hand, and abduction has occurred. Abduction occurs in the frontal plane about an anterio-posterior axis. However horizontal abduction takes place in the horizontal or transverse plane.

Adduction

Adduction is the opposite of abduction and concerns movement towards the midline of the body or body part. For example, by lowering the arm back to the sides of the body, movement towards the midline has occurred and is termed adduction. Adduction occurs in the frontal plane about an anterio-posterior axis. However horizontal adduction takes place in the horizontal or transverse plane.

Circumduction

Circumduction occurs where a circle can be described by the body part and is simply a combination of flexion, extension, abduction and adduction. True circumduction can only really occur at ball and socket joints of the shoulder and hip.

As circumduction is a combination of flexion, extension, abduction and adduction it occurs in the median and frontal planes.

Rotation

Rotation of a joint occurs where the bone turns about its axis within the joint. Rotation towards the body is termed **internal** or **medial** rotation, while rotation away from the body is called **external** or **lateral** rotation. Rotation occurs in the horizontal plane about a longitudinal axis.

To explain this further attempt the following exercise:

1 Grip a ruler at the bottom with your right hand.
2 Now raise your arm up in front of your body and move the ruler in an anticlockwise movement. Medial rotation has occurred at the shoulder joint.
3 Now move the ruler clockwise so that it ends up pointing to the side. This is lateral rotation and has once again occurred at the shoulder.

Pronation

Pronation occurs at the elbow and involves internal rotation between the radius and humerus. It typically occurs where the palm of the hand is moved from facing upwards to facing downwards. Pronation occurs in the horizontal plane about a longitudinal axis.

Supination

Supination is the opposite of pronation and again takes place at the elbow. This time the movement is external rotation between the radius and humerus and generally occurs when the palm of the hand is turned so that it faces upwards. Supination occurs in the horizontal plane about a longitudinal axis.

Plantarflexion

Plantarflexion occurs at the ankle joint and is typified by the pointing of the toes. Plantarflexion occurs in the median plane about a horizontal axis.

Dorsiflexion

This also occurs at the ankle and occurs when the foot is raised upwards towards the tibia. Dorsiflexion occurs in the median plane about a horizontal axis.

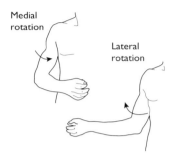

Medial rotation
Lateral rotation

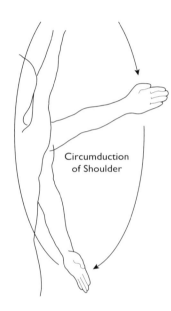

Circumduction of Shoulder

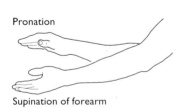

Pronation
Supination of forearm

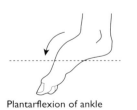

Plantarflexion of ankle

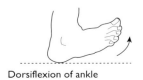

Dorsiflexion of ankle

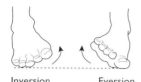

Inversion   Eversion

Inversion

This occurs when the sole of the foot is turned inwards towards the midline of the body. Inversion occurs in the frontal plane.

Eversion

Eversion occurs when the sole of the foot is turned laterally outwards. Eversion occurs in the frontal plane

Using an articulated skeleton, or a partner, examine the joints listed below. Describe the type of joint and the movements possible:

- **knee joint**
- **elbow joint**
- **hip joint**
- **shoulder joint**
- **skull and cervical vertebrae**
- **ribs and thoracic vertebrae**
- **lumbar region.**

What movement patterns occur at:

- **the shoulder and elbow during the performance of a tennis serve?**
- **the hip and knee during a squat thrust?**
- **the hip, knee and ankle during the 'recovery' and 'kick' phase in the breaststroke?**

Exercise and the skeletal system

Exercise has many beneficial effects for the skeletal system:

1 Skeletal tissues become stronger since exercise imposes stress upon the bones, which encourages the laying down of bony plates and the deposition of calcium salts along the lines of stress. This reinforces the criss cross matrix and improves the tensile stress of the bone. Strength training will be particularly beneficial in developing the strength of skeletal tissues.
2 Hyaline cartilage thickens which aids the cushioning of the joint, and therefore protects the bones from wear and tear.
3 Tendons thicken and can withstand greater muscle force.
4 Flexibility and mobility training may enable ligaments to stretch slightly to enable a greater range of movement at the joint.

Participate in a circuit training session. For each activity, state what movement patterns are occurring at the various joints.

Summary

- The skeleton has five basic functions: support, protection, movement, blood production, mineral storage.
- The axial skeleton consists of those bones that provide the greatest support and include the skull, vertebral column and the rib cage.
- The appendicular skeleton consists of the bones of the limbs and their respective girdles.

- The vertebral column is divided into five areas: cervical vertebrae, thoracic vertebrae, lumbar vertebrae, sacral vertebrae and coccygeal vertebrae.
- The rib cage is composed of twelve pairs of ribs which together provide protection for the vital organs and enables the process of inspiration.
- Bones can be categorised as either long, short, flat, irregular or sesamoid.
- There are three types of cartilage in the body: hyaline or articular cartilage, white fibrocartilage, and yellow elastic cartilage.
- Bone is a rigid non-elastic tissue composed of mineral and organic tissue. There are two types of bone: compact or hard bone and cancellous or spongy bone.
- Ossification is the process of bone formation. It can occur within the membranes (intramembranous) or through replacement of cartilage (endochondral).
- Joints are classified according to the degree of movement allowed. There are three basic types of joint; fixed or fibrous joints, and cartilaginous joints.
- Movement at synovial joints can be classified as flexion, extension, abduction, adduction, rotation, pronation, supination, plantar flexion, dorsiflexion, inversion and eversion.
- The whole of the skeletal system can be strengthened through performing exercise.

Review Questions

1 Name the bones that articulate at the following joints:
   a Knee
   b Hip
   c Shoulder
   d Elbow

2 How is the knee joint structured for stability?

3 List the types of movement that occur in the medial plane.

4 Explain how it is possible for us to bend down and touch our toes. What movement patterns are brought about during this action?

5 What is the function of articular cartilage?

6 How is the shoulder structured to enable the different types of movement patterns of which it is capable?

7 List four types of movement that take place in the horizontal plane.

8 State the functions of the following:
   a bursae
   b cruciate ligaments
   c patella
   d carpals
   e thoracic vertebrae
   f collagen
   g the atlas and axis.

9 Outline the benefits that training has on the skeletal tissues.

10 Analyse the action of a tennis serve. State the movement patterns and joint actions that occur at the shoulder and elbow. State the planes in which these movements take place and the axes about which they occur.

chapter 2

Muscular Considerations

No study of human movement or exercise is complete without a study of the muscular system. The muscles interact with the skeleton to provide movement. We will now examine in detail how this happens.

The chapter highlights the structural and functional characteristics of **muscle tissue**, including types of muscle, properties of skeletal muscle (skeletal muscle is particularly relevant to the study of movement, so it will be examined in the greatest detail), the structure of skeletal muscle at molecular level, and the process and types of muscular contraction.

To emphasise the importance of muscle action in sporting situations, a unit on **kinesiology** has been included, which will encourage the reader to examine the muscle actions required to produce effective movement in different sporting situations. Links to the skeletal system will be made specifically at this stage, and a discussion concerning the benefits of exercise and training upon the muscular system will take place towards the end of the chapter.

What is a muscle?

Muscles comprise approximately 45% of the total body weight, and total in excess of 600.
There are three types of muscle tissue:

1 **Skeletal** muscle, which is external and used primarily for movement of the skeleton. These often occur in layers, with 'deep' muscles lying underneath 'superficial' muscles.
2 **Cardiac** muscle which is found only in the heart and used to force blood into the circulatory vessels.
3 **Smooth** muscle which lies internally and has several functions including forcing food through the digestive system (peristalsis) and squeezing blood throughout the circulatory system via arteries and arterioles.

As skeletal muscle is responsible for the body's mechanical movement, and is central to our study of movement analysis, its properties and functions are now examined.

Table 2.1   COMPARING MUSCLE TYPES

SKELETAL	CARDIAC
• voluntary • contract by impulse from the brain • parallel fibres • less/smaller mitochondria • motor unit organisation	• involuntary • generates own impulses (myogenic) • interwoven, intercalating fibres • more/larger mitochondria • auto-ventricular network of fibres

flexion (bending of the arm) is the biceps brachii, and the muscle which produces the desired joint movement is called the **agonist** or **prime mover**. However, in order for the bicep muscle to shorten when contracting, the tricep muscle must lengthen. The tricep in this instance is known as the **antagonist**, since its action is opposite to that of the agonist. The two muscles however must work together to produce the required movement.

    Fixator muscles or stabilisers also work in this movement. Their role is to stabilise the origin so that the agonist can achieve maximum and effective contraction. In this case the trapezius contracts to stabilise the scapula to create a rigid platform. **Neutralisers** or **synergist** muscles in this movement prevent any undesired movements which may occur, particularly at the shoulder where the bicep works over two joints.

    It can thus be seen that for this apparently simple movement of elbow flexion, integrated and synergistic (harmonious) muscle actions are required to enable the necessary smooth movement.

    Furthermore, the roles of each muscle are constantly changed for changing actions. For example, in the action of elbow extension, the roles of the bicep and tricep are reversed so that the tricep becomes the prime mover or agonist (since the tricep is an extensor and thus produces this movement pattern), while the bicep becomes the antagonist, to enable the smooth and effective contraction of the tricep.

Fig. 2.7 DIAGRAM OF ANTAGONISTIC MUSCLE ACTION

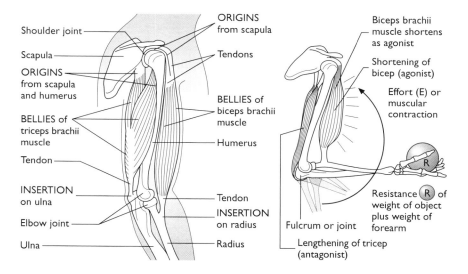

 **Explain the antagonistic muscle action occurring in the leg during a kicking action.**

Types of muscular contraction

In order to produce the vast range of movements of which it is capable, the body's muscles either shorten, lengthen or remain the same length whilst contracting. Indeed, muscle contractions are classified depending upon the muscle action which predominates:

- **Isotonic** contractions refer to those instances when the muscle is moving while contracting. This can further be divided into concentric and eccentric muscle actions.
- **Concentric** contractions involve the muscle shortening while contracting as happens in the bicep during the upward phase of a bicep curl performance or in the tricep during the upward phase of a push-up.

Table 2.5   MUSCLE FUNCTIONS, ORIGINS AND INSERTIONS

MUSCLE	FUNCTION	INSERTION	ORIGIN
pectoralis major	flexes upper arm adducts upper arm	humerus	sternum clavicle rib cartilage
latissimus dorsi	extends and adducts upper arm	humerus	vertebrae (T6–L5) iliac crest
deltoid	abducts, flexes and extends upper arm	humerus	clavicle scapula acromion
biceps brachii	flexes lower arm	radius	scapula
triceps	extends lower arm	olecranon process	humerus scapula
iliopsoas	flexes trunk flexes thigh	ilium vertebrae femur	ilium vertebrae femur
gluteus maximus	extends thigh	femur	ilium sacrum coccyx
gluteus medius gluteus minimus	abducts thigh	femur	ilium
hamstring group biceps femoris semimembranosus semitendinosus	flexes lower leg extends thigh	tibia fibula	ischium femur
quadricep group rectus femoris vastus medialis vastus lateralis vastus intermedius	extends lower leg flexes thigh	tibia (via patella tendon)	ilium femur
sartorius	flexes hip and knee	anterior superior iliac spine	tibia
adductors longus magnus brevis	adducts thigh	femur (linea aspera)	pubic bone
gastrocnemius	plantar flexion flexes knee	calcaneus	femur
soleus	plantar flexion	calcaneus	fibula tibia

As a rule of thumb, the origin of a muscle *is the nearest flat bone*, the insertion is the bone that the muscle *puts into action*

- **Eccentric** contractions on the other hand involve the muscle lengthening whilst contracting (remember that a muscle is not always relaxing while lengthening!). This can be seen in the bicep during the downward phase of the bicep curl or in the tricep during the downward phase of the press-up. The eccentric contraction of the bicep during the downward phase is used to counteract the force of gravity. This is because gravity acts on the mass of the weight and forearm causing extension at the elbow. If the bicep does not contract to control the rate of motion caused by gravity, then the movement will be very quick resulting in injury.

Table 2.6   TYPES OF MUSCLE CONTRACTION

	ISOTONIC		ISOMETRIC
	concentric	eccentric	static
muscle action	muscle shortens	muscle lengthens whilst contracting	muscle remains the same length whilst contracting
example	bicep: when raising a weight	bicep: when lowering a weight	bicep: holding a weight in a static position

Table 2.7   ANALYSIS OF JOINT ACTIONS

JOINT	ACTION	PLANE	MUSCLES USED	DIAGRAM
hip	flexion	median	psoas iliacus rectus femoris	 2.1a 2.1a, 2.4a
	extension	median	gluteus maximus biceps femoris semimembranosus semitendinosus gluteus medius (posterior)	2.1b, 2.4b 2.1b, 2.4b 2.1b, 2.4b 2.1b, 2.4b 2.1b, 2.4b
	abduction	frontal	gluteus medius gluteus minimus tensor fasciae latae	2.1b, 2.4b 2.1a, 2.4a
	adduction	frontal	adductor magnus adductor brevis adductor longus pestineus gracilis	2.1a, 2.1a,
	medial rotation	horizontal	gluteus medius gluteus minimus tensor fasciae latae	2.1b, 2.4b 2.1a, 2.4a
	lateral rotation	horizontal	gluteus maximus adductors	2.1b, 2.4b 2.4a
knee	flexion	median	semitendinosus semimembranosus biceps femoris popliteus gastrocnemius	2.1b, 2.4b 2.1b, 2.4b 2.1b, 2.4b 2.1a, 2.4a, 2.4b
	extension	median	rectus femoris vastus medialis vastus lateralis tensor fasciae latae	2.1a, 2.4a 2.1a, 2.4a 2.1a, 2.4a 2.1a, 2.4a
	medial rotation (when flexed)	horizontal	sartorius semitendinosus	2.1a, 2.4a 2.1b, 2.4b
	lateral rotation (when flexed)	horizontal	tensor fasciae latae biceps femoris	2.1a, 2.1a 2.1b, 2.4b

Table 2.7 CONTINUED

Joint	Action	Plane	Muscles used	Diagram
ankle	dorsi flexion	median	tibialis anterior extensor digitorum longus peroneus tertius	2.1a, 2.4a 2.1a, 2.4a 2.1a, 2.4a
	plantar flexion	median	gastrocnemius soleus peroneus longus peroneus brevis tibialis posterior flexor digitorum longus	2.1a, 2.4a 2.1a, 2.1b, 2.4b 2.1a, 2.4a 2.1a
	inversion	frontal	tibialis anterior tibialis posterior gastrocnemius soleus	2.1a, 2.4a 2.1a 2.1a, 2.4a 2.1a, 2.1b, 2.4b
	eversion	frontal	peroneus longus peroneus brevis	2.1a, 2.4a
shoulder	flexion	median	anterior deltoid pectoralis major coracobrachialis	2.1a, 2.2a, 2.3a 2.1a, 2.2b
	extension	median	posterior deltoid latissimus dorsi teres major	2.1b, 2.2b, 2.3b 2.1b, 2.2b, 2.1b, 2.2b
	adduction	frontal	latissimus dorsi pectoralis major teres major teres minor	2.1b, 2.2b 2.1a, 2.2b 2.1b, 2.2b 2.1b, 2.2b
	abduction	frontal	medial deltoid supraspinatus	
	horizontal abduction	horizontal	posterior deltoid trapezius rhomboids latissimus dorsi	2.1b, 2.2b, 2.3b 2.1b, 2.2b,2.3b 2.1b, 2.2b
	medial rotation	horizontal	subscapularis	
	lateral rotation	horizontal	infraspinatus teres minor	2.1b, 2.2b 2.1b, 2.2b
elbow	flexion	median	biceps brachii brachialis brachioradialis	2.1a 2.1b, 2.3a
	extension	median	triceps	2.3b
	pronation	horizontal	pronator teres pronator quadratus brachioradialis	 2.1b, 2.3a
	supination	horizontal	biceps brachii supinator	2.1a
wrist	flexion	median	wrist flexors	2.1a, 2.3a
	extension	median	wrist extensors	2.1b, 2.3b

movement of the trunk	flexion	median	rectus abdominus internal obliques external obliques	2.1a, 2.2b 2.1a b, 2.2 a b
	extension	median	erector spinae iliocostalis spinalis	2.1b
	lateral flexion	frontal	internal oblique rectus abdominis erector spinae quadratus laborum	2.1a, 2.2b 2.1b
	rotation	horizontal	external oblique rectus abdominis erector spinae	2.1a b, 2.2a b 2.1a, 2.2b 2.1b
movement of the scapulae	elevation	frontal	levator sapulae trapezius rhomboids	2.1b, 2.2b,2.3b
	depression	frontal	trapezius (lower) pectoralis minor serratus anterior (lower)	2.1b 2.1a, 2.2b
	protraction	frontal	serratus anterior	2.1a, 2.2b
	retraction	frontal	rhomboids trapezius	2.1b, 2.2b,2.3b
	upward rotation	frontal	trapezius (upper) serratus anterior	2.1b, 2.2b,2.3b 2.1a, 2.2b
	downward rotation	frontal	rhomboids levator scapulae	

Fig. 2.8 TYPES OF
MUSCLE CONTRACTION
IN THE BICEP BRACHII

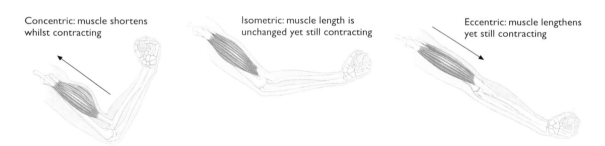

Concentric: muscle shortens whilst contracting

Isometric: muscle length is unchanged yet still contracting

Eccentric: muscle lengthens yet still contracting

Plyometrics is a type of strength training which is based on a muscle contracting eccentrically. Sometimes, however, a muscle can contract without actively lengthening or shortening; in this instance the muscle is going through **isometric** contraction – the muscle remains the same length while contracting. In fact the majority of muscles will contract isometrically in order for us to maintain posture. Static contractions occur while holding a weight in a stationary position or when performing a handstand.

Normally when a muscle contracts the angular velocity of the muscle shortening or lengthening varies throughout the contraction. However specialist hydraulic machines have been devised so that it is possible to keep the speed at which the muscle lengthens or shortens constant, but not necessarily the resistance applied. The speed of the movement cannot be increased. Any attempt to increase the velocity results in equal reaction force from the machine. In this way **isokinetic** exercise, as it is called, is excellent for strength training.

Levers and turning effects

Levers
Efficient and effective movement is made possible by a system of **levers**. These are mechanical devices used to produce turning motions about a fixed point (called a **fulcrum**). In the human body, bones act as levers, joints act as the fulcrum and muscle contractions provide the force to move the lever about the fulcrum.

A basic understanding of lever systems can be used to explain rotational motion, and help athletes develop the most efficient technique for their sport.

There are three types of levers, and each is determined by the relationship of the fulcrum (F), the point of application of force or effort (E) and the weight or resistance (R).

1 **First class** lever: the **fulcrum** lies between the **effort** and the **resistive force**.
2 **Second** class lever: the **resistance** lies between the **fulcrum** and the **effort**.
3 **Third** class lever: the **effort is** between the **fulcrum** and the **weight** – see fig 2.9.

The majority of movements in the human body are governed by third class levers.

Functions of levers

Levers have two main functions:

1 increase the resistance that a given effort can move.
2 increase the speed at which a body moves.

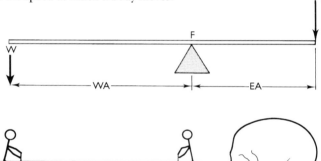

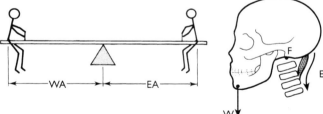

Fig. 2.9A The first order of levers

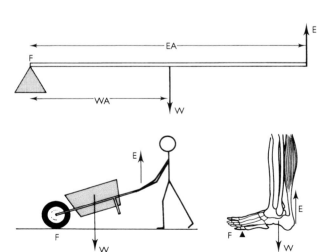

Fig. 2.9B The second order of levers

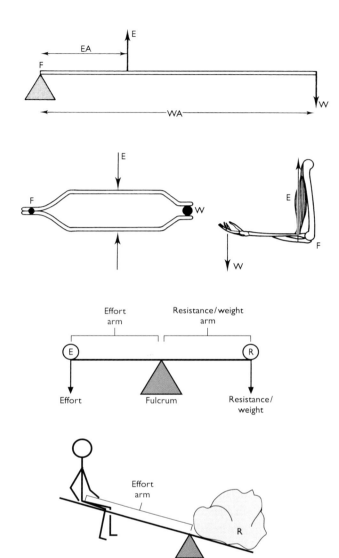

Fig. 2.9c THE THIRD ORDER OF LEVERS

Fig. 2.10 COMPONENTS OF A
LEVER SYSTEM

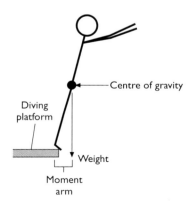

Fig. 2.11 THE MOMENT ARM OF A DIVER —
BY LEANING OUT IN PREPARATION FOR A DIVE,
THE MOMENT ARM IS INCREASED (LENGTHENED),
INCREASING THE ROTATIONAL EFFECT

First class levers can increase both the effects of the effort and the speed of a body; **second** class levers tend only to increase the effect of the effort force; **third** class levers can be used to increase the speed of a body. An example of a third class lever in the body is the action of the hamstrings and quadriceps on the knee joint, which causes flexion and extension of the lower leg. The extent to which this can increase, depends upon the relative lengths of the **resistance arm** and the **effort arm**:

1 The resistance arm (RA) or weight arm (WA) is the part of the lever between the fulcrum and the resistance: see fig 2.10. The longer the resistance arm, the greater speed can be generated.

2 The effort arm (EA) is the distance between the fulcrum and the effort; the longer the effort arm, the less effort required to move a given resistance. In sport, implements are often used such as rackets or bats to increase the length of the effort arm which will increase the force that an object such as a ball is struck. However the optimal length of an implement should be determined by the strength of the person handling it which is why, for example, junior tennis rackets have been designed.

The relative efficiency of the lever system is expressed as the mechanical advantage (MA) which can be determined as follows:

$$MA = \frac{\text{effort arm}}{\text{resistance arm}}$$

Levers and turning effects

The levers of the human body are capable of rotational movement only, so the majority of movements in sporting activity are of an angular nature about a joint (fulcrum). The twisting or turning effect of an applied force is known as the **moment of force** or **torque**, and is directly related to the distance between the point of application of the force (muscle insertion) and the fulcrum (joint). This is the **moment arm** (MA) and can be applied either to the effort arm or the resistance arm.

The largest turning effect or rotation will occur where the moment arm is at its longest or the force applied is at its greatest. For example:

- when preparing to dive from a platform, by leaning out before the dive the moment arm is lengthened and the rotational effect is increased – see fig 2.11.

The moment of a force is equal to the product of the force applied multiplied by the length of the moment arm:

Moment of force = magnitude of force × the perpendicular distance between the line of action of the force and the pivot

$$M = F \times MA$$

Eccentric force

The turning effect of the diver is produced by a force which is not passing through the centre of gravity. This off centre force is called the **eccentric force**, and is vital for rotation to occur. Look at fig 2.12. When the force is applied through the centre of gravity as in figure (a) the resulting motion will be **linear**, but when the force is applied outside the centre of gravity as in figure (b), the resulting motion will be **angular**. By moving the centre of gravity, the diver can produce an eccentric force to perform either a clockwise rotation (front somersault) or an anticlockwise rotation (back somersault).

Look at fig 2.13. When holding such a weight, there is a tendency for this moment to turn the lever clockwise. In order to balance the lever at the fulcrum and hold the weight in a static position, the bicep must produce a force equal to the clockwise moment.

Total clockwise moment = total anticlockwise moment

Clockwise moment = force × distance to fulcrum

Anticlockwise moment = force (of muscle) × distance of muscle insertion from the joint

y (force of resistance) = z (force of muscle)

This is commonly known as the **principle of moments**, and explains how a system can be balanced about a fulcrum

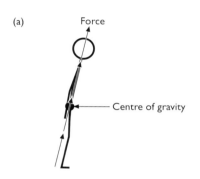

(a)

Force

Centre of gravity

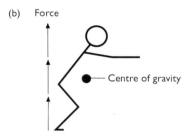

(b) Force

Centre of gravity

Fig. 2.12 ECCENTRIC FORCES (A) WHEN APPLYING A FORCE THROUGH THE CENTRE OF MASS, THE RESULTING MOTION WILL BE LINEAR (B) WHEN APPLYING A FORCE WHICH DOES NOT PASS THROUGH THE CENTRE OF GRAVITY, THE RESULTING MOTION WILL BE ANGULAR

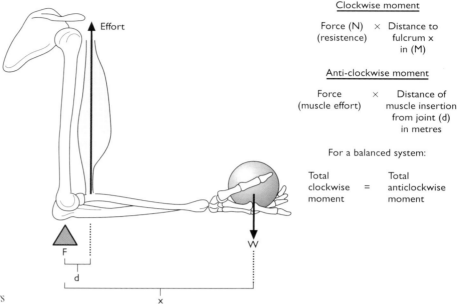

Clockwise moment

Force (N)	×	Distance to
(resistence)		fulcrum x
		in (M)

Anti-clockwise moment

Force	×	Distance of
(muscle effort)		muscle insertion
		from joint (d)
		in metres

For a balanced system:

Total	=	Total
clockwise		anticlockwise
moment		moment

Fig. 2.13 THE PRINCIPLE OF MOMENTS

Movement Analysis

Kinesiology Kinesiology is the study of body movement, and thus includes muscle action. When studying this unit it is helpful to consider the following:

- the function of the muscles contracting
- how the muscle is contracting (eg, concentric or eccentric)
- the movement patterns occurring at joints as a result of the movement
- the plane in which the movement occurs
- the axis about which the movement occurs.

Table 2.8 shows joint movement used in basketball. Think of other sporting situations and complete the table accordingly.

Table 2.8 VARIETY OF JOINT MOVEMENTS

SPORT	ACTION	MOVEMENT PATTERN	MUSCLES WORKING	TYPE OF CONTRACTION	PLANE
basketball	jump shot	extension at knee	quadricep group: rectus femoris vasti muscles	concentric	median

For each of the following joints, state which muscles are used for the movement patterns shown in brackets:

- **Knee (flexion and extension)**
- **Hip (flexion, extension, abduction, adduction)**
- **Shoulder (flexion, extension, abduction, adduction)**
- **Ankle (plantar flexion, dorsi flexion, inversion, eversion).**

Skeletal muscle

Structure

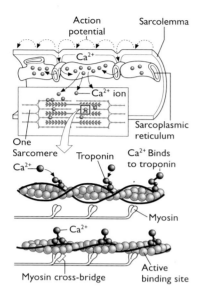

Fig. 2.14 THE STRUCTURE OF ACTIN AND MYOSIN

When viewed under the microscope, skeletal muscle can be seen at molecular level.

The muscle belly is surrounded by a layer of **epimysium** (Fig 2.16a), a thick connective tissue surrounding the entire surface of the muscle. This is continuous and eventually forms tendons which join the muscle onto bones. The muscle belly is composed of many bundles of fibres known as **fasiculi** (Fig 2.16a). Each fibre within a single fasciculus contains many smaller fibres called **myofibrils** (Fig 2.16b) which provide the contractile unit of the muscle. These myofibrils have characteristic dark and light bands (striations) which represent a **sarcomere** (Fig 2.16c). This pattern is repeated along the length of the myofibril.

Sarcomeres have a highly organised structure, and at the most fundamental level the sarcomere is composed of two protein-based myofilaments:

- a thick **myosin** filament, and
- a thinner **actin** filament.

The interaction and overlapping of these two myofilaments enables muscles to contract through the **sliding filament theory**; see below.

Each actin filament is composed of two components:

1 **Fibrous actin** (F. Actin) which provides active sites to which myosin molecules can bind during muscle contraction.
2 **Tropomyosin** molecules and **troponin** molecules which during relaxation prevent the attachment of the myosin cross bridge. Calcium ions are released during innervation (nervous stimulation of the muscle tissue) from the sarcoplasmic reticulum surrounding the myofibrils which cause the troponin to change shape and remove the inhibitory effect of the tropomyosin and allow the myosin cross bridge to attach to the actin filament forming the actmyosin complex.

Myosin filaments are composed of many myosin molecules, which are made up of two parts: a rod, and a head, which together form a golf-club shaped molecule. The heads of each molecule contain ATPase, an enzyme used to break down adenosine triphosphate (ATP), which, in doing so, releases energy for muscular contraction (see p71). This energy is used to bind the myosin cross bridge onto the actin filament, thereby allowing muscular contraction.

The sliding filament theory

The sliding of the filaments past each other takes the form of a ratchet mechanism, whereby the myosin cross bridges continually attach, detach, reattach etc. It is the sweeping action or the 'power stroke' of the myosin head which causes the actin filaments to be pulled towards the centre and slide past the myosin filaments. It is the break down of ATP which releases the energy which enables the attachment and detachment of the myosin head.

The action of the sliding filaments during contraction causes shortening of all sarcomeres, and therefore all muscle fibres.

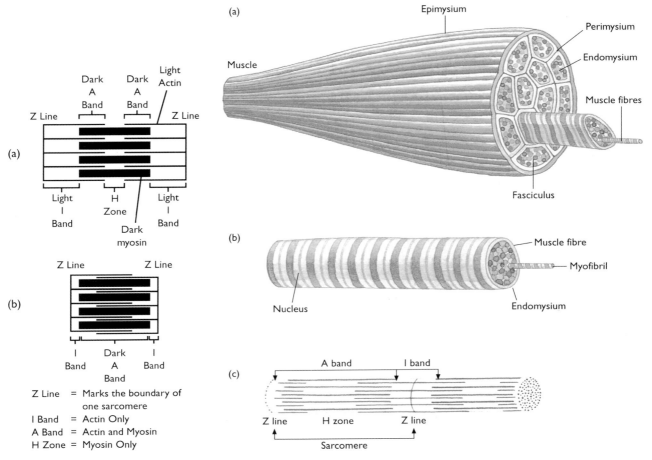

Fig. 2.15 THE SLIDING FILAMENT THEORY (A) RELAXED (B) CONTRACTED — NOTICE THAT THE H ZONE HAS DISAPPEARED AND THE Z LINES HAVE BEEN DRAWN TOGETHER

Z Line = Marks the boundary of one sarcomere
I Band = Actin Only
A Band = Actin and Myosin
H Zone = Myosin Only

Fig. 2.16 (A) THE STRUCTURE OF SKELETAL MUSCLE (B) SINGLE MUSCLE FIBRE, SHOWING CHARACTERISTIC STRIATIONS (C) MYOFIBRIL, ILLUSTRATING A SARCOMERE

Muscle relaxation

The relaxation of muscle is a passive process: the cross bridges uncouple, causing the sarcomere to lengthen and return to its pre-contracted length.

Muscle contraction

To understand how skeletal muscle contracts, a basic understanding of the nervous system is needed, as muscle contraction involves the interaction of the muscular system with the nervous system (neuromuscular interaction).

When a muscle is required to contract, an electrical impulse is emitted from the **central nervous system**. The electrical impulse begins at the brain and is transmitted to a muscle via the spinal cord and by nerve cells called **motor neurones**.

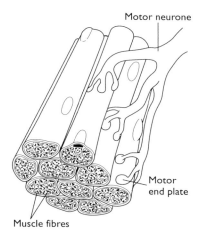

Fig. 2.17 A MOTOR UNIT

One motor neurone (nerve) cannot stimulate the whole muscle, but is only capable of stimulating a number of fibres within it. The motor neurone, and the fibres it stimulates, is called a **motor unit**, which is the functional unit of skeletal muscle.

The number of fibres innervated by a single motor unit varies, depending upon the precision of movement required. For example the eye, which requires a great deal of control and precision in order to focus, will possess between one and five fibres per motor neurone, while the rectus femoris muscle of the quadricep group requires greater power to enable a basketball player to perform a jump shot, and therefore possess up to 2,000 fibres per motor neurone.

Note: the fibres within a particular motor unit will usually be of the same type, either *fast* twitch or *slow* twitch.

Motor units are therefore recruited depending upon the activity being undertaken, and the recruitment is based upon twitch response time or speed of contraction. A powerlifter therefore will only recruit motor units that are composed of fast twitch (type 2b) fibres, whilst a marathon runner will largely recruit motor units consisting of slow twitch or type 1 fibres. These motor units can resist fatigue and contract repeatedly due to their greater aerobic capacity and ability to store glycogen.

Muscle fibre innervation

A muscle fibre is innervated when an impulse is of suitable strength. The point at which the motor nerve meets the muscle fibre is known as the **motor end plate**, and forms the **neuromuscular junction**.

When a nerve impulse arrives at the motor end plate, calcium ions enter the synaptic knob and a transmitter substance called **acetylcholine** is released; this aids the spread of the impulse to the muscle fibre across a small gap called the synaptic cleft. If sufficient acetylcholine is released, there is a change in the permeability of the sarcolemma to sodium and potassium ions; now the muscle fibre is said to have '**action potential**' – which is the capability to contract.

An incoming response may be either excitatory or inhibitory. An excitatory response which causes muscle contraction will produce an excitatory post-synaptic action potential (EPSP), which will cause a contraction of muscle fibres if a given threshold or intensity is reached or exceeded. If this threshold is not attained, then the sum of the individual effects of several impulses can be used until the threshold is exceeded. Once this point is reached, a depolarisation or decrease in the electrical potential across a membrane occurs, which triggers the release of calcium ions from the sarcoplasmic reticulum; this in turn removes the inhibitory effect of tropomyosin and enables the myosin cross bridge to attach to the actin filament to cause muscle fibre contraction.

Following excitation, a chemical called **cholinesterase** is released which blocks the effect of acetylcholine and prepares the muscle fibre for the arrival of subsequent stimuli, so that the muscle fibres in a given motor unit can once again contract.

The all or none law

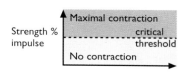

Fig. 2.18 THE ALL OR NONE LAW

Each fibre within a motor unit contracts according to the all or none law. This principle states that when a motor unit receives a stimulus of sufficient intensity to elicit a response, all the muscle fibres within the unit will contract at the same time and to the maximum possible extent. If, however, the stimulus is not of significant intensity, the muscle fibres will not respond and contraction will not take place.

The degree to which a muscle contracts is dependent upon several factors, including the number of motor units recruited by the brain. This will determine the force that can be generated within the muscle. The greater the strength required, the greater the number of motor units (and therefore the number of muscle fibres) that contract. For example, more motor units will be recruited in the biceps brachii when the body weight is being lifted in a chin-up, than when performing a bicep curl with a very light weight.

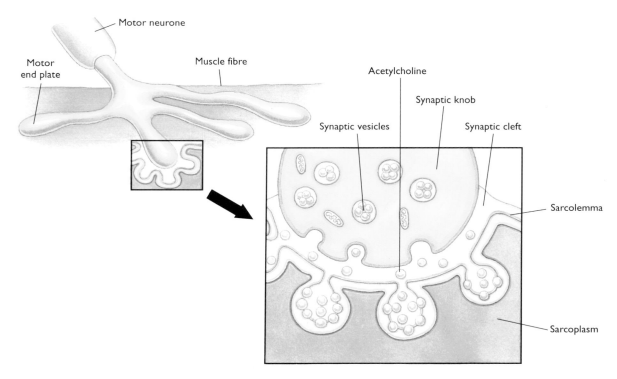

Fig. 2.19 The neuromuscular junction, showing synaptic stimulation of a muscle fibre

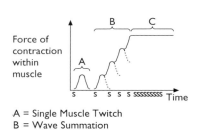

A = Single Muscle Twitch
B = Wave Summation
C = Tetanus

Fig. 2.20 Muscle twitch and contraction

A second consideration is the frequency with which impulses arrive at the muscle fibres. The motor unit will respond to a stimulus by giving a 'twitch' – a brief period of contraction followed by relaxation. When a second impulse is applied to the motor unit before it completely relaxes from the previous stimulus, the sum of both stimuli occurs, increasing the total contraction. This process is known as **multiple wave summation**. Furthermore, when rapid firing of stimuli occurs, giving muscles little or no time for relaxation, **tetanus or tetanic contraction** takes place, increasing the total contraction still further. This is illustrated in Fig 2.20. This increase in total contraction can be explained by the augmented release of calcium ions which causes greater cross bridge attachment of myosin onto actin.

Further reading

Arnould-Taylor, *A Text Book of Anatomy and Physiology*, (Stanley Thornes Publishers Ltd, 1988)
Clegg, *Exercise Physiology* (Feltham Press, 1996)
Davis, Bull, Roscoe and Roscoe, *Physical Education and the Study of Sport* (Wolfe Medical Publishers, 1991)
Kapit and Elson, *The Anatomy Colouring Book* (Harpers Collins College Publishers, 1993)
Hay and Reid, *Anatomy, Mechanics and Human Motion* (Prentice Hall, 1988)
Seeley, Stephens and Tate, *Anatomy and Physiology* (Mosby Year Book Inc., 1992)
Sharkey, *Physiology of Fitness* (Human Kinetics, 1990)
Wilmore and Costill, *Physiology of Sport and Exercise* (Human Kinetics, 1994)
Wirhead, *Athletic Ability and the Anatomy of Motion* (Wolfe Medical Publishers, 1989)

Summary

- There are three types of muscle tissue: Skeletal, Smooth and Cardiac.
- Skeletal muscle properties include extensibility, elasticity and contractility.
- Functions include movement, support and posture, and heat production.
- Muscles can be classified according to shape, either fusiform or pennate.
- There are two basic types of muscle fibre: Slow twitch or type 1 and fast twitch or type 2 fibres. Fast twitch fibre can be further subdivided into fast oxidative glycolytic or type 2a and fast twitch glycolytic or type 2b.
- Muscle are attached to bones via tendons. The origin of a muscle is that attachment onto a stable bone, usually the nearest flat bone. The insertion is the muscle attachment onto the bone that the muscle puts into action.
- Muscles often work together in order to produce co-ordinated movements: antagonistic muscle action. A muscle directly responsible for the joint movement is the agonist. An antagonist often lengthens in order for the agonist to shorten.
- Muscles can contract in several ways: isotonic (shortening or lengthening), concentric (the muscle shortens), eccentric (the muscle lengthens). A muscle can also contract without any visible movement (isometric).
- Skeletal muscle fibres are composed of many smaller myofibrils. Each myofibril is characterised by dark and light bands which represent sarcomeres. Sarcomeres are composed of two proteins – actin and myosin. Interaction of the actin and myosin causes muscular contraction (the sliding filament theory).
- Muscular contraction: interaction of the muscular system and nervous system.
- A motor unit is the functional component of skeletal muscle and consists of a motor neurone and a number of muscle fibres that that motor neurone controls. A single muscle can possess thousands of motor units
- Each fibre within a motor unit will contract maximally or not at all and depends upon the intensity of the stimulus. This is known as the all or none law.
- Strength of contraction can be determined by the number of motor units recruited by the brain to perform a specific task, or by considering the frequency that impulses arrive at muscle fibres.
- Muscle action is controlled by internal regulatory mechanisms which include proprioceptors, muscle spindle apparatus, and Golgi tendon organs.
- The analysis of muscle contraction and joint action is called kinesiology.

Review Questions

1 Explain how the properties of skeletal muscle enable it to perform its function when sprinting. Use the correct names of muscles, where appropriate.

2 Skeletal muscle is composed of different types of fibre. What are they? Explain how the structure of these fibres is suited to the requirements of performers in a variety of sports.

3 When performing a jump shot in basketball, many different muscles work in the lower body. Identify the muscles working on the hip, knee and ankle joints, and state the specific roles that each of these muscles have (ie, are they agonists, fixators etc.)

4 What are the essential ingredients to successful analysis of movement? Use these to analyse an overhead clear in badminton, with particular reference to the shoulder, elbow and wrist actions.

5 Identify one stroke in swimming. State the muscles that are contracting in each phase of the stroke (eg, either the 'kick' or 'recovery' phase in the leg action) and state the **type** of contraction taking place in each muscle.

6 Give definitions of the following terms: Epimysium, Fasciculi, Myofibrils, Sarcomere, Actin, Myosin, Tropomyosin, Troponin.

7 Outline the process of muscle fibre innervation. What is the function of 'acetylcholine'?

8 Why is an understanding of 'the all or none law' important to an athlete undertaking a weight training programme?

9 Analyse the human lever system. Classify the type of lever in operation at as many joints as possible. Give sketch diagrams to show the lever system in action.

10 What is the importance of calcium and ATP in muscle contraction?

chapter 3

Cardiovascular Considerations

This chapter will examine the structure and function of the cardiovascular system, including the heart, the vascular system, and the blood and its performance when performing physical activity.

The second part of the chapter will focus upon the response of the cardiovascular system to exercise, looking in particular at factors such as cardiac dynamics including changes in heart rate, stroke volume and blood pressure.

We will learn how the heart, blood vessels and blood adapt in response to the demands of exercise; links are made to Chapters 8 and 10, on training and health-related implications.

The cardiovascular system

The human body is an amazing machine, and at the centre of its operation is the heart. The heart is a muscular pump that beats continuously, over 100,000 times per day, which together with the blood vessels and the blood provides the tissues and cells with the essentials for life itself – oxygen and nutrients.

The structure and function of the heart

The heart lies behind the sternum (breastbone) and ribs, which offer protection. In adults, it is about the size of a clenched fist – although trained athletes often experience **cardiac hypertrophy**, which is an enlargement of the heart.

In terms of structure, the heart is composed of four chambers:

- The two chambers at the top or superior part of the heart are called the **atria**.
- The two lower or inferior chambers are termed **ventricles**.

The ventricles are much more muscular than the atria since it is here that the pumping action of the heart which circulates the blood all over the body occurs.

As well as being divided transversely (into upper and lower portions), the heart can also be divided into left and right halves (sagitally) due to a muscular partition called the septum. This separation into left and right is essential for the heart to carry out its function effectively, since each side has slightly different roles:

- The left side of the heart is responsible for circulating blood throughout the entire body.
- The right side is responsible for ensuring that oxygen-poor blood is pumped to the lungs where it can be reoxygenated.

The major vessels act as entry and exit points for the blood to enter or leave the heart, and are all situated towards the top of the heart. To ensure a smooth passage of blood through the heart, a number of **valves** exist. These valves make sure that the blood only flows in one direction and are

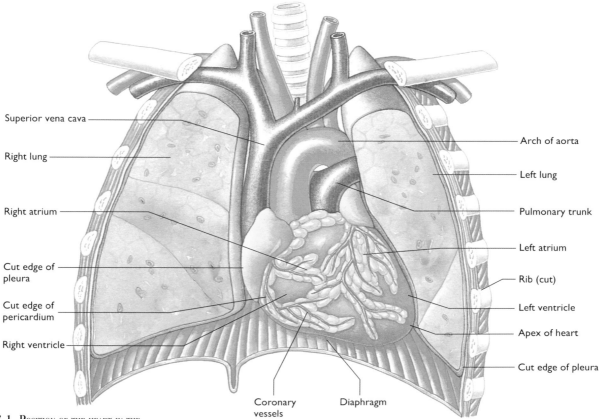

Fig. 3.1 POSITION OF THE HEART IN THE
THORACIC CAVITY

also responsible for the 'lub-dup' sounds of the heart. The 'lub' results from the closure of the atrio-ventricular valves (also known as the bicuspid and tricuspid valves), and the much sharper 'dup' sound occurs when the semi-lunar valves (pulmonary and aortic valves) snap shut. These valves also prevent back flow of blood, ensuring a uni-directional flow through the heart.

The thick muscular wall of the heart is called the **myocardium** and is composed of cardiac muscle fibres. It is situated between the **endocardium** on the inside, a thin squamous epithelial layer which lines the chambers, and the **pericardium** on the outside (a visceral membrane forming the pericardial sac in which the heart sits).

Covering the exterior of the heart are **coronary arteries** which feed the heart muscle with blood; being a muscle, it still requires the fuel to keep the pump working continually. Blockages of these arteries are responsible for many problems of the heart, and in particular cardiovascular diseases such as hypertension, angina pectoris and myocardial infarctions (heart attacks).

 ACTIVITY 1

1 Place the following terms in the correct sequential order to explain the flow of blood returning to the heart from the body and its path through the heart:
- **aorta**
- **lungs**
- **bicuspid valve**
- **left ventricle**
- **pulmonary vein**
- **tricuspid valve**
- **venae cavae**
- **right atrium**
- **pulmonary valve**
- **left atrium**
- **right ventricle**
- **aortic valve**
- **pulmonary artery**

2 Describe the location of the heart.

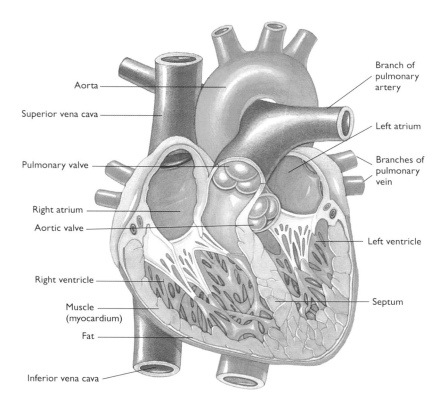

Fig. 3.2 STRUCTURE OF THE HEART

The cardiac cycle

The cardiac cycle refers to the process of cardiac contraction and blood transportation through the heart. As mentioned above, the heart can be viewed as two separate pumps to serve its dual purpose, and the cardiac cycle explains the sequence of events that takes place **during one complete heartbeat**. This includes the filling of the heart with blood and the emptying of the blood into the arterial system.

Each cycle takes approximately 0.8 seconds and occurs on average 72 times per minute. There are four stages to each heartbeat:

1 atrial diastole
2 ventricular diastole
3 atrial systole
4 ventricular systole.

Each stage depends upon whether the chambers of the heart are *filling* with blood while the heart is relaxing (**diastole**) or whether they are *emptying*, which occurs when the heart contracts (**systole**) and forces blood from one part of the heart to another or into the arterial system, and subsequently to the lungs and the body.

The first stage of the cardiac cycle is **atrial diastole** (0.7 sec). The upper chambers of the heart are filled with blood returning from:

• the body via the venae cavae to the right atrium; and
• the lungs via the pulmonary vein to the left atrium.

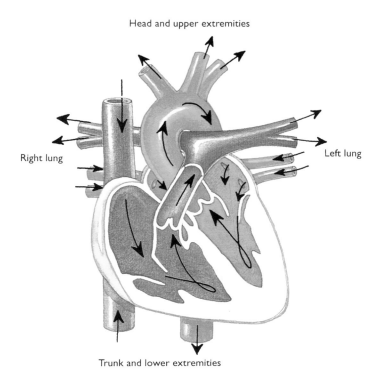

Head and upper extremities

Right lung

Left lung

Trunk and lower extremities

Fig. 3.3 THE PATH OF BLOOD THROUGH
THE HEART
Source: Tortora (1991)

At this time the atrioventricular valves are shut but as the atria fill with blood, atrial pressure overcomes ventricular pressure. Since blood always moves from areas of high pressure to areas of low pressure, the atrioventricular valves are forced open, and **ventricular diastole** (0.5 sec) now takes place. During this stage the ventricles fill with blood and the semi-lunar valves remain closed. The atria now contract, causing **atrial systole** (0.1 sec) which ensures that all the blood is ejected into the ventricles. As the ventricles continue going through diastole, the pressure increases, which causes the atrioventricular valves to close. Ultimately, the ventricular pressure overcomes that in the aorta and the pulmonary artery. The semi-lunar valves open and the ventricles contract, forcing all the blood from the right ventricle into the pulmonary artery and the blood in the left ventricle into the aorta. This is **ventricular systole** (0.3 sec), and once completed, the semi-lunar valves snap shut. The cycle is now complete and ready to be repeated. It is interesting to note that trained athletes have been reported to have a longer diastolic phase of the cardiac cycle, enabling a more complete filling of the heart. In this way, the trained athlete can increase venous return and therefore stroke volume (refer to Starling's law of the heart) during resting periods, which accounts for the decreased resting heart rate often experienced by trained atheletes.

How the heart works

The heart works by producing impulses which spread and innervate the specialised muscle fibres. Unlike skeletal muscle, the heart produces its own impulses (ie, it is **myogenic**), and it is the conduction system of the heart which spreads the impulses throughout the heart and enables the heart to contract.

The electrical impulse begins at the pacemaker: a mass of cardiac muscle cells known as the **sino-atrial node (S.A. node)** located in the right atrial wall. It is the rate at which the pacemaker emits impulses that determines heart rate. As the impulse is emitted, it spreads to the adjacent inter-connecting fibres of the atrium, which spreads the excitation extremely

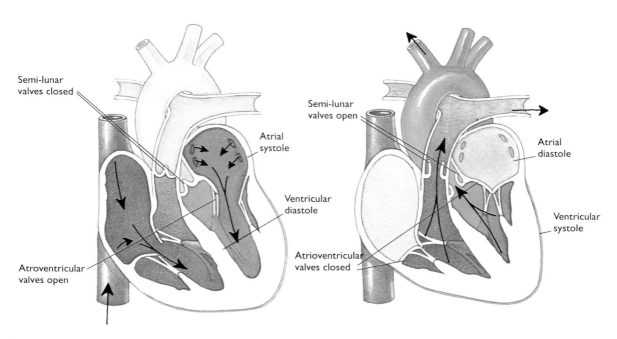

Fig. 3.4 STAGES OF THE CARDIAC CYCLE
Source: Tortora (1991)

rapidly and causes the atria to contract. It then passes to another specialised mass of cells called the **atrioventricular node (A.V. node)**. The A.V. node acts as a distributor and passes the action potential to the bundle of His, which, together with the branching Purkinje fibres, spreads the excitation throughout the ventricles.

There is a delay of about 0.1 second from the time when the A.V. node receives stimulation to when it distributes the action potential throughout the ventricles. This is crucial to allow completion of atrial contraction, before ventricular systole begins. The relationship between the electrical activity of the heart and the cardiac cycle can be shown through an electrocardiogram trace (ECG). From figure 3.6, it can be seen that three clearly visible

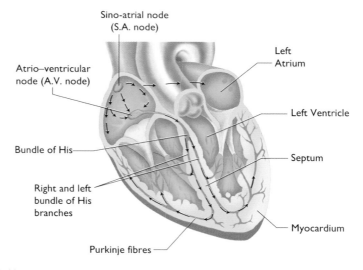

Fig. 3.5 THE CONDUCTION SYSTEM OF THE HEART

waves accompany each cycle. The first, the P wave, indicates the spread of an impulse throughout the atria (atrial depolarisation) which causes atrial systole. The second wave, the QRS complex, is a much larger wave and indicates the spread of the impulse throughout the ventricles (ventricular depolarisation). The T wave shows atrial repolarisation which occurs just before the ventricles can relax. The trace does not exhibit an atrial repolarisation since the large QRS wave masks it.

Heart regulation

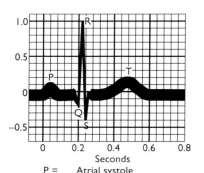

P = Atrial systole
QRS = Ventricular systole

Fig. 3.6 AN ELECTROCARDIOGRAM TRACE

The heart is governed by the **autonomic nervous system (ANS)** which operates without us having to think about it. In respect to the heart, it is the ANS which determines the rate at which the pacemaker (S.A. node) sends out impulses. The sympathetic and parasympathetic nervous systems are the two sub-divisions of the autonomic nervous system. They are fundamental to the regulation of the heart and work antagonistically as follows:

1 The **sympathetic nervous system** increases heart rate by releasing adrenaline and noradrenaline from the adrenal medulla. Adrenaline increases the strength of ventricular contraction, and therefore stroke volume, while noradrenaline (a transmitter substance) aids the spread of the impulse throughout the heart, and therefore increases heart rate.

2 The **parasympathetic nervous system**, on the other hand, releases acetylcholine, which slows the spread of impulses and therefore reduces heart rate, returning it to the normal resting level.

Regulation during exercise

At rest, the parasympathetic system overrides the sympathetic system, and keeps heart rate down. However, once exercise begins, the sympathetic system increases its activity, the parasympathetic system decreases in activity, and so heart rate is allowed to rise. Increased metabolic activity causes an increased concentration of carbon dioxide and lactic acid content in the blood, which increases acidity and decreases blood pH. These changes are detected by **chemoreceptors** sited in the aortic arch and carotid arteries. They inform the sympathetic centre in the upper thoracic area of the spinal cord to increase heart rate in order to transport the carbon dioxide to the lungs where it can be expelled. Messages from the sympathetic centre are sent to the S.A. node via **accelerator nerves** which release adrenaline (epinephrine) and noradrenaline (norepinephrine) upon stimulation.

Other factors which increase heart rate during exercise include:

• increased body temperature (and therefore decreased blood viscosity)
• increased venous return (a result of the increased action of the muscle pump).

Both of these factors will result in a greater cardiac output.

Once exercise ceases, sympathetic stimulation decreases and the parasympathetic system once again takes over. The parasympathetic system responds to information from **baroreceptors** – the body's in-built blood pressure recorders. When blood pressure is too high, messages are sent from the cardiac inhibitory centre to the S.A. node via the vagus nerve. The parasympathetic nerve then releases acetylcholine, which decreases the heart rate.

This continuous interaction of the sympathetic and parasympathetic system ensures that the heart works as efficiently as possible, and enables sufficient nutrients to reach the tissue cells to ensure effective muscle action.

Adrenaline and noradrenaline released from the adrenal medulla (situated at the top of the kidneys) generally have the same effect – increasing heart rate and increasing the strength of contraction. They also help to increase metabolic activity, convert glycogen into its usable form – glucose, make glucose and free fatty acids available to the muscle and help redistribute blood to the working muscles. The release of such hormones, controlled by the sympathetic system, results from many factors including exercise, emotions, excitement and stress.

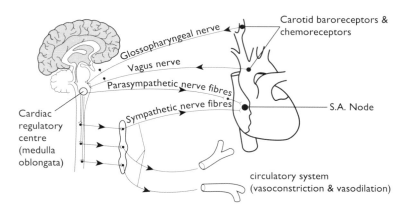

Fig. 3.7 THE REGULATION OF HEART RATE

1 **Fill in the missing gaps:**
   The _____ is a bundle of specialised cardiac muscle cells which generate action potentials and govern the heart rate. Impulses are spread across the atria and reach the _____ which delays the action potentials from spreading through the ventricles via the _____ and branching _____ .
2 **Discuss the difference between cardiac and skeletal muscle in terms of structure and function (you may wish to refer to page 21).**
3 **Describe the structure and function of the heart's conducting system.**
4 **Explain the role of the autonomic nervous system before, during and after embarking upon a distance run.**

Cardiac dynamics

Cardiac output

Cardiac output is the amount of blood that is pumped out of the heart from one ventricle per minute. Cardiac output is generally measured from the left ventricle, and is equal to the product of stroke volume and heart rate.

$$\text{Cardiac Output} = \text{Stroke Volume} \times \text{Heart Rate}$$
$$Q = \text{S.V.} \times \text{H.R.}$$

- The stroke volume is the amount of blood ejected into the aorta in one beat.
- The heart rate reflects the number of times the heart beats per minute.

On average, the resting stroke volume is 75 cm^3 per beat, and the resting heart rate for a person is 72 beats per minute. Therefore, cardiac output at rest is:

$$Q = \text{S.V.} \times \text{H.R.}$$
$$= 75 \text{ cm}^3 \times 72 \text{ bpm}$$
$$= 5,400 \text{ cm}^3 \ (5.4 \text{ Dm}^3)$$

However, during exercise the cardiac output may rise to 30 Dm^3 per minute – a six fold increase!

Training signals an improvement in cardiac output *during exercise*, brought about by an increase in stroke volume due to the larger volume of the left ventricle, and the hypertrophy (enlargement) of the heart (sometimes referred to as 'athletes' heart'). At rest, cardiac hypertrophy plays an important role, since increased stroke volume (which accompanies hypertrophy) allows the resting heart rate to decrease. This is known as **bradycardia**. The increased size of the ventricular cavity in trained athletes allows a longer diastolic phase during which time the heart can fill up with more blood. This stretches cardiac fibres and increases the strength of contraction, with the resultant effect of increasing stroke volume. Consequently, cardiac output does not change at rest following training.

Bradycardia occurs as a result of an increase in parasympathetic activity and a decrease in cardiac sympathetic activity, often to the extent that resting heart rate decreases to 60 bpm and below. During exercise, the hormones have a great influence on stroke volume and cardiac output. Adrenaline and noradrenaline increase the force of cardiac contraction, by increasing the contractility of cardiac muscle fibres. Muscle fibres are elastic and can stretch during the diastolic phase of the cardiac cycle which allows a more complete filling of the heart and thus increases cardiac output. This relationship is known as **Starling's law** and there appears to be a linear relationship between cardiac output and exercise intensity.

What is cardiac output, and how is it measured?

The trained heart

We have examined how the heart responds and adjusts to exercise in the short time of an exercise session. Let us now turn our attention to the effects of long term training on the heart.

As mentioned above, the heart of an athlete is larger than that of a non-athlete and often displays greater vascularisation. Cardiac hypertrophy is characterised by a larger ventricular wall and a thicker myocardium. Endurance athletes tend to display larger ventricular cavities, while those following high resistance or strength training régimes display thicker ventricular walls.

Cardiac hypertrophy is accompanied by a decreased resting heart rate. This can easily be demonstrated by comparing the resting heart rates of trained and untrained people. When the heart rate falls below 60 bpm, bradycardia is said to have occurred, and is due to a slowing in the intrinsic rate of the atrial pacemaker (S.A. node) and an increase in the predominance of the parasympathetic system acting upon the pacemaker. Since the resting cardiac output for an athlete is approximately the same as that of a non-athlete, the athlete compensates for the lower resting heart rate by increasing stroke volume. This increased resting stroke volume is greatest among endurance athletes, due to the increased size of the ventricular cavity. The increase can also be as a result of improved contractility of the myocardium, which is highlighted by the increased **ejection fraction** reported by athletes. The ejection fraction represents the percentage of the blood entering the left ventricle which is actually pumped out per beat. On average this is approximately 60% but can reach 85% following training.

The vascular system

Having examined how the heart works to pump the blood into the network of blood vessels, we will now take a closer look at how the blood supports the functioning of the body and how the blood vessels ensure that sufficient blood reaches the body's tissues.

The blood

Blood consists of cells and cell fragments surrounded by a liquid matrix known as **plasma**. The average male has a total blood volume of 5–6 litres, and the average female blood volume is approximately 4–5 litres.

Functions of blood

The blood's functions are fundamental to life itself and include:

- transportation of nutrients
- protection
- the maintenance of homeostasis.

The blood is responsible for transporting oxygen to the body's cells and removing metabolites such as carbon dioxide from the muscle to the lungs. The blood also transports glucose from the liver to the muscle, and lactic acid from the muscle to the liver where it can be converted back to glucose. Further functions include the transportation of enzymes, hormones and other chemicals all of which have a vital role to play in the body, no more so than during exercise.

The blood protects the body by containing cells and chemicals which are central to the immune system. When damage to blood vessels occurs, the blood clots in order to prevent cell loss.

The blood is vital in maintaining the body's state of equilibrium; eg, through hormone and enzyme activity, and the buffering capacity of the blood, the blood's pH should remain relatively stable. In addition the blood is involved in temperature regulation and can transport heat to the surface of the body where it can be released. All these factors are particularly important during exercise to ensure optimal performance.

Blood composition

1 **Plasma** (55% of blood composition) – this is a pale yellow fluid composed of water (90%), proteins (8%) and salts (2%).
2 **Erythrocytes** – these are red corpuscles which contain **haemoglobin**, an iron-rich protein which is responsible for all the oxygen transport in the blood. The ability of the blood to carry oxygen is determined by haemoglobin concentration, which may be increased through endurance training.
3 **Leucocytes** – these are white blood cells, and are involved in combating infection. Although larger than red blood cells, white blood cells are fewer in number.
4 **Thrombocytes** – thrombocytes or platelets are small bits of cytoplasm derived from the bone marrow, which play an important role in blood clotting, and so limit haemorrhaging.

Blood viscosity

Viscosity refers to the thickness of the blood and its resistance to flow. The more viscous a fluid, the more resistant it is to flow. The greater the volume of red blood cells, the greater the capacity to transport oxygen. However, unless it is accompanied by an increase in plasma, viscosity may also increase, and restrict blood flow. Viscosity may also increase when plasma content decreases due to dehydration (which may accompany endurance based exercise).

Haematocrit is the percentage of the total blood volume composed of red blood cells and typically varies between 40% and 45%.

- Haemoconcentration is an increase in the proportion of red blood cells in the blood, and is usually as a result of a decrease in blood plasma volume.
- Haemodilution is a decrease in red blood cell volume, due to an increase in plasma volume.

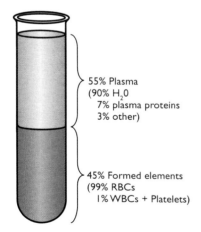

55% Plasma
(90% H$_2$0
  7% plasma proteins
  3% other)

45% Formed elements
(99% RBCs
  1% WBCs + Platelets)

Fig. 3.8 THE CONSTITUENTS OF BLOOD

Training brings about an increase in total blood volume, and therefore an increase in the number of red blood cells. However the plasma volume increases more than blood cell volume so the blood viscosity decreases. This facilitates blood flow through the blood vessels, and improves oxygen delivery to the working muscles.

List the functions and characteristics of blood.

Blood vessels

The vascular network through which blood flows to all parts of the body comprises of arteries, arterioles, capillaries, veins and venules.

Arteries and arterioles

Arteries are high pressure vessels which carry blood from the heart to the tissues. The largest artery in the body is the aorta which is the main artery leaving the heart. The aorta constantly subdivides and gets smaller. The constant subdivision decreases the diameter of the vessel arteries, which now become arterioles. As the network subdivides blood velocity decreases, which enables the efficient delivery and exchange of gases.

Arteries are composed of three layers of tissue:

1 an outer fibrous layer – the tunica adventitia or tunica externa
2 a thick middle layer – the tunica media
3 a thin lining of cells to the inside – the endothelium or tunica intima.

The tunica media is comprised of smooth muscle and elastic tissue, which enables the arteries and arterioles to alter their diameter. Arteries tend to have more elastic tissue, while arterioles have greater amounts of smooth muscle; this allows the vessels to increase the diameter through **vasodilation** or decrease the diameter through **vasoconstriction**. It is through vasoconstriction and vasodilation that the vessels can regulate blood pressure and ensure the tissues are receiving sufficient blood – particularly during exercise. This is explained in more detail on p 55.

Arteries and arterioles have three basic functions:

• to act as conduits carrying and controlling blood flow to the tissues
• to cushion and smooth out the pulsatile flow of blood from the heart
• to help control blood pressure.

Veins and venules

Veins are low pressure vessels which return blood to the heart. The structure is similar to arteries, although they possess less smooth muscle and elastic tissue. Venules are the smallest veins and transport blood away from the capillary bed into the veins. Veins gradually increase in thickness the nearer to the heart they get, until they reach the largest vein in the body, the **vena cava**, which enters the right atrium of the heart.

The thinner walls of the veins often distend and allow blood to pool in them. This is also allowed to happen as the veins contain pocket valves which close intermittently to prevent back flow of blood. This explains why up to 70% of total blood volume is found in the venous system at any one time.

Capillaries

Capillaries are the functional units or the vascular system. Composed of a single layer of endothelial cells, they are just thin enough to allow red blood cells to squeeze through their wall. The capillary network is very well developed as they are so small; large quantities are able to cover the muscle, which ensures efficient exchange of gases. If the cross-sectional area of all the capillaries in the body were to be added together, the total area would be much greater than that of the aorta.

Distribution of blood through the capillary network is regulated by special structures known as pre-capillary sphincters, the structure of which will be dealt with later in this chapter.

The circulatory system

The blood flows through a continuous network of blood vessels, which form a double circuit. This connects the heart to the lungs, and the heart to all other body tissues.

The double circulatory system

Pulmonary circulation transports blood between the lungs and the heart. The pulmonary artery carries blood low in oxygen concentration from the right ventricle to the lung, where it becomes oxygen-rich and unloads carbon dioxide. The pulmonary vein then transports the freshly oxygenated blood back to the heart and into the left atrium.

The blood returning to the left atrium is pumped through the left side of the heart and into the aorta, where it is distributed to the whole of the body's tissues by a network of arteries. Veins then return the blood, which is now low in oxygen and high in carbon dioxide concentration, to the heart where it enters the right atrium via the venae cavae. This circuit is known as **systemic circulation**.

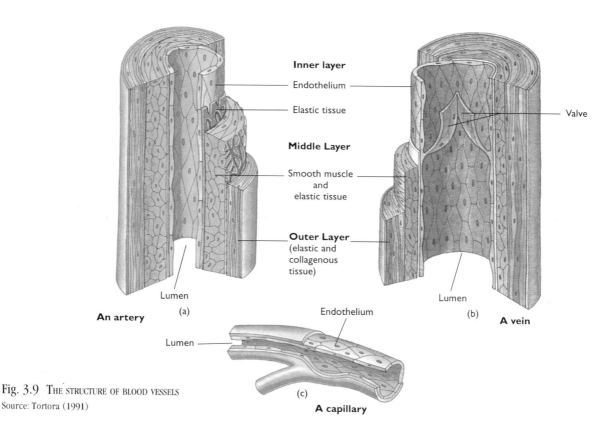

Fig. 3.9 The structure of blood vessels
Source: Tortora (1991)

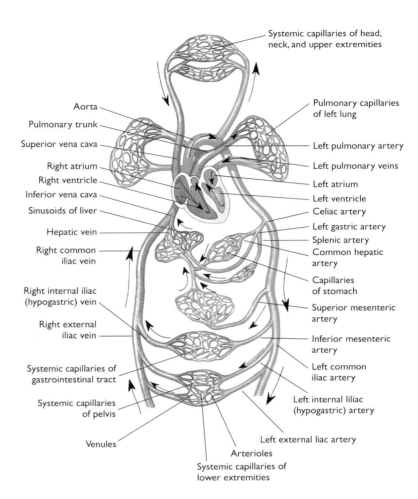

Fig. 3.10 THE DOUBLE CIRCULATORY SYSTEM
Source: Tortora (1991)

The venous return mechanism

Venous return is the term used for the blood which returns to the right side of the heart via the veins. As mentioned above, up to 70% of the total volume of blood is contained in the veins at rest. This provides a large reservoir of blood which is returned rapidly to the heart when needed. The heart can only pump out as much blood as it receives, so cardiac output is dependent upon venous return. A rapid increase in venous return enables a significant increase in cardiac output due to Starling's law (see p 49).

Fig. 3.11 THE MUSCLE PUMP AND VENOUS RETURN

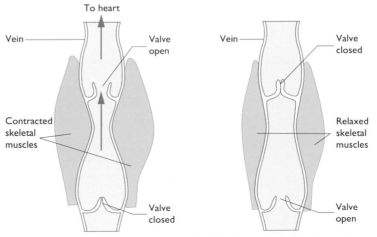

The massaging action of the muscles squeezes blood back towards the heart increasing venous return and therefore cardiac output.

There are several mechanisms which aid the venous return process:

1 **The muscle pump** – As exercise begins, muscular contractions impinge and compress upon the veins, squeezing blood towards the heart. Pocket valves prevent any backflow of blood that might occur. This is illustrated in fig 3.11.

2 **The respiratory pump** – During inspiration and expiration, pressure changes occur in the thoracic and abdominal cavities which compress veins and assist blood return to the heart.

These two mechanisms are essential at the start of exercise. As exercise commences the muscles contracting squeeze the vast amount of blood within the veins back towards the heart to enable stroke volume to increase and optimal delivery of nutrients to the working muscles.

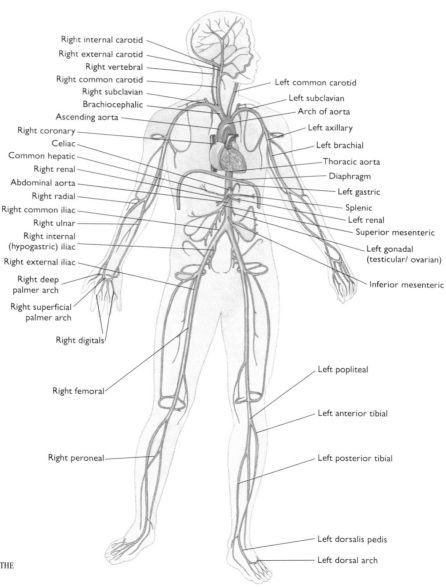

Fig. 3.12 MAJOR ARTERIES OF THE SYSTEMIC SYSTEM (ARTERIES)

The pulse rate

The pulse is a pressure wave which is generated from the heart each time the left ventricle pumps blood into the aorta. The increased pressure causes slight dilation of the arteries as the blood travels through the arteries around the body and this can be felt at various sites on the body. The most common sites where the pulse can be palpated are:

- the radial artery
- the carotid artery
- the femoral artery
- the brachial artery
- the temporal artery.

1 Record your pulse for a 10 second count at each of the following sites:
- carotid artery
- radial artery
- brachial artery.

Remember to start counting from zero.

2 Multiply your scores by six to achieve your heart rate score in beats per minute.

3 Account for any differences in your heart rate scores at the different sites.

4 Why should you never use your thumb to measure your pulse?

An investigation to examine heart rate response to varying intensities of exercise.

Equipment: stop watch, gymnastics bench, metronome

1 Record resting heart rate for a 10 second count at the beginning of the class.

2 Record heart rate for a 10 second count at the carotid artery immediately prior to exercise.

3 Start exercising by stepping onto and off the bench at a low intensity, keeping in time with the metronome.

4 Record your pulse after one, two and three minutes of exercise. After the third minute of exercise, stop the test. Continue to record your pulse each minute during recovery.

5 Once your heart rate has returned to its resting value (or within a few beats) repeat the test at a medium intensity. Record your results as before.

6 Repeat the exercise for a third time but at a very high intensity. Once again record your results.

7 Convert your heart rate scores into beats per minute by multiplying by six.

8 Now use your results to plot a graph for each of the three workloads. Plot each graph using the same axes, placing heart rate along the 'Y' axis and time along the bottom 'X' axis. Don't forget to show your resting heart rate values on the graph.

9 For each of your graphs explain the heart rate patterns prior to, during and following exercise.

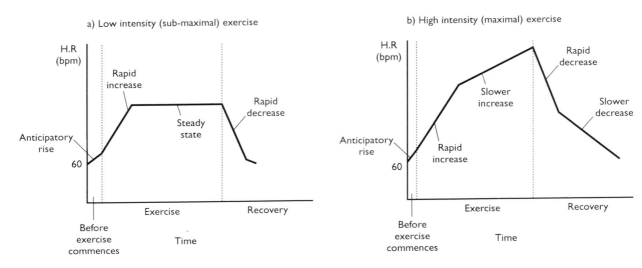

Fig. 3.17 EXPECTED HEART RATE CURVES
FOR DIFFERENT INTENSITIES OF EXERCISE

Using Fig 3.17 account for the different patterns in heart rate for sub-maximal and maximal exercise.

Cardiovascular adaptations to training

Following endurance training, many cardiovascular adaptations arise. In the first instance, the actual size of the heart may increase – **cardiac hypertrophy**. This enables the heart to work more efficiently, particularly at rest. The increase in thickness of the myocardium (cardiac tissue) enables the left ventricle to fill more completely with blood during the diastole phase of the cardiac cycle. This allows the heart to pump more blood per beat since the thicker walls can contract more forcefully, pumping more blood into the systemic system and ultimately to the muscles.

Consequently, stroke volume increases both at rest and during exercise. With an increase in **stroke volume at rest**, the heart will no longer need to pump as many times per minute to achieve the same amount of blood flowing to the body's tissues.

Since the heart seeks to work as efficiently as possible resting heart rate decreases as a result of the endurance training that has taken place.

When resting heart rate falls to below 60 beats per minute, **bradycardia** results, which explains the very low resting heart rates often experienced by top endurance athletes; for example, Indurain, the many times Tour de France champion is reported to have a resting heart rate of around 30 bpm!

As an athlete's stroke volume increases, the cardiac output of the trained athlete also increases. Cardiac output may increase by up to 30–40 min in trained individuals. However it is important to note that there is little or no change in the values of resting cardiac output, due to the decrease in resting heart rate that accompanies endurance training.

The adaptations mentioned above have centred on the structure and function of the heart. We now need to discuss those training-induced changes that occur in the **vascular** and **circulatory** systems:

1 One reason that accounts for greater performances in aerobic events following training is the increased **capillarisation** of trained muscles. New capillaries may actually develop which enables more blood to flow to the muscles and enables more oxygen to reach the tissues. Furthermore, existing capillaries become more efficient and allow greater amounts of blood to reach the muscles, which also become more efficient at extracting the oxygen due to the muscular adaptations mentioned above.

2 Improvements in the vasculature efficiency (especially the arteries) to **vasoconstrict** and **vasodilate**, improve the redistribution of blood by shunting the supply to the active muscles and tissues, so that there is a greater supply of oxygen for energy production in these working muscles.

3 These efficiency gains also result in a **decreased resting blood pressure** following endurance training, although blood pressure during exercise of a sub-maximal or maximal nature remains unchanged.

4 Increases in blood volume following training can be attributed to an **increase in blood plasma** (the water component of the blood). This has the important function of decreasing the blood viscosity and enabling the blood to flow around the body more easily, thus enhancing oxygen delivery to the muscles and tissues.

5 An increase in **red** blood cell volume and **haemoglobin** content is also higher in the trained athlete which further facilitates the transport of oxygen around the body. However although haemoglobin content increases, the increase in blood plasma is greater and consequently the blood haematocrit (the ratio of red blood cell volume to total blood volume) is reduced, which lowers the viscosity of the blood and facilitates its progress around the body.

 **ACTIVITY 11**

Complete the table below showing the responses of the cardiovascular system to exercise.

FACTOR	INCREASE/DECREASE	EXPLANATION
heart rate		
stroke volume		
cardiac output		
blood pressure		
blood flow to working muscles		
a-$\bar{V}O_2$ diff		
blood acidity		
parasympathetic activity		
sympathetic activity		

Summary

- The structure of the heart is specially adapted to its function.
- Valves within the heart ensure a unidirectional flow of blood.
- The sounds of the heart are a result of these valves snapping shut. The Lub sound results from the closing of the atrioventricular valves, whilst the Dub results from the closure of the semi-lunar valves.
- Typically the heart is composed of three layers: an outer pericardium, a thick muscular layer called the myocardium, and a smooth inner endocardium.
- Coronary arteries ensure the heart receives an adequate supply of blood.
- The cardiac cycle explains the passage of blood through the heart. It consists of four stages: Atrial Diastole, Atrial Systole, Ventricular Diastole and Ventricular Systole.
- The heart is myogenic – it creates its own impulses.
- The impulse is emitted from the S.A. node the surrounding fibres are innervated causing the atria to contract. The impulse eventually arrives at the A.V. node, where it is dispersed down the bundle of His and throughout the Purkinje fibres, causing the ventricles to contract.
- The heart rate is governed by the parasympathetic and sympathetic nervous systems. The sympathetic nervous system increases heart rate by releasing adrenaline and noradrenaline, whilst the parasympathetic nervous system slows the heart down through the action of another hormone acetylcholine.
- Increases in heart rate during exercise are largely the result of increased metabolic activity increasing the concentration of carbon dioxide.
- Cardiac output is the volume of blood pumped out of one ventricle in one minute. Stroke volume is the volume of blood pumped out of one ventricle in one beat and heart rate the number of times the heart beats per minute.
- Cardiac hypertrophy is the enlargement of the heart often resulting from endurance training.
- Bradycardia is the reduction in resting heart rate (usually below 60bpm) which accompanies cardiac hypertrophy.
- The vascular system encompasses the blood and blood vessels.
- The blood's main functions are the transportation of oxygen and the maintenance of homeostasis.
- Typically blood is composed of Plasma (water, proteins and salts) Erythrocytes, Leucocytes, and Thrombocytes.
- Major blood vessels consist of arteries, arterioles, capillaries, venules and veins.
- The continuous network of blood vessels in the body is known as the circulatory system, which is composed of the pulmonary and systemic circuits.
- Blood returning to the heart via the veins is known as venous return. It is aided by the muscle and respiratory pumps.
- Blood pressure is the force exerted by the blood on the inner walls of the blood vessels. It is a product of cardiac output and resistance of the vessel walls.
- Blood flow is controlled by the vasomotor centre which causes blood vessels to vasodilate and vasoconstrict and determines the degree of blood reaching various parts of the body.

Review Questions

1 Describe the path that blood takes through the heart, from the point at which it enters via the vena cava to where it exits via the aorta.

2 When using a stethoscope, is it possible to hear the heart beating? What creates the heartbeat and when do these sounds occur during the cardiac cycle?

3 Describe the action of the sympathetic and parasympathetic nervous system on the heart before, during and following exercise.

4 Outline the major functions of the blood. Explain the importance of blood when exercising.

5 Sketch and label a graph showing the heart rate pattern expected from an athlete completing a 400m run in a personal best time of 45 seconds followed by a 15 minute recovery period. Account for these changes.

6 Outline the major factors which affect cardiac output during exercise.

7 During exercise the return of blood to the heart is paramount. Explain how the body achieves this and relate to Starling's law.

8 Explain what you would expect to happen to blood pressure in the following instances:
(a) an athlete undertaking a steady swim (b) an athlete completing a 100m sprint
(c) a weight lifter performing a maximal lift (d) an athlete completing the cycling stage of a triathlon.

9 Endurance training results in significant benefits to the heart and vascular system. What are these benefits and how do they contribute to a 'healthier lifestyle'?

chapter 4

Respiratory Considerations

T his chapter examines the structure and function of the respiratory system, including detail on the lungs and the respiratory airways. It also looks at the mechanics of breathing, the process of inspiration and expiration and definitions of lung volumes and capacities. Simple investigations of measurement of these volumes are also included.

The chapter studies gaseous exchange, partial pressures and the transport of gases in the body; factors that may influence oxygen delivery and uptake; and oxygen consumption and the response of the respiratory system to training. Links can be made to other chapters of the book, particularly Chapters 5 and 6, on training and fitness.

The respiratory system is often studied in combination with the cardiovascular system, since the two systems work together to ensure an efficient and continuous supply of oxygen to the body's cells.

Respiration can be divided into two processes – external respiration and internal respiration.

External respiration

External respiration involves the movement of gases into and out of the lungs and the exchange of gases between the lungs and the blood is known as pulmonary diffusion.

On its journey to the lungs, air drawn into the body passes many structures as outlined below:

Nasal passages

Air is drawn into the body via the nose. The nasal cavity is divided by a cartilaginous septum, forming the nasal passages. The interior structures of the nose help the respiratory process by performing the following important functions:

1 the mucus membranes and blood capillaries moisten and warm the inspired air
2 the ciliated epithelium filters and traps dust particles which are moved to the throat for elimination
3 the small bones known as chonchae increase the surface area of the cavity to make the process more efficient.

The oral pharynx and larynx

The throat is shared by both the respiratory and alimentary tract. Air entering the larynx passes over the vocal chords and into the trachea. In swallowing, the larynx is drawn upwards and forwards against the base of the epiglottis, thus preventing entry of food.

The trachea

The trachea or windpipe is approximately 10 cm in length and lies in front of the oesophagus. It is composed of 18 horseshoe shaped rings of cartilage which are also lined by a mucous membrane and ciliated cells which provide the same protection against dust as the nasal passageways. The trachea extends from the larynx and directs air into the right and left primary bronchi.

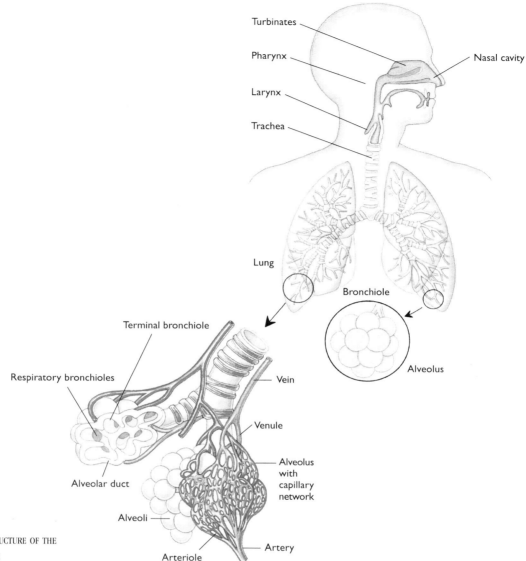

Fig. 4.1 THE STRUCTURE OF THE
RESPIRATORY SYSTEM

Intercostal
muscles
contract and
swings ribs
upwards

Sternum

Spine

Fig. 4.2 MODEL SHOWING THE ACTION OF
THE RIB CAGE

The bronchi and bronchioles

The trachea divides into the right and left bronchus which further subdivide into lobar bronchi (three feeding each lobe on the right, two feeding each lobe on the left). Further subdivision of these airways form bronchioles which in turn branch into the smaller terminal or respiratory bronchioles. The bronchioles enable the air to pass into the alveoli via the alveolar ducts, and it is here that pulmonary diffusion occurs (see p 67).

Alveoli

The alveoli are responsible for the exchange of gases between the lungs and the blood. The alveolar walls are extremely thin and are composed of epithelial cells which are lined by a thin film of water, essential for dissolving oxygen from the inspired air.

Surrounding each alveolus is an extensive capillary network which ensures a smooth passage of oxygen into the pulmonary capillaries. The tiny lumen of each capillary surrounding the alveoli ensure that red blood cells travel in single file, and that they are squeezed into a bi-concave shape increasing the surface area and enabling the greatest possible uptake of oxygen. It has been estimated that each lung contains up to 150 million alveoli, providing a tremendous surface area for the exchange of gases. The alveoli walls also contain elastic fibres which further increase the surface during inspiration.

Breathing mechanics

The lungs are surrounded by pleural sacs containing pleural fluid which reduces friction during respiration. These sacs are attached to both the lungs and the thoracic cage, which enables the lungs to inflate and deflate as the chest expands and flattens. The interrelationship between the lungs, pleural sacs and thoracic cage are central to the understanding of the respiratory processes of inspiration and expiration.

Inspiration

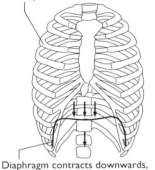

Intercostal muscles cause the rib cage to pivot on the thoracic vertebrae and more upwards and outwards.

Diaphragm contracts downwards, increasing the 'depth' of the thoracic cavity.

Fig. 4.3 ACTION OF THE RIB CAGE DURING INSPIRATION

The process of inspiration is an active one. It occurs as a result of the contraction of the respiratory muscles, namely the **external intercostal** muscles and the **diaphragm**.

The external intercostal muscles are attached to each rib. When they contract, they cause the rib cage to pivot about thoracic vertebral joints and move upwards and outwards, much like the handle of a bucket as it is lifted. The diaphragm, a dome shaped muscle separating the abdominal and thoracic cavities, contracts downwards during inspiration, increasing the area of the thoracic cavity. As the chest expands through these muscular contractions, the surface tension created by the film of pleural fluid causes the lungs to be pulled outwards along with the chest walls. This action causes the space within the lungs to increase and the air molecules within to move further apart.

As pressure is determined by the rate at which molecules strike a surface in a given time, the pressure within the lungs (intrapulmonary pressure) decreases and becomes less than that outside the body. Gases always move from areas of higher pressure to areas of lower pressure, so that air from outside the body rushes into the lungs via the respiratory tract. This process is known as **inspiration**.

During exercise, greater volumes of air can fill the lungs since the sternocleido-mastoid and scaleni muscles can help increase the thoracic cavity still further.

Expiration

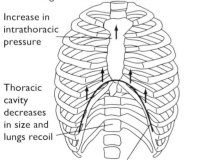

Relaxation of respiratory muscles cause the rib cage to move downwards and inwards.

Increase in intrathoracic pressure

Thoracic cavity decreases in size and lungs recoil

Diaphragm relaxes into a dome shape.

Fig. 4.4 ACTION OF THE RIB CAGE DURING EXPIRATION

The process of expiration is generally a passive process and occurs as a result of the relaxation of the respiratory muscles used in inspiration. As the external intercostal muscles relax, the rib cage is lowered into its resting position, and the diaphragm relaxes and domes up into the thoracic cavity. The area of the lungs is thus decreased and intrapulmonary pressure increases to an extent where it is greater than atmospheric pressure. Air inside the lungs is forced out to equate the pressure inside and outside the body.

During exercise, the process of expiration becomes more active as the **internal intercostal muscles** pull the ribs downwards to help increase the ventilation rate. These muscles are ably assisted by the abdominals and the latissimus dorsi muscles.

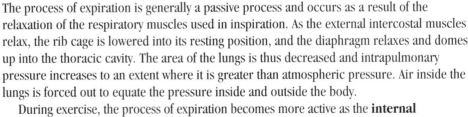

1 **Name the respiratory muscles used both at rest and during exercise.**
2 **How might training affect them?**

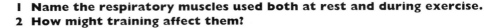

Pulmonary diffusion

Pulmonary diffusion is the term used to explain the process of gaseous exchange in the lungs. It has two major functions:

1 to replenish the blood with oxygen where it can then be transported to the tissues and muscles
2 to remove carbon dioxide from the blood which has resulted from metabolic processes in the tissues.

Partial pressure of gases

Central to the understanding of gaseous exchange is the concept of partial pressure. The partial pressure of a gas is the individual pressure that the gas exerts when it occurs in a mixture of gases. The gas will exert a pressure proportional to its concentration within the whole gas. Thus the partial pressures of each individual gas within a mixture of gases should, when added together, be equal to the total pressure of the gas.

For example, the air we breathe is composed of three main gases: nitrogen (79%), oxygen (20.9%) and carbon dioxide (0.03%). The percentages show the relative concentrations of each gas in atmospheric air.

At sea level, total atmospheric pressure is 769 mmHg which reflects the pressure that atmospheric air exerts. For example:

- The concentration of O_2 in the atmosphere is approximately 21%
- The concentration of nitrogen in the air is approximately 79%
- Together they exert a pressure of 760 mmHg at sea level.

Therefore the PO_2 (partial pressure of oxygen) is calculated as:

$$PO_2 = \text{Barometric pressure} \times \text{fractional concentration}$$
$$= 760 \times 0.21$$
$$= 159.6 \text{ mmHg}$$

Partial pressure of gases explain the movement of gases within the body, and account for the processes of gas exchange between the alveoli and the blood, and between the blood and the muscle or tissue.

Gaseous exchange at the lungs

It is the imbalance between gases in the alveoli and the blood that causes a pressure gradient, which results in a movement of gases across the respiratory membrane (which facilitates this movement by being extremely thin, measuring only 0.5 mm). This movement is two way, with oxygen moving from the alveoli into the blood and carbon dioxide diffusing from the blood into the alveoli. The partial pressure of oxygen (PO_2) in the atmosphere is approximately 159 mmHg (0.21×760 mmHg), which drops to 105 mmHg in the alveoli since the air combines with water vapour and carbon dioxide which is already present in the alveoli. Fig 4.5 illustrates this point.

Blood in the pulmonary capillaries which surround the alveoli has a PO_2 of 45 mmHg, since much of the oxygen has been already used by the working muscles. This results in a pressure gradient of approximately 60 mmHg which forces oxygen from the alveoli into the blood, until such a time that the pressure is equal on each side of the membrane.

In the same way, carbon dioxide moves along a pressure gradient from the pulmonary capillaries into the alveoli. With a PCO_2 of 45 mmHg in the blood returning to the lungs and a PCO_2 of 40 mmHg in the alveolar air, a small pressure gradient of 5 mmHg results. This

Fig. 4.5 PARTIAL PRESSURES OF OXYGEN AND CARBON DIOXIDE AT VARIOUS SITES IN THE BODY

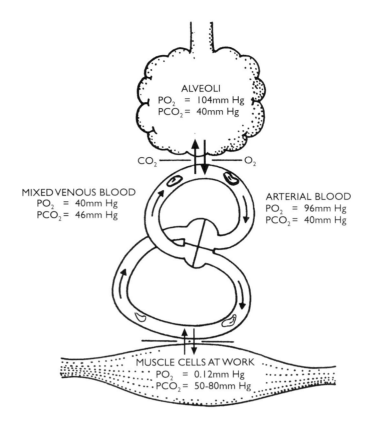

causes CO_2 to move from the pulmonary blood into the alveoli, which is later expired. Although the pressure gradient is relatively small, the CO_2 can cross the respiratory membrane much more rapidly than oxygen, as its membrane solubility is 20 times greater.

Endurance athletes, with larger aerobic capacities will have greater oxygen diffusion ability (the rate at which oxygen diffuses into the pulmonary blood from the alveoli) as a result of increased cardiac output, increased alveoli surface area, and reduced resistance to diffusion.

The effect of altitude

With altitude there is a decrease in atmospheric pressure but the percentages of gases within the air remains identical to that at sea level (nitrogen 79%, oxygen 20.9%, carbon dioxide 0.03%). However it is the partial pressure of the gases that changes in direct proportion to an increase in altitude.

For example: At rest the PO_2 of arterial blood is approx 100 mmHg whilst that in resting muscles and tissues is 40 mmHg. The difference between the two indicates the pressure gradient and ensures an efficient movement of oxygen from the blood into the muscle. The PO_2 of arterial blood at an altitude of 8,000 ft drops significantly to approximately 60 mmHg whilst that in the muscles remains at 40 mmHg causing the pressure gradient to fall to 20 mmHg at altitude. This dramatic reduction in the pressure gradient reduces the movement of oxygen into the body's muscles and performance decreases.

Many endurance athletes often undertake a period of altitude training before major events.

1　**Explain what is meant by the partial pressure of a gas.**
2　**State how this affects gaseous exchange around the body.**

The transport of oxygen

The majority of oxygen is carried by the red blood cells combined with haemoglobin; this is an iron-based protein which chemically combines with oxygen to form oxyhaemoglobin.

Haemoglobin $+$ Oxygen $\rightarrow$ Oxyhaemoglobin
Hb $+$ O_2 $\rightarrow$ HbO_2

Each molecule of haemoglobin can combine with four molecules of oxygen, which amounts to approximately 1.34 ml. The concentration of haemoglobin in the blood is about 15 g per 100 ml, thus each 100 ml of blood can transport up to 20 ml of oxygen (1.34×15). However, the amount of oxygen that can combine with haemoglobin is determined by the partial pressure of oxygen (PO_2). A high PO_2 results in complete haemoglobin saturation, while at lower PO_2, haemoglobin saturation decreases.

Haemoglobin is almost 100% saturated with oxygen at a PO_2 of 100 mmHg (which is the PO_2 in the alveoli). Therefore, at the lungs, haemoglobin is totally saturated with oxygen, and even if more oxygen were available, it could not be transported. As the PO_2 is reduced, haemoglobin saturation decreases accordingly. This is largely due to the increased acidity of the blood (decrease in blood pH), caused by an increase in CO_2 content or lactic acid, and causes a shift in the haemoglobin saturation curve to the right. This is known as the **Bohr shift**, and explains how oxygen is disassociated from haemoglobin at lower pH values in order to feed the tissues.

During exercise, increased CO_2 production causes a greater disassociation of oxygen due to the decrease in muscle pH. A further cause is the increase in body temperature that accompanies exercise; as oxygen unloading becomes more effective, the disassociation curve shifts to the right.

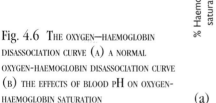

Fig. 4.6 THE OXYGEN–HAEMOGLOBIN DISASSOCIATION CURVE (A) A NORMAL OXYGEN-HAEMOGLOBIN DISASSOCIATION CURVE (B) THE EFFECTS OF BLOOD pH ON OXYGEN-HAEMOGLOBIN SATURATION

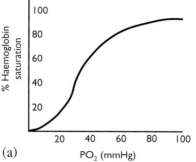

(a)

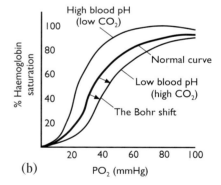

(b)

The overall efficiency of oxygen transport is therefore dependent upon haemoglobin content, and many athletes have sought to increase haemoglobin content through the illegal practice of blood doping. By removing blood which is subsequently replaced by the body, the athlete reinfuses it, to increase blood volume and more importantly haemoglobin content. Results of research on the practice of blood doping are conflicting, and it should always be remembered that it is illegal under the current Olympic Committee doping rules.

More recently the preferred cheater's drug has been EPO – a synthetic version of erythropoietin, a glycoprotein that occurs naturally in the body and stimulates the production of red blood cells. The drug's advantages are that it can increase the oxygen carrying capacity of the blood and therefore improve endurance performance. But EPO has a potentially fatal side, as well as being illegal for competition, it is expensive and several top cyclists have died following misuse of the drug. Thankfully a new test has recently become available to detect use of this potentially fatal drug.

The transport of carbon dioxide

Carbon dioxide produced in the body's tissues is also transported in the blood in various ways:

- approximately 8% is dissolved in the blood plasma
- up to 20% combines with haemoglobin to form carbaminohaemoglobin
- up to 70% of carbon dioxide is transported in the form of bicarbonate ion.

Initially carbon dioxide reacts with water to form carbonic acid. However, **carbon anhydrase**, an enzyme found in red blood cells, quickly breaks down to free a hydrogen ion (H^+) and form a bicarbonate ion (HCO_3^-).

$$CO_2 + H_2O \rightarrow H_2CO_3 \ (+ \ CA) \rightarrow H^+ + HCO_3^-$$

The hydrogen ion (H^+) combines with haemoglobin to form haemoglobinic acid. This causes oxygen to disassociate from the haemoglobin, and shifts the oxygen disassociation curve to the right (the Bohr shift):

$$H^+ + HbO_2 \rightarrow HHb + O_2$$

In this way, the bicarbonate ion frees oxygen for tissue respiration and can aid in the removal of carbon dioxide and other metabolites such as lactic acid. As the blood returns to the lungs, the PCO_2 is low and the H^+ and bicarbonate ion reassociate to form carbonic acid once again. The instability of this acid causes it to split further into water and carbon dioxide, where particles can diffuse into the alveoli and be expired:

$$H^+ + HCO_{3-} \rightarrow H_2CO_3 \rightarrow CO_2 + H_2O$$

This reduction in hydrogen ion concentration of the blood is central to the body's **buffering** system, a system which tries to negate the effects of lactic acid accumulation. When blood pH falls during high intensity exercise, the bicarbonate ion helps to resist the change in pH by absorbing damaging hydrogen ions which have been given up by acids such as lactic acid.

ACTIVITY 3

1. **Explain how the oxyhaemoglobin disassociation curve can aid our understanding of gaseous exchange. How might increases in blood acidity affect the curve?**
2. **Outline how CO_2 is transported in the body. What is the role of the bicarbonate ion in this process?**

Gas exchange at the muscles and tissues

We have seen how oxygen is brought into the lungs and transported to the capillary beds on the muscles. We now need to turn our attention to how the oxygen can enter the muscle cell.

The process is similar to the exchange of gases at the lungs: the partial pressure of the gases in the blood and tissues determines the movement of oxygen and carbon dioxide into and out of the tissue cells. The high partial pressure of oxygen in the arterial blood and the relatively low PO_2 in the muscles causes a pressure gradient which enables oxygen to disassociate from haemoglobin and pass through the capillary wall and into the muscle cytoplasm. Conversely, the high PCO_2 in the tissues and low PCO_2 in the arterial blood cause a movement of carbon dioxide in the opposite direction. The production of carbon dioxide in fact stimulates the disassociation of oxygen from haemoglobin as we learned in the previous section, and this (together with greater tissue demand for oxygen) increases the pressure gradients during exercise.

Once oxygen has entered the muscle cell, it immediately attaches to a substance called **myoglobin**, which is not dissimilar to haemoglobin and transports the oxygen to the

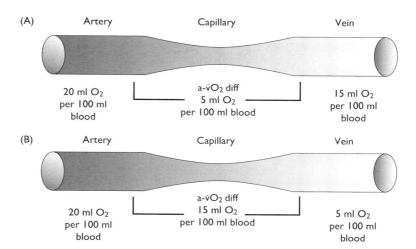

Fig. 4.7 THE ARTERIOVENOUS OXYGEN DIFFERENCE BEFORE AND DURING EXERCISE (A) AT REST (B) INTENSE EXERCISE

mitochondria, where **glycolysis** can take place. The concentration of myoglobin is much higher in the cells of slow twitch muscle fibres, as these are more suited to aerobic energy production. Myoglobin has a much higher affinity for oxygen than haemoglobin and also acts as an oxygen reserve, so that when demand for oxygen is increased, as for example during exercise, there is a readily available supply.

The arterial-venous oxygen difference (a-$\bar{\text{V}}$O$_2$ diff) is the difference in oxygen content between the arterial blood and venous blood, and can measure how much oxygen is actually being consumed in the muscles and tissues. At rest only about 25% of oxygen is actually used; this however increases dramatically during intense exercise to up to 85%. Fig 4.7 illustrates the a-$\bar{\text{V}}$O$_2$ diff at rest and during intense exercise.

Draw diagrams to show how and why gases move between:
- **the alveoli and the pulmonary capillaries**
- **the systemic capillaries and the muscle.**

Lung volumes and capacities

Lung volumes

During normal quiet breathing, we inspire approximately 500 ml of air; the same amount is exhaled during the process of expiration. This volume of air inspired or expired is known as **tidal volume**. Of this 500 ml, only about 350 ml makes its way to the alveoli. The other 150 ml remains in the passageways of the nose, throat and trachea and is known as **dead space**. The volume of air which is inspired or expired in one minute is called **minute ventilation**, and is calculated by multiplying tidal volume by the number of breaths taken per minute. On average we breathe 12 to 15 times per minute, so our resting minute ventilation can be calculated as follows:

$$\text{VE} = \text{T.V.} \times \text{f}$$
$$= 500 \text{ ml} \times 15$$
$$= 7{,}500 \text{ ml/min} \ (7.5\text{l/min})$$

However, at rest we can still inspire much more air than our normal tidal volume. This excess volume of air inspired is the **inspiratory reserve volume**. It can be defined as the maximum volume of air inspired following normal inspiration, and measures approximately 3,300 ml. Following normal expiration at rest we can also expire more air; this volume is known as the **expiratory reserve volume** and measures approximately 1,200 ml. The lungs can never completely expel all the air they contain. Approximately 1,200 ml remains in the alveoli to keep them slightly inflated and regulate pressure; this volume is called the **reserve volume**.

Lung capacities

Lung capacities can be calculated by adding together different lung volumes. For example:

1 inspiratory capacity is the sum of tidal volume and the inspiratory reserve volume, and amounts to 3,800 ml.
2 functional residual capacity is the sum of expiratory reserve volume and residual volume, and accounts for approximately 2,400 ml.
3 vital capacity is the amount of air that can be forcibly expired following maximal inspiration and is the sum of tidal volume, inspiratory reserve volume and expiratory reserve volume; this measures about 5,000 ml.
4 total lung capacity is the sum of all volumes and on average is approximately 6,000 ml.

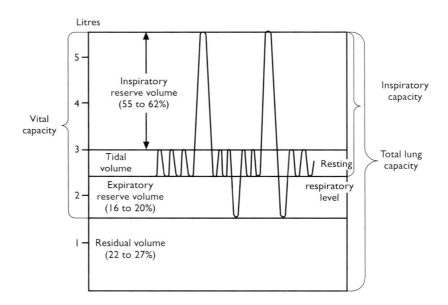

Fig. 4.8 Lung volumes shown by a spirometer trace

The **Forced Expiratory Volume** (FEV1) is the percentage of vital capacity that can be expired in one second. This is approximately 85% and gives an indication of the overall efficiency of the airways. A low reading may assume that the airways are resisting the passage of air during expiration and consequently the efficiency of the gaseous exchange process at the lungs may decrease. A summary of lung volumes and capacities, their values and the effect of exercise is outlined in table 4.1.

Respiratory complications

Many of us probably have or know someone who suffers from **asthma**. Asthma causes bronchial airways to constrict and inflammation of mucous membranes, which results in shortness of breath and restriction to ventilation. However, asthma should not prevent asthmatics from participating in an exercise programme. In fact many past Olympic athletes have asthma and have competed at the top level. What is important is that asthmatics follow a few simple rules before and during their exercise session. Medication is obviously vital. The purpose of asthma medicines is to control asthma so that individuals can fully undertake what they wish to do without allowing their asthma to get in the way, this includes exercising. There are two main types of asthma medicines – bronchodilators which relieve the symptoms of asthma and anti-inflammatories which help prevent asthma attacks, and assuming both are used correctly they should enable individuals to participate fully in exercise programmes.

Tips for exercising with asthma:

- Do not start exercising if you have symptoms of your asthma.
- Follow appropriate warm-ups prior to and cool downs following exercise.
- Stop if an asthma attack develops.
- In cold or damp conditions try to exercise indoors.
- Always train with a partner in case an attack develops.

If these tips are followed, asthmatics should fully benefit from their exercise programme and it may help to actually control their symptoms to boot!

Define the lung volumes and capacities. Discuss how and why each changes with exercise.

Ventilation during exercise

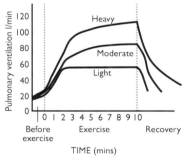

NOTE: The anticipatory rise prior to exercise and the continual increase in ventilation during intense exercise

Fig. 4.9 RESPIRATORY RESPONSE TO VARYING INTENSITY OF EXERCISE

During exercise, both the depth and rate of breathing increases. The tidal volume increases by utilising both the inspiratory reserve volume and the expiratory reserve volume; consequently both these volumes decrease during exercise, while tidal volume may increase six-fold. Since both tidal volume and the frequency of breathing increase during exercise, minute ventilation increases dramatically – values up to 180l/min have been recorded for trained endurance athletes.

Changes in ventilation occur before, during and after exercise as shown in fig 4.9. Before exercise starts there is a slight increase in ventilation; this is called the **anticipatory rise** and is the result of hormones, such as adrenaline, stimulating the respiratory centre. Once exercise begins there is a rapid rise in ventilation caused by nervous stimulation. During submaximal exercise this sudden increase in ventilation begins to slow down and may plateau into what is known as the **steady state**. This assumes that the energy demands of the muscles are being met by the oxygen made available, and that the body is expelling carbon dioxide effectively. During maximal exercise however, this steady state does not occur, and ventilation continues to increase until the exercise is finished. This is thought to be due to the stimulation of the respiratory centre by carbon dioxide and lactic acid, and suggests that it is the body's need to expel these metabolites rather than its desire for oxygen which determines the pattern of breathing. If exercise intensity continues to increase to a point near the athlete's $\bar{V}O_2$ **max** (the **maximum** amount of oxygen that can be taken in, transported and utilised in one minute) then the amount of oxygen entering the body is not sufficient to meet the demands of the working muscles. Because the athlete is working at maximal levels they are unable to meet the body's requirements and the athlete may need to stop exercising, or at the very best, significantly reduce the intensity of the exercise. In this way oxygen supply can once again meet the demands imposed by the body.

During recovery from exercise, ventilation drops rapidly at first, followed by a slower decrease. The more intense the preceding exercise, the longer the recovery period and the longer ventilation remains above the normal resting level. This is largely due to the removal of by-products of muscle metabolism such as lactic acid and will be discussed further in Chapter 6.

Complete the table below showing the responses of the respiratory system to exercise.

FACTOR	INCREASE/DECREASE	EXPLANATION
respiratory rate		
expiratory reserve volume		
oxygen content of arteries		
minute ventilation		
tidal volume		
oxygen consumption		
max. oxygen comsumption		
a-$\bar{V}O_2$ diff		
action of respiratory muscles		
transport of carbon dioxide		

Respiratory regulation

Ventilation is controlled by the nervous system, and this enables us to alter breathing patterns without consciously thinking about it. The basic rhythm of respiration is governed and co-ordinated by the respiratory centre, situated in and around the medulla area of the brain. The pneumotaxic area is responsible for regulating the rate of breathing, whilst the apneustic area regulates the depth of breathing. During inspiration nerve impulses are generated and sent via the phrenic and intercostal nerves to the inspiratory muscles (external intercostals, and diaphragm) causing them to contract. This lasts for approximately two seconds after which the impulses cease and expiration occurs passively by elastic recoil of the lungs.

During exercise however, when breathing rate is increased, the expiratory centre may send impulses to the expiratory muscles (internal intercostals) which speeds up the expiratory process.

It is however the chemical composition of the blood which largely influences respiration rates, particularly during exercise. The respiratory centre has a chemosensitive area which is sensitive to changes in the blood acidity. Chemoreceptors located in the aortic arch and carotid arteries assess the acidity of the blood and in particular the relative concentrations of CO_2 and O_2. If there is an increase in the concentration of CO_2 in the blood, the chemoreceptors detect this and the respiratory centre sends nerve impulses to the respiratory muscles which increase the rate of ventilation. This allows the body to expire the excess CO_2. Once blood acidity is lowered, fewer impulses are sent and respiration rates can once again decrease. This regulation of breathing is aided by a series of stretch receptors in the lungs and bronchioles, which prevent over-inflation of the lungs. If these are excessively stretched the expiratory centre sends impulses to induce expiration – this is known as the **Hering–Breur reflex**.

1 **Explain the process of increased breathing rates during exercise.**
2 **Why do breathing rates remain high following exercise, even though exercise has ceased?**

Respiratory adaptations to training

Endurance performance is dependent upon oxygen transportation and utilisation, but no matter how good the functioning of these are, improvements in performance will not happen unless we can get oxygen into the body. The respiratory system is responsible for receiving oxygen into the body and dealing with the waste products associated with muscle metabolism. Respiratory functioning does not usually hinder aerobic performance, and the adaptations that take place merely aid the improved cardiovascular functioning.

Following training, there is a reduction in both resting respiratory rate and the breathing rate during submaximal exercise. This appears to be a function of the overall efficiency of the respiratory structures induced by training.

Surprisingly there are only very small increases in lung volumes following training. Vital capacity (the amount of air that can be forcibly expelled following maximum inspiration) increases slightly, as does tidal volume during maximal exercise. One factor to account for these increases is the increased strength of the respiratory muscles which may facilitate lung inflation.

Pulmonary diffusion (the exchange of gases at the alveoli) will become more efficient following training, especially when working at near maximal levels. The increased surface area of the alveoli during exercise together with their increased capillarisation, ensures that there is ample opportunity for gaseous exchange to take place, and thus guarantees sufficient oxygen is entering the blood.

Table 4.1 LUNG VOLUMES AND CAPACITIES DEFINED; RESTING VALUES AND CHANGES DURING EXERCISE

LUNG VOLUME OR CAPACITY	DEFINITION	CHANGES DURING EXERCISE	APPROXIMATE NORMAL VALUES (ML)
tidal volume (TV)	volume inspired or expired per breath	increase	500
inspiratory reserve volume (IRV)	maximal volume inspired from end-inspiration	decrease	3,300
expiratory reserve volume (ERV)	maximal volume expired from end-expiration	slight decrease	1,000–1,200
residual volume (RV)	volume remaining at end of maximal expiration	slight decrease	1,200
total lung capacity (TLC)	volume in lung at end of maximal inspiration	slight decrease	up to 8,000
vital capacity (VC)	maximal volume forcefully expired after maximal inspiration	slight decrease	5,500
inspiratory capacity (IC)	maximal volume inspired from resting expiratory level	increase	3,800
functional residual capacity (FRC)	volume in lungs at resting expiratory level	slight increase	2,400
dead space	volume of air in the trachea/ bronchi etc. that does not take part in gaseous exchange		150
minute ventilation	volume of air inspired/expired per minute $VE = TV \times F = 500 \times 15$ $= 7,500$ ml		7,500

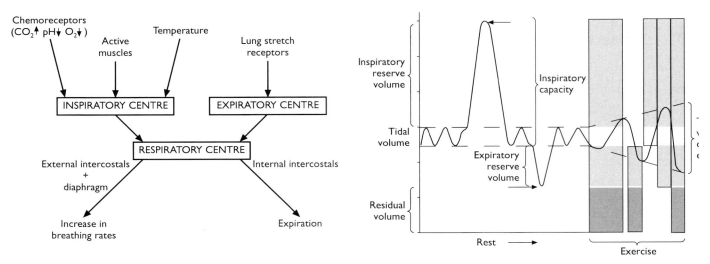

Fig. 4.10 The respiratory regulation mechanism

Fig. 4.11 The effect of exercise on lung volumes

Summary

- Respiration can be divided into external and internal respiration.
- External respiration is the process of getting air into and out of the lungs.
- Inspiration occurs when the respiratory muscles contract, lifting the ribcage upwards and outwards and lowering the diaphragm. The resultant pressure differential causes air to rush into the lungs.
- Expiration at rest is a passive process, simply a result of the intercostals and diaphragm relaxing. This once again causes a pressure differential and air is forced out of the lungs.
- Oxygen enters the blood stream at the alveoli through the process of diffusion.
- Gaseous exchange occurs as a result of differences in concentration of oxygen and carbon dioxide around the body.
- The partial pressure of a gas is the individual pressure the gas exerts when in a mixture of gases and explains the movement of gases in the body.
- Oxygen is transported around the body by combining to haemoglobin to form oxyhaemoglobin.
- Carbon dioxide is largely transported as a bicarbonate ion. Some however combines with haemoglobin to form carbominohaemoglobin and some dissolves in the blood's plasma.
- Respiration is governed by various levels within the brain. The main regulatory mechanism is performed by chemoreceptors within the aortic arch and carotid arteries. These assess the concentration of carbon dioxide within the blood.

Review Questions

1 Trace the path of inspired air, outlining the structures it passes on its journey from the nasal cavity to the alveoli.

2 Identify the muscles used in respiration at rest and during exercise.

3 Sketch a graph to show what happens to oxygen consumption (VO_2) during an exercise session that gets progressively harder (eg, the multi-stage fitness test).

4 Identify and explain four factors that influence the efficiency of gaseous exchange between the lungs and the pulmonary capillaries.

5 Explain the importance of the partial pressure of gases in the respiratory process.

6 How are oxygen and carbon dioxide transported in the body?

7 Outline and explain the changes that occur to lung volumes and capacities during exercise.

8 What is asthma, and what precautions might an asthmatic need to take before participating in exercise?

9 What factors influence the respiratory system during exercise?

10 How does the body combat increases in blood acidity resulting from intense exercise?

chapter 5

Physical Fitness

Sports physiology is the study of how the body's structures and functions adapt in response to exercise, and in particular how training can enhance the athlete's performance. Fundamental to sports physiology is a knowledge of fitness and training. This chapter explores the whole realm of fitness, and in particular, the complexities involved in defining fitness. A detailed investigation into the components of fitness and fitness testing is the main crux of this chapter, using information gathered from my own research and case studies from the fitness testing laboratory at Lilleshall National Sports Centre. This provides a complete guide to fitness measurement and assessment.

This chapter will form an excellent introduction to Chapter 10, Training Implications.

Fitness considerations in physical activity

The term 'fitness' is difficult to define, since it means many different things to different people. For example one individual may see himself as being 'fit' if he can run for the bus without getting too out of breath, whereas a physically active person may seek a quick heart rate recovery as a measure of fitness, following a distance run. However in the search for an acceptable definition that encompasses most individuals, Dick (1989) has defined fitness as

'... the successful adaptation to the stressors of one's lifestyle ...'

This suggests therefore that all of us must look closely at the stressors of our everyday activities, and see how well we cope with those stressors if we are to gauge our fitness levels satisfactorily.

Another frequently quoted definition is

'... the ability to undertake everyday activities without undue fatigue ...'

This once again is a very generic definition which encompasses everybody; athletes and non-athletes alike. The everyday activities undertaken by an athlete in heavy training for a major competition are obviously going to be very different from those experienced by a non-athlete.

When considering physical activity however, it would not be acceptable to rely solely upon this definition, since the fitness requirements of various activities differ dramatically from each other. We therefore need to be a little more specific in our definitions. For example: the different fitness requirements of a 100 m sprint and a marathon run:

1 The sprint requires a tremendous amount of power, strength and speed in order to travel a relatively short distance in the quickest time possible. It also requires the muscles to work in the absence of oxygen and as such the composition of the muscle tissue will need to be specialised to accommodate this.
2 The marathon run requires the body to work for an extended period of time, and therefore relies upon the endurance capabilities of the cardiovascular and muscular systems. Oxygen consumption is essential in this instance and similarly the body will have become adapted to take in, transport and utilise as much oxygen as possible during the run.

Fig. 5.1 A 100 M SPRINTER

The components of fitness

The components of fitness relate to the requirements of a given sporting activity, and can help to explain success or failure in sport.

A distinction can be made between components which are generally considered to be **health-related** (health benefits may be gained through improvements in these components), and those that are **skill-related**, although both will affect performance in sport.

Health-related factors are **physiologically based** and determine the ability of an individual to meet the physical demands of the activity; the **skill-related factors** are based upon the **neuromuscular system** and determine how successfully a person can perform a specific skill. Both are required in all activities, but the relative importance of each dimension may differ. For example, a person may be physically suited to tennis, possessing the necessary speed, endurance and strength requirements, but may not possess the hand-eye co-ordination needed to strike the ball successfully. In this instance the individual may be best advised to switch to an activity that requires fewer skill-related components.

Table 5.1   COMPONENTS OF FITNESS

HEALTH RELATED FACTORS	SKILL RELATED FACTORS
• strength	• agility
• speed	• balance
• cardio-respiratory endurance/ aerobic capacity	• co-ordination
• muscular endurance	• reaction time
• flexibility	• power
• body composition	

Health-related components of fitness

Strength

Strength relates to the ability of the body to apply a force and although the recognised definition of strength is *the maximum force that can be developed in a muscle or group of muscles during a single maximal contraction*, it is how we apply strength that is important when analysing sporting activity. Three classifications of strength have been identified:

- maximum strength
- elastic strength
- strength endurance.

An athlete who requires a very large force to overcome a resistance in a single contraction, such as we see in weight lifting, or performing a throw in judo, will require **maximum strength**. An athlete who requires to overcome a resistance rapidly yet prepare the muscle quickly for a sequential contraction of equal force will require **elastic strength**. This can be seen in explosive events such as sprinting, triple jumping or in a gymnast performing tumbles in a floor routine. Finally, an athlete who is required to undergo repeated contractions and withstand fatigue, such as a rower or swimmer, will view **strength endurance** as a vital determining factor to performance.

Strength is directly related to the cross-sectional area of the muscle tissue as well as the type of muscle fibre within the muscle. Fast twitch (white fibres) can generate greater forces than slow twitch (red fibres).

The optimum age to develop strength appears to be in the early to mid-twenties. As the body ages, less protein becomes available in the body for muscle growth, and the stress and anaerobic nature of strength training also makes it an inappropriate method of training during old age.

In this age of gender equality it is highly appropriate to dismiss the notion of a weaker sex. In fact, relative to cross-sectional area of pure muscle tissue, men and women are equal in terms of strength. It is the greater fat content of women and the higher testosterone levels in men that can create the difference in the cross-sectional area of muscles and therefore strength, to the advantage of males.

Fig. 5.2 A WEIGHT LIFTER — STRENGTH IS VITAL TO SUCCESSFUL PERFORMANCE

Speed

– the ability to put body parts into motion quickly, or the maximum rate that a person can move over a specific distance.

Speed is a major factor in many high intensity, explosive activities such as sprinting, vaulting in gymnastics or fast bowling in cricket. However speed is not simply concerned with the rate at which a person can move his/her body from point A to point B. Although this may be important during sprinting or when running down the wing in rugby, other sports require the athlete to put his/her limbs into action rapidly such as when throwing the javelin. Our definition of speed therefore encompasses both aspects of speed. A fast bowler in cricket for example does not necessarily need to run at maximum pace but must be able to put his arm into action rapidly to achieve an effective outcome. Speed tends to be genetically determined due to the physiological make-up of the muscle, and as such is least affected by training and can take some time to develop. Once again, fast twitch (FTG) muscle fibres tend to be beneficial in activities where speed is essential, since they can release energy for muscular contraction very rapidly. There are many physiological factors that help to determine speed, which include: the ability to select motor units accurately, the elasticity of muscle tissue, and the availability of energy supply (ie the ATP-PC system). However the role of body mechanics and the efficiency of the body's lever systems are also integral in determining speed of the body or body part, and in this way developing appropriate technique is essential.

Cardio-respiratory endurance is:

– *the ability to provide and sustain energy aerobically*. It is dependent upon the ability of the cardiovascular system to transport and utilise oxygen during sustained exercise.

Cardio-respiratory endurance is the component of fitness that underpins all aerobic activities which include long distance running, cycling or swimming, as well as being a contributory factor to many other sporting situations. Physiological factors that determine aerobic performance include the possession of a large proportion of slow twitch muscle fibres, a proliferation of mitochondria and large myoglobin stores. These help in the production of large amounts of energy via the aerobic pathway. Perhaps the major influencing factor of cardio-respiratory performance is the maximum volume of oxygen an individual can consume ($\dot{V}O_2$ max). This has a very large genetic component, and is influenced little by training. Factors affecting cardio-respiratory endurance are dealt with in more depth later in this chapter.

Muscular endurance

– *the ability of a muscle or group of muscles to sustain repeated contractions against a resistance for an extended period of time*. Slow twitch muscle fibres will ensure they receive a rich supply of blood to enable the most efficient production of aerobic energy.

This enables the muscles to contract repeatedly without experiencing the fatigue due to the build-up of the lactic acid. Activities that require muscular endurance are numerous but can best be highlighted by using the example of rowing. Individual muscle groups are required to contract at high intensity for a period of approximately five minutes (or as long as it takes to complete the 2000m course!). Muscular endurance relies upon the efficiency of the body to produce energy under both anaerobic and aerobic conditions, together with an ability of the body to deal with and 'buffer' the lactic acid.

Flexibility

Flexibility can be defined as *the range of movement possible at a joint*.

Flexibility is determined by the elasticity of ligaments and tendons, the strength and opposition of surrounding muscles (including antagonists) and the shape of the articulating bones. Although flexibility is most commonly associated with activities such as trampolining and gymnastics, it is in fact a requirement in all sports since the development of flexibility can lead to both an increase in speed and power of muscle contraction. Often the degree of movement is determined by the type of joint, since joints are designed either for stability or mobility. The knee joint for example is a hinge joint and has been designed with stability in mind. It is only truly capable of movement in one plane of direction (it is uniaxial), allowing flexion and extension of the lower leg. This is due to the intricate network of ligaments surrounding the joint, which restricts movement. The shoulder joint on the other hand is a ball and socket joint and allows movement in many planes (it is polyaxial) since few ligaments cross the joint. However, the free movement at the joint comes at a price, as the shoulder joint can easily become dislocated. Flexibility training is even more important for athletes, since there is a distinct reduction in mobility from the age of 8 years, and during periods of inactivity.

Body composition

Body composition is concerned with the physiological make-up of the body with regard to the relative amounts and distribution of muscle and fat. Body composition is commonly defined as: *the component parts of the body in terms of the relative amounts of body fat compared to lean body mass.* For an average 18-year-old, men range from 14–17% fat, while women range from 24–29%. Body composition has an important role for élite athletes and more generally in health and well-being. Excessive body fat can lead to obesity and the associated complications such as cardiovascular diseases. Whilst for the athlete high body fat can result in a reduction in muscle efficiency and contributes to greater energy expenditure, since more weight requires more energy to move around. Body composition requirements vary with different sports but generally the less fat the better. Muscle mass is desirable for those activities or sports that require muscular strength, power and endurance.

The relative shape of the body or **somatotype** can also be mentioned at this point. Somatotyping is a method used to measure body shape. Three extremes exist:

1 **Endomorphy** – the relative fatness or pear-shapeness of the body.
2 **Mesomorphy** – the muscularity of the body.
3 **Ectomorphy** – the linearity or leanness of the body.

Fig. 5.3 SOMATOTYPING: THE THREE EXTREMES OF BODY TYPE

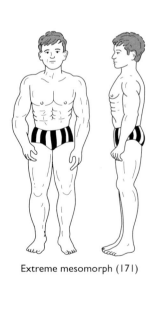

Extreme mesomorph (171)

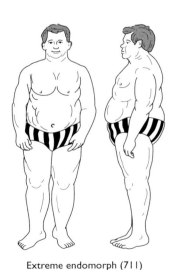

Extreme endomorph (711)

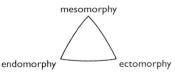

Extreme ectomorph (117)

The characteristics of a performer's body can be categorised according to these somatotypes and plotted on the delta shaped graph.

It is very rare that an individual would be classed as an extreme endo, meso or ectomorph at the apex of the delta. More realistically they would possess characteristics of all three, but the relative contributions of each somatotype would differ depending upon the activity. For example rowers tend to be very lean yet very muscular with little body fat, and are placed accordingly (see fig 5.4).

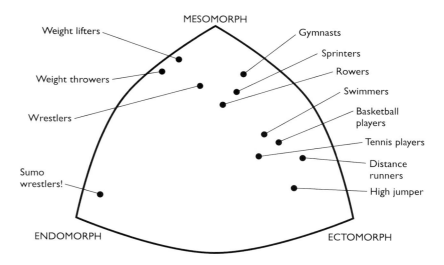

Fig. 5.4 SOMATOTYPING RELATES BODY COMPOSITION TO SPORTING ACTIVITY

Skill-related components of fitness

Agility

Agility is defined as:

the ability to move and change direction and position of the body quickly and effectively while under control.

With reference to this definition we can see that many factors are involved in agility including balance, co-ordination speed and flexibility. However agility is required in a range of sporting activities from tumbling in gymnastics to retrieving balls in volleyball. Although activities can be undertaken to improve agility, development of this skill-related component is limited.

Fig. 5.5 A GYMNAST ON A BEAM REQUIRES BOTH STATIC AND DYNAMIC BALANCE

Balance

Balance is defined as:

the maintenance of the centre of mass over the base of support. This can be while the body is static or dynamic (moving).

Balance is an integral component in the effective performance of most activities. In gymnastics, for example, it may be necessary to maintain a balanced position when performing a handstand. This is static balance. However in games such as rugby, players must maintain balance whilst moving, for example when side-stepping or staying on their feet in the tackle in rugby, also requires balance – this is known as dynamic balance.

Again balance can be improved only slightly through training, but one effective method involves the maintaining of balance on a 'wobble' or balance board.

Co-ordination

Co-ordination is defined as: *the interaction of the motor and nervous systems and is the ability to perform motor tasks accurately, and effectively.* When serving in tennis for exxample, the tennis player must co-ordinate the toss of the ball with one hand with the striking of the ball with the racket head at the optimum position. This requires co-ordination. A swimmer performing breaststroke must co-ordinate the pull of the arms with the strong kick phase to ensure effective performance.

Reaction time

Reaction time can be defined as:

the time taken to initiate a response to a given stimulus.

Table 5.2   COMPONENTS OF FITNESS FOR DIFFERENT ACTIVITIES

ACTIVITY	SPEED	STRENGTH	CARDIO-VASCULAR ENDURANCE	MUSCULAR ENDURANCE	FLEXIBILITY	POWER	REACTION TIME	AGILITY	BALANCE	COORDINATION	BODY COMPOSITION
swimming											
squash											
marathon											
tennis											
cycling											
rugby											
sprinting											
x-country skiing											
aerobics											
basketball											
judo											
gymnastics vault											
badminton											
netball											
cricket											

This stimulus may be visual, for example in responding to a serve in tennis, or aural in responding to a gun in athletics or verbal guidance from players and coaches. Colin Jackson, one of the fastest starters in the world, explains his success by 'going on the 'B' of the Bang'. Reaction time is dependent upon the ability of an individual to process information and initiate a response by the neuro-muscular system. Reaction time can be improved through training.

Power

the amount of work done per unit of time; the product of strength and speed.

Power can also be thought of as explosive strength where the ability to exert a large force over a short period of time is paramount. It relies on the interactionof the neuro-muscular system to recruit fast twitch fibres as rapidly as possible.

Complete table 5.2 by ticking one health-related and one skill-related component of fitness that you consider to be the most important for each activity listed.

Having established the various requirements and components of fitness of a given activity, an athlete must constantly assess and measure the components in order to gauge improvement.

The measurement and assessment of fitness

Why test? In order to measure fitness levels, a battery of recognised tests has been developed, which are easily administered and evaluated. These tests are outlined below.
    Through testing it is possible to:

1 identify the strengths and weaknesses of the athlete
2 provide baseline data for monitoring performance
3 provide the basis for training prescriptions
4 assess the value of different types of training and help to modify training programmes
5 predict physiological and athletic potential
6 provide comparisons with previous tests and other élite performers in the same group
7 can be used to identify overtraining syndrome
8 talent identification
9 enhance motivation
10 form part of the educational process.

Measuring your fitness levels: complete the tests outlined below and record your results. Make sure you warm up thoroughly and perform the tests under the guidance of your teacher.

Strength Strength can be measured with the use of dynamometers which give an objective measure of the force generated within various muscles or muscle groups. The easiest strength test to administer is using the **Handgrip Dynamometer** which measures grip strength generated by the muscles in the forearm; see fig 5.6.
    Record the maximum reading from three attempts for both left and right hands. See Appendix 2 for grip strength norms.

Advantages
• a simple and objective measure

Fig. 5.6 THE HANDGRIP TEST

Disadvantages
- the validity of the handgrip test has been questioned, since it only indicates strength of muscles of the forearm.

Another common test of strength is the **one repetition maximum test** (1RM test). This assesses the maximal force a subject can lift in one repetition using free weights or other gym equipment.

Advantages
- weight training equipment is easily accessible.

Disadvantages
- when performing maximal lifts the threat of injury is more apparent and so safety is essential.

Speed

The simplest measure of speed is a **30 m sprint**. Mark out 30 m on a non-slip surface and sprint as hard as you can from a flying start over the course. Record the time taken. See Appendix 2 for 30 m sprint test ratings.

Advantages
- equipment is readily available.

Disadvantages
- timing can be affected by error.
- effects of weather and running surface may affect the results.

Cardiovascular endurance

Cardiovascular endurance can be assessed by measuring a person's **VO_2 max**: the maximum amount of oxygen that an individual can take in, transport and utilise per minute (for a fuller explanation, see page 92). A simple prediction of $\dot{V}O_2$ max can be made through the **NCF multistage fitness test**. This is a progressive shuttle run test which means that it starts off easily and gets increasingly difficult. See Appendix 2 for test ratings.

Equipment
- 20 m track (or flat non-slippery surface)
- NCF cassette tape
- Tape player
- Tape measure and marking cones

Follow the instructions given on the tape. Subjects are required to run the 20 m distance as many times as possible, keeping in time to the bleeps emitted from the tape. Each shuttle of 20 m should be timed so that the individual reaches the end line as the bleep is emitted.

The difficulty increases with each level attained, and speed of running will need to be increased accordingly. Continue to run as long as possible until you can no longer keep up with the bleeps set by the tape. If you fail to complete the 20 m shuttle before the bleep is emitted you should withdraw from the test, ensuring that the level and shuttle number attained has been recorded.

Advantages
- scores can be evaluated by referring to published tables
- large groups can participate in the test at once
- limited equipment required.

Disadvantages

- the test is maximal and to exhaustion and therefore relies, to a certain extent on subject's levels of motivation
- the test is only a **prediction** and not an absolute measure of VO₂ max
- the test may favour subjects more used to running. Swimmers for example may not perform as well as they might in a swimming pool.

Another test of aerobic capacity is the **PWC170 Test**. PWC stands for '**Physical Work Capacity**' and this sub-maximal test measures an individual's aerobic capacity. Subjects are required to perform three consecutive workloads on a cycle ergometer, whilst the heart rate is monitored. Initially a workload is set that increases the subject's heart rate to between 100 and 115 beats per minute. The heart rate is measured each minute until the subject reaches steady state. The test is repeated for a second and third workload which increases the heart rate to between 115 and 130, and 130 and 145 beats per minute respectively. Each steady state heart rate and respective workload is graphed and used to predict a workload that would elicit a heart rate response of 170 beats per minute. The score can then be compared to standard tables and a prediciton of *VO₂ max* given.

Advantages

- cycle ergometers often contain a pulse monitor, and therefore the heart rate is easily monitored.

Disadvantages

- as the test is performed on a bicycle it may favour cyclists.

Muscular endurance

A test for muscular endurance will assess the ability of one muscle or muscle group to continue working repeatedly. A simple test to measure the endurance of the abdominal muscle group is the NCF **Abdominal Conditioning Test**. See Appendix 2 for test ratings.

Equipment

- NCF abdominal conditioning tape
- Tape recorder
- Stopwatch
- Gym mat

Follow the instructions given on the tape. Subjects are required to perform as many sit-ups as possible, keeping in time to the bleeps emitted from the tape. Get a partner to count the number of sit-ups completed correctly, and time the duration of the work period. Subjects should withdraw from the test when they can no longer keep in time to the bleeps, or when technique deteriorates noticeably.

Advantages

- easy to administer with little equipment
- large groups can participate in the test at once
- the abdominal mucscles can be easily isolated.

Disadvantages

- correct technique is essential for successful completion of the test
- the test is maximal and therefore relies upon participant's motivation
- full sit-ups are not recommended to be undertaken on a regular basis, due to excessive strain being placed on the lower back region.

Other simple tests of muscular endurance include assessing the **number of press-ups** or **pull-ups completed in 30 seconds**. Although these tests are easy to administer and require little equipment, their reliability in terms of assessing muscular endurance of a particular muscle group is limited.

Flexibility

The **Sit and Reach test** can be easily administered. It gives an indication of the flexibility of hamstrings and lower back. See Appendix 2 for test ratings.

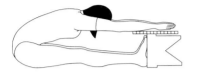

Fig. 5.7 THE SIT AND REACH TEST

Equipment

- Sit and reach box

Sit down on the floor with your legs out straight and feet flat against the box. Without bending your knees, bend forwards with arms outstretched and push the cursor as far down as possible and hold for two seconds. Record your score.

Advantages
- an easy test to administer
- there is plenty of data available for comparison

Disadvantages
- the test only measures flexibility in the region of the lower back and hamstrings, so it cannot give an overall score of flexibility
- the extent to which a subject has warmed up may be well affect results, when comparing to norms.

Another test of flexibility involves the use of a **goniometer**, a piece of equipment used to measure the range of motion at a joint. The 'head' of the goniometer is placed at the axis of rotation of a joint whilst the arms are aligned longitudinally with the bone. A measurement in degrees can be taken which gives a very *objective* reading that can be used to assess improvement. One small disadvantage of this piece of equipment is that it is not always easy to identify the axis of rotation of a joint.

Body composition

You will recall body composition is primarily concerned with the distribution of fat and muscle in the body. Body fat is measured in a variety of ways:

1 **Hydrostatic weighing** considers water displacement when the body is submerged in water, but requires a large hydrostatic weighing tank, and a knowledge of the subject's residual volume is required for the calculation.
2 **Biolectrical impedance** is another popular objective measure whereby a small electrical current is passed through the body from wrist to ankle. As fat restricts the flow of the current, the greater the current needed, the greater the percentage of body fat. Although this test requires specialist equipment, it is becoming more accessible with the introduction of simple scales which transmit an electrical current.
3 The most common and simplest measure of body fat is made through the **Body Mass Index** (BMI). Through calculation of an individual's BMI, body fat can be predicted. The body mass index is calculated by measuring the body mass of the subject (weight in kg) divided by the height (in metres) of the individual squared.

ie: $$\mathbf{BMI} = \frac{\text{weight in kg}}{\text{height in m}^2}$$

The higher the score, the greater the levels of body fat.

healthy   20–25
overweight   25–30
obese   >30

Although this test is very quick and a prediction can be made instantaneously, it can obviously be inaccurate since it does not make a difference between fat and muscle. So large, lean muscular athletes may well fall into the wrong category.

4 **Skinfold measures** using callipers: by far the simplest measure. On the left side of the body, take measures at the following sites:

- biceps
- triceps
- sub scapular
- supra iliac

Add the totals together in millimetres and record your results.

At this stage, you may wish to make some other anthropometrical measures such as length of bones and overall height, muscle girths or circumferences, and condyle measures at the joints.

Advantages
- a simple test that is widely used
- scores can be used to identify changes in body fat over time.

Disadvantages
- the testing procedure can vary between tester. For example was the measurement taken iin exactly the correct place.

As well as measuring these physical or health related factors, it is also possible to assess skill related components.

Fig. 5.8 BODY FAT MEASUREMENT

1 Triceps
With the pupil's arm hanging loosely, a vertical fold is raised at the back of the arm, midway along a line connecting the acromion (shoulder) and olecranon (elbow) processes.

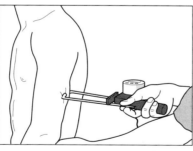

2 Biceps
A vertical fold is raised at the front of the arm, opposite to the triceps site. This should be directly above the centre of the cubital fossa (fold of the elbow).

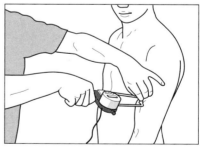

3 Subscapular
A fold is raised just beneath the inferior angle of the scapula (bottom of the shoulder-blade). This fold should be at an angle of 45 degrees downwards and outwards.

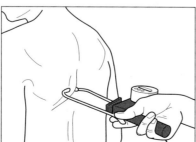

4 Anterior suprailiac
A fold is raised 5-7 cm above the spinale (pelvis), at a point in line the anterior axillary border (armpit). The fold should be in line with the natural folds downward and inwards at up to 45 degrees.

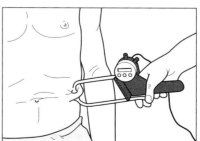

Agility

Agility is most commonly measured via the Illinois agility run. See Appendix 3 for test ratings.

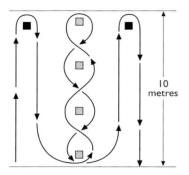

Equipment

- tape measure
- cones
- stopwatch

Place four cones 3.3 m apart. Starting by lying flat on the floor, then run the course as fast as you can on the signal issued by a partner. Ask your partner to time you and record your results.

Advantages

- the testing procedure is simple to administer with litle equipment required
- a widely used test with easily accessible rating

Disadvantages

- since agility is influenced by many other factors such as speed, balance and co-ordination, the validity of test scores could be questioned
- this test is not sport specific. The agility demanded for different sports is very specific. For example in some games such as hockey the player must be agile whilst using a stick to control the ball. Where possible, agility tests should show relevance to the particular activity for which the athlete is being tested.

Reaction time

Although the most accurate measures of reaction time will involve the use of a computer programme, a simple test is the stick drop test. See Appendix 2 for test ratings.

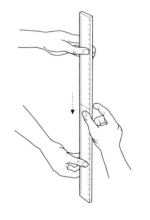

Equipment

- A metre ruler

A partner holds a metre rule in front of you. Place your index finger and thumb either side of the 50 cm calibration without making contact with the ruler itself. Without warning the partner should release the ruler, and you must catch it with your finger and thumb as quickly as possible. Record the calibration at the point your index finger lies.

Advantages

- the testing procedure is simple and easy to administer with little equipment required

Disadvantages

- the relevance of a stick drop test to sporting activity is questionable. Where possible the testing environment should reflect the environment of the game or activity for which the athlete is being tested.
- the test only measures visual reaction time, but in many sporting situations, such as the 100m sprint, reaction time to an audio cue is required.

Power

Power can be measured with the help of a jump metre. See Appendix 2 for test ratings.

Equipment

- jump metre

Standing with your legs straight on the mat of the jump metre, pull the string taut. In one smooth movement, bend the knees and explode upwards, record the score. Repeat and take the highest score. If a jump metre is not available, the vertical jump test is similar.

Testing the élite athlete

The above fitness measures are well recognised and simple to administer which makes them very appropriate for this level of study. However, élite athletes may require greater objectivity in their results if they are to compare themselves accurately with other elite performers in their group. Specialised laboratories have therefore been established which dedicate themselves to sports testing. One such laboratory is the Human Performance Centre at Lilleshall; another is the National Sports Medicine Institute at St Barts Hospital, and what follows is an example of some of the tests they now administer on the élite sports performer.

The anaerobic capacity test

This test is designed to assess each player's ability to exercise anaerobically without experiencing the effect of fatigue through lactic acid build up. The longer an individual is able to work flat out at high intensity, the greater his/her anaerobic capacity. See Appendix 2 for test ratings.

Each subject is required to perform a maximal 30-second bout of exercise (sprint) on a bicycle ergometer which has been specially linked to a micro computer. During the bout of exercise the computer records the peak power reached, which relates to the body's explosive power ability as well as the mean power. This is an indication of the body's ability to sustain high intensity effort. The percentage of fatigue sustained can also be recorded. Those subjects who are able to sustain and achieve high levels of power throughout the test are those with the greatest ability in anaerobic events.

OBLA test (Onset of Blood Lactate Accumulation)

The lactate threshold, or point of onset of blood lactate accumulation, is the point at which the body appears to convert to anaerobic energy production and lactic acid starts to accumulate. Below the lactate threshold the body works aerobically and prolonged exercise can take place, with a blood lactate volume of 2–3 mmol per litre of blood. Exercise above the lactate threshold (which usually occurs at 4 mmol per litre of blood) can only usually be sustained for approximately one minute. (To highlight this, think of how your legs feel at the end of a flat out 400 m run!)

The test is performed in four stages where subjects are required to run at speeds of 8, 9, 10 and finally 11 miles per hour. At the end of each stage blood samples are taken by a small prick on the finger, and analysed for blood lactate. The point at which blood lactate rises significantly (usually 4 mmol/litre of blood) indicates the point of onset of blood lactate accumulation, and the running speed which corresponds to this is recorded. Improvements in endurance ability can be observed where lower lactate levels are recorded for the same intensity of exercise; this shows that the body has adapted to cope better with this intensity of exercise through buffering lactic acid.

Maximum oxygen uptake test ($\dot{V}O_2$ max test)

The multistage fitness test gives a reasonable prediction of $\dot{V}O_2$ max, but it is purely a prediction and not a truly objective measure of the volume of oxygen that the body can take in, transport and utilise.

There are a wealth of tests to achieve this objective measure, but the most accurate is gas analysis. Subjects are measured at progressively increasing intensities on one of many laboratory ergometers (treadmills, cycle or rowing machines tend to be the most popular), while breathing through respiratory apparatus which is linked to a computer. The computer analyses the relative concentrations of oxygen and carbon dioxide inspired and expired. Since the concentrations of these in the surrounding environment are known, it is fairly simple to calculate the amount of oxygen consumed and the amount of carbon dioxide produced over time.

The subject continues to work at increasingly higher work intensities, until such a time is reached when the body's oxygen consumption does not increase further with increasing workloads. At this point the subject's body is working at its aerobic limit, and any further increments in workload must be met through anaerobic means. This is the point of maximal oxygen uptake, and the amount of oxygen being consumed can now be recorded. $\dot{V}O_2$ max can be measured in absolute terms: ie, 1/min for non-weight bearing activities such as swimming, cycling and rowing, or relative to body weight in ml kg^{-1} min^{-1} (millimetres of oxygen per kilogram of bodyweight per minute). The higher the value of $\dot{V}O_2$ max, the more efficient the body is at exercising under aerobic conditions.

The results of the lactate threshold test and maximal oxygen uptake test can be used in conjunction to determine the percentage of maximum oxygen uptake the subject uses when exercising at the point of lactate threshold (an individual will rarely be able to exercise at a 100% of $\dot{V}O_2$ max). The higher the value, the better the subject will be able to sustain exercise at fairly high intensities for long periods of time without getting fatigued, since they can delay the onset and effects of lactic acid which can inhibit muscle action (see fig 5.12a and 5.12b).

Haematology

Haematology is the study of blood and its component parts which can significantly affect our performance during exercise.

The first part of this test considers haemoglobin content at rest. This component transports oxygen from the lungs to the muscle site and other organs. Low haemoglobin levels can lead to premature fatigue as there is a limit to the oxygen carrying capabilities of the body. Low levels can easily be rectified by increasing the amount of iron consumed in the diet. Recommended normal values for males are 14.0–18.0 grammes per decilitre of blood.

This test involves taking a sample of blood via a simple thumb prick which is then analysed.

Haematocrit

Haematocrit measures the amount of fluid in the blood – ie, its current state of hydration, which concerns the proportion of solids (blood cells) to plasma in the blood. Normal haematocrit for males occur in the region of 42–45%. If blood haematocrit is too high, there may be too many red blood cells in the blood relative to plasma; as a result the blood viscosity increases which slows down the flow, and hinders oxygen transport to the muscles. This high value can also reflect that dehydration has occurred, which is obviously a problem in endurance events. Drinking plenty of fluids is essential to prevent performance from deteriorating and to keep the body in an adequate state of hydration.

Muscle power and strength

Muscle force can be tested by an isokinetic dynamometer linked to a computer. It measures muscle strength at different angles and speeds of contraction and can be linked to the speeds most appropriate to the athlete's event. By exerting a force against the dynamometer, muscle strength and power can be assessed.

 ACTIVITY 3

See table 5.3 for each of the components of fitness; give a recognised test, a brief description of the test and how each test can be evaluated.

Table 5.3   TESTS FOR COMPONENTS OF FITNESS

FITNESS COMPONENT	RECOGNISED TEST	DESCRIPTION OF TEST	EVALUATION
aerobic fitness			
anaerobic fitness			
strength			
muscular endurance			
flexibility			
body composition			
speed			

Discuss the merits of fitness testing. Outline some tests you may use to assess an athlete's level of fitness and how you would evaluate them.

Validity and reliability of testing

Validity of testing is concerned with whether the test measures exactly what it sets out to. We have discussed for example, that the sit and reach test is a valid test for the assessment of flexibility in the lower back and hamstrings but not at the shoulder. The validity of a test is further improved if the test is sport specific ie, the testing environment should resemble the activity being tested, so that specific muscle groups and fibres together with specific actions from the sport are actually being assessed. We would have to question therefore the validity of the multi-stage fitness test to a swimmer. A much more appropriate test of $\dot{V}O_2$ max for a swimmer would be conducted in the confines of a swimming pool. Reliability on the other hand questions the accuracy of the test results. If a test is reliable it should be possible to gain the same or similar result during a re-test, ie, the results should be consistent and reproducible. The testers should be experienced and equipment should be standardised. The sequencing of tests is also important since if more than one test is to be conducted during the same session the order of the tests could affect results. When any type of testing is undertaken, it must be remembered that many things contribute to performance, and fitness tests look solely at one aspect. Other factors to be considered when testing include motivation and the testing environment – is the athlete really pushing him/herself in the tests, particularly when some tests require the athlete to work to near exhaustion? Submaximal tests are therefore often favoured over maximal tests since they do not require the athlete to undergo the duress and strain of maximal tests and therefore increase the reliability of the results – are the tests truly replicating the sporting environment accurately? In order to maximise the reliability of a specific test, it may be necessary to repeat the test several times in order to minimise the possibility of human error. Other factors to take into account when conducting tests are safety, the ability to interpret the results and ensuring that correct standardised testing procedures and protocols are used. All these factors should ensure that any tests conducted are valid and reliable.

Maximal oxygen uptake (V.O₂ max) and the anaerobic threshold (OBLA)

In the previous section we learnt how to measure an athlete's aerobic capacity, through testing their $\dot{V}O_2$ max. We are now going to look in detail at how maximal oxygen uptake can be specifically related to successful endurance performance. Maximal oxygen uptake can be defined as the maximal amount of oxygen that can be taken in, transported and consumed by the working muscles per minute. It is largely dependent upon the difference in oxygen content of inspired and expired air.

When exercise commences, the volume of oxygen increases sharply at first, and then levels out into a steady state. This steady state in oxygen consumption represents a balance between the energy demands of the muscle and the amount of oxygen supplied to the muscle to meet these demands. At this steady state, a cyclist (for instance) should be able to continue exercising for a long period of time, theoretically until his energy stores (of glycogen and fat) are depleted. If the cyclist then comes up against a hill, oxygen consumption must increase in order to meet the increased energy demands (assuming the cyclist remains at the same speed).

Steady state may once again occur when energy demands are met by oxygen supply. If the cyclist subsequently comes up against a steeper hill, oxygen consumption will again need to increase until steady state is reached once again. If exercise intensity continues to increase in this manner, oxygen consumption will continue to increase, until such a point is reached where the body cannot consume any more oxygen – this point is known as the maximal oxygen uptake or $\dot{V}O_2$ max.

Once this point has been reached, if there is a subsequent increase in intensity (such as cycling up a steeper slope or increasing speed), then the body must meet the extra energy requirements through anaerobic means. This causes severe problems to the cyclist or athlete since anaerobic respiration causes an onset of lactic acid and ultimately fatigue. The only way that this can be prevented is by reducing the intensity of the exercise so oxygen consumption can fall below the point of $\dot{V}O_2$ max. However this may decrease all chance of a successful performance.

The point at which lactic acid starts to accumulate in the body is known as the anaerobic threshold, or onset of blood lactate accumulation (OBLA). It is measured as the percentage of $\dot{V}O_2$ max reached before lactic acid starts to accumulate.

$$\%\dot{V}O_2 \text{ max utilised} = \frac{\dot{V}O_2 \text{ (amount of } O_2 \text{ used)}}{\dot{V}O_2 \text{ max (maximum potential)}}$$

For example:

$$\frac{\dot{V}O_2 \text{ used}}{\dot{V}O_2 \text{ max}} = \frac{30 \text{ ml/kg/min}}{60 \text{ ml/kg/min}} = \frac{30}{60} = 50\% \text{ of } \dot{V}O_2 \text{ max used}$$

The athlete in this example is not utilising his aerobic capacity efficiently, which could be a result of poor training methods or a lack of training.

$\dot{V}O_2$ max can only increase by 10–20% however, through training, as it has a 93% genetic component. This assumes that an athlete with a $\dot{V}O_2$ max of 50 ml/kg/min may expect to increase this to 60 ml/kg/min through training. In order to assess our physiological potential in terms of endurance capacity it may well be necessary to take a look at our parents and grandparents!

However, the anaerobic threshold or OBLA is a **product** of training and can be heightened through following an appropriate training programme, so that aerobic efficiency is improved by utilising a greater percentage of $\dot{V}O_2$ max before the onset of lactic acid. The reasons for this are discussed in Chapter 6.

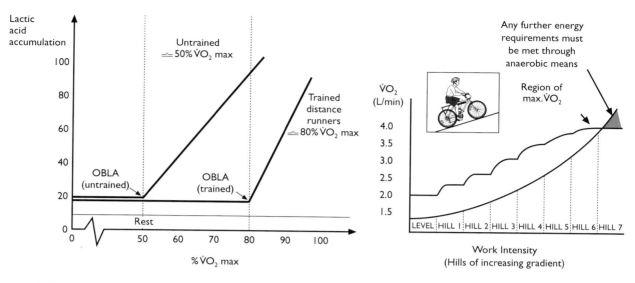

With appropriate endurance training the anaerobic threshold (OBLA) can be heightened, so that a greater amount of aerobic capacity can be utilised. Aerobic performance therefore improves

Fig. 5.12A A COMPARISON OF THE ANAEROBIC THRESHOLD (OBLA) BETWEEN THE TRAINED AND UNTRAINED

Fig. 5.12B OXYGEN CONSUMPTION DURING A CYCLE RIDE OF PROGRESSIVE INTENSITY

1 **How could a knowledge of maximal oxygen uptake ($\dot{V}O_2$ max) help the coach and athlete in the design of training programmes?**
2 **Outline the $\dot{V}O_2$ max scores expected from a rugby player, a shot putter and a triathlete.**
3 **Explain the concept of the anaerobic threshold (OBLA). How would a knowledge of this help to improve endurance performance?**

Summary

- Fitness requirements differ tremendously between athletes and activities.
- Health related components of fitness are largely physiologically based and include strength, speed, cardiorespiratory endurance, muscular endurance, flexibility and body composition.
- Skill related components of fitness include agility, balance, co-ordination, reaction time and power and are dependent upon the interaction of the nervous system with the muscular system.
- Fitness testing is imperative for the élite athlete since it can identify weaknesses and assess the value of the training programme.
- Any fitness tests conducted should be repeated regularly to ensure validity.
- Maximal Oxygen Uptake of $\dot{V}O_2$ max is the maximum amount of oxygen that can be taken in, transported and consumed by the working muscles per minute. It is the best predictor of aerobic capacity and can only increase through training by 10–20% since it has a 93% genetic component.
- The anaerobic threshold or onset of blood lactate accumulation (OBLA) is the point at which lactic acid starts to accumulate. It is measured as a percentage of $\dot{V}O_2$ max reached before lactic acid accumulation. The anaerobic threshold is a product of training and therefore increases through endurance training.

Review Questions

1 Identify two physical fitness components and two motor fitness components that will be required in **a)** sprint running and **b)** gymnastics. Give details of when each component will be needed within the activity.

2 Identify two tests to assess each of: **a)** muscular endurance **b)** aerobic capacity. State how each can be evaluated.

3 In any test, validity and reliability are important. How would you ensure that an investigation was valid and reliable?

4 Critically evaluate the validity and reliability of the multi-stage fitness test as a measure of aerobic capacity.

5 Explain the division of physical fitness into general fitness and specific fitness.

6 Using the example of basketball, suggest how you might adapt a test of agility to make it more specific.

7 What factors contribute to aerobic capacity of an individual?

8 Construct a somatotype delta graph and show where you would place **a)** a rock climber, **b)** a rugby prop forward, **c)** a tour cyclist and **d)** a heavyweight boxer.

chapter 6

Training Implications

This chapter seeks specifically to investigate how training can improve and enhance fitness levels.

The chapter consists of two main sections. The first discusses the principles and types of training that can be employed in a training régime, culminating in considerations needed when designing long-term training programmes. Having acquired this knowledge it is hoped that the reader will be able to design such a programme for the athlete. Throughout this section, the benefits of training on the body systems are highlighted; the second part of this chapter synthesises this information, so that a complete picture is given of the adaptive responses of the body to exercise and explains just what happens to the body to account for improved performance.

The principles of training

Specificity

The principles of training are essentially the rules or laws that underpin a training programme. If these rules are not followed then any training undertaken will become obsolete and worthless. There are many principles of training that the coach and athlete must bear in mind in the design of an effective training regime.

The law of specificity suggests that any training undertaken should be relevant and appropriate to the sport for which the individual is training. For example, it would be highly inappropriate for a swimmer to carry out the majority of his/her training on the land. Although there are certainly benefits gained from land-based training, the majority of the training programme should involve pool-based work.

The specificity rule does not govern just the muscles, fibre type and actions used but also the energy systems which are predominantly stressed. The energy system used in training should replicate that predominantly used in the event. The energy systems should also be stressed in isolation of each other so that high intensity work (stressing the anaerobic systems) should be done in one session, whereas more aerobic and endurance based work should be completed in a separate session. When designing a weight training programme for a shot putter, for example, the coach will ensure specificity by using weights or exercises, (such as an inclined bench press) that replicate the action of shot putting. He will ensure that the exercises use the same muscle group and muscle fibres that the athlete recruits during the event and that the repetitions are undertaken explosively, using the alactic (ATP–Pc system) energy pathway, which of course is the predominant energy system used during the shot putt.

Progressive overload

This rule considers the intensity of the training session. For improvement and adaptation to occur, the training should be at an intensity where the individual feels some kind of stress and discomfort – this signifies **overload** and suggests that the old adage 'no pain, no gain' has some truth in it, especially for the élite athlete. Overload for the shot putter may therefore involve lifting very heavy weights, or indeed using a shot that is heavier than that used in competition. If exercise takes place on a regular basis the body's systems will adapt and start to cope with these stresses that have been imposed. In order for further improvement to occur, the intensity of training will need to be gradually increased – this is **progression** and can be done by running faster, lifting heavier weights, or training for longer.

Reversibility

Also known as 'regression' or detraining, this explains why performance deteriorates when training ceases or the intensity of training decreases for extended periods of time. Quite simply, if you don't use it you lose it!

Seven weeks of inactivity has been shown to have the following physiological effects. Significant decreases in maximum oxygen uptake have been recorded – up to 27%, which reflects a fall in the efficiency of the cardiovascular system. In particular, stroke volume and cardiac output can decrease by up to 30%. During exercise, increases in both blood lactate and heart rate have been shown to increase for the same intensity of exercise. Muscle mass and therefore strength also deteriorate but at a less rapid rate. Now you may be able to understand why pre-season training feels so tough even after just 6–8 weeks of inactivity..

Individual difference

These suggest that the benefits of training are optimised when programmes are set to meet the needs and abilities of an individual. What may help one athlete to improve may not be successful on another. The coach must therefore be very sympathetic to the needs of the individual athlete and adjust training programmes accordingly.

The F.I.T.T. regime

The coach may also wish to consider the F.I.T.T. regime when designing the training programme. These letters stand for:

- F = frequency of training
- I = intensity of exercise
- T = time or duration of exercise
- T = type of training.

'F'

– the **frequency** of training. The élite athlete will need to do some sort of training most days, depending upon the activity being undertaken. Endurance or aerobic type activities can be performed five or six times per week, but more intense or anaerobic activities such as strength or speed work should be performed three or four times per week, as sufficient rest days are required for the body tissues to repair themselves following this high intensity work.

'I'

– the **intensity** of the exercise. This also depends upon the type of training occurring, and can be quite difficult to objectively measure. For aerobic work, exercise intensity can be measured by calculating an individual's 'training zone'; this is represented by the training heart rate and so involves observing heart rate values, which has become much easier with the advent of the heart rate monitor.

The most established method of calculating the training zone is known as the **Karvonen Principle**. Karvonen developed a formula to identify correct training intensities as a percentage of the sum of the maximum heart rate reserve and resting heart rate. Maximum heart rate reserve can be calculated by subtracting resting heart rate (HRrest) from an individual's maximum heart rate (HRmax):

Maximal heart rate reserve $= HR(max) - HR(rest)$

Where an individual's maximal heart rate can be calculated by subtracting their age from 220:

Maximal heart rate $= 220 - age$

Karvonen suggests a training intensity of between 60–75% of maximal heart rate reserve for the average athlete, although this can obviously be adapted to account for individual differences.

Training heart rate 60% = 0.60 (maxHR reserve) + HRrest

Consider the following example to illustrate the value of this measure of intensity:

A twenty year old rower, with a resting heart rate of 65 bpm is aiming to build up his endurance capacities for a forthcoming event. He is advised to train between 60–75% of his training heart rate reserve in the weeks prior to the event. To calculate his training zone, the rower used the Karvonen formula as follows:

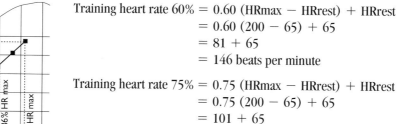

Training heart rate 60% = 0.60 (HRmax − HRrest) + HRrest
= 0.60 (200 − 65) + 65
= 81 + 65
= 146 beats per minute

Training heart rate 75% = 0.75 (HRmax − HRrest) + HRrest
= 0.75 (200 − 65) + 65
= 101 + 65
= 166 beats per minute

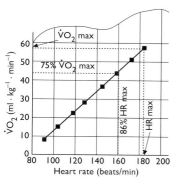

Fig. 6.1

Thus the rower now has some precise figures to measure and ensure that he is training at the correct intensity. In order for some kind of aerobic adaptation to occur, the rower must be exercising within his target zone, between 146 and 166 beats per minute.

This is a valued measure of exercise intensity since it relates closely to both the stress being imposed on the heart and the vascular system and the percent of $\dot{V}O_2$ max at which the athlete is working.

Another method of monitoring the intensity of training is through working the athlete at a percentage of $\dot{V}O_2$ max. For the élite endurance athlete, this should be no less than 70% of $\dot{V}O_2$ max, whilst those exercising for health-related reasons will see benefits from training at just 50% of their $\dot{V}O_2$ max. Fig 6.1 shows the linear relationship between heart rate and oxygen consumption ($\dot{V}O_2$).

A coach could also use lactate tests working sufficiently hard and analyse oxygen consumption and carbon dioxide production to determine the respiratory exchange ratio. The **Respiratory Exchange Ratio** (RER) or Respiratory Quotient is a method of determining which energy providing nutrient is predominantly in use during exercise. It is represented as follows:

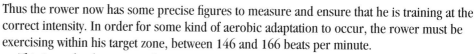

$$RER = \frac{\text{Volume of } CO_2 \text{ expired per minute}}{\text{Volume of } O_2 \text{ uptake per minue}}$$

The closer the value is to 1.0 the more likely it is the body is using glycogen as a fuel, whereas the expected value for fats is 0.7. Intermediate figures suggest that a mixture of fuels is being utilised which is obviously the expected norm. Obviously the harder the athlete is working the more he or she relies on using glycogen as a fuel.

'T'

– the **time** or **duration** that the exercise is in progress. For aerobic type activities, the athlete should be training within his/her training zone for a minimum of 20–30 mins. However duration should not be considered in isolation since intensity of training often determines the duration of the training session.

'T'

– the **type** or **mode of training** that is undertaken. This is explained on p 100.

1 Using table 6.1, calculate your training zone (between 60 and 75% of your maximum heart rate reserve).

2 Now complete a 15 minute run, ensuring your heart rate lies at 70% of your MHR.

3 Sketch the heart rate curve expected.

Table 6.1   THE TRAINING ZONE

AGE		20	25	30	35	40	45	50	55	60	65	70	75	80
55%	19	18	18	17	17	17	16	16	15	15	14	14	13	13
60%	21	20	19	19	19	18	18	17	17	16	16	15	15	14
70%	24	23	23	22	22	21	20	20	19	19	18	18	17	16
80%	27	27	26	25	25	24	23	23	22	21	21	20	19	19
90%	29	28	28	27	26	26	25	24	23	23	22	21	21	20

Use this table as a calculator to work out your target training zone at various intensities. All scores reflect your heart rate for a 10 second count. Don't forget to start counting from zero! If you fall between age ranges take the next stage group up. For example, if you are 18 and wish to train at 70% of your maximum heart rate, find the age group 20 along the top of the table and move down until you come to 70% of MHR. Your target 10 s pulse rate should be 23 beats. You may wish to convert this to beats per minute, in which case multiply the figure in the box by six.

Warm-ups and cool-downs

Warm-up

Although one might not immediately think of warm-ups and cool-downs as a principle of training as they should be undertaken prior to and following the training session and will improve the effectiveness of training, it seems highly appropriate to discuss them here. Before embarking upon any type of exercise, it is imperative to perform a warm-up. As it is fundamental to safe practice, it has often been considered as a principle of training and thus seems appropriate to discuss here.

A warm up should make the body ready for exercise. It can prevent injury and muscle soreness, and has the following physiological benefits:

- The release of adrenaline will increase heart rate and dilate capillaries, which in turn enable greater amounts and increased speed of oxygen and blood delivery to the muscles.
- Increased muscle temperatures associated with exercise will facilitate enzyme activity; this increases muscle metabolism and therefore ensures a readily available supply of energy through the breakdown of glycogen.
- Increased temperatures also lead to decreased viscosity within the muscle. This enables greater extensibility and elasticity of muscle fibres which ultimately leads to increased speed and force of contraction.
- Warm-ups also make us more alert, due to an increase in the speed of nerve impulse conduction.
- Increased production of synovial fluid ensures efficient movement at the joints.
- Certain psychological benefits can also occur through a warm-up, particularly if the individual has certain superstitions or rituals they follow. Think of the New Zealand All Blacks Rugby Team performing the Haka, prior to kick off.

Design a circuit training session for an activity of your choice. Give reasons for the exercises you have chosen and explain how the principle of progressive overload could be applied.

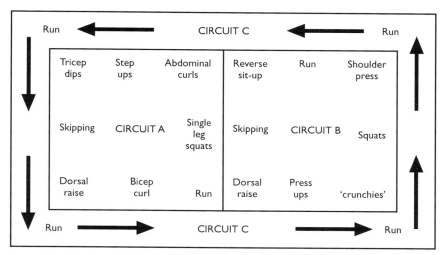

Each participant is to complete each circuit.

Circuit A = 8 exercises x 30 secs = 4 mins
Circuit B = 8 exercises x 30 secs = 4 mins
Circuit C = Run around outside = 4 mins
Repeat 2 or 3 times

Each participant is to complete circuit A, B and C with 60 secs walking recovery between circuit.

Fig. 6.4 A GENERAL FITNESS CIRCUIT

Table 6.3   EXERCISES TO INCLUDE IN A CIRCUIT

cardiovascular exercises	running around the gym skipping step ups cycling on an ergometer bounding exercises on a mat
trunk exercises	abdominal curls crunchies dorsal raises trunk twists
arm exercises	press ups/box press bicep curls tricep dips shoulder press squat thrusts chin ups to beam
leg exercises	single leg squats any of the cardiovascular exercises outlined above

Strength training

Strength gains are sought by many athletes and usually occur either through weight or resistance training methods, or through a further type of training known as plyometrics.

With advances in technology and the improvement in the quality of weight machines, weight training has increased in popularity in both athletic and recreational training regimes. It can be used to develop several components of fitness, including strength, strength endurance and explosive power. Which of these are stressed at a particular time is determined by manipulating the weight or resistance, the number of repetitions and the number of sets. Central to the devising of an effective weight training programme is the principle of one repetition maximum (1RM). The 1RM is the maximum amount of weight the performer can lift with one repetition. Once this has been found for each exercise the coach can design a programme adjusting the resistance as a percentage of the athlete's maximum lift.

For activities where maximum strength is required, such as power lifting or throwing the hammer, training methods which increase muscle strength and size will be required. Essentially this will involve some form of very high resistance, low repetition exercise. For example:

- Performing 3 sets of 2–6 repetitions at 80–100% of maximum strength, with full recovery between sets.

Key points for power development are:

a) that the movement and contraction period must be explosive to ensure the muscle works rapidly

b) to use very high loads or resistance which will encourage the muscle to recruit all its motor units

c) to ensure the muscle recovers fully between sets, enabling the relevant energy system to recover.

Fig. 6.5 STRENGTH TRAINING: LEG EXTENSION

To train for activities which require strength endurance, such as swimming or rowing, a different approach to training will be required. In order to perform more repetitions, a lighter load or resistance is needed and the following programme might be prescribed:

- 3 sets of 20 repetitions at 50–60% of maximum strength with full recovery between sets.

Plyometrics

Power is determined by the force exerted by the muscle (strength) and the speed at which the muscle shortens:

Power = Force × Velocity

It thus follows that by improving either strength or speed of shortening, power may be improved. One method of training which may improve the speed at which a muscle shortens is plyometrics.

It has long been established that muscles generate more force in contraction when they have been previously stretched. Plyometrics enables this to occur by taking the muscle through an eccentric (lengthened) phase before a powerful concentric (shortening) phase. This stimulates adaptation within the neuromuscular system whereby the muscle spindles within the muscle cause a stretch reflex, which prevents muscle damage and produces a more powerful concentric contraction of the muscle group. This has important consequences for sprinting, jumping and throwing events in athletics, as well as in games such as rugby, volleyball and basketball where leg strength is central to performance.

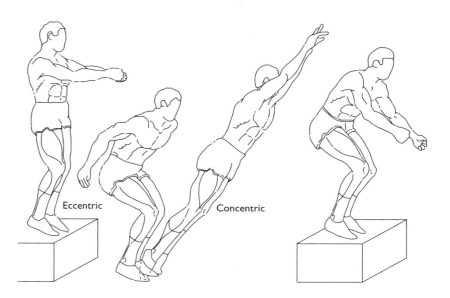

Fig. 6.6 EXAMPLES OF PLYOMETRIC EXERCISES

Exercises that might form part of the plyometrics session include:

- bounding
- hopping
- leaping
- skipping
- depth jumps (jumping off and onto boxes)
- press-ups with claps
- throwing and catching a medicine ball.

Taking the example of depth jumping (Fig 6.6), here the athlete drops down from a box or platform 50–80 cm high. On landing the quadricep muscle group lengthens, pre-stretching the muscle. A stretch reflex causes the muscle to give a very forceful concentric contraction driving the athlete up onto a second platform. Furthermore the exercise becomes more effective if the athlete spends as little time as possible in contact with the ground when landing. This particular plyometric activity can also be made sport specific. For example a basketball player could perform a rebound after dropping down from the box or a volleyball player perform a block etc. Due to the high impact nature of the plyometrics individuals would need to be screened for injury and participants would need to undergo a thorough warm-up. The strength gains and muscle hypertrophy associated with strength training may only start to become evident after about eight weeks of training, and are largely due to the increase in size and volume of the myofibrils.

A triple jumper requires some advice on improving leg strength. Design a strength programme, stating which type of strength is being developed.

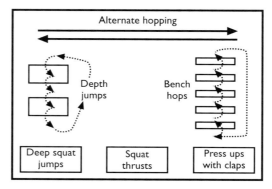

Fig. 6.7 A PLYOMETRICS CIRCUIT

Mobility training

Mobility training is the method employed to improve flexibility. It is often a neglected form of training, but should be incorporated into every athlete's training programme. Effective flexibility training can improve performance and help prevent the occurrence of injury.

The method of stretching used in mobility training should centre on the connective tissue and the muscle tissue acting upon the joint, as these tissues have been shown to elongate following a period of regular and repeated stretching. Two types of stretching have been identified and outlined below.

Active stretching

The athlete performs voluntary muscular contractions, and holds the stretch for a period of 30–60 seconds. By consciously relaxing the target muscle at the limit of the range of motion, muscle elongation may occur following regular contraction.

Passive stretching

This refers to the range of movement which can occur with the aid of external force. This is generally performed with the help of a partner who can offer some resistance, although gravity and body weight can also be used.

One method of flexibility training that has emerged from passive stretching is **proprioceptive neuromuscular facilitation** (PNF). This seeks to decrease the reflex shortening of the muscle being stretched, which occurs when a muscle is stretched to its limit. A simple PNF technique is now outlined:

1 Move slowly to the limit of your range of motion with a partner aiding (passive stretch).
2 Just before the point of discomfort, isometrically contract the muscle being stretched for between 6 and 10 seconds.
3 After the hold, the muscle will release, having stimulated a Golgi tendon organ (GTO) response which causes further relaxation of the muscle and enabling further stretching of the muscle with the aid of a partner. PNF stretching relies on the fact that when a muscle contracts isometrically when stretched, the stretch reflex mechanism of the muscle spindles is switched off, and therefore enables the muscle to stretch further than previously.

With continued practice of PNF, a new limit of the muscle stretch may occur, but, don't forget that pain is the body's signal that damage is occurring, and athletes should not stretch beyond the slight discomfort.

Furthermore, stretching and mobility training should only be performed after a thorough warm-up where an increase in body temperature has occurred. This is easily achieved by performing a period of light cardiovascular exercise, centreing upon those muscle groups that are to be stretched. In addition, wear warm clothing while performing the stretches to maintain body temperature; if possible, perform in a warm environment.

Altitude training

Altitude training is a method of training based on the principle that with an increase in altitude, the partial pressure of oxygen (pO_2) in the atmosphere decreases by about a half, causing the body to adapt by increasing red blood cell mass and haemoglobin levels to cope with a lower pO_2. It is widely used by endurance athletes to enhance their oxygen carrying capacity and when athletes return to sea level these increases remain, yet the pO_2 has increased which means that the body can transport and utilise more oxygen, giving improved endurance performance. However there appears to be contradictory evidence concerning the

Table 6.4 Types of training

Type	Advantages	Disadvantages
Continuous	• time efficient • trains cardiovascular and muscular endurance • easy to follow routine programme • can be sports-specific, eg, distance running • less chance of injury because lower intensity	athletes may need higher intensity can be monotonous may not be specific to some activities, eg, team sports
Fartlek	• adds variety of pace • train at higher intensity than in continuous training	may not be sports-specific higher intensity may increase risk of injury
Interval	• adds variety of pace and duration • can be very sports-specific, eg, sprinting	more time is needed increases risk of injury due to higher intensity
Circuit	• trains cardiovascular and muscular endurance as well as strength • time efficient • can be very sports-specific	not maximal improvements in endurance and strength need access to equipment
Aerobic circuit	• time efficient • can train at high intensity • can be very sports-specific	need access to equipment higher risk of injury

From Abernethy *The Biophysical Foundations of Human Movement Human Kinetics* 1997

Table 6.5 THE DEVELOPMENT OF DIFFERENT TYPES OF STRENGTH

OBJECTIVE	INTENSITY OF TRAINING LOAD	REPETITIONS IN EACH SET	NUMBER OF SETS	RECOVERY BETWEEN SETS	EVALUATION PROCEDURES	TRAINING OF VALUE FOR
development of maximum strength	85–95%	1–5	normal 2–4 advanced 5–8	4–5 mins	maximum lift dynamometer	weight lifting, shot, discus, hammer, javelin, jumping events rugby and contact sports men's gymnastics
development of elastic strength	75–85%	6–10	(4–6)	3–5 mins	standing, long and vertical jump capability	all sports requiring 'explosive' strength qualities – sprinting, jumping, throwing, striking
development of advanced level of strength endurance	50–75% of maximum		(3–5)	30–45 s	maximum reps possible	rowing, wrestling, skiing, swimming, 400 m, steeplechase etc.
development of a basic level of strength endurance	25–50% of maximum	15–20	(4–6)	optimal	maximum reps possible	generally required for all sports suitable for young and novice competitors and fitness participants

Source: Leeds University, 1988

benefits of altitude training and recent evidence suggests that living at altitude whilst training at sea level produces the greatest endurance performance and in doing so athletes can increase oxygen carrying capacity of the blood by up to 150%.

Responses and adaptations to training

We have already mentioned that the reason behind training is to improve our components of fitness, the capacity of each energy system and overall performance. The body responds to the stresses that training imposes upon it and subsequently adapts and adjusts to meet the demands of the exercise that is occurring.

Short term responses

Short term responses to exercise are the ways in which the body's systems adjust to cope with the exercise *during* a training session. At the end of the exercise period the body will return to its normal resting state.

Cardiovascular and respiratory responses to exercise

We have established that many adjustments are made by the cardiovascular system during exercise to ensure adequate delivery of oxygen and nutrients to the muscle and efficient removal of metabolites from the muscle. Such adjustments include an increased heart rate of between 60–80 bpm at rest to between 160–180 bpm during exercise.

We also see a slight increase in stroke volume during exercise, with the élite athlete increasing stroke volume from 110 ml/beat to 170 ml/beat while exercising; this is due to Starlings law.

There is also an increase in cardiac output (cardiac output is a product of heart rate and stroke volume). Cardiac output may increase from 5–6 l at rest to 30 l during exercise.

More importantly, however, is the adjustment made in the redistribution of blood being pumped around the body. At rest, only about 20% of the cardiac output is distributed to the working muscles. During exercise however, when there is greater demand for oxygen up to 85% of cardiac output may be distributed to the working skeletal muscles. This can occur through accommodation and shunting of blood from inactive tissues such as the stomach and kidneys to the working muscles. Adjustments in blood pressure are also seen during exercise due to the increased blood flow and vasoconstriction of blood vessels which ensure a rapid flow of blood to the working muscles.

Respiratory responses occur largely because of the increase in muscle metabolism which takes place as a result of the increased activity. Increased muscle glycogen breakdown results in greater amounts of carbon dioxide production, which decreases blood pH and stimulates the respiratory centre to increase ventilation. With higher exercise intensity (usually exceeding 60% of $\dot{V}O_2$ max), increased production of lactic acid may occur. This also increases acidity and again stimulates the respiratory centre to increase ventilation.

Long term adaptations

Long term physiological adaptations are those changes that occur in the body as a result of following a long term training programme.

Muscular adaptations

Depending upon the type of the prior training, different adaptations will occur in the muscle. We are first going to look at the changes that occur following a period of aerobic training and then take a look at the anaerobic changes that may arise.

Aerobic adaptations

These occur in the muscle as a result of following an endurance based training programme. Examples of activities that can be performed include swimming or jogging, although any continuous type activity will lead to some adaptation.

Regular stimulation of the muscle through aerobic based exercise will cause changes to occur within the muscle cell. In particular, the structure of the muscle fibres may alter. Since the performance of endurance exercise stresses the slow twitch muscle fibres, these respond by enlarging by up to 22%. This gives greater potential for aerobic energy production since larger fibres mean a greater area for mitochondrial activity.

Indeed, endurance training leads to an increase in both size and number of **mitochondria**. Some studies have reported mitochondria size to increase by up to 40% and the number by over 100%. Since the mitochondria are the factories that produce our aerobic energy, increases in size and number can be associated with the economies of scale achieved by large businesses and an increase in production of energy will result.

Endurance training may also increase the activity of our **oxidative enzymes** which work on breaking down our food fuel to release the energy stored within. As a result, there is more scope to use glycogen and fat as a fuel. The oxidation of both these fuels increases, providing greater amounts of energy. With hypertrophy of slow twitch muscle fibres there is a corresponding increase in stores of **glycogen** and **triglycerides** which ensures a continuous supply of energy, enabling exercise to be performed for a longer period of time.

A further benefit of aerobic training is the increase of up to 80% in **myoglobin** content within the muscle cell. Myoglobin is the substance within the muscle that carries oxygen to the mitochondria, and is similar in structure to haemoglobin. With greater amounts of myoglobin, more oxygen can be transported to the mitochondria which further improves the efficiency of aerobic energy production.

All of these aerobic adaptations associated with endurance training ensure that a higher percentage of $\dot{V}O_2$ max can be attained before the anaerobic threshold is reached and thus the onset of fatigue can be delayed. Generally, $\dot{V}O_2$ max is not a product of training as it is largely genetically determined but these metabolic adaptations within the muscle that occur as a result of training may slightly increase an individual's $\dot{V}O_2$ max (maximum oxygen uptake) in the region of 10–20%.

Anaerobic adaptations

The anaerobic or lactate threshold is a product of training, and improvements in this will certainly improve endurance performance.

While training at very high intensity, eg, sprint or strength training, **hypertrophy** of fast twitch muscle fibres takes place. Increases in levels of **ATP and PC** within the muscle occurs which increases the capacity of the ATP-PC or alactic energy system. The efficiency of this system is further improved through increased activity of the **enzymes** responsible for breaking down ATP and PC. These include creatine phosphokinase and myokinase.

Training at high intensities for up to 60 seconds has also been shown to increase the **glycolytic** capacity of the muscle, largely through increasing the activity of glycolytic enzymes. This improves the muscles' ability to break down glycogen in the absence of oxygen and means that the athlete can exercise for longer periods of time before feeling the effects of fatigue.

This is further aided by improvements in the **buffering** capacity of the muscle, which enables the muscles to tolerate lactic acid more effectively. When lactic acid accumulates in the muscle, hydrogen ions (H^+) are released, inhibiting glycolytic enzyme activity and interfering with the contractile elements of the muscle. Bicarbonate ions existing in the muscle and the blood mop up these hydrogen ions reducing acidity. By following an anaerobic training programme, the buffering capacity of the body increases substantially, and enables the body to work for longer periods of time and at higher levels of acidity.

Cardiovascular adaptations to training

Following endurance training, many cardiovascular adaptations arise. In the first instance, the actual size of the heart may increase – **cardiac hypertrophy**. This enables the heart to work more efficiently, particularly at rest. The increase in thickness of the myocardium (cardiac tissue) enables the left ventricle to fill more completely with blood during the diastole phase of the cardiac cycle. This allows the heart to pump more blood per beat since the thicker walls can contract more forcefully, pumping more blood into the systemic system and ultimately to the muscles.

Consequently, stroke volume increases both at rest and during exercise. With an increase in **stroke volume at rest**, the heart will no longer need to pump as many times per minute to achieve the same amount of blood flowing to the body's tissues.

Since the heart seeks to work as efficiently as possible resting heart rate decreases as a result of the endurance training that has taken place.

When resting heart rate falls to below 60 beats per minute, **bradycardia** results, which explains the very low resting heart rates often experienced by top endurance athletes; for example, Indurain, the many times Tour de France champion is reported to have a resting heart rate of around 30 bpm!

As an athlete's stroke volume increases, the cardiac output of the trained athlete also increases. Cardiac output may increase by up to 30–40 min in trained individuals. However it is important to note that there is little or no change in the values of resting cardiac output, due to the decrease in resting heart rate that accompanies endurance training.

The adaptations mentioned above have centred on the structure and function of the heart. We now need to discuss those training-induced changes that occur in the **vascular** and **circulatory** systems:

1 One reason that accounts for greater performances in aerobic events following training is the increased **capillarisation** of trained muscles. New capillaries may actually develop which enables more blood to flow to the muscles and enables more oxygen to reach the tissues. Furthermore, existing capillaries become more efficient and allow greater amounts of blood to reach the muscles, which also become more efficient at extracting the oxygen due to the muscular adaptations mentioned above.

2 Improvements in the vasculature efficiency (especially the arteries) to **vasoconstrict** and **vasodilate**, improve the redistribution of blood by shunting the supply to the active muscles and tissues, so that there is a greater supply of oxygen for energy production in these working muscles.

3 These efficiency gains also result in a **decreased resting blood pressure** following endurance training, although blood pressure during exercise of a sub-maximal or maximal nature remains unchanged.

4 Increases in blood volume following training can be attributed to an **increase in blood plasma** (the water component of the blood). This has the important function of decreasing the blood viscosity and enabling the blood to flow around the body more easily, thus enhancing oxygen delivery to the muscles and tissues.

5 An increase in **red** blood cell volume and **haemoglobin** content is also higher in the trained athlete which further facilitates the transport of oxygen around the body. However although haemoglobin content increases, the increase in blood plasma is greater and consequently the blood haematocrit (the ratio of red blood cell volume to total blood volume) is reduced, which lowers the viscosity of the blood and facilitates its progress around the body.

Respiratory adaptations to training

Endurance performance is dependent upon oxygen transportation and utilisation, but no matter how good the functioning of these are, improvements in performance will not happen unless we can get oxygen into the body. The respiratory system is responsible for receiving oxygen into the body and dealing with the waste products associated with muscle metabolism.

Respiratory functioning does not usually hinder aerobic performance, and the adaptations that take place merely aid the improved cardiovascular functioning.

Following training, there is a reduction in both resting respiratory rate and the breathing rate during submaximal exercise. This appears to be a function of the overall efficiency of the respiratory structures induced by training.

Surprisingly there are only very small increases in lung volumes following training. Vital capacity (the amount of air that can be forcibly expelled following maximum inspiration) increases slightly, as does tidal volume during maximal exercise. One factor to account for these increases is the increased strength of the respiratory muscles which may facilitate lung inflation.

Pulmonary diffusion (the exchange of gases at the alveoli) will become more efficient following training, especially when working at near maximal levels. The increased surface area of the alveoli during exercise together with their increased capillarisation, ensures that there is ample opportunity for gaseous exchange to take place, and thus guarantees sufficient oxygen is entering the blood.

A student decides to take up distance running and joins a local running club. After following a training programme for three months, a distinct improvement in performance is noted. From a physiological standpoint, account for these changes.

We have seen from this chapter that training will induce changes in the muscular, cardiovascular and respiratory systems which make their functioning more efficient and hopefully improve endurance performance. We now need to discuss how a coach or an athlete can design a training programme to guarantee and maximise the effects of these adaptations.

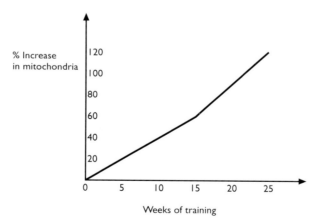

Fig. 6.8 THE INCREASE IN THE SIZE AND NUMBER OF MITOCHONDRIA AS A RESULT OF ENDURANCE TRAINING

A 120% increase in the number of mitochondria following a 25 week endurance programme.
Size of mitochondria may also increase in size by up to 40%

Designing a training programme or personal exercise programme

Training programmes do not come in a standard package that suits everybody; they have to be made to measure and designed specifically for the individual. For example, Colin Jackson would need a very different programme to one designed for a marathon runner.

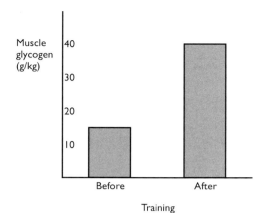

Muscle glycogen (g/kg)

Before   After

Training

Fig. 6.9 THE INCREASE IN MUSCLE GLYCOGEN CONTENT FOLLOWING ENDURANCE TRAINING

A 20 week, 4 day/week endurance training programme.

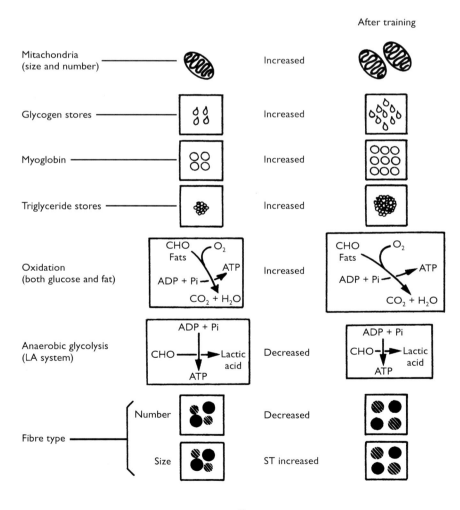

Fig. 6.10 A SUMMARY OF PHYSIOLOGICAL EFFECTS OF ENDURANCE TRAINING ON THE MUSCLE

Source: Davis, Kimmet and Auty (1986)

The problem that a coach faces when designing a programme is that not only are all athletes different but each sport requires different components of fitness at varying levels of importance. A programme should therefore be balanced yet specific enough to ensure that the demands of both the athlete and sport are being met.

When planning a training programme, the following factors should be considered to ensure a worthwhile experience for the athlete:

- the performer's needs
- the sport and related fitness components
- the principles of training
- the types of training that can be employed
- the training year
- the major competitions of the year, and when do they occur.

We have discussed the first four considerations earlier in this chapter. There now follows a short explanation of how a training programme can be structured to ensure optimal performance of the athlete.

1 **For your chosen activity prioritise the relevance of each of the fitness requirements outlined in table.**

2 **Make a list of the key competitive periods of the training year. This might include major athletic meets or swimming galas or indeed league or cup games for game players. An example is shown below. Having completed this task you will be better equipped to determine the requirements of your training programme and optimise the performances of yourself or others.**

The training year

It is important to structure the training programme so that the athlete can achieve the best possible improvements in performance, and that optimal performance occurs in the climax of the competitive season. To ensure this, the training programme should be viewed as a year-long process divided into specific periods designed to prepare the athlete for optimal performances. This is known as **periodisation**. The long term training plan which is usually one year in length but can be longer, (perhaps for an athlete preparing for the Olympic Games or a Soccer player preparing for a World Cup competition) is known as a **macro-cycle**. This macro-cycle is subdivided into periods of 2–6 weeks which concentrates training on particular areas – these phases are known as **meso-cycles**. Meso-cycles are further divided into individual or weekly training sessions known as **micro-cycles** which again have specific aims and objectives.

Typically the periodised year has three periods:

- the preparation period
- the competition period
- the transition period.

Fig 6.11 outlines the periodised year for a rugby player. Phases 1 and 2 relate to the preparation period, phase 3 is the competition period – notice this is at the peak or apex of the triangle to mirror peak performance during the competitive phase, whilst phase 4 relates to the transition period.

The preparation period

The preparation period includes the off-season and pre-season aspects of the periodised year.
During the off-season stage, general conditioning is required through a well rounded programme of aerobic endurance training, mobility training and training to maintain strength.

During the pre-season stage there is a significant increase in the intensity of training. This is the time when much of the strength work should be undertaken, through lifting heavier weights or working against greater resistances, and working at higher speeds. Towards the end of this period the coach should employ some competition specific training; eg, working on sprint starts for the sprinter.

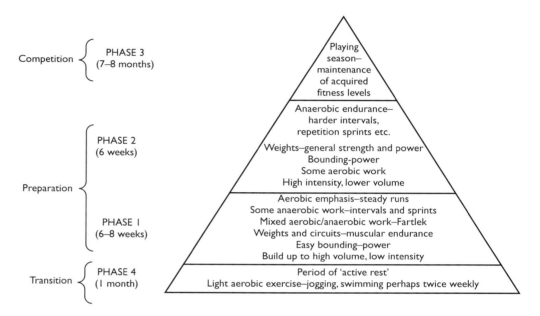

Fig. 6.11 THE PERIODISED YEAR FOR A RUGBY PLAYER

The competition period

Training during the competition period should be aimed at maintaining levels of conditioning achieved during the pre-season phase. Maximum strength training is reduced and much of the training should be centred on competition specific aspects. For the endurance athlete however, training at high intensity is still important in preparation for competition. In order to ensure that the athlete is perfectly prepared and can 'peak' for competition a process known as **tapering** may be undertaken. Tapering involves manipulating the volume and intensity of training 2–3 weeks prior to competition to ensure that athlete is fully recovered from any hard training undertaken, and that muscle glycogen stores can be fully replenished, without the effects of de-training occurring. The two key factors to successful tapering are to:

a) maintain intensity of training

b) decrease the volume of training by approximately one-third. For example if I normally train at 80% HRmax for 45 mins, when tapering I should maintain the intensity, ie, continue to train 80% HRmax but reduce the volume of training to 30 mins. This should hopefully lead to optimal performance during competition.

The transition period

Following a hard season of competition the body needs to recuperate, and the transition period bridges the gap between the season passed and the next training year. Essentially the transition period should be a period of active rest with some low intensity aerobic work such as swimming or cycling. The transition period is vital and should not be omitted; as well as giving the body a break from all the hard work in psychological terms, it can enhance motivation for training during the following periodised year.

Overtraining

Overtraining is a common problem to élite athletes as they strive for greater improvement. It is caused by an imbalance between training and recovery, which usually occurs when insufficient time has been left for the body to regenerate and cause adaptation before embarking upon the next training session. In their search for the best possible performance in competition, élite athletes are often tempted to increase training loads and frequency of training above optimal levels, which can lead to symptoms of overtraining. These symptoms include enduring fatigue, loss of appetite, muscle tenderness, sleep disturbances and head colds. The coach can identify overtraining syndrome by physiological testing, which may show the athlete having an increased oxygen consumption, heart rate and blood lactate levels at fixed workloads. In order to combat overtraining the coach should advise prolonged rest, and a reduction in training workloads for a period of weeks or months. This should restore both performance and competitive desire.

Summary

- In order for a training programme to be successful the athlete must follow the laws or 'principles of training'. These include specificity, progressive overload, reversibility, individual differences, frequency, intensity, time, type, warm-ups and cool-downs as well as many others.
- There are a number of training methods that can be employed by an athlete. These include continuous methods such as Fartlek or intermittent training methods such as interval training, circuit training, weight training and plyometrics. Mobility training is often neglected and athletes should incorporate some form of stretching activity into every session.
- A well planned training programme will cause the body to adapt positively. The adaptive responses can be categorised into the following categories: aerobic muscular changes, anaerobic muscular changes, cardiovascular adaptations, and respiratory adaptations.
- When designing a training programme the coach must ensure that it is tailor-made for the athlete. The training year should be structured initially into three main phases: the preparation period, the competition period and the transition period.

Review Questions

1 What structural changes are brought about within a muscle as a result of:
   - a strength training programme using weights
   - an endurance training programme?

2 State the importance of flexibility to sporting activity. How might you begin to improve flexibility? Use sporting examples where necessary.

3 Discuss ways in which training intensity can be determined.

4 Design a circuit training programme for a specific group of people. State the exercises you would use and explain why. What other considerations might be necessary?

5 Outline some training régimes designed to improve
   • the aerobic system
   • the anaerobic systems.

6 Explain how the principle of specificity can be applied to the design of a training programme for a squash player.

7 Explain how the periodised year can lead to optimal performance in competition.

8 How might you construct a training programme to ensure that overtraining syndrome does not occur to athletes in your charge?

Introduction

Sport sociology is an approach which attempts to determine the place of physical activity in the cultural hierarchy. Society is a dynamic concept as it is constantly changing and adapting, sometimes gradually evolving over centuries, and in other instances revolutionary changes are experienced almost overnight. Sport will reflect and influence the society of which it forms an integral part.

Cultural research in this area has expanded to include other societies which are modelled on different plans and motivated by different ideals. Societies ranging from primitive to modern industrial are now studied: the organisation of physical activities and type of participation are viewed as an essential part of that society.

The following chapters will hopefully highlight to you the impact society has on sport and vice versa, how this process is ongoing, continuing to affect **your** personal experiences of participating in sporting activities. Imagine a situation where you have no facilities to train, no clubs to belong to, and where the system of coaching is so underdeveloped athletes cannot improve. Imagine living a hundred years ago, how different our experiences in terms of leisure, recreation, sport and education would have been. In comparison to the Victorian era there is now:

- more equality of opportunity for different social classes, ethnic groups and women
- sport has enhanced international communication
- sport as big business has created questions about ethics and the politics of sport
- perhaps more importantly, experiencing the human emotions connected to participation in sporting activities is what makes it a valuable subject of study.

These are relevant issues and where necessary we will use the discipline of sociology to help us gain a wider understanding.

Factors affecting sport in society

Several factors can influence and be influenced by the system of sport and they are outlined in the diagram below. The arrows suggest the symbiotic relationship.

Interrelating aspects of society which affect the system of sport:

- Economic
- Educational
- Historical
- Political
- Religious
- Social and Cultural
- Demographic
- Ecological

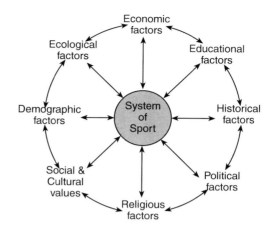

DIAGRAM. 1   SPORT IN SOCIETY

Task

Consider each factor and try and extend them into sub categories. For example, Education could include:

- state and private schools
- facilities
- government policies
- National Curriculum
- physical education and so on

It is useful at this stage to choose one factor that interests you and research what influence it may have had on sport or vice versa in the past or present day.

This should have given you some understanding of the type of issues that will be covered in later chapters. We will study the:

- social and cultural make-up of the United Kingdom
- the conceptual understanding of Play, Leisure, Recreation, Physical Education and Outdoor Education/Recreation and Sport
- the system of sport and physical education in the United Kingdom
- the historical development of physical activities, sports and physical education

First of all it is necessary to understand clearly what is meant by the terms Play, Leisure, Recreation, Physical Education, Outdoor Education, Recreation and Sport.

chapter 7

Concepts of Physical Activity

The aim of this chapter is to explore the various concepts of physical activity: play, leisure, physical education and sport. We have already used some of these terms, but it is necessary at this stage to explore each term in its own context; ie, what characterises each concept, its uniqueness and also its common elements. We will also follow the theory of each concept with a brief look at how the theory has affected the development of the activity in society.

For ease of study we will start from the least organised, play, and move on to the most highly organised, sport: see fig 7.1.

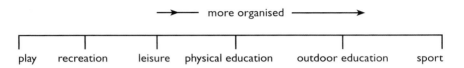

Fig. 7.1 THE PHYSICAL ACTIVITY CONTINUUM

Play

Play is something which children *and* adults do. It takes different forms and has different motives and benefits for each, but it can assume a great significance and importance to people's lives. A quick look in the dictionary to investigate what we mean by the word 'play', reveals that it conjures up many different meanings; eg, 'to occupy or amuse oneself in a sport; to fulfill a particular role – he played defence; a dramatic production; play fair'. It is very difficult to extract one meaning alone, but we must attempt to tease out the common characteristics which are relevant to our field of study and have been developed by psychologists such as Huizinga, Piaget, Callois and Ellis.

Play to the Ancient Greeks was associated with childhood. Play served to integrate children into Greek culture, acting as a form of social control, as well as developing the mental, physical and social well-being of the youngsters. The philosopher Aristotle believed children should have an early diet of games, tales and stories. These would better serve the developing child than formal lessons.

In the Middle Ages, the Church focused on the preparation of the soul for the after life. Play was therefore given a low status, being seen as a threat to the social order and a waste of time. Work for salvation attained high status and the two concepts were separated. This coincided with the harsh life many children experienced, which carried on into the nineteenth century where many were sent to work at a very early age. However, it was also at this time that French Philosopher Rousseau reinstated play as an important part of 'getting back to nature' in the text *Emile*. He claimed that simplicity and freedom should be an important part of a child's development into an adult, allowing spontaneity and self expression. However, it would be some time before most children experienced this concept.

Classical theories of play

Play

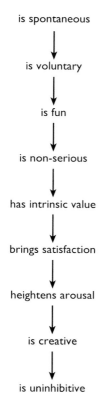

is spontaneous

↓

is voluntary

↓

is fun

↓

is non-serious

↓

has intrinsic value

↓

brings satisfaction

↓

heightens arousal

↓

is creative

↓

is uninhibitive

Fig. 7.2   VALUES OF PLAY

1 **Surplus Energy**
2 **Preparation**
3 **Recapitulation**
4 **Relaxation**

These theories tend to concentrate on the instinctive nature of man and tend to reflect only certain aspects of play behaviour.

J Huizinga

The contribution of Huizinga, a Dutch cultural historian, lies in the detailed way he describes play; he provides observations but does not attempt an explanation of play. His descriptions include the following:

- Play is creative; it is repeated, alternated, transmitted; it becomes tradition.
- Play is a stepping out of real life.
- Play is uncertain. The end result cannot be determined.
- All play has rules, and as soon as the rules are transgressed, the whole play world collapses.
- Play is social. A play community generally tends to become permanent, encouraging the feeling of being together in an exceptional situation, of mutually withdrawing from the rest of the world.

'Play is a voluntary activity or occupation exercised within certain fixed rules of time and place, according to rules freely accepted but absolutely binding, having its aim in itself and accompanied by a feeling of tension, joy, and the consciousness that this is different from ordinary life'   *(Huizinga, 1964)*.

Piaget

Piaget, a Swiss psychologist, claimed that play is:

- an end in itself
- distinguished by the spontaneity of play as opposed to the compulsion of work
- an activity for pleasure
- devoid of organised structure.

Piaget believed that play was the most effective aspect of early learning. Much educational thinking has been influenced by this thought. Play is crucial for development and intelligence: the child uses its intelligence in play and is manipulative; s/he adapts to the environment by modifying feelings and thoughts through:

- assimilation – child imposes own knowledge on reality, thus can change reality
- accommodation – child fits into environment.

Callois

Callois, a French sociologist, developed a theory which suggested that play is a reflection of society. He used Greek terms to develop four forms of play:

1 **Agon** (competition) – contest or struggle, eg, competitive games.

2 **Alea** (chance) – the end is determined by chance or fate.

3 **Mimicry** (role taking) – eg, children playing mummies and daddies.

4 **Ilynx** (vertigo) – eg, fast-moving activities which induce giddiness.

These can all be distinguished from each other by two other aspects:

- **Paidia** – the pure ideal of children's play, where fun is the key element
- **Ludus** – when activities become more organised.

When we move from play to sport, the ludic element becomes more prominent.

Place the following activities on table 7.1:

- **lottery, children dressing up, theatre, skiing, abseiling, fencing, merry go rounds, tag, mummies and daddies, hockey, kite flying, chess.**

Try to think of other activities to fill in the table.

Table 7.1   CATEGORISING ACTIVITIES

	AGON	ALEA	MIMICRY	ILYNX
paidia ludus				

Ellis

Recent theories of play tend to be concerned with the 'individual' explanation of play. Ellis summarises five major theories:

1 **Generalisation** and **compensation** – people select activities which will either reflect or compensate for their world of work.
2 **Catharsis** – the purging and consequent release of strong emotions. It suggests that aggressive tendencies can be subdued, but research suggests that experiencing aggression, such as involvement in sport, can lead to more aggression.
3 **Psychoanalytic** – the Freudian idea that play is motivated by pleasure.
4 **Development** – Erikson's idea that children can learn through play, the ability to master reality.
5 Play is ritualised to provide social traditions.

Modern theories

Play is regarded as stimulus-seeking behaviour. In his book, Why people play?, Ellis developed the notion that play involves the integration of three theories:

- learning
- developmental
- arousal seeking behaviour (behaviour is motivated to maintain an optimal level of arousal).

He claims that:

'When the primary drives are satisfied the animal continues to emit stimulus seeking behaviour'.

However, when the situation is too complex it reduces arousal; at the opposite end, if the outcome is too predictable, the lack of uncertainty will also reduce arousal. Imagine a sporting contest where the opponents are not well matched. Both know the result is a foregone conclusion, so an intermediary level is sought. This theory has the advantage of incorporating work and play, rather than separating them.

The following definition is a useful amalgamation of the different theories of play.

'Play is activity – mental, passive or active. Play is undertaken freely and is usually spontaneous. It is fun, purposeless, self initiated and often extremely serious. Play is indulged in for its own sake; it has intrinsic value; there is innate satisfaction in the doing. Play transports the player, as it were, to a world outside his or her normal world. It can heighten arousal. It can be vivid, colourful, creative and innovative. Because the player shrugs off inhibitions and is lost in the play, it seems to be much harder for adults, with social and personal inhibitions to really play'.

(Adults play but children just play more *G. Torkildsen*).

Implications of play

Education

The importance given to play in terms of children's ability to learn more effectively, has been taken seriously by many educationalists. Certainly in the early years there is a focus on play activities through which children will learn.

Exploratory learning led to a more **heuristic** teaching style (a device or strategy that serves to stimulate investigation). The teacher's role changed from being purely instructional to one of initiating a guidance form of learning.

Physical education lessons

There are aspects of physical education which do not match the concept of play. For example: it is compulsory; the content is chosen by the teacher; the teacher is in authority over the group; the group does not initiate the activity spontaneously.

Recreation

Recreation managers should also take note of the positive experiences which play can generate in everyone's lives, not only children's.

1 **What strategies as a teacher could you use to help inject a more playful element in a PE lesson, while achieving your educational objectives? (The following section on physical education may give you some ideas).**
2 **What possible constraints can operate on the play world of children?**
3 **Taking a play activity of your choice say how and why spontaneity can exist.**

Recreation

The word 'recreation' originates from the Latin word 'recreatio', which means to restore health. Recreation has long been connected with relaxation and recuperation of the individual. It has been particularly valued during the nineteenth and twentieth centuries, with the emergence of an industrialised, machine controlled workforce. Recreation is thought to be useful in restoring people's energies for work. However, as with other concepts of physical activity, people participate for many different reasons. Many sections of the community are not in paid employment and yet participate in recreation. Physical recreation is where the activity requires the individual to expend a reasonable amount of energy. This is also known as 'active leisure'.

Other ideas focus on recreation as being: activity based; not an obligation; socially acceptable; morally sound; an emotional response; an attitude; a way of life.

Theories of recreation

Serving the needs of human beings

J. B. Nash evaluates recreation as creative social contribution and a way of satisfying human inner urges. He developed the participation model where the recreative lifestyle is 'active participation experience'. Nash regards play as the childhood preparation for recreation in adult life and as a practice for work.

A leisure time activity

The most widely accepted view of recreation is simply activities in which people participate during their leisure time. One problem with this viewpoint is that many people are biased towards thinking that recreation can only be sport or physical activity.

1 List the numerous activities that you, your family and peers take part in, as recreation.

2 Can you classify these in any way? For example, physical and non physical; individual or team/group situations; creative or informative?

Recreation

is activity based

|

is an extension of play

|

occurs in leisure time

|

not an obligation

|

socially acceptable

|

morally sound

|

an emotional response

|

valuable to individuals
and society

Fig. 7.3   VALUES OF RECREATION

M. Neumeyer describes recreation as any activity, either individual or collective, which is pursued during one's leisure time. Recreation has four elements:

1 behavioural expression
2 intrinsically valuable
3 rewards found within the activity
4 socioculturally conditioned.

Valuable to individual and society

Many theorists (H. Meyer; C. Brightbill; G. Butler) espouse the idea that recreation must be of 'value', either to the individual or society. This is always a problem area, because whose values are more important? This is particularly significant when considering the provision for recreation by the public and voluntary agencies. What are the presumptions under which they organise their services?

Recreation as re-creation

J. S. Shivers concentrates on the idea of recreation as an 'experience'. Recreation wholly absorbs the individual at any one moment and helps provide 'psychological homeostasis', ie, the satisfying of psychological needs, and the process of mental re-balancing. Recreation is the harmony and unity experienced between mind and body. This occurs at the *time* of the experience; the *value* is felt later.

    The degree to which individuals feel this 'completeness' of recreation will vary, probably will only occur in its purest sense on a few occasions. Those occasions would undoubtedly be extremely memorable and personally uplifting. Do you have any such experiences?

A social process

J. Murphy believes recreation is a *process*, which requires exploration, investigation, manipulation and learning behaviour. This theory is similar to theories of play, examined earlier. He claims that the physical, psychological, social and educational processes are the outcome of recreation, and lead to self realisation.

A social institution

R. Kraus takes a different slant:

- Voluntary activities must to some degree be determined by the choices made available. This involves the social institutions and agencies which have developed, eg, churches, schools, industries, voluntary agencies, government departments, etc.
- Skill levels associated with many activities take time to master.
- Motivation to participate is rarely completely intrinsic.

Recreation planning

- Services should be developed so that people can find recreation and fulfil individual needs.
- Programmes should take a holistic approach, ie, concern for the whole person.
- Access should be available to all citizens
- Planning for recreation *activities* can be measurable and operable, but planning cannot guarantee a recreation *experience* (a particular incident or feeling).

Recreation planning certainly has its place within this modern and rapidly changing society, but for many people, true recreation is not about having their leisure time organised in the same way that the world of work is organised, as this brings its own constraints. Improvements can be made:

1 **Recreation managers** need to create an environment where recreation is most likely to occur.
2 **Work** conditions can be improved to give people greater chances of self expression, recreation activity and recuperation.
3 **Education** can be extended to include leisure skills, helping people to realise and achieve their potential.

Discuss the following:

1 **Why is play a more important aspect of a child's life and recreation more significant for adults?**
2 **What is the significance of the word 'process'?**
3 **What are the suggested outcomes of participating in recreational activities?**
4 **Give an example of a distinct value orientation of a stated institution.**

Summary of theories of recreation

'Recreation consists of activities or experiences carried on within leisure, usually chosen voluntarily by the participant – either because of satisfaction, pleasure or creative enrichment derived, or because he perceives certain personal or social gains to be gained from them. It may also be perceived as the process of participation, or as the emotional state derived from the involvement.' (R. Kraus, 1971)

Recreation can be viewed as:

- an extension of the 'play' experience
- a personal experience – the value to the individual
- the nature of an activity
- an institution and structural framework
- a process – what happens to an individual.

Leisure

The Ancient Greeks regarded 'leisure' as important for the development of the 'whole' man, his mind and body. This, however, was a state reserved only for the wealthy members of society. The growth of Christianity had a negative effect on leisure time, believing it to have little value in the preparation of the soul for the later life. The Puritan work ethic is a concept developed in the sixteenth and seventeenth centuries which valued the benefits of labour as opposed to the temptations of idleness. It has had far reaching effects on how we view leisure; even today, work is given a much higher status than leisure activities.

Theories of leisure

There are four major approaches to looking at leisure.

Leisure as time

This refers to **surplus** time; ie, time left over when practical necessities have been attended to. These necessities were referred to by the Countryside Recreation Research Advisory Group in 1970 as 'work, sleep, and other needs' (including family and social duties). C. Brightbill claims that people need the time, opportunity and choice to enjoy true leisure. He contrasts true leisure with enforced leisure, such as illness, unemployment or forced retirement.

1 **Fill in a weekly timetable with all the 'necessities' mentioned above, including sleep, paid work, college/school work, domestic responsibilities etc. Then try and approximate the amount of time you have left as leisure.**
2 **Fill in the activities you consider to be part of your leisure time.**

Leisure as activity

Leisure activities can be subdivided into different categories of interest: sport; home entertainment; hobbies and pastimes; reading; public entertainment; holiday activities such as sightseeing.

J. Nash believes that leisure activities occur on four levels:

1 passive
2 emotional
3 active
4 creative involvement.

Each is attributed a value; those at the apex are considered more worthy as leisure than those at the base.

Other theories claim that it is the meaning the activities have for the individuals participating which is more important than the activities themselves.

J. Dumazadier believes that leisure must be freely chosen and should benefit the individual in terms of relaxation, diversion or broadening of horizons. He uses the term 'semi leisure' to include such activities as DIY which can be pleasurable as well as being functional.

Leisure as an end in itself

This contradicts the idea of free time being leisure. The state of mind with which a person approaches this free time is crucial. In its ideal state, leisure should be an opportunity for self expression (J. Pieper; C. Brightbill; S. de Grazia).

Leisure

is free time
|
opportunity
|
choice
|
relaxes the individual
|
allows self fulfilment
of the individual

Fig. 7.4   VALUES OF LEISURE

The holistic approach

J. Dumazadier believes leisure has three main functions:

1 relaxation
2 entertainment
3 self fulfilment.

In other words, leisure holds a meaning for people and this is what is most important. It can relieve stress, be an antidote to boredom and allow freer movement than is allowed in many work places.

The concept of leisure is still undergoing changes. Many people are now motivated to work, not for the sake of work but to allow them the opportunity to enjoy their leisure status. Many feel their true identity is not that which occurs at work, but that which emerges during leisure.

Leisure and work

- Leisure is generally something people do not have to do, whereas most people have to work to earn a living.
- Work and leisure can both create a sense of self worth, creativity and personal development within a person.
- The common belief that people have more free time for leisure in the modern world, can be challenged by the fact that economic circumstances can force people to take on extra work.

In modern industrial societies, work can determine:

- how much time a person has for leisure
- how much energy they can bring to their leisure
- whether leisure can be pursued through work.

Purposeful leisure

'Purposeful leisure' is a term used by communist governments who, as they operate an authoritarian system, require as much control over their population in leisure in the same way as other areas of social life. This is social control, extolling the belief that rebellious tendencies can be curbed and political messages can be equally learnt through the leisure situation.

Growth and change in leisure time

There are many reasons for the growth and change in leisure time in the UK:

- working hours have been reduced by the application of technology
- labour-saving gadgets enable people to spend much less time on domestic chores in the home
- increase in life expectancy
- increase in disposable incomes
- decline in the role of traditional social structures like the church and family
- education for everyone
- mobility of a large section of the population
- public provision of leisure facilities including the ability to hire equipment which would otherwise be out of reach of the majority of the population
- early retirement
- high unemployment.

Popular (low) culture

Individuals choose their own leisure within the context of their own culture, values and identity; the majority of the population will also be exposed to marketing forces of leisure. Popular culture is therefore defined by what is available and what represents social development.

Popular culture can also create change and trends, eg, skateboarding, public marathons. Different aspects are given prominence at different times but generally there is less of a tendency to maintain traditional established practices. The far-reaching effects of the mass media as it transmits Western popular culture across the world can however result in a uniformity of cultures, rather than the richness and variety of cultures which characterise different countries.

Consider the following factors and suggest how they can affect and be affected by leisure:

- **occupation**
- **trends**
- **levels of participation**
- **leisure provision in society**
- **women's lives**
- **media.**

High culture

This traditionally refers to the cultural pursuits of the higher social classes and they usually reflect the privileged lifestyles of wealth, education and more free time. Activities pursued by this group of people are often not made easily accessible to the lower social classes, and there is a sense of cultural separation. These activities are often considered to operate on a more intellectual and refined manner to those of popular culture.

Fig. 7.5   SUMMARY OF LEISURE

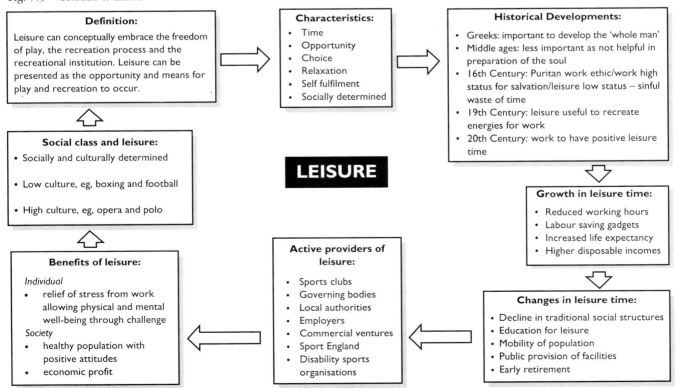

1 **Select activities which can be categorised as popular or high culture.**
2 **Discuss the elements which make them different.**
3 **Investigate the different approaches taken by the media towards activities from the two ends of the spectrum.**

Summarise theories of leisure.

Integrating play, recreation and leisure

Each concept has its own distinct nature, but that they also have similarities; they are multi-dimensional and link together.

Similarities

- freedom
- self expression
- satisfaction
- quality
- self initiated
- no pressure or obligation to take part
- range of activities
- experiential

Differences

- emphasis, eg, play has a strong emphasis on childlike spontaneity and unreality.
- functions, eg, for learning, refreshing, recreating or just being!

Interrelationships

Leisure can be the pivot upon which the other two concepts can be embraced

> '*leisure can conceptually embrace the freedom of play, the recreation process and the recreation institution. Leisure can be presented as the opportunity and the means for play and recreation to occur.*'
> (*Torkildsen*).

A recreation programme combines planning, scheduling, time tabling and implementation, using resources, facilities (eg, swimming pools, parks, natural resources etc) and staff to offer a wide range of services and activities. The activities will range from allowing spontaneity to being completely structured.

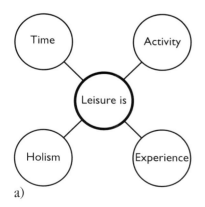

a)

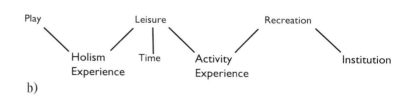

b)

Fig. 7.6   (A) MULTI-DIMENSIONAL CONCEPT OF LEISURE (B) A SIMPLE PLR DIAGRAM

1 **What factors should recreation managers take into account when building and planning services?**
2 **Explain the difference between the terms 'leisure' and 'recreation'.**
3 **Name two home based leisure activities and two non-home based leisure activities.**

4 Select two categories of people who are known to have low participation rates in the non-home based activities. For each category explain why their participation is low and suggest strategies which could help to rectify the situation.

Fig. 7.7   PLAY, RECREATION, LEISURE OR SPORT?

Physical education

What is physical education?

Physical education is an academic discipline (an organised, formal body of knowledge), which has, as its primary focus, the study of human movement. It may be viewed as a field of knowledge, drawing on the physical and human sciences and philosophy, with its main emphasis on physical activity. As this field of knowledge has broadened, the subject specific areas have increased. Sub-disciplines have emerged which have diversified the subject and related it to career opportunities; examples are – sport sociology, biomechanics, sports medicine, exercise physiology, sport philosophy, history, psychology, sports management. You will probably recognise some of these from your own 'A' level physical education course.

Physical education at this level may seem a far cry from what you have experienced over the last twelve years at school. At this stage it is necessary to know what is meant by the term and to appreciate that a philosophy has developed over the last century, and will continue to do so, sometimes changing radically the practice of our subject.

Consider these philosophical viewpoints:

- All participants, regardless of athletic ability, should have equal amounts of playing time on the school curriculum.
- Physical educators should be role models and practise on the playing fields what they preach in the classroom.
- Physical education is only useful in that it provides a break from academic lessons.
- Physical education should be compulsory.

Physical education is an educational process which aims to enhance total human development and performance through movement and the experience of a range of physical activities within an educational setting. Total development means acquiring activity specific skills and knowledge, as well as fostering positive attitudes and values which will be useful in later life. Physical education can help us to achieve a quality of life and a vitality which can be lacking in sedentary lifestyles.

The key words are:

- **Range of physical activities**
- **Movement**
- **Activity specific skills**
- **Knowledge**
- **Values**
- **Educational setting.**

Aims and objectives

Physical activity involves doing, thinking and feeling. Children need to know *how* to perform or express themselves, know *about* physical activities and also benefit from the enriching experience of knowing how it *feels* to perform.

Already we have given physical education some very difficult challenges. We are assuming that all the outcomes are positive, but this is clearly not the case. Among your peers are those who have enjoyed their physical education experiences but also those who definitely did not! Before we can hope to achieve the positive benefits, we must clarify the aims, objectives and desired outcomes from the physical education curriculum.

Aims

Physical education aims to:

- develop a range of psycho-motor skills
- maintain and increase physical mobility and flexibility, stamina and strength
- develop understanding and appreciation for a range of physical activities
- develop positive values and attitudes like sportsmanship, competition, abiding by the rules
- help children acquire self esteem and confidence through the acquisition of skills, knowledge and values
- develop an understanding of the importance of exercise in maintaining a healthy lifestyle.

Objectives

Physical education can affect different areas of development. For example:

- The children will be able to complete a 20 minute run – physical development.
- The children will execute the correct technique for a gymnastic vault – motor development.
- The children will be able to explain the scoring system in badminton – cognitive development.
- The children will display enthusiasm and enjoyment and participate in the extra-curricular activities – affective or emotional development.

Ask a group of your peers about their experiences of physical education (including the types of activities, what they enjoyed most or least). You can ask general or more specific questions.

Imagine you are taking a practical session with Year 9; a team game within the physical education timetable. Using table 7.2 as a guide, draw up a detailed plan of your lesson.

(This could assist students following the CCPR Community Sports Leaders Award or on teaching practice, and can be used as a role play situation within your academic group.)

Table 7.2   THE STRUCTURE AND FUNCTION OF A PRACTICAL SESSION: DEFINITION OF TERMS, RELATING TO A PRACTICAL SESSION

TERM	DEFINITION	RELATED TO EDUCATIONAL SETTING
structure	the way in which something is constructed or organised; the arrangement and interrelationship of parts	a lesson within a school timetable; compulsory; age, size, sex and ability of group; location; authority structure
function	the special activity or purpose of a thing or person	
objectives	something one is trying to achieve or reach	transmit knowledge and skills; safety; success for all abilities; enjoyment; fitness
strategies	the planning and directing of the whole operation of a curriculum or lesson; a plan to achieve something (such as the objectives)	effective grouping; personal knowledge; varied teaching styles (instruct, guide); discipline; differentiated tasks to cater for varying abilities; rewards systems
content	the substance of a thing or occasion	change kit; warm up; skills; small/conditioned game; full game
constraint	to confine, restrain, inhibit, restrict	duration of a lesson; ability of group; condition of facility or equipment
evaluation	to set the value of; to judge or assess the worth of something	to test (physical, verbal, written) at end of session or block; own feeling or judgement of lesson (should be ongoing)
authority	the power or right to control; a position that commands power	headteacher, teacher, prefect, captain
conflict	a state of opposition between ideas, which can lead to tension	relationships (teacher/child, child/child, teacher/teacher); ideas (compulsory, kit, showers)
dysfunction	any disturbance or abnormality in the function of a group	discipline problems

A balanced physical education programme

A balanced programme should attempt to offer a variety of activities selected from each group in table 7.3, in order to maximise fully the opportunities to be gained from the different activities. There should be a balance of activities which are:

- team orientated
- individual
- competitive
- non-competitive movement based.

Table 7.3   A BALANCED PHYSICAL EDUCATION PROGRAMME

GAMES				MOVEMENT
INVASION	NET	STRIKING/FIELD	REBOUNDING	gymnastics dance trampolining athletics swimming
football netball hockey rugby	tennis volleyball table tennis	cricket rounders softball	squash	

1 Study the aims of physical education and see how you might link these to the activities shown in table 7.3.
2 Tick the activities which you experienced during your secondary education. Do you think that you received a balanced physical education programme?
3 Conduct a survey of approximately six schools in your local area. Try and find out what they offer their pupils. Can you find parallels or many variations? Does what is on offer reflect the different nature of the schools?

Who chooses the physical education programme?

In the United Kingdom there is a decentralised system where the teacher and individual school have their the power to produce own programme, though increasingly bound by government guidelines. The National Curriculum now sets out which subjects are to be taught at each Key Stage of a pupil's schooling. Physical education is compulsory from Key Stage 1 (ages 5 to 7) through to Key Stage 4 (up to age 16).

At this point it will be useful to remind yourself about the meaning of the terms centralised and decentralised.

Centralised: means to draw under central control – the central government directs policy across a country. State legislation co-ordinates and supports policies such as an education curriculum. France is an example of a centralised system whereby teachers are instructed what to teach, when to teach and sometimes how to teach. Although the United Kingdom is not completely centralised in this manner the National Curriculum brought in after the Education Reform Act 1988 was a move in this direction.

Advantages of a centralised system:

- provides uniformity of experience
- is a co-ordinated system
- funded by the Government.

Disadvantages of a centralised system:

- can be rigid and inflexible
- may not cater for different local needs
- can be difficult to monitor the system effectively, particularly in large countries
- can reduce the initiatives of individuals such as good teachers.

Decentralised: means dispersal away from the centre towards outlying areas. It is a system of government, which is organised into smaller, more autonomous units. Examples are local authorities in the United Kingdom and the individual States in the United States of America. The government in power often gives guidelines, which can be interpreted, at a local level.

What are the advantages and disadvantages of a decentralised education system?

National Curriculum
[www.dfee.gov.uk/nc]

The National Curriculum attempts to raise standards in education and make schools more accountable for what they teach. Physical education continues to be one of only five subjects which pupils of all abilities must pursue, from their entry to school at age 5 until the end of compulsory schooling at age 16.

Attainment targets and programmes of study have been written for physical education. Children are required to demonstrate the knowledge, skills and understanding involved in areas of various physical activities, including dance, athletics, gymnastics, outdoor and adventurous activities and swimming. There are 4 Key Stages.

In the document 'Sport: Raising the Game', the government went one step further, and produced a revised PE curriculum which took effect in August 1995.

This has been superseded by Curriculum 2000 changes, being brought more into line with other National Curriculum subjects. The programmes of Study and Attainment Targets are outlined below.

The importance of Physical Education

Physical education develops pupils' physical competence and confidence, and their ability to use these to perform in a range of activities. It promotes physical skilfulness, physical development and a knowledge of the body in action. Physical education provides opportunities for pupils to be creative, competitive and to face up to different challenges as individuals and in groups and teams. It promotes positive attitudes towards active and healthy lifestyles.

Pupils learn how to think in different ways to suit a wide variety of creative, competitive and challenging activities. They learn how to plan, perform and evaluate actions, ideas and performances to improve their quality and effectiveness. Through this process pupils discover their aptitudes, abilities and preferences, and make choices about how to get involved in lifelong physical activity.

Key Stage 1

During key stage 1 pupils build on their natural enthusiasm for movement, using it to explore and learn about their world. They start to work and play with other pupils in pairs and small groups. By watching, listening and experimenting, they develop their skills in movement and coordination, and enjoy expressing and testing themselves in a variety of situations.

Breadth of study
During the key stage, pupils should be taught the knowledge, skills and understanding through dance activities, games activities and gymnastic activities.

FIG. 7.8   KEY STAGE 1 — PROGRAMME OF STUDY

Key Stage 2

During key stage 2 pupils enjoy being active and using their creativity and imagination in physical activity. They learn new skills, find out how to use them in different ways, and link them to make actions, phrases and sequences of movement. They enjoy communicating, collaborating and competing with each other. They develop an understanding of how to succeed in different activities and learn how to evaluate and recognise their own success.

Breadth of study
During the key stage, pupils should be taught the knowledge, skills and understanding through five areas of activity:

   a)   dance activities
   b)   games activities
   c)   gymnastic activities

and two activity areas from:

   d)   swimming activities and water safety
   e)   athletic activities
   f)   outdoor and adventurous activities.

FIG. 7.9   KEY STAGE 2 — PROGRAMME OF STUDY

Key Stage 3

During key stage 3 pupils become more expert in their skills and techniques, and how to apply them in different activities. They start to understand what makes a performance effective and how to apply these principles to their own and others' work. They learn to take the initiative and make decisions for themselves about what to do to improve performance. They start to identify the types of activity they prefer to be involved with, and to take a variety of roles such as leader and official.

Breadth of study
During the key stage, pupils should be taught the knowledge, skills and understanding through four areas of activity. These should include:
  a) games activities

and three of the following, at least one of which must be dance or gymnastic activities:

  b) dance activities
  c) gymnastic activities
  d) swimming activities and water safety
  e) athletic activities
  f) outdoor and adventurous activities.

FIG. 7.10   KEY STAGE 3 — PROGRAMME OF STUDY

Key Stage 4

During key stage 4 pupils tackle complex and demanding activities applying their knowledge of skills, techniques and effective performance. They decide whether to get involved in physical activity that is mainly focused on competing or performing, promoting health and well-being, or developing personal fitness. They also decide on roles that suit them best including performer, coach, choreographer, leader and official. The view they have of their skilfulness and physical competence gives them the confidence to get involved in exercise and activity out of school and in later life.

Breadth of study
During the key stage, pupils should be taught the knowledge, skills and understanding through two of the six activity areas.

FIG. 7.11   KEY STAGE 4 — PROGRAMME OF STUDY

Attainment Targets

Level 1
Pupils copy, repeat and explore simple skills and actions with basic control and coordination. They start to link these skills and actions in ways that suit the activities. They describe and comment on their own and othersí actions. They talk about how to exercise safely, and how their bodies feel during an activity.

Level 2
Pupils explore simple skills. They copy, remember, repeat and explore simple actions with control and coordination. They vary skills, actions and ideas and link these in ways that suit the activities. They begin to show some understanding of simple tactics and basic compositional ideas. They talk about differences between their own and others' performance and suggest improvements. They understand how to exercise safely, and describe how their bodies feel during different activities.

Level 3
Pupils select and use skills, actions and ideas appropriately, applying them with coordination and control. They show that they understand tactics and composition by starting to vary how they respond. They can see how their work is similar to and different from others' work, and use this understanding to improve their own performance. They give reasons why warming up before an activity is important, and why physical activity is good for their health.

Level 4
Pupils link skills, techniques and ideas and apply them accurately and appropriately. Their performance shows precision, control and fluency, and that they understand tactics and composition. They compare and comment on skills, techniques and ideas used in their own and others' work, and use this understanding to improve their performance. They explain and apply basic safety principles in preparing for exercise. They describe what effects exercise has on their bodies, and how it is valuable to their fitness and health.

Level 5
Pupils select and combine their skills, techniques and ideas and apply them accurately and appropriately, consistently showing precision, control and fluency. When performing, they draw on what they know about strategy, tactics and composition. They analyse and comment on skills and techniques and how these are applied in their own and others' work. They modify and refine skills and techniques to improve their performance. They explain how the body reacts during different types of exercise, and warm-up and cool-down in ways that suit the activity. They explain why regular, safe exercise is good for their fitness and health.

Level 6
Pupils select and combine skills, techniques and ideas. They apply them in ways that suit the activity, with consistent precision, control and fluency. When planning their own and others' work, and carrying out their own work, they draw on what they know about strategy, tactics and composition in response to changing circumstances, and what they know about their own and others' strengths and weaknesses. They analyse and comment on how skills, techniques and ideas have been used in their own and others' work, and on compositional and other aspects of performance, and suggest ways to improve. They explain how to prepare for, and recover from, the activities. They explain how different types of exercise contribute to their fitness and health and describe how they might get involved in other types of activities and exercise.

Level 7

Pupils select and combine advanced skills, techniques and ideas, adapting them accurately and appropriately to the demands of the activities. They consistently show precision, control, fluency and originality. Drawing on what they know of the principles of advanced tactics and compositional ideas, they apply these in their own and others' work. They modify them in response to changing circumstances and other performers. They analyse and comment on their own and others' work as individuals and team members, showing that they understand how skills, tactics or composition and fitness relate to the quality of the performance. They plan ways to improve their own and others' performance. They explain the principles of practice and training, and apply them effectively. They explain the benefits of regular, planned activity on health and fitness and plan their own appropriate exercise and activity programme.

Level 8

Pupils consistently distinguish and apply advanced skills, techniques and ideas, consistently showing high standards of precision, control, fluency and originality. Drawing on what they know of the principles of advanced tactics or composition, they apply these principles with proficiency and flair in their own and others' work. They adapt it appropriately in response to changing circumstances and other performers. They evaluate their own and others' work, showing that they understand the impact of skills, strategy and tactics or composition, and fitness on the quality and effectiveness of performance. They plan ways in which their own and others' performance could be improved. They create action plans and ways of monitoring improvement. They use their knowledge of health and fitness to plan and evaluate their own and others' exercise and activity programme.

Exceptional performance

Pupils consistently use advanced skills, techniques and ideas with precision and fluency. Drawing on what they know of the principles of advanced strategies and tactics or composition, they consistently apply these principles with originality, proficiency and flair in their own and others' work. They evaluate their own and others' work, showing that they understand how skills, strategy and tactics or composition, and fitness relate to and affect the quality and originality of performance. They reach judgements independently about how their own and others' performance could be improved, prioritising aspects for further development. They consistently apply appropriate knowledge and understanding of health and fitness in all aspects of their work.

FIG. 7.12   ATTAINMENT TARGETS - END OF KEY STAGE DESCRIPTIONS

This initially sounds encouraging and positive but fig 7.13 shows data published by the European Union of Physical Education Association. The survey shows the amount of time spent per week on physical education in schools, in the USA and the UK. At the primary level the UK is ninth out of ten and at secondary level the UK is placed at the bottom of the table.

The DfES also conducted a survey in 1995, which showed that some schools are still not devoting two hours a week to physical education as recommended.

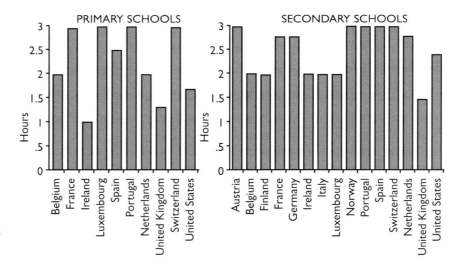

Fig. 7.13   THE AMOUNT OF TIME DEVOTED TO PE IN SCHOOLS IN THE UK COMPARED TO THE REST OF EUROPE AND USA

Source: European Union of PE Associations

1 **Summarise the general requirements for each key stage of the National curriculum.**
2 **What factors may a teacher have to take into account when devising a syllabus?**
3 **What are the advantages and disadvantages of a decentralised education system?**

Assessment in physical education

Aims and objectives will depend on how achievement is evaluated and how well the children have progressed is one element within the evaluation. Several types of assessment are used in physical education departments, such as longitudinal student profiles, purely quantitative data like fitness tests or generalised comments.

Children need to be able to show what they know, what they can do and what they understand. They can show this through written and verbal language, and in a performance situation.

Assessment should be made of the whole person, not just physical skills. Aspects of their personality such as their ability to work with groups or individually, and their ability to abide by rules should be assessed.

Study fig 7.14, which gives the results of two students' assessment tests.

1 What comments might you make about the strengths and weaknesses of the two candidates?
2 What does an average score for each reveal?

Administration of physical education in the UK

The UK has a system of private and state school education, and of comprehensive and grammar schools. The nature of schools can be as diversified as the people they house. Local authorities used to have a large influence on how education operates in their areas; they would be the middle man between the schools and the government. During the 1980s, the government implemented increasingly centralised policies, such as the National Curriculum, the Local Management of Schools (LMS) and the growing number of grant maintained schools (GMS), which resulted in them leaving local authority control. The government sought more direct control of education, and through the Education Reform Acts of 1986 and 1988, they have restricted the freedom of teachers, schools and local authorities to construct their own syllabus.

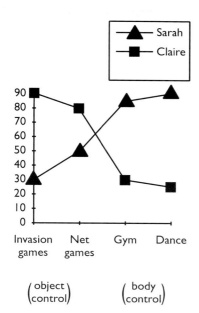

Fig. 7.14   An assessment graph

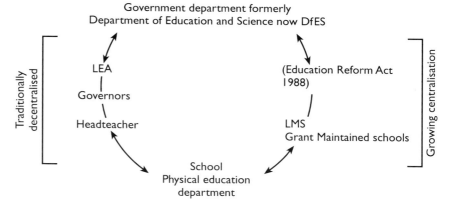

Fig. 7.15   Changes in administration: the government can now deal directly with the school, rather than through the LEA

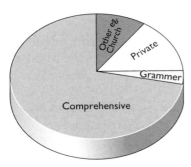

Fig. 7.16

Private schools

Education in this country began with private schooling for the social élite. Pupils enjoyed extensive facilities and focused on the 'character building' aims of education, as preparation for responsibilities in later life as employers, officers, members of the clergy and so on. Competitive team games developed to serve these aims. There was always a concentration on sport rather than a physical education emphasis and this is still prevalent today. As a result sport coaches still tend to be employed often for their specialist sporting prowess. This is particularly evident for schools wishing to continue a sporting tradition. Competitive fixtures are a recognised feature and the prestige which arises from winning helps to distinguish it from other schools.

State education – primary schools

State education began after the Forster Education Act 1870 which initiated compulsory schooling for all. Compulsory schooling begins at the age of five. As mentioned above, in the state system physical education is compulsory and is a core subject of the National Curriculum: students must spend at least two hours a week on this subject. The class teacher is usually in charge, though is not usually a specialist. Some schools may hire specialist help for certain activities, eg, swimming.

The content of the lessons is usually based on movement and ball skills. Learning by moving and doing is considered essential to the physical, emotional, intellectual and social education of young children. Children's own play is generally very physical and enjoys a lot of repetition, as this enables them to master skills which increases their sense of worth. The physical education programme can use this as a foundation. Variety is also important as their concentration span can be limited and they need to be stimulated by interesting situations.

In addition to the curriculum, many schools also offer club activities like gymnastics, netball, soccer, country dancing, etc. This tends to be at the discretion and goodwill of the teachers.

Secondary education

As children approach the end of the compulsory years of schooling, it is necessary to foster in them an awareness of the opportunities available in the community. As a result of the philosophy of educating children for their leisure time, schools began to offer options programmes in the later years where a wider variety of activities, sometimes using community facilities, could be experienced. Smaller groups guided by additional non-specialist staff made this possible. Students should be informed about and put into contact with local clubs and sports centres. This is an area of weakness in the United Kingdom; there are traditionally poor links between schools and community sport, as a result of trying to keep a distance between sport and physical education. This will be discussed in more detail later.

Physical education as an examination subject has flourished. A rapidly growing number of students opt to take GCSE and 'A' level examinations, and some GNVQs offer sport and physical education as a focus.

Developments in school sport

The term 'sport' refers to the 'physical activities with established rules engaged in by individuals attempting to outperform their competitors' (Wuest, Bucher, 1991). Its main focus is on improving performance standards rather than the educational process and mainly takes place outside the formal curriculum. It is usually viewed as an opportunity for children to extend their interest or ability in physical activities.

Fig. 7.17 SCHOOL SPORT ENCOURAGES TEAMWORK

The changes in society and education in the last 20 years have affected school sport (ie, the extra-curricular opportunities), with a reduction in emphasis on the sporting élite, which sometimes required a disproportionate amount of resources for a few children. Extra-curricular clubs, open to all, became more acceptable. The situation did not change overnight, however; many teachers continued to focus on competitive sports, and extra-curricular activities were affected by these factors:

1 The teachers' strikes in the early 1980s – the contractual hours and lack of monetary incentives tended to diminish teachers' goodwill, and clubs were disbanded.
2 Financial cuts were felt in terms of transport.
3 The local management of schools allowed schools to supplement their funds by selling off school fields.
4 The increasing amount of leisure and employment opportunities for children meant they were less attracted to competing for their school team.
5 The anti-competitive lobby became more vocal: they espoused the theory that competition in sport was not good for children's development.

This all led to the claim that school sport was in decline, although the report produced in 1995 by the Office of Her Majesty's Chief Inspector of Schools, 'Physical Education and Sport in Schools – A Survey of Good Practice', concluded 'that there was little to support the notion of irrevocable decline'.

Table 7.4 ADVANTAGES AND DISADVANTAGES OF COMPETITIVE SPORT

ADVANTAGES	DISADVANTAGES
Children have natural competitive instinct, and as more motivated to practise, enjoyment of sport increases	Continued feelings of failure can cause stress and anxiety
Can raise self esteem and learn how to cope with failure and success	The need to win can encourage unsporting behaviour

 ACTIVITY 16

1 **What strategies would you use in order to teach a competitive game situation to a group of mixed ability 11-year-olds, producing the more positive aspects of competition?**

2 ***Night and Day***
   The ball nears his feet, he kicks and he misses
   A groan from the crowd, some boos and hisses
   A thoughtless voice, – "take off the bum"
   Tears in his eyes. This is no fun.
   Tempted to shout or to groan?
   Remember, it's a boy out there, alone
   A boy don't forget
   And not a man yet.

   a) What issues are raised in this poem?
   b) What are the pressures on young children in the arena of Sport?
   c) What measures can be taken to reduce these pressures?

'Sport: Raising the Game'

The focus of the 1995 document is mainly on reinstating the status of school sport within school life. It formed part of the Conservative government's overall strategy to develop an effective sporting continuum.

The publication of this document showed a recognition that school sport had declined, and the government wanted to rectify the situation:

1 **The Sportsmark** scheme recognises the best schools with additional gold star awards for the most innovative. Teachers who make an extra commitment to school sport can, *at the governors' discretion* receive additional salary points.

2 The weak links with community sport have already been highlighted. To attempt to overcome this the government welcomed the idea of improving links by accepting and encouraging the voluntary assistance offered by coaches. However, this is dependent on the initiative of the individual teachers and schools. Finance, needless to say, is also limited.

3 Schools must record in their annual prospectuses their sporting aims and their provision for sport.

 **Review the extra-curricular provision for sport in your education institution, and lay it out as a timetable as suggested below.**

	Lunch	After school
Monday		
Tuesday		

Physical education or sport?

This is an ongoing debate, which re-surfaced in this document with the government's decision to give competitive sport a higher status. The terms 'physical education' and 'sport' are complex. There is an overlap between them but their central focuses are different. The aim of the former is to educate the person, while the latter has other purposes, eg, achieving excellence, fitness, earning an income, etc. A good physical education programme can be the foundation on which the extra-curricular opportunities can be extended and enhanced. However, physical education teachers should not necessarily feel pressured into allowing a 'sport' ethos to creep into the curriculum.

A C T I O N
A g e n d a

SPORTSMARK CRITERIA

To achieve a Sportsmark schools might expect to:

i.   offer a minimum of two hours a week of formal PE lesson time;

ii. offer at least four hours each week of structured sport outside formal lessons: schools will be expected to provide all interested pupils with the opportunity to participate in sport at lunch-times, in the evenings and at weekends;

iii. devote at least half the time spent on PE both inside and outside formal lessons to sports which, if not the full game, should be played in a form judged appropriate for the year group by the relevant sports governing body;

iv. encourage teachers and others involved in extra-curricular sport to gain coaching qualifications or leadership awards enabling them to lead sports matches;

v.   encourage teachers to improve their individual coaching skills by taking advantage of the different levels of awards/qualifications provided by the national governing bodies of sport;

vi. ensure in secondary schools that pupils of all ages have the opportunity to take part in competition if possible, and promote competition within their own school and against other schools;

vii. have established links with local sports clubs: schools will be expected to have developed links with a number of local sports clubs as a way of providing pupils with further sporting opportunities outside school hours. Sportsmark schools are likely to be among those successfully competing for the Sports Council's challenge fund for school–club links; and

viii. encourage pupils to take part in sports governing bodies' award schemes.

Fig. 7.18 EXTRACTS FROM *PLAYING THE GAME*

Fig. 7.19   Sportsmark award results 1998–1999

Sportsmark Award Results 1998–1999			
	ALL SECONDARY SCHOOLS	SPECIAL SCHOOLS	MIDDLE SCHOOLS
Sportsmark	342	26	24
Sportsmark Gold	23	5	2

Some people were concerned that the Conservative government's agenda appeared to be about the winning of major international and World Cup events. Is it the aim of schools to set the foundations for success at international level? If so, the professional coaches should perhaps have as much contact with school teams as the physical education teacher has.

The problem of liaison and contact with outside agencies appears to be more of a problem. Initiatives have begun and are being successful, such as TOP Play, BT TOP Sport, and Champion Coaching (which involves 145 local authorities). The aim is to guide the young person from school to community sport and provide coaching training and experience for teachers and coaches involved. This is a top priority for the Sports Council and National Coaching Foundation, and the traditional notion of keeping sport coaching out of schools is being challenged.

Sports College status

The sports college initiative was launched in June 1996 with the first schools viable in September 1997. It is part of a specialist schools programme, which include centres for technology, arts and modern languages. It is an attempt to allow schools with particular strengths to build upon them attracting pupils with those interests. Out of approximately 800 schools it is envisaged that 100 will be sports colleges. It is hoped these schools will be more than just schools, rather a centre for sport and physical education encompassing all sectors of the community.

Objectives:

- Extend the range of opportunities available to children which best meet their needs and interests.
- Raise the standard of teaching and learning for PE and sport in schools.
- Develop characteristics which identify the schools to the local community and local schools.
- They should be of benefit to local schools, called the 'family of schools' network.
- Attract local sponsors who should take an active role in the schools development.
- A school that wishes to apply needs to raise £50,000 sponsorship for a capital project to improve existing sports facilities.
- The development plan drawn up by the school will show its vision.

Organisations involved:

The government Department for Education and Skills [DfES] lays down the guidelines. The Youth Sports Trust, a charitable organisation employed by the DfES, offers development and sponsorship guidance.

Funding:

Successful schools will receive:

- a one off capital grant of £100,000
- recurrent funding for four years of £120 per pupil
- opportunity for a further three years of funding for schools who have met their targets.

What are the differences and similarities between sports colleges and the specialist residential sports schools mentioned in chapter 9?

The National Council for School Sport

Membership is open to national sports organisations in England and Wales responsible for the development of their sport in schools. The aims of the Council are to:

- coordinate the work of the schools' national sports associations
- encourage the formation of new associations
- provide a forum for discussion
- encourage involvement in the International School Sport Federation.

The official journal is the *Sports Teacher* magazine.

Outdoor education

Outdoor education and recreation refers to the participation in outdoor pursuit activities within the natural environment. The difference between the two is that recreation is done in one's own free time, while outdoor education takes place within an educational setting.

1 List as many activities as you can which take place in the natural environments of water, mountains, air and countryside.
2 Where people do not have easy access to these areas, how could you adapt the urban environment for them to learn the basic skills of some of these sports?

These activities can place the individual in situations which are dangerous and challenging, and which induce exhilaration, fear and excitement. They can be competitive, but more often against the elements or the human body, than against another person. Generally, there are no officials with rules, though there are codes and ethics of practice which are usually adhered to.

The personal qualities required for and enhanced by these activities include:

- self reliance
- decision making
- leadership
- the ability to trust others
- the ability to be trusted.

These activities are not usually done alone, and the ability to work with others to overcome obstacles and find solutions is important; so too is the need to conquer fear of danger and the unpredictable. They often create unique situations which cannot be found playing in sports such as netball or soccer.

Risk and adventure

There has been a considerable growth both in the traditional (eg, canoeing, rock climbing, abseiling, climbing) and 'new' (eg, jet skiing, snow boarding, mountain biking) adventure sports. The reasons for this growth can be explained by:

- increasingly sedentary lives, which makes some people seek a more active and exciting leisure time
- increased leisure time and standards of living, which make these activities more accessible

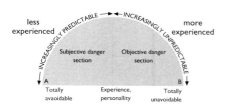

Fig. 7.20 MORTLOCK DIAGRAM

source The Adventure Alternative. C.Mortlock

- the development of new and exciting technology sports
- the appreciation of the natural environment particularly as a release from urban pressures.

According to Mortlock, there are four broad stages of adventure:

1 **Play** – little challenge in developing skills/boredom could set in
2 **Adventure** – more challenging environment/skills developed under safe conditions
3 **Frontier Adventure** – the individual is placed in more difficult terrain where well learned skills can be put to the test/challenge/conquest
4 **Misadventure** – where things go wrong either due to lack of preparation or due to more extreme terrain and climatic conditions.

As a leader you would hopefully aim for stages 2 and 3.

I If you were a leader of a mixed ability group, which stages would you aim to achieve for your group and which factors would you aim to avoid?

2 Plan an activity which could come under the outdoor education umbrella. Note the pitfalls which could arise.

Are outdoor pursuit activities for everyone?

These activities should be available to everyone, regardless of wealth, race, sex or health. Many of these activities are being made more available to people with disabilities in the community, particularly through organisations such as the Calvert Trust; at their centres near Keswick, Exmoor and Kielder Water, the emphasis is on ability, achievement and enjoyment, and a range of disabilities such as physical, mental and sensory disabilities, is catered for. The Commission concluded that more information about these activities should be directed towards people from ethnic minorities to increase their participation. 'A Countryside for Sport' (1993) sets out the Sports Council's policy on encouraging newcomers. Established in 1994, 'The Foundation for Outdoor Adventure' should assist in providing information to ethnic community leaders.

Outdoor education and the school curriculum

There are strong reasons why outdoor education should be included in the school curriculum; namely, the benefit to the personal and social education of children, through experiential learning. The National Curriculum does not require that outdoor education is taught, though schools can arrange for it to be included. The skills which can be directly experienced and learned are an intrinsic element of Key Stages 3 and 4 of the adventurous activity option in physical education.

In an already constricted timetable, few schools have the commitment to the subject to support and sustain outdoor education:

1 The Education Reform Act 1988 increased the problems schools experienced in offering these activities.
2 The fundamental changes to the way in which schools are funded have also seriously affected the opportunities for teachers to gain valuable in-service training in order to achieve the appropriate qualifications.
3 Local education authorities may no longer have access to sufficient funds to provide for this training.
4 The law regarding charging pupils for out of school activities may cause schools to limit or abandon such activities, as voluntary contributions may not be sufficient. This could mean that only the wealthier schools are able to participate, so these activities would retain their élite image.
5 The increasing concern over safety issues is another problem for schools.

Fig. 7.21   OUTDOOR ACTIVITIES SHOULD BE AVAILABLE TO EVERYONE

Other subjects could also utilise and benefit from outdoor education as it has useful cross-curricular implications; environmental issues which can be highlighted are inequalities in wealth distribution, land use, forestation and deforestation, energy sources and the problems caused by people and pollution. However, it must not lose its own unique contribution in its own right. The United Kingdom lags far behind many other countries in its provision, and many outdoor education residential centres have been threatened with closure.

Tourism and environmental safeguards

Outdoor pursuit activities are growth sports, but there are also some problems which need to be addressed. The areas in which they often take place are country parks, nature reserves, green belt areas, areas of outstanding natural beauty and national parks. Conflicts can emerge between the sport participants, land owners and the environment. The UK is a relatively small island with a high density population. Problems caused by the growth in tourism and outdoor activities will be more keenly felt than in much larger, low population density countries such as the USA and France.

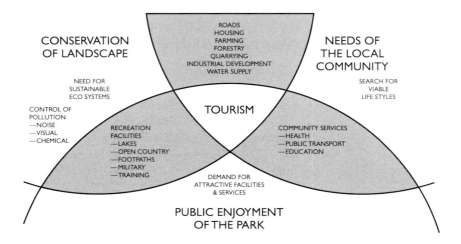

Fig. 7.22   CAUSES OF CONFLICT IN A NATIONAL PARK

Some of the problems caused are:

- erosion of land and river banks
- pollution caused by motor sports
- the increase in the number of vehicles disturbing wildlife and local residents.

The most radical solution would be to *ban* the activities, but it might be more viable to *plan* for these activities in order to minimise the damage done to the environment. The agencies concerned need to liaise together to produce effective strategies. These would include the Sports Council, the CCPR, the governing bodies of the individual sports, the local authorities, the Countryside Commission and the National Parks Authorities.

National parks

There are ten national parks in the United Kingdom: the Brecon Beacons, Dartmoor, Exmoor, the Lake District, Snowdonia, the Norfolk and Suffolk Broads, the North York Moors, Northumberland, the Peak District, the Pembrokeshire Coast and the Yorkshire Dales.

Locate the national parks on a map of the United Kingdom.

These areas are governed by the national park authorities, which are local government bodies consisting of local councillors plus members appointed by the Secretary of State for the Environment. They have two statutory duties:

1 to protect and enhance the character of the landscape
2 to enable the public to enjoy the recreational opportunities of the area.

They also need to protect the social and economic well being of the local community.

National parks cater for a wide range of interests: they provide walkers with pleasant open countryside for enjoyment, accommodation for tourists and a livelihood for farmers and foresters, quarrymen and gamekeepers, rangers. The movement to establish these parks came from two main sources:

- access to mountains and moorlands (ramblers in the North of England)
- landscape preservation (Southern England middle class amenity lobby).

Increasing industrialisation and urbanisation amidst the changing relationships between rural and urban areas were important factors in the formation of the parks. See Chapter 10 for further information.

The Outward Bound Trust

The Outward Bound Trust began to pioneer outdoor activities in the 1940s. It has five centres in Britain, including Aberdovey in Wales, Ullswater in the Lake District and Loch Eil in Scotland. The organisation is now worldwide. Outward Bound works in partnership with the Duke of Edinburgh's Award Scheme. Its main aim is to promote personal development training for young people, placing them in challenging situations, such as physical expeditions, skill courses and the city challenge which is the urban equivalent. The challenging and often rugged activities include living in the wilderness, mountain climbing, canoeing, skiing and touring on bicycles. The first school was founded in Wales in 1941 by Kurt Hahn, an educator, to help young sailors who were 'outward bound' to sea.

Sport

What is sport? We know that Sport England refers to numerous activities as sport; we have sports clubs; hunting is called a sport; a person can be referred to as 'a good sport', and so on. In general we use the term loosely in normal conversation, but when we are relating important sociological concepts to sport (such as discrimination, concepts of femininity and its relationship to physical education), it is necessary to focus quite specifically on what we mean by the term. See Chapter 10 for a comprehensive history of sport.

A definition of sport would be useful, to examine the key elements. Sport can be defined as:

'institutionalised competitive activities that involve vigorous physical exertion or the use of relatively complex physical skills by individuals whose participation is motivated by a combination of intrinsic and extrinsic factors'

(Coakley, 1993).

What do we mean by some of these terms?

Institutionalised:
- A standardised set of behaviour recurs in different situations.
- Rules are standardised.
- Officials regulate the activity.
- Rationalised activities involve strategies, training schedules and technological advances.
- Skills are formally learned.

Physical activities:
- skills, prowess, exertion
- balance, coordination
- accuracy
- strength, endurance

The extent of the physical nature of the activity can vary and can lead us to question whether an activity such as darts, is a sport. Darts is referred to as a sport via the media, but the fact that it does not require much physical exertion can place it lower down on the sport continuum, even though it meets other criteria for inclusion as a sport. Any activity which does not meet all the criteria listed above would have less status as a sport.

Intrinsic:
- self satisfaction
- fun
- enjoyment
- own choice
- 'play spirit'.

Extrinsic:
- money
- medals
- fame
- obligation
- praise.

Most people will combine both of these motivations in the approaches they adopt towards sport participation. Colin Montgomerie says:

"I used to get tense about the money angle of it, the financial situation you found yourself in when suddenly you had to putt for a prize the size of someone's salary. Now it's not the financial side, it's trying to beat my peers. I don't need to be paid. Don't tell the sponsors that. But when I finish a tournament and I've beaten my peers, I don't need to be paid. The feeling I have is terrific, of success and freedom, if you like. That's what I do it for."   *[The Daily Telegraph Sat. Oct. 16,1999]*

Huizinga also identified characteristics of sport. These are:

- **dexterity** – involves an element of skill
- **strategy** – aspect of planning or tactic
- **chance** – sporting outcomes are usually unpredictable based on luck, injury, weather etc
- **exultation** – the 'feel good' factor/intrinsic elements of fun and enjoyment.

I Think of a couple of activities you regularly participate in but possibly at different levels with different attitudes. List the reasons why you may participate in both.

Progression from play → Recreation → Sport

The following situation may help clarify this complex concept as we have developed the argument so far:

Two friends who kick a football in the street are involved in an informal, social occasion. Physical exertion is present and skills are developing, but the people are involved in recreation rather than sport. If they challenged two other friends to a competition, this has moved to a situation called a contest or match. It is competitive but still under informal conditions. Only when they follow formalised rules and confront each other under standardised conditions can their situation be called sport.

Using a variety of equipment, devise a game within a group.
- **What characterised the development of this game?**
- **What would you have to do to change it into a PE lesson?**
- **What would you have to do to turn this game into an Olympic activity?**

Merely playing a recognised physical activity is not enough to allow us to call it sport. The situation under which it is operating is also important and needs consideration.

I Suggest other activity situations where this level of analysis could be applied.
2 How can the institutionalised sporting activities, such as football and hockey, be made more enjoyable for young children, creating a more educational environment?

Amateurism and professionalism

There are two types of sports performers:

1 A person who competes as an **amateur** does so on the grounds that they will not receive monetary reward for their involvement in sport.
2 A **professional** sportsperson is one who earns an income from their sport.

See Chapter 10 for more information on this issue.

Benefits of sport

Sport can:

- act as an emotional release.
- offer individuals an opportunity to express their own individuality.
- help in the socialisation of people, ie, encourage a collective spirit and persuade people away from social unrest.
- help people achieve success when other avenues of achievement are not available to them.
- help highlight issues which can be changed.
- help achieve health and fitness
- have economic benefits to individuals [income] and nations' economies
- create a challenge and provide enjoyment.

Problematic areas

- Sport can help to retain and reinforce discrimination.
- Too much emphasis can be placed on winning, and financial rewards intensify this.
- Competition, if not handled well can be damaging.
- Excessive behaviour can be encouraged through sport.
- Spectator sport can begin to outweigh active participation.
- Media coverage can dominate sports and their type of coverage can determine the wealth of a sport.

Classification of sporting activities

When we examined the nature of physical education, in particular, the need for children to experience a balanced physical education programme, we referred to activities such as games and movement. These in turn could be classified into further categories: the Council of Europe and the Sports Council have identified four main categories of sporting activity:

1 Conditioning activities
2 Competitive games and sports
3 Outdoor adventure activities (covered on p 146)
4 Aesthetic movement or gymnastic movements.

Conditioning activities

These are activities which are primarily designed to improve the physical and mental condition of the performer. Examples of such activities would be aerobics and also circuit and weight training. A programme of work is set and should be followed on a regular basis if it is to have the desired effect. They are easily adaptable for both the recreational and more serious performer. Some participants will participate purely for the general conditioning effect, while others will use it to achieve fitness for a particular sport. In some cases, they have developed into competition sports in their own right, for example, weight lifting and aerobics. They have competitions at all levels with rules, regulations and scoring systems.

Competitive games and sports

The main aim of competitive participation is to find out who is the best given equal circumstances. For example, athletes are matched within categories of level of ability, such as club, county or national standard; by age, weight and often gender, to make the competition as fair as possible. They adhere to the same standardised rules, which makes the unpredictability of the outcome more exciting. Their skill level, physical and mental fitness will be the main criteria of winning.

 **ACTIVITY 25**

1 Why is a pyramid a useful way of categorising competition?
2 What strategies could you use to increase the amount of people who reach the élite level?

As one unit wins, another must lose. However, during a game an individual can still make successful contributions like winning a contest within the game; eg, the defender who marks an opposing attacker out of the game. A player can enjoy the game even though they lost, simply because the effort, challenge and physical work was worthwhile.

Athletics

This category includes races, field athletics and weight lifting. The athlete who wins the 100 m is the person who reaches the tape first. All race events, whatever the form of locomotion, are decided in this way: the high jumper clears the bar; the thrower achieves the furthest distance in the competition. The explosive or sustained power of the athlete is tested. In order to be fair to their opponents, athletes adhere to strict rules and also may take it in turns. This is called a quantitative, **objective** method of assessment, where scientific criteria is applied. The advances in the level of technology used have allowed extremely fine units of measurement to be used.

 **ACTIVITY 26**

1 List as many ways as you can of scientifically measuring the outcomes of athletic contests.
2 Consider arguments for and against calling synchronised swimming a sport.

Games

This category includes ball, fighting and target sports. Within a game situation, competitors interact with each other, and in the case of team games, with their own team mates. Interaction will take the form of verbal communication like calling out, coding messages and in preparing strategies; non-verbal communication takes place through signals, signs and facial expressions. Players need the ability to process a lot of information which is constantly changing and this requires them to make decisions either quickly, or more slowly, as in a strategic approach to the activity. Players will bring to the game situation their own skill level, attitudes, and previous experiences. They will have certain expectations also. They will want to play well and have their achievements recognised, will want to win and socialise with other players.

In a game of hockey, identify situations where a player is

- **processing information**
- **aiming at a stationary and moving target.**

The wide variations of activities existing in this category enable us to sub-divide them further.

Invasion games

These are games where one team invades the territory of their opponents. Examples would be hockey, netball, basketball and football. Scoring is usually in the form of goals and points, and the winner is the team who achieves the most goals or points within the allocated time period. The contest can last for one match or extend over a longer period of time, as in a league.

Invasion games are about maintaining possession of the ball by passing effectively within your team or creating possession by tackling or intercepting. Some invasion games allow personal *contact*, while others have strict rules forbidding it. The principles of play are based mostly on attacking and defending, and numerous strategies will be worked on to achieve the advantage. A range of skills and techniques are developed. They are usually 'open' (flexible) skills, as the game situation is always changing and the player is usually reacting to another's move. However, in situations like a penalty stroke in hockey, the skill could be described as closed.

Net games

This category includes tennis, volleyball and badminton, and constitutes a situation where opponents are separated by a net. These can be individual or team games. The winner is decided by who wins the most games, sets or rubbers. Domination in this instance is achieved by playing shots which the opponent is unable to return. The skills are again mainly 'open' except in the serve situation where the server has control; this is why so much importance is placed on the serve. All net games start with a serve, though they vary as to how points are scored in relation to the serve.

Rallies involve opponents hitting the object into each other's territory. The players must return the object immediately and on the rebound. Only in volleyball does a team have the option to move the ball around before returning it over the net.

A further category of net games are called 'rebounding' games, where the principles of play are the same but where a net is not used. Such activities include squash, fives, racquetball and rackets.

Innings games

Games such as cricket, baseball, softball and rounders are included in this category. An innings is the opportunity a team has to score. The playing area is defined as infield and outfield. The infield gives the opportunity for striking the ball in order to score runs, while the outfield is used to field or defend the ball and cut down on the opportunities for the opposing side to score runs. The aim is to get the other team out. A contest will occur between the bowler and batter who are put in a one-on-one situation.

Target games

The main characteristic of these games (archery, snooker, golf, darts, ten pin bowling) are that they require a high degree of accuracy when aiming at a target, which may be stationary or moving.

Gymnastic movements

These activities rely on the repetition of a movement pattern. Technical expertise (technique) and artistic interpretation are the two main factors which are assessed. The body is used as an art form, with appearance and individuality forming an important element. The 'performance' is assessed.

In activities such as ice skating where the winners are chosen by judges, there can be more questionable outcomes, than in competition sports. This type of assessment is called qualitative or **subjective** assessment.

1 Rearrange the following activities listed below under these Categories – Adventure, Conditioning Dance and Sport

Trampolining	White water rafting	Circuit Training
Hockey	Lacrosse	Skiing
Judo	Jet ski	Tap Dance
Aerobics	Rugby	Basketball
Swim Racing	Tai Chi	Rhythmic Gymnastics
Weight Training	Ballet	Netball

2 We have already shown how the Game category can be further subdivided. Give the following game activities a subclass and consider similar games that could be allocated to each subdivision.

Basketball   Golf   Boxing   Rounders   Tennis

Analysis of Activities

Beashel and Taylor (1996) analyse each sporting activity by breaking the activity down into component parts.

Structural
- nature of sport problem
- scoring system
- rules
- behaviour of players
- roles of officials
- penalties for rule infringements

Strategic
- planning and decision making
- directly related to sport problem eg, moves or sequences in gymnastics, technical difficulty or tariff, artistic interpretation
  or, series of shots/rallies in net games, play a winner or force an error, pre-planned but subject to change

Technical
- techniques – perfect movement and its outcome
- requires controlled movement of body to produce specified patterns and outcomes
- skills – performer's learned capacity to reproduce the technique eg, types of skills, open/closed etc

Physical
- body conditions required for success
- varies depending on the sport of performer's role within the sport, eg, types of fitness/cardiovascular/flexibility

Psychological
- mental and psycho-social conditions required for successful sport performance
- mental battle involved in competitive sport
- controlled aggression/assertiveness
- pain involved
- concentration
- limelight role
- anticipation.

Take a sport you have an intimate knowledge of and analyse it, using the above criteria.

Summary

- You should have a clearer picture of differences between the concepts of play, recreation, leisure, physical and outdoor recreation/education and sport; their unique features and also features which complement and relate with each other.
- People become involved in sport for various reasons and at various levels; each activity provides different challenges and experiences.
- Play is the least formal of the activities and sport is the most organised.
- Each of the concepts has implications for the individual and for society.
- For both leisure and Physical Education it is useful to understand how they have both developed over a period of time.
- Very often the physical activities used are the same – it is the attitude with which they are undertaken which makes the difference.

Using an A3 sheet of paper, list as many key words as you can under play, recreation, leisure, physical education, outdoor recreation and sport.

Review questions

1   Give five characteristics of the concept of Play.

2   What word does the term 'recreation' derive from and what does it mean?

3   What is the implication of the words 'activity' and 'experience' when applied to the term recreation?

4   How can work affect people's leisure time?

5   What factors have led to the growth in leisure time?

6   What do the terms 'high and 'low' culture mean?

7   What are the key terms that characterise the term Physical Education?

8   Name five aims of Physical Education.

9   Describe the Sportsmark Award.

10   What is the main difference between Outdoor Education and Outdoor Recreation?

11   What constraints determine the level of Outdoor Education whilst at school in the United Kingdom?

12   Briefly describe the work of the Outward Bound Trust.

13   What are some of the benefits and problems associated with participating in sporting activities?

14   What are the four main classifications of sporting activities?

15   What do the terms 'structural', 'strategic', 'technical', 'physical' and 'psychological' mean when attempting to analyse sporting activities?

chapter 8

Sport, Politics and Culture

This chapter explores the role that sport and physical education assume in the political arena. It examines the organisation, administration and policy making process of sport which should help you to reflect on major issues such as policies for school physical education sport, policies for increasing sport participation by groups such as women, ethnic minorities, disabled, low socio economic groups and such.

The politics of sport

Before we explore the concept of how sport and politics interact, we may find it useful to begin with a definition of politics:

'the science and art of government; dealing with the form, organisation and administration of a state or part of one, and of the regulation of its relations with other states ... Political [means] belonging to or pertaining to the state, its government and policy'.

(*Oxford English Dictionary*).

Let's take some of the key words and look at their possible meaning to sport.

Administration

The administration of sport can be seen as developing from the community, for example, a local sports club forms the base of the pyramid, and is surmounted by its regional, national and international counterparts. The international governing bodies of sport (the International Olympic Committee, the Commonwealth Games Federation and the European Sports bodies) are political bodies. They are concerned with governing sport, making decisions, creating and distributing finances and resources, and often their dealings must reflect the political climate in which they operate.

Relations with other states

The relationships between states with regard to sport began as soon as worldwide travel and unified rules of competition developed. Sport can provide international goodwill: it can promote cultural empathy and understanding between nations, and athletes are seen as ambassadors of their country. The Olympic Charter promotes the view that sport promotes world peace by improving international understanding and respect.

However, sport can also reinforce conflict: the sense of belonging to a country encourages a sense of patriotism and nationalism, and thus is all the more powerful when conflict is prevalent, be it war or sport. Sport represents and reinforces images and feelings of communal, regional and national identity. Powerful symbols are used, eg, national anthems, team colours, flags and ceremonies. Sporting conflict results in winners and losers. Winners can be viewed as superior and powerful, whereas losers are inferior and powerless. Sport is often portrayed as being more than just a contest between two opposing sides, and success is attributed to countries as much as to the athletes themselves. For example, the Scottish rugby ground at Murrayfield evokes vivid messages and images of Scottish identity and nationhood, and England is often portrayed as the 'old enemy'.

Policy

Policy suggests decision making based on the ideology (set of ideas) or philosophy of those in power. This is relevant from local to international situations. Numerous indicators can be used to determine the importance a government places on sport:

- the expenditure for sport
- the position or status of sports ministers within a government
- the type and amount of sport legislation produced.

Politics reflects the power systems within a culture – who has the power and how do they use it? Sport and physical activities have sometimes been used by various governments, individuals and administrators for political reasons. The British government used to be in control of many of the world's sports organisations, but there has been a shift in power, and Britain is no longer so prominent.

The commercial world plays an extremely important role in sports decision making, at local, national and international level. The cost of staging sports events, particularly at international level, is extraordinarily high:

1 The constructing of stadiums requires capital which often only governments can raise.
2 The running of events increasingly involves those who pay international television fees.
3 Revenue for major events requires huge commitment from governments.

Equally, sport is now a major market for governments, and the trend in the United Kingdom has been for the government to receive more money from sport than it contributes.

Political uses of sport

Social factors

Sport can be used to introduce or reinforce social harmony. Government inquiries into inner city riots usually include reference to the need to provide better sporting facilities. This can be taken to have various meanings:

1 Boredom creates dysfunctional activity; by providing the highest standard of sporting facilities and by educating people to use them constructively in their leisure time, we can help to improve people's quality and enjoyment of life, giving them less reason to involve themselves in anti-social activities.
2 The 'bread and circuses' theory: this is more controversial, and claims that sport can be used to divert the attention and energy of the masses away from the problems of the political and social system in which they live.

Sport as 'character-building'

Sport would also seem to have socialising qualities, which can be used as a political tool. In the nineteenth century, English public schools placed great importance on the values gained from the boys' involvement in team games, such as the ability to work in a team, cooperation, leadership and the response to leadership, obeying rules, respecting authority and so on.

Propaganda

Sport can be used as political propaganda; eg, in the 1930s, the Nazi Youth groups aimed to indoctrinate young people in the values of Nazi Germany.

Defence and work

Sport has also been used to raise the fitness level of populations in order to better prepare them for defending their country and to make them more productive in the workplace:

1 Following heavy losses in the Boer War, attention was focused on the physical deterioration of the British troops in the nineteenth century.
2 Physical fitness among the working classes became official policy in Britain by introducing compulsory fitness exercises in state schools in the early twentieth century.
3 In the old Soviet Union, a national fitness campaign called 'Ready for Labour and Defence' was compulsory for its citizens and was still operational in the latter half of the twentieth century.

Thus, we can see there are various reasons why national governments become involved in sport. See fig 8.1 for a summary of these points.

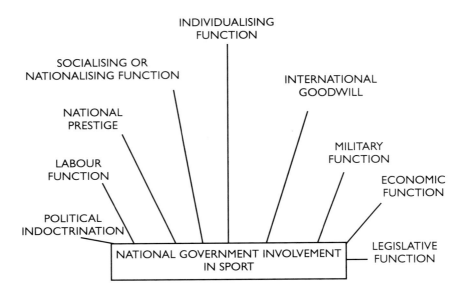

Fig. 8.1   NATIONAL GOVERNMENT INVOLVEMENT IN SPORT

1 **Choose four functions of sport from fig 8.1. Explain in detail how each operates.**
2 **Consider the stance of the Department for Culture, Media and Sport. Which of these functions is the British Government most concerned with ?**

State intervention

We have already established that it is extremely difficult to keep sport and politics separate. However, a crucial point can be the nature of the involvement and the *type* of political system which operates:

Centralised political system

A centralised system at a simple level means to draw under central control – the central government directs policy across the country. An example of this is the former Soviet Union. The Soviet Union under Communist rule was not initiating a 'new' use of sport when it sought to make use of sport's ability to improve the health and hygiene of the population, boost morale, production and military effectiveness, integrate a diverse nation of peoples with varying cultural backgrounds, and to provide an international image for their regime. What was new was the extent of the **central control**, with state legislation to coordinate and support policies. Sport and its usefulness was considered too important to be left to chance. Sport would have the same attention, assistance and planning as other social agencies, such as education.

Decentralised political system

A decentralised system is one where the administration of government is reorganised into smaller, more autonomous units. Examples are local authorities in the United Kingdom; and the individual States of America, who control their own affairs while the federal government becomes involved in matters of national importance. The government in power can give guidelines, but would not normally enforce them. The local authority could then use the guidelines to suit their particular needs.

What are the advantages and disadvantages of:

1   a decentralised system
2   a centralised system?

Sport and politics in the United Kingdom

We have been suggesting that sport cannot be seen as an activity which only has relevance to those who practise it; it also serves various functions of a society.

In the United Kingdom, sport and politics have traditionally been kept separate. The reverse side of the coin is that many people genuinely defend the right of sport to be free from direct political control, seeing it as a danger to the autonomy of the traditional sporting governing bodies and not necessarily having the best interests of sport at heart. Many wish sport to be above the concerns of politics; they do not wish sporting heroes to be the object of sociological analysis, or for sport to be tarnished by political concerns – sport should be an escape from the everyday world.

Traditional social class barriers, the development of sport through the 'grass roots' and the dominant sporting ethos of amateurism, have had an important impact on the relationship between the political and sporting agencies in the UK. The amateur code was an important part of the nineteenth century tradition of team games in public schools: sport was regarded as important for the individual benefits rather than for financial gain. However, it must not be forgotten that amateurism itself was a code based on a political model. It was the privilege of the gentry to be able to participate in sport for 'the love of it', while other social classes were excluded, lacking the time and money. The ideals of amateurism should be viewed in this light: we have clung on to this tradition in a modern and fast-changing society, and sportspeople are having to fight for their right to earn a living from sport. They are often in conflict with their own sports administration; eg, the lengthy negotiations in 1996 between the English Rugby Football Union and the English rugby clubs.

Today the issue of sport and politics is never far away. The number of politically motivated sports organisations in Britain is still increasing. The issue of the building of the new national stadium is one such case. UK Sport, Sport England, the British Olympic Association, UK Athletics, Wembley National Stadium Limited, the Department for Culture, Media and Sport, and the Football Association all had their own interests and solutions with the resulting confusion over the choice of venue and design. Labour's manifesto at the 1997 general election promised that Britain would bid for the Olympics and other world class events. The 52-year wait for a major championships to be held in Britain is coming to a close.

The Home Secretary's decision to bend the immigration laws to admit Mike Tyson reveals the power of sport especially when allied with commercial interest.

We will now look at the major organisations involved in recreation and sport in the U.K.

The Organisation of Sport in the United Kingdom

This chapter should help you to understand the general cultural background of the United Kingdom and an understanding of how sport is organised within it. It is first useful to have a general understanding about the nature of British society.

Fig. 8.2   THE UNITED KINGDOM

Historical
- First industrialised country
- Modern sport evolved in the UK
- Codes and administration
- British Empire resulted in export and import of cultural activities
- Present day Commonwealth countries

Climate and Population
- Temperate, western maritime
- Less rainfall on east coast
- Four seasons have traditionally had an impact on sport
- High density population (596 per sq. mile)
- Urban-industrial conurbation's surrounded by green belts

UNITED KINGDOM

Nationalism
- Four major racial groups – English, Welsh, Scots and Irish seeking more independence
- England the 'old enemy' in sporting fixtures
- County championships allow regional loyalty to be expressed
- Post WWII influence of Afro-Caribbean's and Asian immigrants

Terrain and Communications
- Mainly rolling countryside with Pennines and Cotswold as major hill features (ideal for family rambling and field sports)
- East Anglian Fens
- Mountainous Areas mainly Scottish Highlands, Lake District and Welsh mountains
- Extensive roads and rail network
- All Areas in Britain can be reached in a day

Political
- Monarchy – Head of state little political influence
- Two houses of parliament – Lords and Commons
- Western Democracy
- Minister of sport works in the Department of Culture, Media and sport
- Major sporting organisations remain autonomous
- 1980's and 1990's saw an increase in centralisation, with policies such as the National Curriculum and more government involvement in sporting matters

The organisation of Sport and Physical Education is a dynamic aspect and therefore it is important and more interesting if you attempt to keep up to date with changes as they occur.

The web sites for some of the major organisations are given. These are correct at the time of writing.

The following organisations will be studied:

National Organisations

Central Government through the Department for Culture, Media and Sport [www.culture.gov.uk]

Minister for Sport

Sport England [www.sportengland.org] and the Home Country Sports Councils

UK Sport [www.uksport.gov.uk]

Sport Coach UK (formerly National Coaching Foundation) [www.sportscoachuk.org]

Central Council of Physical Recreation [CCPR] [www.ccpr.org.uk]

Governing Bodies [can be accessed via the Sport England web site]

Local Authorities [www.iga.gov.uk]

Disability Sport England [www.euroyellowpages.com/dse/dispeng.htm]
British Paralymic Association [www.paralympics.org.uk]

At the end of this chapter you should be able to understand the structure, function and funding arrangements for the major organisations that are significantly involved in the administration of and policy-making decisions for sport, physical education and recreation in the United Kingdom.

Structure: the way in which something is constructed or organised: the arrangement or interrelationship of parts. An example in a school would be Governors/Headteacher/Senior Staff/Teaching Staff/Students.

Function: the special activity, purpose or role of an organisation or person. An example of the function of a school would be to educate young people.

Funding: income that is generated, for example internally or externally, and expenditure incurred to meet the function of the organisation.

The role of central government

The role that a national government adopts towards any social factor can be indicative of the importance placed upon it. The government of the UK has tended to have legislation which is **permissive** rather than **mandatory** in matters regarding sport and recreation. An example of this is that local authorities provide for sport but are not required by law to do so.

Fig. 8.3   ORGANISATION OF SPORT IN
THE UK

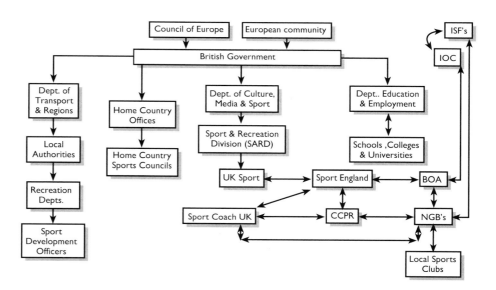

Traditionally the system of sport in the UK has been significantly free from political control.

A decentralised political system has also contributed to this position (ie, dividing the organisation of government amongst local authorities). Greater powers were given to local authorities after World War II; they were able to make their own policy decisions, relating to their own unique regional characteristics. However, successive Conservative governments in the 1980s and '90s have implemented a shift towards centralising power again, and this has affected policy for sport among other social factors. A brief summary of these changes:

- increasingly centralised policies, eg, the National Curriculum and the Educational Reform Act 1988
- a gradual reduction in emphasis on the welfare state
- market solutions to service provision, ie, privatisation of leisure services management and Compulsory Competitive Tendering (CCT) [See p 140].

Minister for Sport

In the 1960s, the creation of the post of Minister for Sport provided a focus for the coordination and formulation of policy. This was long overdue as six government departments previously had a significant responsibility for sport and recreation. The involvement of so many government departments had posed considerable problems of coordination for the Minister for Sport.

The creation of the position had two main purposes:

1 to enable sport and recreation to perform a key role across a wide range of government policy: to improve the nation's health, to alleviate social deprivation, and to channel the energies of the young.
2 to enable governing body representatives and volunteers to serve sportsmen and women, providing a financial, advisory and legal framework.

The Department of National Heritage was founded in 1992, and the Minister for Sport moved to it from the Department of the Environment, locating sport firmly within a wider cultural and leisure brief and giving sport a voice at cabinet level. There were two main advantages:

1 Sport was located firmly within a wider cultural and leisure brief.
2 Sport now had a voice at cabinet level.

However, the department also had responsibility for the arts, broadcasting, films, tourism and heritage. It was also responsible for the funding of national galleries and museums, and sport had to compete in this arena.

Structure

The Minister for Sport has a Sport and Recreation Division (referred to from now on as SARD). The allocation of responsibility can be seen in fig 8.4. Coordination is mainly gained through informal contacts – but not many issues have affected all departments at the same time. SARD is administered by civil servants, and sport policy can sometimes be overshadowed by other issues, such as health, education and defence. This has led to an ad hoc approach, with SARD having little contact with the main providers of sports opportunities for the majority of the public, that is, the local authorities.

This fragmentation of responsibility and interest is apparent at all levels of sports policy. Certain limitations are apparent with the role of the Minister for Sport:

1 The role of the Minister is to advise and consult, not to direct.
2 S/he co-ordinates sport rather than controls it.
3 S/he now comes under the Department for Culture, Media and Sport (DCMs), which also has competing responsibilities.

However, these limitations should not be overstated for the Minister can exert considerable influence on policy, when required. This would mainly depend on:

- the prominence of sporting issues to the government
- the quality, ambition and style of the Minister in office.

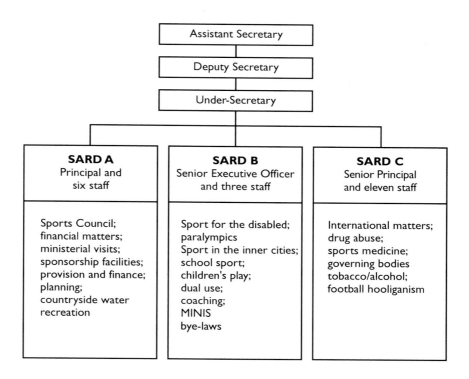

Fig. 8.4 THE ORGANISATION OF THE SPORT AND RECREATION DIVISION AND THE ALLOCATION OF RESPONSIBILITY

Research some instances of the involvement of specific Ministers of Sport; for example, Denis Howell, Neil McFarlane, Colin Moynihan and Tony Banks.

Make sure you know who the current Minister of Sport is and try to keep track of any initiatives, opinions or events with which s/he becomes involved.

In 1995 the Prime Minister, John Major, produced a statement laying out his aims for the development of Sport in the UK, entitled 'Raising the Game'. Figure 8.5 relates the most important sections.

1 **What values did John Major assign to participation in sporting activities?**
2 **What four 'pillars' of education does he refer to?**
3 **Give reasons why there may be a significant drop out rate in sport participation on leaving school.**
4 **John Major refers to a continuum from the primary school to Olympic standard. What suggestions does he make to realise this transition?**

I set up the Department of National Heritage to protect, enhance and develop the arts, leisure and sport. That is why we are publishing ideas to rebuild the strength of every level of British sport.

These new plans are the most important set of proposals ever published for the encouragement and promotion of sport. I want us to bring about a seachange in the prospects of British sport – from the very first steps in primary school right through to the breaking of the tape in an Olympic final.

The existence of the National Lottery has transformed forever the prospects of British sport. Indeed, this was one of my principal aims when I decided to create the Lottery. It was a way to provide resources for sport – and other good causes – that would be unlikely ever to come directly from the taxpayer.

The £300 million a year that the Lottery in full flood will provide for sport will revolutionise it over the years ahead. It will make possible the creation of a new British Academy of Sport for the best of our young men and women. It will help generate the resources for some of our other targets – for example, to achieve the target I am setting today, to bring every child in every school within reach of adequate sports facilities by the year 2000.

In this initiative I put perhaps highest priority on plans to help all our schools improve their sport. Sport is open to all ages – but it is most open to those who learn to love it when they are young. Competitive sport teaches valuable lessons which last for life. Every game delivers both a winner and a loser. Sports men must learn to be both. Sport only thrives if both parties play by the rules, and accept the results with good grace. It is one of the best means of learning to live alongside others and make a contribution as part of a team. It improves health and opens the door to new friendships.

My ambition is simply stated. It is to put sport back at the heart of weekly life in every school. To re-establish sport as one of the great pillars of education alongside the academic, the vocational and the moral. It should never have been relegated to be just one part of one subject in the curriculum. For complete education we need all of those four pillars of school life to be strong.

Sports education is only the first step to a lifetime's enjoyment of sport. Sporting opportunities must continue after school. So we shall be looking to colleges and universities to do more to promote sport among their students. At present, too many teenagers find it difficult to transfer their sporting interests to the world outside school. So we will also aim to improve the sporting links between school and club sport. In that way we can improve access to high quality coaching and promote sensible arrangements to share facilities and equipment. There is much to gain in this, both for clubs and for schools.

Fig. 8.5   EXTRACTS FROM JOHN MAJOR'S ADDRESS, 12 JULY 1995

After the publication of this report a more streamlined structure for the organisation of sport in the United kingdom emerged:
- Under the revised system the Great Britain Sports Council disappeared and the newly established English Sports Council [now Sport England] assumed responsibility for the development of sport in England.
- The Home Country Sports Councils [NI, Wales and Scotland] remained largely unchanged.
- A new organisation – UK Sport took responsibility for issues that required a nation-wide approach such as doping control and the siting of the national Sport Institute.
- Governing bodies drew up their plans to meet the requirements.
- School sport was given encouragement in the form of a variety of initiatives:
  Sportsmark and Sportsmark Gold Awards
  Sports college status
  Schools and sport clubs to form firmer links
  National Junior Sports Programme.

Department of Culture, Media and Sport [DCMS]
www.culture.gov.uk

Following the restructuring of sport this Department assumed control of sport, becoming the central Government Department responsible for Government policy on the arts, sport and recreation, the National Lottery, libraries, museums and galleries, broadcasting, films, to mention a few. Sport therefore has to compete alongside these other areas.

It is headed by the Secretary of State and then there are the Parliamentary Under Secretaries of State, one of which represents sport.

In 1999 a radical new structure to strengthen the role of UK Sport was introduced. A "Sports Cabinet" was set up under the chairmanship of the Secretary of State for Culture, Media and Sport to work alongside UK Sport and to bring together Ministers with responsibility for sport in the four Home countries.

The Department promotes its policies for the range of sectors that can be broadly defined as "culture". It intends to take an across sectoral view where policy is concerned. The themes to this approach are:

- the promotion of access for the many not just the few
- the pursuit of excellence and innovation
- the nurturing of educational opportunity
- the fostering of the creative industries.

In relation to sport this can be translated as:

- Sport for All, aiming to widen access to sport and recreation to the masses.
- Achieving Excellence in national and international competition.
- The Youth Sports Unit promotes the importance of Physical Education and Sport for young people, in conjunction with the Department for Education and Employment [DfEE] and also has responsibility for children's play, via education and training.
- Major international events are a high priority such as attracting the 2006 World Cup and the 2003 World Athletics Championships. The Department will support the relevant organisations in terms of bidding for and staging the events.

Quangos

A large number of quangos exist outside government departments, with varying degrees of independence. They have clearly defined functions specialising in their own area, but this has tended to increase the problem of co-ordination rather than improve it.

Quangos are not under the direct control of Parliament but linked to the government in some way, either financial, policy accountability or its statutory obligations. Some common characteristics can be identified:

- Quangos tend to be funded directly by the Treasury.
- The board in control is usually elected by the appropriate Minister.
- They tend to perform promotional or developmental activities.
- They tend to have specialist expertise not found elsewhere in the government.
- They remain slightly politically detached from sensitive issues such as racial and sexual equality, creating a 'buffer zone' for the government.
- Paradoxically, they could help the former Conservative government to bypass contentious local authorities (usually under Labour control).

However, quangos are often fragmented, lack co-ordination, are administratively cumbersome and contain increasing numbers of interested and sometimes competing parties.

An example of a quango is the Countryside Commission.

Sport England
www.sportengland.org

Sport England began its role in January 1997 and is accountable to Parliament through the Secretary of State for Culture, Media and Sport who operates under the Department for Culture, Media and Sport [DCMS]. Sport England also operates ten regional offices across England providing partnerships across public and private sectors.

Objectives:

The objectives of Sport England are to lead the development of sport in England by influencing and serving the public. Its aim is:

- more people involved in sport
- more places to play sport
- more medals through higher standards of performance in sport.

Members of the Council are appointed by the Secretary of State for Culture, Media and Sport. Their responsibilites include:

- approving all policy matters and operational and corporate plans for Sport England
- bringing independent judgement to issues such as strategy and resources
- ensuring all financial matters are regulated and operate efficiently.

A series of advisory panels guide Sport England in the following areas:

- Lottery
- Local authorities
- Women and sport
- Disability
- Racial equality
- Government body investment.

Funding:

The work of Sport England is jointly funded by:

- the Exchequer for maintaining England's sports infrastructure and
- through the National Lottery via the Sport England Lottery Fund which is earmarked for the development of sport in England
- sport as part of the overall social inclusion policy and neighbourhood regeneration work.

Many of these policies will be discussed in greater detail in chapter 9.

Sport is funded via UK Sport [which is also the National Lottery distributor] and Sport England who in turn provides grants to governing bodies, advice and support to schools, local government and sports clubs.

Some of the achievements of Sport England are the:

- Active Sports Programme
- Millennium Youth Games

'Sport for all'

Although Sport for All campaigns are no longer the main functions of Sport England it is nevertheless useful to have some idea of previous campaigns. This campaign in 1972 was on a nationwide basis regardless of sex, age, race or social class. To achieve this aim they targeted groups with low participation such as 13–24 years; 45–59 years; women; people with disabilities and the unemployed. Within the wider campaign certain specialist campaigns were set up.

 **Research the Sports Council's campaigns from 1975 onwards.**

UK Sport
www.uksport.gov.uk

Established in 1997 by Royal Charter, as part of the re-structuring programmes, UKS took responsibility for issues that need to be dealt with at UK level. UK Sport's mission is to help our athletes become world class performers. It is to take on a role above that of the Home Country Sport Councils on issues that require strategic planning, administration, co-ordination or representation for the benefit of the UK as a whole. It is funded through Exchequer and Lottery Funding. In 1999–2000 it will receive approximately £12 millions and £20.5 million respectively to fund sporting projects of UK significance. It has a remit to:

- encourage and develop higher standards of sporting excellence in the UK
- identify sporting policies that should have a UK-wide application
- identify areas of unnecessary duplication to avoid administration waste
- develop and deliver appropriate grant programmes in conjunction with the governing bodies and home country sport councils
- oversee policy on sport science, sports medicine, drug control, coaching and other areas where there is a need for a consistent UK – wide policy
- co-ordinate policy for bringing major international events to the UK
- represents the UK internationally and increase the influence of the UK at an international level.

Fig. 8.6   UK SPORT

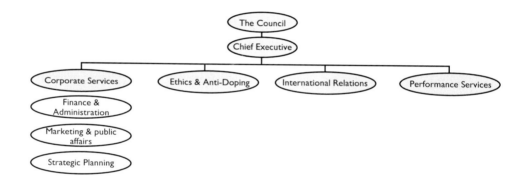

It performs these aims through four key directorates:

- **Performance Development** – provides advice to UK/Governing Bodies on their planning processes; allocates Exchequer funding; advises on applications for Awards from the Lottery Sports Fund.
- **UK Sports Institute** – Central Services will be based in London with regional network centres. The Olympic sports will be mainly catered for and it will be primarily for potential and élite athletes including, athletes with disabilities. The main support services of Sport Science, Sports Medicine, Lifestyle Management Services, Information services and a range of facilities will help to create an environment where world class athletes are more likely to develop.
- **International Relations and Major Events** – the globalisation of sport and the cultural, social and economic benefits accrued by events such as the Olympic Games and World Cup make it imperative for the UK to be in a strong position at the centre of international decision making. There is a need to promote and enhance the position and reputation of the UK sports system internationally. It links with organisations such as the European Union and British Council to develop initiatives in place like South Africa.
- **Ethics and Anti-doping** –   the directorate is responsible for the co-ordination of an effective testing programme and a comprehensive education programme. Its quality work was recognised in 1997 by the awarding of certification of management, the first organisation in the world to receive one.

Fig. 8.7   The location of National Coaching Centres in the UK

This trend towards co-ordinating policies for sporting excellence began in the 1980s and the formation of the National Coaching Foundation now Sport Coach UK was an integral part of this movement.

Sport Coach UK

This was established in 1983 to provide a range of educational and advisory services for all coaches and to complement the award schemes of the individual governing bodies. This has enjoyed increasing success. It oversees the running of the 16 National Coaching Centres which are primarily based in Institutions of Higher Education (see fig 8.7).

The aims of Sport Coach UK and the means by which they will deliver their intentions are:

- lead and develop the national standards of coaching and the various other qualifications available. Examples are the Diploma in Professional Studies; the Coaching for Teachers courses; BSc [Hons] in Applied Sports Coaching.
- working with organisations such as the local authorities, governing bodies, the British Olympic Association and Higher Education to improve the standards and professional development of coaches
- provide high quality education programmes products and services, such as coaching literature, videos, seminars and workshops, factsheets and databases, that reflect the needs of coaches and are accessible to them. Most are available from 'Coachwise Limited' Sport Coach UK's wholly owned trading company.

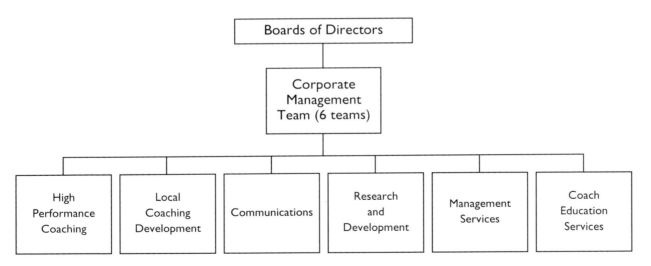

Fig. 8.8   Structure of Sport Coach UK

Funding is provided by the:

- United Kingdom Sports Council [UKSC] and Sport England 66% grant aid
- 29% earned income [including 4% subscription]
- 5% other grant aid donations.

What are National Standards?

Like performers, coaches develop depending on their interest, knowledge, commitment, skills and opportunities. One coach may aspire to work to become the National Coach, while others are keen to develop their skills to be the best coaches working with beginners. The

National Coach will be the one that media attention focuses on. However, both coaches are fundamental to the sport. We recognise that different levels and types of performers require different levels and types of coaches.

Table 8.1 illustrates the *vertical* progression that a coach maytake.

LEVEL OF COACH	WHAT SHOULD A COACH BE ABLE TO DO?	HOW NGBs MIGHT DESCRIBE A COACH
Level 5	Coaches having significant and repeated success at the highest level of the world stage. Competent to assume full responsibility for the organisation, management and delivery of all elements of a world class performer's (team's) preparation for competitive international success	National Coach
Level 4	Coaches with substantial and proven practical coaching experience at club and representative level. Competent to take full responsibility for the management of every aspect of a performer's (team's) preparation for competition at an international level.	Regional Coach Mentor Coach
Level 3	Coaches competent to plan, coach and evaluate an annual coaching programme for committed club level and representative performers competing at county, regional and/or national levels.	Advanced Coach Club Coach Senior Coach
Level 2	Coaches competent to plan, coach and evaluate a series of sessions for recreational participants and those competing in local leagues.	Coach Instructor Teacher
Level 1	Competent to assist more experienced coaches and lead sections of safe, fun, recreational sessions.	Assistant Coach Leader

Table. 8.1   LEVELS OF COACHING.

Disability Sport England www.euroyellowpages.com/dse/dispeng.htm

This organisation was formally known as the British Sports Association for the Disabled which was founded in 1961 by Sir Ludwig Guttman, a neuro-surgeon who worked from Stoke Mandeville hospital.

Disability Sport England is about:

- promoting the benefits of sport and making it accessible to everyone regardless of ability
- helping talented athletes reach the highest levels such as the Paralympic Games.

Fig. 8.9   DISABILITY SPORT ENGLAND — ORGANISATION

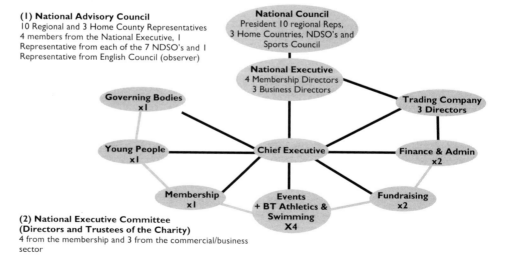

(1) **National Advisory Council**
10 Regional and 3 Home County Representatives 4 members from the National Executive, 1 Representative from each of the 7 NDSO's and 1 Representative from English Council (observer)

National Council
President 10 regional Reps, 3 Home Countries, NDSO's and Sports Council

National Executive
4 Membership Directors
3 Business Directors

Governing Bodies
x1

Trading Company
3 Directors

Young People
x1

Chief Executive

Finance & Admin
x2

Membership
x1

Events
+ BT Athletics &
Swimming
X4

Fundraising
x2

(2) **National Executive Committee**
(Directors and Trustees of the Charity)
4 from the membership and 3 from the commercial/business sector

Liaison with the Sports Councils will mean a more co-ordinated approach towards setting foundations in developing young people; talent development; coaching; national governing bodies; local authorities; membership services and management administration.

The aims

- **To provide** opportunities for disabled people to participate in sport.
- **To promote** the benefits of sport and physical recreation by disabled people.
- **To support** organisations in providing sporting opportunities for disabled people.
- **To educate** and make people aware of the sporting abilities of disabled people.
- **To enhance** the image, awareness and understanding of disability sport.
- **To encourage** disabled people to play an active role in the development of their sport.

Central Council of Physical Recreation

www.ccpr.org.uk

Fig. 8.10   Structure of the Central Council of Physical Recreation

This organisation was originally founded in 1935 to have responsibility for sport and recreation in the UK. It had three main objectives:

1 to encourage as many people as possible to participate in physical activity
2 to provide the governing bodies with a separate organisation to represent their collective interests to the Sports Council (now Sport England)
3 to increase public awareness and knowledge of the importance of sport.

They set up regional offices and the first national sport centres, and as such, the organisation was a precursor to the Sports Council. In 1972, the Sports Council took over the overall responsibility for sport, and the personnel of the CCPR were merely transferred from one to the other. It was inevitable perhaps that similar policies would be adopted, at least until each organisation defined its individual roles more clearly. Thus, the CCPR became the **representative** and **consultative body** to the Sports Council. It became the chief means of preserving the traditionally voluntary and independent nature of organised sport in the UK.

A useful way of simplifying one of its roles is to visualise it as the middle man between Sports England and the autonomous governing bodies whose interests it represents. The CCPR can liaise across a wide range of sporting activities and bring together specialist bodies. There are however some limitations, mainly the organisational weakness and the rivalry between the CCPR and the Sports Council.

The CCPR Executive Committee has divided sport and recreation into six divisions: see fig 8.10.

Write a list of specific physical activities which would come under each category heading.

CCPR policy towards current issues

It supports 'dual use' policy: this recommends increased access to sporting facilities but protests against Compulsory Competitive Tendering, viewing it as a threat to the British tradition of the provision of public sporting facilities. This emphasises the nature of the CCPR – an organisation which looks after the interests of sport for the people.

Financing the CCPR

The CCPR is financed from five main sources:

1 subscriptions and donations from its members
2 support from industry and commerce
3 sponsorship by individuals or companies of particular events and projects under the CCPR
4 sales of its own publications and research findings
5 contractual support from the Sports Council.

CCPR achievements

The CCPR is concerned about the sale of playing fields in schools and is firm in its campaign to stop this happening.

'A Sporting Chance' The CCPR National Conference of Sport and Recreation November 1999. The issues addressed are those of equity issues and explores sports role tackling Social Exclusion and providing Equality of Opportunity.

British Sports Trust [BST]

The British Sports Trust is the charitable arm of the Central Council of Physical Recreation. In 1998 43,000 people were trained to become leaders of sport in their communities. Many of these people were aged between 14–25. This was achieved via the Sports Leader Awards which aim to achieve five core values:

- personal development
- a stepping stone to employment
- developing leadership
- volunteering in communities
- reaching youth crime.

Local authorities

We have already mentioned the burden on local authorities to provide leisure facilities in their area. This is decreed under mainly permissive legislation, such as the Physical Training and Recreation Act 1937 and the Local Government Miscellaneous Act 1976, which stated that a local authority 'may provide ... such recreational facilities as it thinks fit'.

The following factors stimulated local government involvement:

- The creation of the Sports Council (1972), the Tourist Boards (1969) and the Countryside Commission (1968).
- The creation of new sporting and recreational facilities, in particular leisure centres and country parks.
- Increased leisure and a steady rise in the standard of living.
- Increase in the rate and frequency of sport and recreation participation.
- Creation of 'service' departments within local authorities following the restructuring of local government in 1974, eg, a leisure service department.

A two-tier structure emerged, of District and County Councils. Leisure provision assumed greater importance, but a lack of coordination halted its progress. Recreational planning was encouraged through government reports, particularly the 1975 White Paper 'Sport and Recreation'.

Leisure, by the 1990s, is mainly the responsibility of one specialist department. Excluding educational provision, authorities' net expenditure on revenue support for sport exceeds **£400 million** a year in England and Wales. In addition, **£100 million** capital expenditure is incurred.

Write to your local leisure officer, asking them for a list of their objectives for leisure provision in your area.

Pressures on local authorities

Local authorities operate within certain restrictions:

1 The community charge and the capital control regimes affect the ability of local authorities to fund new developments and their attitudes to subsidies.

2 Increased competition from the private sector, partly due to the establishment of Compulsory Competitive Tendering and the effects on dual use policies following the Education Reform Act 1988 require improved management on behalf of local authorities.

3 Sport and physical recreation also has to compete with nine other departments: the arts and cultural provision, libraries, entertainment and catering services, museums, heritage and conservation, tourism, youth and community services, adult education and selective social services.

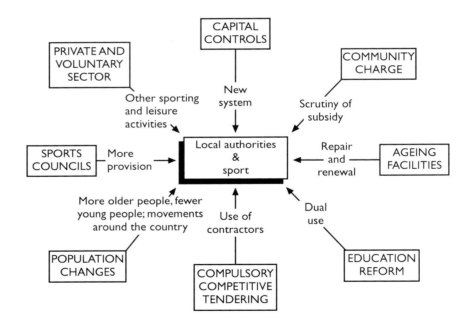

Fig. 8.11   PRESSURES ON LOCAL
AUTHORITY SPORTS POLICY

Table 8.2   VARIOUS LEISURE ACTIVITIES

SPORT	EDUCATION	TOURISM	SOCIAL	CULTURAL
sports centres playing fields ski slopes	libraries swimming pools	museums conservation country parks	youth clubs community centres	theatres art galleries

4 The term 'leisure' encompasses a wide range of activities, like sport and physical recreation, education, tourism, social and cultural. This is illustrated in table 8.2.

As legislation is mainly permissive, it is not surprising that wide variations in provision and expenditure can be found between local authorities.

In the light of some of the problems highlighted, what procedures would you suggest to a local authority in order to improve the level and effectiveness of its leisure services?

Positive aspects

Positive features emerge, nonetheless:

- Financial expenditure has remained reasonably steady.
- Leisure is a popular demand by local residents.
- Leisure is increasingly valued for its own benefits and not just as a means of meeting other policy objectives like reducing vandalism or improving the nation's health.
- Leisure in the 1990s was also perceived to be of economic benefit to a local area, particularly in its ability to attract tourism.

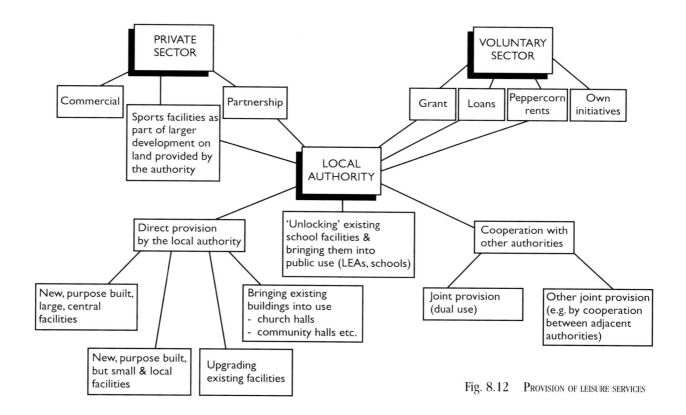

Fig. 8.12   PROVISION OF LEISURE SERVICES

Best Value

Many Local Authorities place sport as a central feature in their work on:

- healthy living
- regeneration
- social inclusion and other key objectives.

Local Government will work closely alongside Sport England in the changing landscape of cultural activity such as Best Value and Regional Cultural Strategies.

The document, 'The Value of Sport' responds to the challenge 'Why invest in sport?' and demonstrates that sport can make a difference to people's lives and to the communities in which they live. It emphasises that for every pound spent on sport there are multiple returns in improved health, reduced crime, economic regeneration and improved employment opportunities.

The document highlights how sport needs to justify continued investment:

- through seeking public support for local authority investment
- making an impact locally within health improvement programmes
- ensuring that it is part of the Government's 'Pathfinder Area' initiatives related to social exclusion and included within programmes in the 'New deal for Communities'.

Research the document 'Best Value through Sport' produced by Sport England. As a group or class consider;

a the social, economic and environment benefits that sport can bring to local communities
b the liaison required between different organisation.

Research some of the work of the Institute of Leisure and Amenity Management (ILAM) (www.ilam.co.uk).

Autonomous organisations

Governing bodies of sport

History

With the increasing popularity of sport during the late nineteenth century, it became necessary for individuals and clubs taking part to agree on a common set of rules or laws. In most areas this led directly to the formation within each sport of a governing body, with the task of agreeing rules for the sport so that all clubs and individuals could compete on equal terms.

The persons responsible for the establishment of the governing bodies were mainly the educated, middle and upper classes, and there is still a tendency for sport administration in the UK to be the domain of the middle classes.

Structure

It is difficult to generalise across all the governing bodies, as some are extremely wealthy (eg, the Football Association), while others are still heavily reliant on grants. However, there are some common characteristics:

- executive boards and officers
- elected by clubs through local, regional and county representatives
- many have separate organisations in the four home nations (England, Scotland, Wales, Northern Ireland)
- many still have separate organisations for men and women.

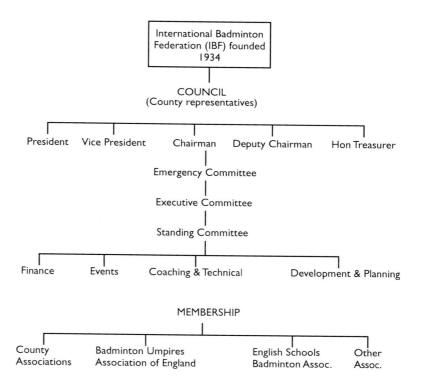

Fig. 8.13 ORGANISATION AND ADMINISTRATION OF THE BADMINTON ASSOCIATION

Below is a list of the professional staff of the Badminton Association, as an example of a governing body. See fig 8.13 for the hierarchical structure.

- Chief Executive
- Accountant
- Director of Coaching and Development
- Coaching Manager
- Events Director
- Tournament and County Liaison Officer
- Press and Public Relations Manager
- P.A. to the Chief Executive
- Coaching Secretary
- Secretarial Staff

There are approximately 300 governing bodies in the UK. Many are unpaid volunteers, though this situation has improved somewhat by the appointment of paid administrators (largely dependent on the size and scale of the individual governing body).

These organisations proudly retain their autonomy from political control and each other. They become a more collective voice when represented to the Sport England by the CCPR, though we have already voiced some concern over this rather strained relationship. Their main functions are to:

- establish rules and regulations (in accordance with the International Sports Federations, ISF)
- organise competitions
- develop coaching awards and leadership schemes
- selection of teams for country or UK at international events
- liaise with relevant organisations such as the CCPR, Sports Council, local clubs, British Olympic Association and the International Sports Federation.

Recent changes for governing bodies

Examples of some changes are:

- growth of new sports, setting a challenge to the older traditional sports
- the decline in extra-curricular school sport and a dependence on the governing bodies to try and fill this gap
- the blurring in definition of amateur and professional sport
- the need to compete internationally with countries who have developed systematic forms of training have made the governing bodies develop the coaching and structuring of competitions and devote more money to the training of their élite sportspeople.

Governing bodies have a variety of **finance** sources: drawn from member clubs, associations and individual members, or receiving grant in aid from Sport England. The last two decades have seen the dominance of television sports coverage and consequently sponsorship affects many sports. Governing bodies have had to meet this challenge and market themselves in the modern world if they wish to take advantage of these opportunities. Sports like snooker, badminton, squash and athletics have moved into the arena of big business. **Commercial sponsorship** is now a desirable form of income.

Research in your class the development of a particular governing body. Choose from different categories, eg, traditional, professional, a new growth sport, or a sport which has recently experienced rapid change etc.

Local Provision For Leisure

Provision for physical recreation in any local area comes from three main sources:

- Private
- Public
- Voluntary

With reference to the financing and management of sports provision for the general public, briefly explain what is meant by:
- The private sector
- The public sector

Private Sector:	Public Sector:	Voluntary Sector:
• Privately owned/registered companies • Trading on normal profit and loss/ self financed • Membership entrance fees • Managed by owners/their employees • Must operate and survive in open market/make a profit/compete	• Business operations run by local authority departments • Trading on set prices/charges etc • According to a pre-set budget • May involve subsidies as a matter of policy/Council tax or equivalent • Managed by local authority employees	• Business operations owned by 'members' • Possibly on trust/charity basis • Trading on normal profit and loss/ break even • Managed through a members committee • May employ staff • Financed by membership fees/fund raising/sponsorship

What are the objectives of each sector?

Facilities

Local authority and local education authority
Outdoor pursuit centres
Community sport centres
Voluntary sports clubs
National sport centres

Our sporting experiences are only made possible by the wealth of public facilities which have developed during the twentieth century. Prior to this, specialised sporting activities had been mainly the preserve of the privileged classes who owned land and built the necessary facilities, eg, real/lawn tennis courts, croquet, etc. Social changes began to take the needs of the lower classes into account, beginning with public baths, urban recreational parks and followed by the provision of facilities for physical education in state schools. From then on there was a rapid expansion in local authority provision of public recreational facilities.

Local authorities

They are the main providers of land and large scale facilities for community recreational use.

1 They maintain playing fields, gymnasia, tennis courts, golf courses, boating lakes, swimming baths and sports centres.
2 Local authorities are able to borrow capital to finance facilities within an overall allocation for 'locally determined schemes'.
3 The Sports Council is able to support local authority sports projects, costs of national centres and local facilities provided by voluntary organisations.

Local education authority

It is a legal requirement for all publicly maintained schools to provide for the physical education of pupils. Considering the vast amount of recreation facilities available at most schools, it makes sense to maximise their use. Most LEAs and district councils now have policies to share facilities. See Dual Use and Joint Planning. Private schools and Higher Education Institutions also have facilities available.

Outdoor pursuit centres

Local education authorities established up to 400 residential outdoor centres between 1960 and 1970. The main aims of these centres were:

• to provide experiences in support of physical education
• to offer residential experience of outdoor adventure activities, to broaden the personal and social development of youth.

They are also widely used in the training of teachers and instructors in the pursuit of national governing body awards.

The primary users of the centres are undoubtedly schools (64%). Other users are the commercial sector, when the centres are used for leadership training. In a recent survey, 65% of centres felt that the user base could be broadened. Thirty per cent of centres operate for about 39 weeks per year. They may need to change this policy as they move into the unprotected, competitive market due to the decline in local authority financing of the centres, eg, the summer holiday period could be an opportunity to promote activity holidays. Most of the full time employed staff are qualified (93%).

Suggest some potential markets which could best increase the usage of these centres.

Community sport centres

They often cater for a range of interests and those with high quality facilities often attract national interest. Examples of these are: the Meadowbank Sports Centre; Harrison's Rock in Kent; Bowles Rocks Outdoor Pursuit Centre; Birmingham National Indoor Arena; Lord's Cricket Ground; Wimbledon Tennis Club.

However, the majority of us are more familiar with a local leisure centre.

Research your local centre (eg, a sports centre, a country park, a water based recreational facility etc).
   Note carefully:

- **its provision of a variety of activities**
- **its costing system**
- **access for the disabled**
- **opportunities for the Sports Council's target groups**
- **ease of access for the local catchment area**
- **opening hours**
- **social areas**
- **club use**
- **competition use of the centre, etc.**

Be as thorough as you can.

   Following your findings write a report which concentrates on the positive as well as the negative, with any recommendations.

Write a list of the possible aims and objectives of a leisure centre manager.

Local voluntary sports clubs

These would normally be affiliated to the national governing body, eg, football, cricket, hockey. However, private clubs may be linked to business firms. Figure 8.14 and table 8.3 give examples of sports club administration and organisation.

Commercial facilities

For example: ten pin bowling; ice and roller skating rinks; squash clubs; golf courses; driving ranges; riding stables.

National sports centres

These are run by Sport England – See fig 8.15. It is recognised that only by providing appropriate training facilities will it be possible for the UK to compete effectively in international sport.

Fig. 8.14   ADMINISTRATIONAL
FRAMEWORK OF A LARGE ATHLETIC CLUB

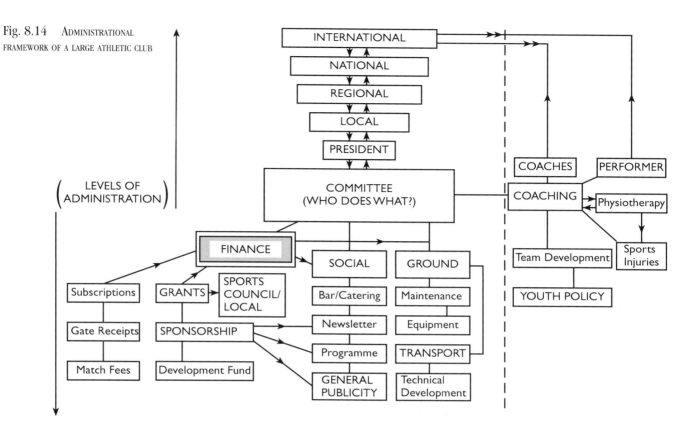

Table 8.3   ADMINISTRATION OF A SPORTS CLUB

ROLE OF OFFICERS	CLUB MEETINGS	FINANCE	PRACTICAL MANAGEMENT	CLUB SAFETY

club president
vice president
club chairman
club secretary
club treasurer
fixtures secretary
social secretary
press officer
club groundsman
captains
bar manager
membership
  secretary
training & coaching
junior section
senior members
	management comm.
	agenda
	minimum attendance
	voting procedures
	minutes
	regularity of meetings
	a.g.m.
		income
		subs
		match fees
		sale of clothing
		bar
		social events
		lotteries
		capital costs
		loans/grants
		breweries
		banks
		local auth.
		sports council
			admin
			staffing
			finance
			bar management
			legal
			facility care
			insurance
				Health & Safety at Work
				  1974
				injuries (rel. to facilities)
				accidents
				governing body reg.
				training awards
				insurance

Fig. 8.15   NATIONAL SPORTS CENTRES IN THE UK

Plas y Brenin

Based in Snowdonia, this is the national centre for mountain activities. It trains leaders and offers courses in the Alps, Scotland and in Snowdonia. They run award schemes and employ full time instructors who work with the governing bodies.

Holme Pierrepont

This centre offers an artificial canoe slalom course, a 200 metre regatta lake and an artificial ski tow, amongst its facilities. The key governing bodies (the British Canoe Union, the British Water Ski Federation and the National Federation of Anglers) make extensive use of this facility.

Lilleshall Hall

This is a multi-purpose centre with a particular specialism in gymnastics and football. Governing bodies account for 75% of use. The human performance fitness testing centre is open to all and signifies the attempt to coordinate the fields of sports medicine, physiotherapy and rehabilitation.

Crystal Palace

Also a multi-purpose facility, it has a world famous stadium, swimming pool, and a variety of indoor facilities and artificial surfaces. A sports injury clinic provides for individual treatment.

Bisham Abbey

The main activities include tennis, squash, hockey, weight lifting and golf. An Excellence partnership has been forged with the British Amateur Weightlifters Association. Elite squads account for approximately 70% of use.

Manchester

It contains the velodrome for cycling, and has been accredited an Olympic training centre by the BOA. This is in recognition of the fact that it provides the very best training opportunities and services for British cyclists. It is managed by the British Cycling Federation on behalf of the Sports Council.

National Cities of Sport

Sport England is developing a more co-ordinated approach toward a coherent sports facilities plan, and as such, designated Birmingham, Sheffield and Glasgow as the first National Cities of Sport. The Cities of Sport Programme aims to create a network of cities with the vision, commitment and resources to bid for and stage major sporting events. It hopes to bid by using a planned, co-ordinated approach supported by an infrastructure at both local and national level, and management expertise; it is very important to develop partnerships among councils, universities, media and business community as well as sports organisations.

New national stadium

Creating a new national stadium at Wembley is a decision of national importance. Millions of pounds of National Lottery money will be spent with the intention of providing a stadium which will cope with modern day seating capacities (80,000) and spectators' expectations (easily accessible, safe and comfortable), and with the capability of attracting European and world single or multi-sports events.

Finance

Government funding
National Lottery funding [www.english.sports.gov.uk/lottery]
Voluntary sector
Governing Bodies
SportAid [previously Sport Aid Foundation] [www.sportsaid.org.uk]
Football Trust
Gambling
Foundation for Sport and the Arts
Sponsorship
Tax

Funding for sport in the United Kingdom is a mixture of Government, private and commercial incentives.

Central Government

The Exchequer funds sport, via the Department for Culture, Media and Sport. Funds are allocated to Sport England and UK Sport for fostering, supporting and encouraging the development of sport and physical recreation. They in turn provide grants to governing bodies in sport. The DCMS is developing new Funding Agreements such as:

- UK Sport is the proposed [1999] distributor of the Lottery funding ensuring equal treatment of all UK athletes. Sport England is responsible for the distribution in England of sport's share of the Lottery funding.
- In 1999/2000 Sport England will receive £4.5m and UK Sport will receive £12.6m in Exchequer funding from the Department for Culture, Media and Sport to assist their work.
- Children's Play is to receive central funding.
- The Football Licensing Authority is to be reconstituted as a Sports Ground Safety authority.
- Responsibility for Sportsmatch to be transferred to Sport England from April 1999.

Sportsmatch

The Conservative government's £1 for £1 Business Sponsorship Incentive Scheme (for grass roots sport) was established in 1992. It will provide funding for over £3.7 million a year in the UK to match funds for the private sector.

It is administered by the ISS in co-operation with Sport England and provides an excellent opportunity for sports bodies and sponsors to double the value of the project investment or to mount extra events or activities. The Sportsmatch Awards Panel which considers grants is particularly interested in developing projects for rural and inner cities which lack sporting resources. The events must be competitive, challenging and physically skilful.

Fig. 8.16a FUNDING ALLOCATIONS 1999–2002

FUNDING (IN £ MILLIONS) ALLOCATIONS				
	1998–99	1999–2000	2000–2001	2001–2002
ESC (of which Sportsmatch)	36.5 3.2	37.9 3.4	38.0 3.4	3.4
UKSC	11.6	12.6	12.6	12.6
Children's Play	0.4	0.5	0.5	0.5
FLA	0.9	0.9	0.9	0.9

Fig. 8.16b

	1997–98	1998–99	1999–2000
SPORTS	**50,144**	**49,434**	**51,923**
of which:	out turn	provision	plans
English Sports Council	36,925	36,489	37,873
of which: Sportsmatch	3,200	3,200	3,373
United Kingdom Sports Council	11,824	11,600	12,600
Children's play	400	400	500
Football Licensing Authority	896	896	900
British Chess Federation	49	49	50
Other sports support	50		

Local Government

Local Authorities spend nearly £900m per annum on sport and active recreation in England. It is a heavy burden for an already over-stretched budget.

Why should a Local Authority spend large sums of money on sport when it is a permissive duty rather than a mandatory one?

The voluntary sector

This is the area in which most sporting activity occurs. Individuals come together to form clubs and associations which are run to benefit the participants. They are generally self-financing; annual subscriptions and match fees provide the bulk of the revenue and indicates the 'grass roots' development of sport in the UK.

Governing bodies

Governing bodies receive their income from grants from the Home Country Sport Councils, sponsorship, affiliation fees, donations, insurance, commission and royalties, marketing, interest receivable and profit on sale of investments.
Expenditure goes on élite squads, matches, publications, salaries and personal expenses, international affiliation fees, promotions, press and publicity, development officers and so on.

Wide variations exist depending on the size and type of governing body. For example, is it a female club in which case sponsorship will be harder to find? Is it a professional organisation where commercial markets are readily available?

Gambling in sport

Commercial betting and gaming is allowed under strict licensing regulations. This includes card games and casinos, but the bulk comes from greyhound and horse racing, and football matches.

Football Trust

With the aim of putting money back into sport, the Football Trust has been set up to supervise the levying of money from football pools and 'Spot the ball' competitions. Its income is over £32 million a year. Much of this money will be used to improve facilities for both performers and spectators (in line with the Taylor Report recommendations).

The Trust has announced plans to establish a nationwide Grass Roots Facilities Scheme. Over £1 million has been allocated and will be available for pitch and changing facilities for local authority owned, non league clubs, schools, voluntary bodies and other organisations.

The Football Trust has received over £150 million since 1990 for safety work at League football clubs, financed from a 3% Pool Betting duty concession extended in the 1999 Budget.

The National Lottery

In 1994 the Sport England Lottery Fund was launched with a broad policy strategy. It achieved many successes including the Priority Areas Initiative; funding for 1000 community projects in the first year; promise of funding for the new national stadium and funding for talented young stars. Problems occurring at this time were: the system was too slow, too bureaucratic and too centralised. The Government has acted to address some of these issues.

At the time of writing UK Sport is being earmarked to be the distributor nationally of the Lottery funding for sport. A two-fund approach has been adopted:

- A Community Projects Fund [small projects below £5000; capital awards over £5000; revenue awards for tackling social exclusion in sport]. By the beginning of 1999 grants totalling £900m had been awarded to capital sports projects.
- World Class Fund.

Fig. 8.17a   DISTRIBUTION OF LOTTERY
FUNDS

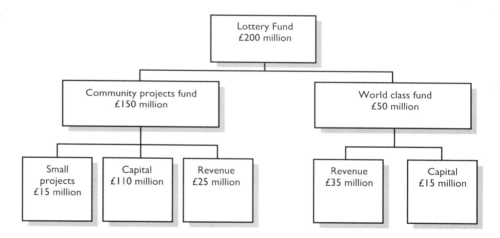

The Lottery Sports fund has earmarked £20.5 million a year for UK Sport to administer to our top UK medal hopes through the World Class Performance Programme and to help attract and stage major sporting events in the UK. Sport now benefits by around £300 million per year from the Lottery.

- World Class Events Programme:

Aim: stage major international events such as the Olympics, Paralympics, World, European and Commonwealth in the United Kingdom
Funds: £3 million p.a. providing 35% of the cost of bidding and staging events

- World Class Start Programme:

Aim: help governing bodies identify and develop young talent by providing qualified support staff
Funds: £10 million p.a.

- World Class Potential Programme:

Award details	
Months and awards	53
Projects founded to date	2936
Total awarded to date	£934,179,807
Total project cost to date	£1,634,854,001
Average projects funded per month	55
Average amount awarded per month	£30,846,302
Number of countries covered	All
Number of sports covered	61

Application details	
Total applications to date	7073
Total amount requested to date	£3,603,486,322
Total project cost to date	£5,555,048,103
Average applications per month	133
Average amount requested per month	£67,990,308
Number of countries covered	All
Number of sports covered	78

Fig. 8.17b

Aim: help governing bodies develop potential medal winners by setting up training and competition programmes
Funds: £15 million p.a.

- World Class Performance Programme

Aim: support our élite athletes
Fund: Since 1997 grants totalling over £64.6m have been committed to over 30 sports in the Programme and 2100 athletes have received support

SCSI School Community Sports Initiative

This has been established to help schools apply for increased levels of funding from the National Lottery Sports Fund, to develop good school/community sports facilities.

ACTIVITY 17 **The National Lottery has had a considerable moral, economic and social impact. What do you consider to be the advantages and disadvantages of the good causes scheme and what suggestions for change would you make?**
What opportunities exist for the funding of amateur athletes?

Foundation for Sport and the Arts

This organisation was set up by the pools promoters in 1991 to channel funds into sport and the arts. It has contributed more than £316 million towards sport projects and is financed from 3% Pool Betting Duty concession extended in the Budget. The pools provide approximately £43.5 million p.a. which can be used for the benefit of sport. It works closely with the Sport England and administers grants. Its main aims are to

- support the improvement of existing facilities
- assist the construction of new sports venues
- help with appropriate sports projects (schools, disabled, Olympic and Paralympic teams).

The sums involved are quite substantial, eg, £1 million to Northern Ireland's Sports Training Centre, £100,000 to Widnes Rugby League FC to assist with the upgrading of the facilities following the Taylor recommendations, £200,000 to Yorkshire & Cleveland Riding for the Disabled.

Sponsorship

The private sector contributes approximately £320 million a year to sport, involving more than 2,000 British companies assisting schemes from national excellence programmes to local grass roots schemes. See Chapter 16 for further information on sponsorship.

The Institute of Sports Sponsorship (ISS)

This is one of the main national organisations concerned with sports sponsorship. It was set up in association with the CCPR Sports Sponsorship Advisory Service, and acts as a grouping of commercial companies and public bodies with an interest in sport.

Tax

The introduction of the Uniform Business Rate in 1990 meant that rates for some sports clubs tripled. This is generally considered as unfair, as they are non-profit making and in addition provide a social service. The British Olympic Association, which receives no Government assistance, have to pay approximately £750,000 on £5 million raised. Britain is the only country to tax its Olympic fund raisers.

Summary:

- Sports policy is characterised by a high degree of fragmentation between central government departments. There is heavy reliance on local government to provide facilities and opportunities for sport and recreation.
- In local authorities, there is a decentralised approach towards the organisation of sport and recreation, reflecting the political system in the UK. There is a slender thread of cohesion through the organisations, but there are also areas of overlap and conflict.
- As with much of the administration of sport in the UK it is a mixture of tradition and compromise.
- There has been a steady expansion in the internationalisation of sport and it has brought challenges for the National Governing Bodies to adjust their rules and take note of the international sporting calendar.
- The pattern of funding for sport in the UK will be dominated by sponsorship. Government grants (local and central) and funds from the governing bodies and private individuals make the next share. Relatively small but important market niches are funded by the SAF (Sports Aid) and the BOA.
- British sports bodies must cast off their traditional amateur, élitist approach to join the modern, professional sports world, if this country is to allow its athletes the same opportunities as those from rival countries.

Review questions:

1 Describe the function of the following organisations:

   Department for Culture, Media and Sport
   Sport England
   Sport Coach UK
   Disability Sport England
   Central Council of Physical Recreation

2 What is the role of the Sports Minister and who is the current sports minister in the United Kingdom?

3 Why were governing bodies for sport initially established? What are the main functions of governing bodies?

4 What changes have governing bodies had to undertake in more modern times?

5 What does the term 'permissive' mean in relation to the provision of leisure by local authorities?

6 Name 6 forms of finance for sport in the United Kingdom.

7   What do the terms private, voluntary and public mean in relation to provision for leisure?

8   Outline the main idea of 'Best Value' as a policy for recreation and sport.

9   What was the effect of the Government report 'Sport: Raising the Game'?

10 Describe the 5 levels of coaching as defined by SportCoach UK.

Government Policies

In the last decade of the twentieth century the British Governments, both Conservative and Labour, have sought increasingly to assume more control over Physical Education and Sport. They represent a change in the development of DCMS policy and funding to promote Social Inclusion in the context of the National Strategy for Neighbourhood Renewal.

Policy Action Team 10 [PAT] has the job of maximising the impact on poor neighbourhoods of Government spending and policies on arts, sport and leisure.
    In conjunction with the Social Exclusion Unit [SEU] success is deemed to depend on community involvement rather than policies being imposed from above.

Why should the government wish to spend money on sport and leisure?

The stance taken is that sport can make a valuable contribution to delivering the four key outcomes of:

• lower long term unemployment
• less crime
• better health
• better qualifications.

It can also develop:

• individual pride
• community spirit to enable communities to run regeneration programmes themselves.

An integrated approach is envisaged in order to dovetail the monitoring and effectiveness of sport activities with other Action Teams, for example, the Department for the Environment, Transport and the Regions, Department for Education and Skills, Department of Health and so on. 'Joined up Government' is the key term.

Neighbourhood Regeneration

Sport should be used to engage those who feel most excluded in society such as disaffected young people and people from ethnic minorities. Organisations that receive public funds should work actively to engage those who have been excluded in the past.

"Arts and sport are not just an 'add-on' to regeneration work. They are fundamental to community involvement and ownership of any regeneration initiative when they offer means of positive engagement in tune with local interests".

[DCMS]

Executive Summary

Findings

Arts and sport, cultural and recreational activity, can contribute to neighbourhood renewal and make a real difference to health, crime, unemployment and education in deprived communities.

1. This is because they:
   a appeal directly to individuals' interests and develop their potential and self-confidence
   b relate to community identity and encourage collective effort
   c help build positive links with the wider community
   d are associated with rapidly growing industries.
2. Barriers to be overcome are:
   a projects being tailored to programme/policy criteria, rather than to community needs
   b short-term perspectives
   c promoting arts/sport in communities being seen as peripheral, both to culture/leisure organisations and in regeneration programmes
   d lack of hard information on the regeneration impact of arts/sport
   e poor links between arts/sport bodies and major 'players', including schools.
3. Principles which help to exploit the potential of arts/sport in regenerating communities are:
   a valuing diversity
   b embedding local control
   c supporting local commitment
   d promoting equitable partnerships
   e defining common objectives in relation to actual needs
   f working flexibly with charge
   g securing sustainability
   h pursuing quality across the spectrum: and
   i connecting with the mainstream of art and sport activities.
4. Social exclusion issues arise with various groups irrespective of their geographic location. This is particularly the case with ethnic minority groups and disabled people where special and systematic arrangements need to be made:
   a to invest in people and capacity within these groups and to build an information base against which future progress can be measured
   b to cater specifically for their needs in general regeneration programmes and culture/leisure policies
   c to engage directly with people within these groups, and actively to value and recognise diversity
   d to develop, monitor and deliver action plans to promote their access and involvement and to meet their needs.

Fig. 8.18   EXECUTIVE SUMMARY – POLICY ACTION TEAM 10
Source: Department for Culture, Media and Sport

NATURE OF BENEFIT	EXPERIENCED BY EXCLUDED	STRENGTH OF EVIDENCE	NATURE OF EVIDENCE			
			LAB/ EXPERIMENTAL	NATIONAL/ LARGE	CASE STUDY SURVEY	META ANALYSIS/ STUDY REVIEW
National identity	−	+			*	*
prestige	+ +	+			*	
reduced health costs	− −	+ +	*		*	*
trade		+ +	*			
Communal community/family coherence	− −				*	*
lower law and order costs (especially for youth)	− − −	+			*	*
job creation	+/−	+			*	*
environmental (created/ renewed)						
Personal physical health (heart, lungs, joints, bones, muscles)						
better mental heath (coping, depression)	− − −	+ + + +	*	*	*	*
better self esteem/image/ competence	+/−	+ +	*		*	*
socialisation/integration/ tolerance	+ + +	+ + +	*		*	*
general quality of life	+ +	+ +	*		*	*

Table. 8.4   THE BENEFITS OF SPORT
Source: Department for Culture, Media and Sport

The strength of positive and negative experience in col 2 and of evidence in col 3 is shown by the number of + and − ; * show where the particular form of evidence is available

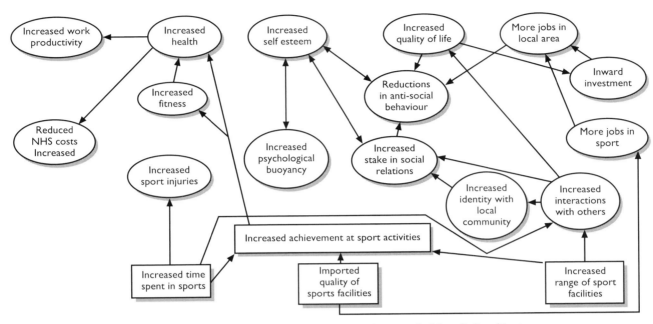

Source: Department for Culture, Media and Sport

Fig. 8.19 MODEL OF RELATIONSHIPS BETWEEN SPORT & WIDER ECONOMIC BENEFITS

Department for Education and Skills [DfES]

"Should encourage schools in the use of creative and sporting activity to support the drive to raise standards of literacy and numeracy, and through the use of these activities as part of Personal and Social and Health Education to build pupils, confidence and self esteem".

[*DCMS*]

Department of Health

"Should encourage health authorities, NHS Trusts, primary care groups/trusts and Health Action Zones to use artistic and sporting approaches to preventing illness and improving mental and physical health".

Department of the Environment, Transport and the Regions [DETR]

"Ensure the Best Value reviews carried out by local authorities consider ways in which art, sport, tourism and leisure provision could contribute to meeting new performance targets in education, crime, health, employment and social inclusion. The best practice principles outlined in this report could usefully form the basis of what Best Value Inspectorate could look for when undertaking their instructions".

[*DCMS*]

Best Value Local Authorities should:

- take on board the principles of community development approach and should build on ways in which leisure strategies and services are developed and provided, creating targeted programmes linked to networked projects

- aim to improve the four key indicators of crime, health, education and employment
- assess provision according to the social, ethnic and professional background of users and potential users
- plan for culture/leisure based community work rather than having isolated policies
- youth services should promote and enhance young people's talents
- seek value for money from their assets/facilities, ensuring the widest feasible use of them[eg, school facilities out of school hours].

Lottery Distributors should:

- fund community run multi-purpose community venues in areas with poor access to facilities, which can flexibly meet local needs rather than isolated use
- consider how to 'market' the Lottery for groups who could be classed as socially excluded and to make use of the flexibility provided by the 1998 Lottery Act by matching funding when assessing applications from neighbourhoods which have regeneration initiatives.

Talented individuals with limited opportunities could benefit from an area bursary scheme designed to help them to develop employment potential. The National Endowment for Science, Technology and the Arts (NESTA). ACE [The Arts Council of England] and Sport England should also seek to involve commercial partners from the relevant industry.

Department for Culture, Media and Sport [DCMS] should:

- ensure neighbourhood renewal is a high priority on the agenda with culture/leisure sector involved
- make effective use of regeneration funds
- involve all groups in society in the sport strategy
- monitor and follow through policies
- monitor impact of sponsored bodies' social inclusion policies through QUEST [Quality, Efficiency and Standards Team].

Sport England should address its basic policy aims:

- to sustain cultural diversity
- to combat social exclusion
- to promote community development.

should consider joint policies with other agencies such as:

- partnerships managing New Deal for Communities Pathfinders to spend on sport related activities
- proposals regarding the allocation of Sportsmatch monies in areas of regeneration
- funding agreements with governing bodies
- ensuring the Voluntary Sector plays a part in community development
- proposals as to how it will tighten the social inclusion objectives and targets given in its funding agreement with DCMS.

1 Which benefits of sport are highlighted in these Case Studies?

CASE STUDY: Community Games

The Community Games (Ireland) is an independent voluntary organisation operating through the local community. It provides opportunities for children and young people to experience a wide range of sporting and cultural activities. Community Games is sponsored and supported by the Government, national sponsors and local authorities.

The Games is a country wide movement – non-political and non-sectarian – which operates at area, county, provincial and national levels. Membership is open to anyone who wishes to participate. Some of its aims and objectives include: encouraging community spirit and a love of sport and culture amongst members of the community and promoting a better understanding between people of different cultures and environments. It also encourages community members to work with children, and many adults have found the Community Games an ideal way of meeting and making new friends.

Liverpool's Community Games (first held in 1998) are based on the same principle, with the main purpose of fostering community development and identity through sporting and cultural endeavour. Piloting initially on a small scale, this is extending to some other parts of Liverpool in 1999 and it is intended that the games will run throughout the city and then eventually throughout the country. It is distinctive to other 'Games' in that it stresses the merits of participation rather than winning

competitions. Recognising that all children are not physically or temperamentally suited to sport, Community Games will aim to provide a balance of other games and cultural activities.

CASE STUDY: Ivybridge Estate, Houndslow

Houndslow Borough Community Recreation Outreach Team, together with Housing Management and Youth Service, devised a programme of activities to benefit all youngsters on the Ivybridge estate. After consulting the youngsters on the estate, it was clear that football coaching sessions would be popular with both boys and girls. An unexpected bonus of the sessions, held in a multi-sport area on the estate, has been the high level of ability and skill shown by the youngsters.

This has resulted in many of the boys being referred to Brentford FC School of Excellence. Two girls have also gone on to join women's football teams and other young people have become involved in coaching and refereeing. As a result of the youngsters asking for refreshments a youth café was established in the estates's community centre, organised and run by the young people during the sessions. Another benefit was that the young people felt included in life on the estate. They have since participated in the Tenants' Association and have been involved in planning a new community centre for the estate.

Source: Department of Culture, Media and Sport

2 What strategies were employed to achieve a measure of success?

Smith and Hoey launch a Sporting Future for all [April 2000]

Chris Smith, the Secretary of State for Culture, Media and Sport and Kate Hoey, the Minister for Sport, launched the government's strategy for sport –'A Sporting Future for All'. They promise a new deal with governing bodies in sport.

The strategy sets out the government's vision for sport in the twenty-first century and highlights the importance of co-ordinating sport between schools, local clubs and organisations.

The strategy includes:

- a new fund of £75 million from the Government over two years with a target of matched funding from the lottery to add to it for primary schools to provide new, multi-purpose sports and arts facilities for pupils and the wider community
- devolved lottery funding to governing bodies in return for modernisation of their administration, increased involvement with schools through coaching and visits by élite performers, and a commitment to invest at least 5% of TV rights revenue in grassroots facilities and activities
- ring-fencing of 20% of lottery sports awards for youth sports projects

- establishment of Sport Direct a national telephone helpline to advise people how to get involved in sport in their local area
- establishment of a fast track system for élite performers to become coaches
- a comprehensive audit of sport facilities to be undertaken by local authorities and Sport England.

Local government involvement in sport

Local government has traditionally had an important role to play in the provision of recreational and sporting facilities for its local area. However, its responsibility has been permissive, rather than mandatory; by law, it is not required to provide for recreation.

The document 'The Value of Sport' produced by Sport England highlights the benefits of sport to local areas. Sport needs to demonstrate tangible benefits to individuals, communities and the nation in its share of limited public resources. Local Authorities will be using the 'Best Value' idea in developing their policies towards sport.

Compulsory Competitive Tendering

Following the Local Government Act 1988, a range of local authority services were tendered, including the management of local authority leisure services. The Conservative government wanted to ensure a more competitive market in order to reduce costs.

Compulsory Competitive Tendering is slightly different from privatisation of large companies. The local authority would still:

- own the facilities
- control the prices
- set quality standards
- influence programming
- retain the ability to decide policy.

Local authorities were to become 'enablers' rather than providers. An 'enabler' needs to plan, coordinate, and facilitate the provision of leisure services. To do this they must think strategically, to identify and make explicit their objectives when planning new capital projects. This is not to suggest they were not doing this before the legislation. Four main areas need to be considered: planning and research; development within the community, eg, Action Sport; management, eg, accessibility, price range and quality experience; marketing, eg, to ensure that target groups are identified on the basis of market research.

Table 8.5   ADVANTAGES AND DISADVANTAGES OF CCT

ADVANTAGES	DISADVANTAGES
Reduce unit costs by 20%	Could result in worse pay and conditions for employees
Free local authorities from the day to day running problems	Sport no longer regarded as a social service
Help to review the use of manpower	CCPR felt it was a serious attack on traditional provision of sports facilities

Law and order

Generally in most countries sports law does not exist. More often established legal principles are applied to new problems generated by sport, such as performance enhancing drugs and legal requirements imposed by sport organisations. A notable exception is the Amateur Sports Act in the United States of America [1978].

Players

There has been an increase in sports legislation and legal challenges to the administrators of sport. Sport has traditionally been perceived as being outside and almost above the law, and as such has retained autonomy for a greater length of time than most other social agencies. But the number of prosecutions of sports players for assaults which occurred within the confines of the game, has increased. Should assaults be viewed separately to a similar occurrence outside a sports setting? On the one hand, players have understood the activity they are taking part in, and by participating they have accepted that the rules of the game control the extent of physical contact which is allowed. On the other hand, a foul could be considered outside the rules and therefore, no contract was entered into.

The results of this type of judicial reasoning have led to convictions of assault. Yet many people would also accept that the rules are not taken literally and terms such as the 'professional foul' are a part of the game. Rugby referees have been prosecuted for allowing a situation to develop which caused harm to a player. Whatever the rights or wrongs of these cases, they evidently have far-reaching consequences for the world of sport.

Drug Misuse

Virtually no sport is without the problem of having to tackle the misuse of drugs. The Diane Modahl case illustrated how entwined sport and the law can become. The Portuguese Athletics Federation in June 1994 tested and found the sample positive with an incredibly high reading of 42:1. The British Athletics Federation [BAF] banned the athlete for four years. Modahl appealed and the focus was on the testing procedure and degradation over time which could cause an increase in testosterone. The result was the first time the BAF sport administrators had been sued for alleged defective procedures. Modahl resumed her athletic career.

Violence

Injury is a part of sport though deliberate intent is not normal. Boxing however intends to inflict harm but is accepted so long as it abides by a proper system of rules. Changes to boxing-related law would require an Act of Parliament, which at the moment seems unlikely. Martial arts have to be recognised by Sport England and so far include karate, tae kwon do and jujitsu. Some kick boxing and Thai boxing groups are not recognised. Soccer and rugby have witnessed criminal proceedings from incidents directly related to the sport. An example occurred in 1995 when Duncan Ferguson was convicted, following a head butt against an opponent. He was the first professional soccer player to be imprisoned for an on-the-field assault. Another notable case was Elliot vs Saunders [1994] following a tackle which ended the career of Elliot. Although the case was not won by Elliot, Liverpool FC accepted liability for its employee's wrongdoing.

Players' Rights

Jean Marc Bosman, a Belgian footballer, forced the authorities to address the issue of players' rights to play the game. The European Court of Justice recognised in this case that there was no reason why professional sports players should not enjoy the benefits of the single market and in particular the free movement of workers. This has resulted in national competitions being open to players throughout Europe and has revitalised major European leagues. The new legislation also abolished transfer fees if a player was out of contract.

Influence of television

Television is mostly responsible for the financial boom in football but the reliability of the income is not guaranteed as is demonstrated in the restrictive practices court case against the Premier League, BSkyB and the BBC. The case is about the League's right to negotiate a television deal on behalf of all the clubs; it is claimed individual clubs should have the right to negotiate their own television contracts. If the case goes against the Premier League and in favour of the clubs the bigger clubs will be able to negotiate very lucrative contracts, making even more money available to players.

Players vs Officials

This is a very controversial issue. In the case of Smolden vs. Whitworth and A.N. other' [1996] the court held a referee liable for crippling injuries suffered by Smolden in a colts rugby union game. At the same time Whitworth was cleared of any liability. The laws of the game were changed to allow fewer than eight players in a scrum and to ban contest scrimmaging. The implications for referees, many of whom are voluntary and amateur, are considerable. Are referees to owe a duty of care to clubs in their application of the laws of the game?

Supporters

The attitude and behaviour of supporters has also been controversial in the eyes of the law. The growth of hooliganism in the 1970s and 1980s brought into question the ability of the football clubs to regulate the behaviour of their supporters.

Education

As we have seen, the Education Act 1988 affected physical education within the wider education system. The traditionally decentralised system of education was being challenged by a Conservative government seeking more control. This necessitated cutting the powers of the local authorities. The capacity for schools to manage their own budgets and the introduction of the National Curriculum reinforced a growing centralisation of policies. The new National Curriculum specified in general terms the content of physical education teaching. This went further in 1995 with the government report 'Raising the Game'.

In April 2000 the following Government policy was launched.

Smith and Blunkett launch radical boost to School Sport

Chris Smith and David Blunkett, Education Minister, launched the five point plan to make schools the nurseries of sports stars of the future:

- a new fund of £75 million over two years from the government matched by the Lottery for primary schools to provide 300 new, multi-purpose sports and art facilities for pupils and the wider community
- goal of having 110 specialist sports colleges in place by 2003 with close links to governing bodies of sport and help for talented young people to tie in with the UK Institute of Sport
- establishment of 600 school sport co-ordinators by Sport England, paid for with lottery money, to develop more inter-school competitive games
- developing after-school sport and physical education. The £240 million out-of-hours learning programme funded jointly by the New Opportunities Fund [£160 million] and the standards fund [£80 million] currently supports sport, art, homework and computer clubs outside normal school hours
- encourage World Class Performance athletes to visit a minimum number of schools each year.

In addition the DfES will set up an advisory panel on school playing fields underpinning the government's rules to prevent sales without rigorous consultation. Sales have been cut from 40 a month to 3 with proceeds ploughed back into schools and school sport.

Summary

- The type of political and economic system is crucial in determining the nature of state intervention; centralised or decentralised, capitalism or communist.

Review Questions

1 What are the nine reasons given for explaining National Government Involvement in sport? Choose two and explain in more detail.

2 What advantages are there to sport being free from political control?

3 Briefly explain what Compulsory Competitive Tendering means and give an example of how it can affect sport.

4 Name four ways in which sport and politics have become entwined in the United Kingdom.

5 What does centralised and decentralised mean?

6 How can sport policies help the Government's overall aim of Neighbourhood Regeneration?

7 Outline the main features of the policy 'A Sporting Future for All'.

8 What is meant by the term policy?

9 List 10 wider economic benefits which can result from sport.

10 Fill in the table below.

ORGANISATION	SPORT POLICY	CHARACTERISTICS OF POLICY
DCMS		
Sport England		

chapter 9

Levels of Sport Participation

This chapter investigates the various levels of participation in sporting activities. This will range from the broad base of the pyramid where the main emphasis is on participation, to the apex of the pyramid where the focus is on the standard of performance. For ease of study, society will be categorised into distinct groups based on age, disability, gender, socio-economics, culture and race, and each will be studied in relation to their sporting participation.

We will concentrate on the previous Sports Council's Target groups and the policies developed to increase their levels of physical activity, and try to establish some of the reasons for low participation.

Many of the qualities assigned to sport are well recognised – opportunity for self knowledge, personal achievement, good health, enjoyment, skill acquisition, social interaction, responsibility, development of confidence and so on. We should therefore be concerned that certain sections of the population are missing the chance to benefit from such an enriching experience.

The issue of participation

The need for a more coordinated and fair approach to the provision of sporting activities addresses two main areas:

1 **sports development:** enabling people to learn basic sports skills with the possibility of reaching a standard of sporting excellence.
2 **sports equity:** redressing the balance of inequalities in sport ie, equality of access for everyone, regardless of race, age, gender or level of ability.

Sport England has a sport development continuum:

- **Foundation:** learning basic movement skills, knowledge and understanding; developing a positive attitude to physical activity.
- **Participation:** exercising one's leisure option for a variety of reasons – health, fitness, social.
- **Performance:** improving standards through coaching, competition and training.
- **Excellence:** reaching national and publicly recognised standards of performance.

Firstly it is important to understand the sociological basis for inequality in sport. It is not intended to be a thorough sociological review – merely a tool to help us achieve a greater understanding of the issue.

Fig. 9.1   Sports development continuum model

All men are equal?

In the descriptive sense this is patently untrue: human beings do not possess the same amount of physical, mental or moral qualities. In the prescriptive sense, however, people ought to treat one another with equal respect, dignity and consideration.

Stratification of society

Society can be divided into layers, as are rocks (ie, rock strata). The divisions are based on biological, economic and social criteria, eg, age, gender, race and social class. The dominant group in society, which controls the major social institutions like the media, law, education and politics, can exercise control over the more subordinate groups. This need not be the majority – take the case of previous minority white rule in South Africa. Using this classification, the dominant group in the UK could be described as white, male and middle class; the subordinate groups would be women, ethnic minorities, people with disabilities and belonging to the working class.

Discrimination can occur when opportunities available to the dominant group are not available to all social groups.

Discrimination means 'to make a distinction: to give unfair treatment especially because of prejudice', and it occurs when a prejudicial attitude is acted upon. Discrimination can be **overt**, eg, laws which form part of the structure of a society, such as the former political system of apartheid, or a membership clause for a private sports club. This can be officially wiped out by changing the law, but **covert** discrimination (hidden or less obvious), eg, people's attitudes and beliefs, can be very hard to dislodge.

When subordinate groups in society are discriminated against, their opportunities are limited, including opportunities of social mobility (the pattern of movement from one social class to a higher or lower one). This can also be affected by whether the social system is closed (an extreme example is the Hindi caste system in India), or open (a true egalitarian democracy).

Sport and stratification

Sport is often described by sociologists as a microcosm of society: it reflects in miniature all facets of society. This includes the institutionalised divisions and inequalities which characterise our society. Sporting institutions are equally controlled by the dominant group in society, and stratification in sport is inevitable when winning is highly valued. It is highlighted even more when monetary rewards are on offer.

Sport is often cited as an avenue for social mobility:

- physical skills and abilities – professional sports requires little formal education
- sport may create progression through the education system eg, athletic scholarships
- occupational sponsorship may lead to future jobs
- sport can encourage values such as leadership and teamwork skills, which may help in the wider world of employment.

Although sport for all campaigns are no longer a direct function of Sport England these target groups are still under represented in sport participation. More recently they are being dealt with at governmental level, under the Department for Culture, Media and Sport using the term 'Social Exclusion Groups'.

Social Exclusion
Aspects of Exclusion:

- Ethnicity
- Gender
- Disability
- Youth
- Age
- Sexuality
- Poverty
- Exclusion in rural areas/cities.

Defining Exclusion

The term can be attributed to Rene Lenoir, Secretary of State for Social Action for the Chirac Government [1974].

In the most intensive study of exclusion Europe wide, it is seen as a consequence of unemployment and low income [Roch and Annesley 1998] leading to exclusion from a fair share of social goods and capital in the form of recognition, income and work. Three main causes of changes in social welfare were identified:

- mass unemployment and insecure employment
- family restructuring with a rapid growth of one parent families and workless households
- growing inequality with a group of really poor separated from the rest – an economic underclass.

The UK is considered a liberal welfare régime. Sport was seen by the British Labour Government of the 1970s as "part of the fabric of the social services"[Sport and Recreation White Paper 1975]. Various concepts emerged during the last two decades of the twentieth century regarding the relationship between recreation, welfare, the individual and the community. This culminated in Ravenscroft [1993] using the term 'inclusive citizenship' arguing that access to leisure and recreation should be seen as part of the concept. The Social Exclusion Unit's definition of social exclusion is 'a shorthand label for what can happen when individuals or areas suffer a combination of linked problems such as unemployment, poor skills, low incomes, poor housing, high crime environments, bad health and family breakdown'.

So what about the role sport can play in this situation?

Many studies have been carried out and moves are under way for improving the perception of recreation from a purely utilitarian one to the earlier nineteenth century one which focused more on the wider benefits to society on which the parks and recreation movement began [see chapter 10]. The following organisations are beginning to take a similar stance:

- The Institute of Leisure and Amenity Management
- Sport England
- New Zealand Hillary Commission for Sport
- Council of Europe.

When considering this area you will need to address the following terms:

- **Descriptive:** explain and give examples of how discrimination occurs for the identified groups in society.
- **Reformative:** suggest solutions to the identified problems.

The following table shows a summary of the nature and strengths of the benefits of sport and also the experiences of the excluded groups without direct action by the state or voluntary organisations.

Study Table 9.1. Which groups suffer the worst levels of constraint? What are the major factors restricting:

- **female participation**
- **older people**
- **ethnic minorities.**

Table 9.1: Constraints and Exclusion in Sport and Leisure DCMS

Group excluded	Youth			Poor/ unemployed	Women	Older people	Ethnic minority	People disabled/ learn diff.
Constraint/exclusion factor	Child	Young people	Young delinq.					
Structural factors								
Poor physical/social environment	+	+	++	++	+	+	++	+
Poor facilities/community capacity	+	+	++	++	+	+	+	++
Poor support network	+	+	++	++	+	+	+	++
Poor transport	++	++	++	++	++	++	+	++
Managers' policies and attitudes	+	+	++	++	+	+	++	++
Labelling by society	+	+	+++	+	+	+	++	++
Lack of time structure	+	+	++	++		+		+
Lack of income	+	+	++	+++	+	++	+	++
Lack of skills/personal and social capital	+	+	+++	+++	+	+	++	++
Fears of safety	++	++	++	++	+++	++++	++	++
Powerlessness	++	++	+++	++	++	++	++++	++
Poor self/body image	+	+	++	++	+	+	++	++

the number of + signs shows the severity of particular constraints for particular groups

Constraints and exclusion in sport

These can be broken down into three main categories:

- Environmental/structural [economic, physical and social factors]
- Personal constraints [internal and psychological]
- Attitudes of society and provider systems [policies and managers practices can act as barriers or enablers].

The evidence suggests that

a large numbers of people are affected
b policies such as discount schemes/ adaptations for disability sport will have little impact if managers do not actively promote their facilities and services. The target population [women, ethnic, poor, aged and disabled] must be made to feel secure in attending these venues.

Main constraint factors

- Poverty is constantly being highlighted as the factor that contributes to 'locking people in', accentuating their feelings of isolation and powerlessness.
- Time [quoted by many groups, rich, poor and retired]
- Chronic unemployed [greatest problems of structuring time].

Combinations of aspects of exclusion can be said to lead to double deprivation, for example, being elderly and from an ethnic minority. If exclusion is prolonged in youth it can have lasting effects in terms of playing recreationally, socialising and competing to achieve.

A recent survey by the previous English Sports Council [ESC] [1998] showed that 38% of élite performers from 14 sports were from the professional and managerial social groups compared to 19% of the population. Only 10% were from the semi and unskilled compared to a quarter of the population. The conclusions drawn by the ESC was 'that the opportunity to realise sporting potential is significantly influenced by an individual's social background. So, for example, a precociously talented youngster born in an affluent family with sport loving parents, one of whom has achieved high levels of sporting success, and attending an independent private school has a 'first class' ticket to the sporting podium'.

Better partnerships and joined up thinking

There has been enough evidence to highlight the problems encountered by certain groups and many schemes to counteract them. Pressures to account publicly on schemes have tended to concentrate on short-term outputs rather than long term ones.

Using the formula of dividing outputs by inputs gives a value for money measure. This is only possible where both have been recorded and many schemes do not do this.

Inputs are financial, human or material resources, including time and whether paid or not. Outputs are short-term products, for example, the number of participants in different groups in an event or programme. A specific example would be the number of new clubs or junior or veterans' sections formed.

Outcomes result in:

- sustained changes in provision and its use
- attitudes, for example, accessibility to facilities
- behaviour, for example, increase in participation
- relationships between individuals and organisations, for example, school–community partnerships to the use of school facilities by the community.

Evaluation of public sector programmes

The following suggestions were put forward by Thomas and Palfrey [1996] as being useful markers for evaluating public sector programmes:

- effectiveness
- efficiency
- equity
- acceptability [equal to customer satisfaction]
- accessibility [information, resources etc]
- appropriateness [relevance to need]
- accountability [to public and investors]
- ethical considerations [values and how conflicts will be resolved]
- responsiveness [speed, accuracy, empathy]
- choice.

Problems with earlier government programmes were outlined in 'Bringing Britain together: a national strategy for neighbourhood renewal' [1998]:

- mainstream services not joined up
- initiative-itis – too many programmes to respond to
- too many rules to be met

- lack of co-operation
- too little investment in people
- patchwork policies displace problems to new areas
- poor links beyond the neighbourhood
- not harnessing community commitment
- neglecting what works.

Select a group affected by exclusion and devise a specific programme to cater for their needs.
What recommendations would you make for any new national or local programmes that were to be initiated?

Race

Race is the physical characteristic of an individual, while ethnicity is the belonging to a particular group, eg, religious, lifestyle. Racism is a set of beliefs or ideas based on the assumption that races have distinctive cultural characteristics determined by hereditary factors, and that this endows some races with an intrinsic superiority. The media promotes the popular idea of sport enabling many individuals to 'climb out of the ghetto' as well as lack of equal opportunities and racism in sport. Sport England and governing bodies have sought to encourage non-discriminatory attitudes to combat racism and to open up organisations to equal opportunities.

Examples of racism in sport

In sport, racism can be seen in a system called '**stacking**'. This refers to the disproportionate concentration of ethnic minorities in certain positions in a sports team, which tends to be based on the stereotype that they are more valuable for their physical skills than for their decision making and communication qualities. In American football there has been a tendency to place ethnic players in running back and wide receiver positions. In baseball, until fairly recently, they have tended to be in outfield positions. According to Grusky's theory of **centrality** (1963), this restricts them from more central positions which are based on coordinative tasks and require a greater deal of interaction and decision making. Significantly, coaches who make these decisions are generally white. Sociological studies have revealed the self-perpetuating coaching subculture which exists in American sport (J Coakley, 1994). When existing coaches need to sponsor a new coach, they are likely to select one with similar ideas.

Attempts to overcome racism in sport

'Let's stamp racism out of football'

This was a large scale, national campaign begun in 1993–4, intended to cut racial harassment out of football. It was supported by CRE/PFA (Commission for Racial Equality and Professional Footballers Association) and supporters' groups, the FA, the Football Trust, the Premier and Endsleigh Leagues. In 1994–5, over 10% of clubs took specific action. It is now simply called 'Kick it Out' and has received support from subsequent Sports Ministers. The anti-racism campaigns were initiated by fans themselves culminating in the national campaign. The focus has now shifted to study to what extent racism exists at the 'institutional' level.

It is a recognition that clubs who reap financial benefits of fielding players from ethnic minorities should also show a greater responsibility and consideration for all its customers or members. It was highlighted in the media as a serious issue requiring action, with particular regard to Paul Ince, Mark Stein and Andy Cole. Concern is also felt that ethnic minority players should experience equal opportunities in reaching the administerial levels of the game.

In a recent study by Malcolm and Last at the Centre for Research into Sport and Society at the University of Leicester their findings suggested that at first it would appear at the élite level there are few barriers for players to overcome.

Fig. 9.2 THE PROPORTION OF BLACK PLAYERS AT FOOTBALL LEAGUE CLUBS
Source: singer & friedlander's review 1998/99 season

	1985/86		1989/90		1995/96	
	Nos	**%**	**Nos**	**%**	**Nos**	**%**
White	1332	92.3%	1302	89.5%	1732	88.3%
Black	111	7.7%	152	11.5%	231	11.7%

Compared to the number who claim to be of Afro-Caribbean origin on the General Household survey [1%] they would appear to be well represented and particularly at the Premiership level 17.5% in 1995/96.

Positional Play:

Over a ten-year period 50% of black players played in forward positions. This can mean occupying glamorous positions, high goal scoring and higher transfer fees. Average black players in the Premier League commanded transfer fees £1 million more than white players.

	1985/1986	1989/1990	1995/1996
Goalkeeper	0.9%	0%	1.8%
Fullback	19.8%	15.8%	
Centreback	12.6%	15.2%	28.7%
Midfield	15.3%	12.5%	21.5%
Forward	51.3%	56.5%	47.9%

Fig. 9.3 POSITIONAL BREAKDOWN OF BLACK PLAYERS
Source: Singer & Friedlander's review 1998/99 season

	WHITE	BLACK	DIFFERENCE ±
Premiership	1 377.1	2 317.2	+940.1
Division 1	306.6	571.9	+265.3
Division 2	67.6	106.3	+38.7
Division 3	22.8	28.3	+5.5
All Divisions	475.9	919.5	+443.6

Fig. 9.4 AVERAGE TRANSFER COSTS OF PLAYERS DURING 1995/96 SEASON (£,000s)

However, the main difference occurs in the different career paths taken by black footballers. Few break their way into management positions, for example as directors, as FA committee members and so on. Also few Asian players have broken through into the professional ranks.

ACTIVITY 3

1 **Imagine you are in charge of a football club. What comprehensive measures would you take to eliminate racism from the game?**
2 **Account for why so few black football players break into coaching and managerial positions.**

Education

There has been a tendency for teachers to act upon a stereotype labelling children from ethnic minority groups and developing certain expectations of them. This can be self-perpetuating, as children can internalise these misconceptions and regard the sport side of educational life as the only successful route for them.

Studies of ethnic minority participation in sport

In 1991, the Greater Manchester Conurbation was selected as a region to try to identify the relationship between ethnicity, culture and participation in sport. African, Bangladeshi, Caribbean, Chinese, East African, Asian, Indian, Pakistani and a comparable British white group were studied. The striking results were the **gender** differences:

- to be female and a Muslim, Hindu, or Sikh is likely to result in a lower participation rate. The higher the importance placed on religion, the more this trend increased, as a strong patriarchal structure operates (Carroll and Hollinshead, 1992–3).
- Women in these research studies did express a wish to increase their participation and this should have implications for sport policies.

Respect for **cultures** must also be considered:

- Asian groups do not rate sport and PE as highly as some of the other groups, and there is a lack of role models.
- Some cultural traditions can conflict with active sport participation habits, such as showing parts of the body, sharing changing facilities, attending co-educational classes.

The biggest provider of facilities for all groups was the local authority. Problems the ethnic groups encountered were 'feeling an outsider', racism, and lack of single sex provision.
To summarise the results of the study:

- Sport is generally popular with ethnic groups – the Asian Games attract thousands of people.
- Special assistance is needed.
- Clubs should be supported but integration not forced.
- Information should be available about sport provision.
- Ease of access is important.
- Group leaders who may persuade other members to participate should be encouraged to train.
- Sport development officers from ethnic minorities should be appointed.
- Greater media coverage, such as Channel 4's Kabbaddi have helped to raise the awareness of the general population.

In sport, Verma and Derby [1994] have given a useful overview of participation in sport by ethnic minorities who are educated alongside their white counterparts. They have the same interests in sport but with more limited opportunities of women and girls, particularly acute in Islamic cultures with traditions against body exposure and participation in mixed groups.

Provision of segregated transport and sessions have been successful in supporting short term participation eg, Asian women's swimming, fitness and sport schemes.

Sport England's Demonstration project in Scunthorpe suggested that making leisure linked to health and education a stronger part of lifestyles is a helpful precursor to promoting particular sports programmes [Macdonald and Tungatt 1991].

Football in the Community Scheme involves them as participants as well as coaches and leaders.

Publications from the previous English Sports Council [1997] gives examples of policy planning [Leicester City], the use of Race Relations advisors and customer care [Birmingham], employment schemes [Watford and Southwark].

 **ACTIVITY 4**

Using your knowledge of a local sports centre, explain why sports providers should give special attention to ethnic minority users.

State what factors may be responsible for the lower levels of participation rates by ethnic minority groups and suggest strategies in overcoming these inequalities.

Gender

Gender means the biological aspect of a person, either male or female; gender roles refer to what different societies and cultures attribute as appropriate behaviour for that sex. These can vary from culture to culture and also change historically within a culture. We learn our expected role through a process called **socialisation**, which simply means the learning of cultural values and is equally applicable to table manners! We learn firstly through primary socialisation (mainly from our close family group at an early age), and then through secondary socialisation from the wider world of institutions. What emerges are the terms **masculinity** and **femininity**, in relation to gender roles.

Gender role models are first asserted in children's play and early in primary schools there are clear differences in the preferences of girls for less structured activities.

1 **Write a list of what you consider to be the dominant characteristics of these two gender roles, masculinity and femininity.**
2 **Write a list of the qualities necessary to succeed in sport at a high level.**
3 **Which gender role best fits the sport role model?**

Matters of self -image and body image – 'sports women being portrayed by the media as either muscle bound superwomen or sleek and fit beyond the reach of normal women'.
Historical factors regarding the role of women cannot be discounted.

- Sport was always seen as a male preserve. Males developed and controlled most of the modern day sports.
- Men, as the dominant group in society, denied or limited opportunities for women in the types of sports they could participate in.
- The role of women was stereotypically seen as being the housewife or mother.
- The types of activities women were encouraged to participate in were those considered appropriate to their role and therefore, socially acceptable.
- Middle and upper class ladies in the nineteenth century began to play sports such as golf, tennis, horse riding, archery and so on. These activities were not particularly physically demanding and did not involve physical contact or aggression.
- Activities that females could play socially with males was also highly valued, for example croquet followed by lawn tennis.
- Working class women had the least leisure opportunities of all. (See Chapter 10 for the influence men had on the participation of women in football.)

In **the present day**, opportunities for women have increased in terms of greater independence via more disposable income and transport; availability of more sports, clubs and competitions, more media coverage and women in positions of responsibility in sports organisations. The overiding feature has been the increasing emphasis placed on health, fitness and the stereotypical feminine figure.

This has led major organisations like Sport England and the previous Sports Councils to target women as being under-represented in sport participation. They have actively pursued policies to promote sport/physical activity to this group.

WOMEN IN THE TWENTIETH CENTURY UNEQUAL SPORTING OPPORTUNITY		
REASONS	EVIDENCE	ACTION REQUIRED
• Domestic role • Social stereotyping • Femininity • Sport's association with male characteristics • Sport's association with muscularity • Blurred leisure time • Male traditionally more money, power, transport, leisure • Less role models • Less media coverage	• Inequalities in PE and Sport • Unequal provision of facilities • Lack of variety of activities • Few female coaches/administrators • Resticted club access • Lack of creche facilities • Unequal financial provision • Less participation than men	• Equal provision in school Sport and PE • More facilities for women • Women only sessions/target group • Better links between schools and clubs • Balance of recreational and competitive sport • Widen women's horizons • Media/advertise/publicise • Create positive role models • Promote health related activities • Positive discrimination of female coaches and administrators

The body as a social construct

The notion that the body might be of sociological interest has become popular since the 1980s. This can relate to the 'ideal' shape of women and men.

There are four main perspectives of interpreting the body: medical, social construct, feminist and phenomenological.

- **Medical model:** The body is viewed as a machine that can break down and need repair. This is the dominant model for health and fitness.
- **Social construct model:** This belief holds the view that the way people view themselves and others is not shaped by biology but rather the sort of society in which they live and the sorts of ideas that are popular at any given moment. In a society like ours a thin body shape is likely to offer high status and be sought after. Douglas' work in 1966 showed that where women lived in societies where they were expected to do hard physical labour, larger body sizes for females are preferred and produced, as women seek to match up to these societal expectations.
- **Feminism:** Gendered expectations exist for both males and females though more negative connotations have become synonymous with the female body mainly due to natural bodily functions such as menstruation and shape. This can involve individuals having extreme responses to dieting and exercise.
  These factors lead people to shape their own self-identity and self-image. This can be called a phenomenological approach.
- **Phenomenological:** This approach is interested in how self-image and identity are affected and how they shape notions of the 'normal' body shape. Body shape can be changed by radical dieting, exercise programmes and cosmetic surgery. Individuals often express how different they feel as people when they undergo changes to their body shape that they consider being more acceptable. This approach concentrates on the perception of the individual rather than on the social or collective ideas about the body and body shape.

 **ACTIVITY 7**

Why is aerobics seen as a more acceptable form of exercise for women rather than bodybuilding?

Sexism in sport

Sexism is the belief that one sex is inferior to the other, and is most often directed towards women. It is sometimes based on the idea that women are not best suited to roles which carry prestige and influence. Traditionally women have been denied the same legal, political, economic and social rights enjoyed by men.

Don't underestimate the long-lasting effect of attitudes which are handed down through the generations. Sexism against women operates in sport in numerous ways:

The Barr Sex Test

This requires a sample of cells to be scraped from the inside of a woman's cheek to determine the amount of 'Barr Bodies' present (chromatins). If the count drops below a minimum percentage, the athlete is disqualified. Princess Anne was the only female Olympic athlete who was not required to take this test.

The Sex Discrimination Act (SDA) 1975

This act made sex discrimination unlawful in employment, training, education and the provision of goods, facilities and services; ie, a female should be treated in the same way as a male in similar circumstances.

- Competitive sport is excluded by section 44 of the Act. Separate competitions for men and women are allowed where 'the physical strength, stamina or physique puts her at a disadvantage to the average man'. Problems have occurred where female referees and PE teachers have been denied promotion on the grounds of being a woman, and some successful appeals have been made.
- Private sports clubs can legally operate discriminatory policies, under Sections 29 and 34. After an appeal in 1987, the EC recommended that all clubs which are not genuinely private must remove any barriers which discriminate against men or women.

Women and professional sport

The Womens Sports Foundation (WSF) is a voluntary organisation promoting the interests of women and girls in sport and recreation. There is a network of regional groups and a wide range of activities and events are organised. Their regular publication is 'Women in Sport Magazine'.

Professional sport still tends to favour men, even in activities such as pool, where physical strength differences could be questioned.

Only women who are very dedicated and committed move through from participation to performance sports. Myths and negative stereotypes still abound, and the media give much less coverage to women's sport:

- Surveys have shown that national newspapers give less than 6% of total sport space to women's sport.
- The Women's Sport Foundation found in a 4-week period in 1991, a 90% male bias in photographs and articles in newspapers.
- Television rarely covers women's team games which the majority of school girls play, even though the national teams are internationally quite successful.
- There are more sport competitions for men.
- Financial constraints affect women more than men, as they attract less sponsorship to help with training, equipment, travelling and general fees.

Female power in sports organisations and levels of administration have not matched the rise in female sport participation.

Table 9.2   PERCENTAGE OF MALE/FEMALE ATHLETES AND COACHES IN THE GREAT BRITAIN SUMMER OLYMPIC TEAMS

	% OF ATHLETES		% OF COACHES	
	MALE	FEMALE	MALE	FEMALE
1976	73	27	96	4
1980	68	32	91	9
1984	68	32	96	4
1988	64	36	90	10
1992	61	39	92	8

Official reports of Olympic Games British Olympic Association.

- Few women reach the top levels of coaching: in 1992 there were only eight female coaches at the Olympics, compared with 92 male coaches (see table 9.2)
- Mixed governing bodies, such as swimming, badminton, tennis, riding and cycling all show a poor ratio of female decision makers in proportion to the amount of female participants.

The problem has increased with a more professional and bureaucratic environment, and perhaps reflects the inappropriateness of the male model of sport, women's lack of access to political systems and the poor recruitment mechanisms operating in these institutions.

However, improvements are occurring slowly. The first woman Vice President of the IOC was appointed in 1997.

Female football in the United Kingdom is going professional. The Football Association is to set up a full-time professional league of women's teams from the year 2000. Millions of pounds will be spent, television will screen fixtures, and women players can train full time. Women's football is confirmed as the UK's fastest growing sport.

- 1993 – 500 clubs
- 2000 – 4,500

2003 should establish England's female league. England ladies have a full time coach and 1000 players attend 30 regional centres of excellence.

What could account for this change in attitude by the Football Association?

Female participation in recent years

In 1996 The General Household Survey (GHS) reported that men were more likely to participate in a sport or physical activity than women. 87% of men compared with 77% of women had taken part in at least one activity during the previous 12 months.

The State of Play

- Six out of ten women (58%) compared with seven out of ten men (71%) participate in either outdoor or indoor sport.
- For both genders, walking was the most popular activity with 73% of men and 64% of women having walked at least two miles in the previous year.
- Women are more likely than men to have received tuition (27% compared with 19% of regular participants).

- Over three times as many males as female participated competitively in the previous 12 months (32% of regular male participants in comparison to 10% of regular female participants)
- Men are more likely to be a member of a sports club.
- The greatest difference in participation between men and women are to be found in:
  - Cue sports (7.9% of women and 32.6% of men)
  - Soccer (1% of women and 24.3% of men)
  - Cycling (16% of women and 27% of men)
  - Weight training (6.1% of women and 27% of men)
  - Golf (4.4% of women and 18.8% of men)
  - Darts (3.9% of women and 14.2% of men)
  - Fishing (1.1% of women and 10.3% of men)
- Participation rates for women are higher than men in:
  - Indoor swimming (37% of women and 32.5% of men)
  - Keep Fit/Yoga (29.4% of women and 10.4% of men)
  - Horse riding (4.1% of women and 1.8% of men)

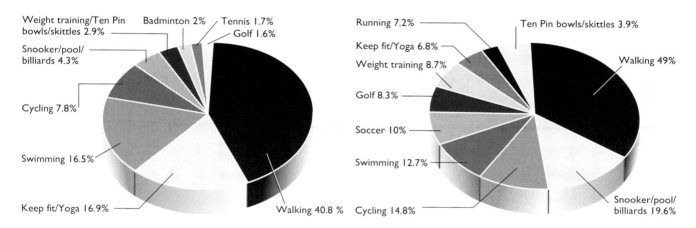

Fig. 9.5   WOMEN'S TOP 10 SPORTS IN GB IN 1996 (GHS)
PARTICIPATION ON ONE OR MORE OCCASIONS IN THE PREVIOUS FOUR WEEKS

Fig. 9.6   MEN'S TOP 10 SPORTS IN GB IN 1996 (GHS)
PARTICIPATION ON ONE OR MORE OCCASIONS IN THE PREVIOUS FOUR WEEKS

The General Household Survey indicates general trends within those sports with the largest participation rates, it fails however to identify significant growth patterns within sports starting from a relatively small participation base.

The following participation figures have been supplied by the respective national governing bodies. They reveal substantial growth in sports which have traditionally been viewed as 'male sports'.

Table 9.3   CRICKET PARTICIPATION RATES IN ENGLAND, OCTOBER 1997–SEPTEMBER 1998

	GIRLS	BOYS
Primary Schools	354,040	625,350
Secondary Schools	138,908	649,067
	WOMEN	MEN
Total No.Club	187	6,697
Participants	4,267	220,784

Table 9.4   FOOTBALL FEMALE PARTICIPATION RATES IN ENGLAND, OCTOBER 1989–SEPTEMBER 1998

SENIORS	1989	1993	1997	1999
Teams	263	400	600	700
Players	7,000	10,000	14,000	17,500
JUNIORS				
Teams	–	80	–	1,000
Players	–	2,000	–	25,000

Table 9.5   GROWTH IN WOMEN'S RUGBY UNION

	1988	1992	1996	1999
Total No. of clubs *	263	400	600	700
No. of youth clubs U16's	7,000	10,000	14,000	17,50
No. of senior registered players	–	80	–	1,000
Other players including students & merit table players	–	2,000	–	25,000

* Many clubs have more than one team.

Kay [1994] confirmed that women are constrained in their leisure time by the needs of housekeeping and caring for dependants and by lower car ownership than men. These effects are stronger for women in the lower socio-economic groups. Women's participation in indoor sport has grown, mainly due to the fitness boom and aerobic classes but is still in decline in terms of outdoor sports. Fears of attack in urban parks and the countryside have been cited as additional problems faced by women in addition to time and transport constraints.

Below are some of the reasons why women have less time for sport than men.

Table 9.6   HOW THE HOURS OF THE WEEK ARE SPENT FOR THE AVERGE MALE AND FEMALE

	FULL-TIME WORKING MALE	FULL-TIME WORKING FEMALE
Work and travel to work	47.2	42.3
Household chores, essential cooking and shopping	12.0	24.5
Other non-discretionary activities (other shopping, caring for children, personal hygiene)	13.9	18.6
Free time	45.9	33.6

Note: this table assumes 7 hours sleep per night

Source: the Henley Centre, 1991

Physical Education Policies

Physical Education policies, through the Government initiatives in the National Curriculum can still appear to show preferences for the competitive team games, sex differentiated programmes and traditional teaching methods that may alienate many girls.

NIKE and the Youth Sport Trust are co-operating in a scheme that aims to support the delivery of Physical Education and sport to girls, 11-14 years of age, in secondary schools.

Women continue to face social, political and prejudicial barriers to sport. Identify as many examples of inequalities as you can under these three categories.

The Brighton Declaration on Women and Sport 1994

In Brighton on the 5–8th May 1994, sport policy and decision makers at both national and international level met. It was organised by the British Sports Council and supported by the British Olympic Committee; 82 countries took part. There was a wish to increase the momentum that had already begun to narrow the gap between male and female sport participation across many continents.

The following points were developed:

1 Equal opportunity should be available through all social structures, and anti-discrimination legislation should be implemented.
2 Facilities should take into account the needs of women, particularly in the provision of childcare and safety.
3 Physical education in particular should take into account the differing approaches and aspirations of girls to active sport involvement, compared with those of boys.
4 Women involved in high performance sport should be supported in terms of competition opportunities, rewards, incentives and recognition.
5 Sporting organisations should develop policies and programmes to increase the number of women coaches, advisers, decision makers, officials, administrators and sports personnel at all levels. Particular attention needs to be directed at recruitment, development and retention.
6 Research and information in sport should equally reflect women's involvement.
7 Action for change must be coordinated. Women themselves can do much to improve the situation but this can only really be effective if they are helped through the social structures operating.

Windhoek Call for Action 1998

By 1998 over 200 organisations worldwide had adopted the Brighton Declaration. In 1998 the second World Conference was held in Windhoek, Namibia, resulting in the Windhoek Call for Action.

From Brighton to Windhoek 'Facing the Challenge' – this is a document produced by the UK Sports Council and the International Working Group on Women and Sport.

The publication charts the progress made from 1994–98 in developing a sporting culture that enables and values the full involvement of women in every aspect of sport. It provides an international overview of strategies and action plans adopted by women and sports in various countries. It considers the challenge that lies ahead and the implementation of the Windhoek Call for Action.

The International Working Group on women and sport [IWG] is an informal co-ordinating body consisting of governmental and non-governmental organisations which was established as an outcome to the Brighton conference with the aim of promoting the development of opportunities for girls and women in sport and physical activity.

What women can do:
* Develop a positive attitude to a healthy lifestyle; find out what is available locally and encourage a friend to go with them; be determined!
* Having developed an interest, join a club to gain access to coaching and facilities; lobby a governing body, local authority and the media to increase availability and opportunity of coaching, facilities, competition and coverage.
* Attend courses to improve career prospects; apply for senior positions; become a coach or administrator; gain relevant qualifications.
* Be aware that family responsibilities can coexist with other aspirations.

Fig. 9.7 WOMEN CAN BE JUST AS AGGRESSIVE AS MEN

The International Working Group on women and Sport [IWG] is an informal co-ordinating body consisting of governmental and non-governmental organisations which was established as an outcome to the Brighton conference with the aim of promoting the development of opportunities for girls and women in sport and physical activity.

What organisations can do:

- Ensure equality of opportunity to acquire sports skills.
- Adopt policies on child care, transport, access, pricing, and programming of facilities.
- Recognise that women do not form an homogeneous group. Women who are disabled, are members of an ethnic minority, have heavy domestic responsibilities, have busy working lives, or school leavers, will all require some specific action directed at them.
- Positive images of women should be widely seen in a variety of sport promotional material and not only the traditionally female sports. This will help provide much-needed role models for young girls.
- Redress inequalities in competition, coaching, financial assistance and improve the talent identification process.
- Review recruitment practices and establish appropriate training and allow flexible working hours.
- Publicise the achievements of women's contributions to sport.

Sport England investigated the specific needs and preferences of women and they came up with five principles called the '5c's':

- promote **confidence**
- a **comfortable** atmosphere
- **choice** of activity
- **convenience** of programmes
- **consultation.**

 **ACTIVITY 10**

What do the four levels of foundation, participation, performance and excellence mean? Discuss the main issues which affect women's involvement in sport.

Sport and people with disabilities

A national survey in 1988 suggested that there are 6.2 million adults with disabilities in Britain; 14.2% of the population. Approximately 5 million have a disability severe enough to limit everyday activities, 1 million have a learning disability, 69% are over the age of 60 and only 5% are under 30 years of age.

Many people experience discrimination which effectively excludes them from active social participation. Yet sport can help to integrate them into the rest of society and add to their quality of life. De Pauw and Gavron [1995] described the barriers as similar to those for women – lack of organised programmes and informal early experiences, role models, access, and of economic, physiological and social factors. In the UK the special needs of disabled athletes are catered for by six national disability sports organisations:

1 The British Amputee Sports Association
2 The UK Sports Association for People with Mental Handicap
3 Cerebral Palsy Sport
4 The British Les Autres Sports Association
5 Disability Sport England, formerly the British Sports Association for the Disabled, probably the most important organisation in the UK for people with disabilities
6 The British Paralympic Association.

A new organisation the English Federation of Disability Sport [EFDS] is to be set up to act as the main supporting and co-ordinating body for the development of sport for all disabled people. This is part of a recently restructured disability sport network. In turn the EFDS has the support and direct involvement of all the major disability sport organisations and will promote a corporate approach at national and regional level to determine priorities and the implementation of programmes.

A growing number of opportunities exist; the National Federation of Gateway Clubs has over 660 affiliated clubs, giving 40,000 disabled people an opportunity to take part in leisure activities.

 **ACTIVITY 11** **Research some of these organisations and pool the information within your group.**

Disability Sport

A term used to suggest a more positive approach towards the participation in sport of disabled people. It covers people with a physical, sensory or mental impairment. The term disability is used when impairment adversely affects performance. Other terms used are handicapped sports; sports for the disabled; adapted sport; wheelchair sport and deaf sport.

Competitive sports have either been designed specifically for the disabled such as goalball, boccia and polybat for the blind or have been modified such as volleyball and wheelchair basketball/tennis.

Fig. 9.8   WHEELCHAIR TENNIS

Current trends tend to focus on the sport rather than on the disability, to allow closer involvement with mainstream sport which previously has not catered for the needs of disabled athletes. The increasing numbers of participation should provide role models for people with disabilities. It is very important that all these organisations, both mainstream and special needs, cooperate and pool their resources in joint programmes of work; the creation of one federated organisation might help the situation.

GOALBALL

- A 3-a-side game.

- Aim is to score a goal by rolling the ball along the floor into your opponent's goal.

- Developed for visually impaired people.

- Features which enable visually impaired people to play:
  The ball has a bell inside
  The playing court has tactile markings
  All players wear eyeshades to ensure that everyone is equal when it comes to visual perception.

- Internationally, Goalball is currently played in 87 countries.

- It is a paralympic sport, and has European and World Championships.

- British Blind Sport (BBS) is the organisation responsible for the sport in the UK.

- Approx. 15 clubs and school teams in the UK.

- The BBS organises 10 one-day tournaments a year, termly national schools competition, national championships and the British Goalball Cup.

- There are at present, no award schemes or coaching courses for Goalball.

POLYBAT

- A one to one hitting game played on a modified table tennis table.

- The table has no net and has panels on the two long sides of the table.

- Aim is to hit the ball past your opponent and off the end of the table or to cause your opponent to lift the ball off the table.

- The name Polybat came from Nottingham Polytechnic who invented the game, and the hitting bat.

- Developed as a result of an increased level of young people who had severe impairments entering the special school system in the 1980's.

- In 1990 the game was introduced into the Disability Sport England National Mini Games and is now played at numerous junior regional events.

- A fast growing sport and is currently played in Brazil, Canada, New Zealand, Spain and the USA.

BOCCIA

- Boccia pronounced 'botcha'.

- Similar to bowls.

- Target game.

- Aim is to get your Boccia balls closer to the jack than your opponents.

- Played individually (1v1), in pairs or in teams of three.

- Originally designed for people with a severe impairment and, in particular for people with cerebral palsy.

- All participants must play from a seated position.

- Played locally in schools and clubs, at regional, national competitions and internationally at the Paralympics and World Games.

- Internationally it is played in over 30 countries.

- An estimated 5000 people play Boccia in UK

- Co-ordinating body is the The British Boccia Federation.

Source: Tutor File Higher Sports Leaders Award British Sports Trust

Integration into mainstream sport does not have to mean participating at the same time as everyone else. It is more significant that facilities, competitions, training and coaching should be equally available to people with disabilities as to able-bodied people.

Inclusiveness

Developing an inclusive approach to all aspects of school life, including physical activity can act as a route into inclusion in the wider community.

The main barrier to the participation of disabled people in the activities of their choice is as much a matter of social attitudes and environmental barriers as their medical condition.

The Inclusion Spectrum, designed by Ken Black, the Inclusive Sport Officer for the Youth Sport Trust, identifies five different approaches:

- **Inclusive:** activities where everyone is included without adaptations or modification
- **Modified Activities:** changes to rules, area or equipment are made in order to include disabled people
- **Parallel Activities:** participants do the same activity but approach the task according to disability
- **Included Activity:** 'reverse integration' where disabled people participate in games adapted specifically with disability in mind such as boccia and goalball
- **Separate Activities:** where disabled people practice an activity on their own or with disabled peers, eg preparing for a disabled sports event.

Fig 9.9 THE INCLUSION SPECTRUM

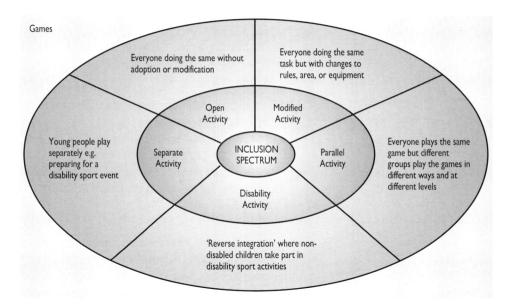

 **Discuss the advantages and disadvantages of completely intergrating disabled people into mainstream sport.**

Improving opportunities

Sport England

Sport England has supported the development of national bodies for disability sport and the appointment of specialised regional and local Development Officers.

The previous Sports Council, Yorkshire and Humberside [1995], showed good practice in governing body schemes in table tennis, canoeing and gymnastics.

Sport England has implemented various projects aimed at improving sporting opportunities for disabled people.

1 The campaign 'Every Body Active' was set up following research which highlighted several major problems encountered by people with disabilities; in particular a lack of awareness amongst maintstream leisure providers and PE teachers as to the special needs of this group of people.
2 The 'Pro-motion' campaign established in 1990 is now a national programme intending to raise awareness, training, liaison and resources.

Much of the Sport England's work is regionally developed and coordination is therefore difficult to achieve. However, several common features emerge:

- promotion and development of training programmes
- inclusion of information about disabled sport in publications
- liaison with relevant organisations
- encouragement of local authorities and governing bodies to consider the needs of people with disabilities
- development of coaching opportunities
- appointment of sport development officers with special interest in this area.

The Sports Council's policy document 'Sport and People with Disabilities' was published in 1993, and is a national statement of intent for which it will be accountable.

The former Conservative government carried out research and published a report, 'Building on Ability'. As a result, the following initiatives were set up:

- the development of a national disability equality training course
- the identification of examples of good practice involving the participation at a local level of young people with disabilities
- a national governing bodies liaison project, involving 40 schemes and promoting integration with 23 governing bodies
- support the Pro-motion programme which seeks to develop sport and recreational opportunities for those with a multiple disability.

Local authorities

Local authorities play a crucial role at local level, because of their leisure departments. The planning and architects departments are also important when trying to build functional and imaginative facilities. When facility tenders are reviewed and renewed under the compulsory competitive tendering regulations, the needs of the disabled must be considered.

10 THERE ARE MANY SPORTS
ADAPTED FOR PEOPLE WITH

Excellence

Excellence in sport performance has grown substantially, both in the number of competitions and variety of activities. The Paralympics (so called because it runs parallel to the Olympics) and the World Championships are the notable examples (see chapter 10).

As knowledge about training, coaching and the input of sport science increases, the performance levels of disabled athletes will undoubtedly improve.

Classification

An attempt to group sport competitors to enable fair competition. This was initially used for sport by gender, where separate competitions developed for men and women, and by weight in sports such as boxing. It is now used to include individuals with disabilities.

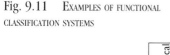 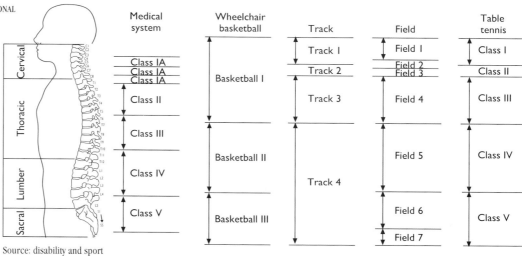

Fig. 9.11   EXAMPLES OF FUNCTIONAL CLASSIFICATION SYSTEMS

Source: disability and sport

CLASS	FUNCTIONAL PROFILES
Class 1	Moderate to severe spasticity – severe involvement of all four limbs. Poor trunk control. Poor functional strength in upper extremities.
Class 2	Moderate to severe spasticity – severe to moderate involvement of upper extremities and trunk. Poor functional strength and control of upper extremities. Propels wheelchair with legs.
Class 3	Fair functional strength and moderate control in upper extremities. Almost full functional strength in dominant upper extremity. Propels wheelchair with one or both arms slowly.
Class 4	Moderate to severe involvement of lower limbs. Functional strength and minimal control problems in upper extremities. Uses wheelchair for daily activities and sports.
Class 5	Good functional strength; minimal control problems in upper extremities. Ambulates on two legs for competition.
Class 6	Moderate to severe involvement of all four extremities and trunk; walks without aids. May use assistive devices for track events.
Class 7	Moderate to minimal hemiplagia. Good functional ability is non-affected side. Walks without aids.
Class 8	Minimally affected hemiplegic or monoplegic. Minimal co-ordination problems. Good balance and is able to run and jump freely.

Note: 1–4 wheelchair for competition, 5–8 ambulatory for competition.

Source: Disability and Sport

Fig. 9.12   CEREBRAL PALSY ATHLETES (USCPAA AND CPN-ISRA) FUNCTIONAL PROFILES

Two types of classification are used:

- **Medical classification:** this developed in the 1940s and was dominant into the 1990s. It was based on the level of spinal cord lesion. It was designed to enable individuals with similar severity of impairment to compete against one another. It was used for wheelchair athletes and amputees. Many other disability sport federations adopted this system resulting in a multiple classification system.
- **Functional classification:** an integrated classification system that places emphasis on sport performance by disability groupings rather than by specific disability. This has enabled disability sport to move on from its original rehabilitation base to élite competitive sport. Wheelchair basketball was the first Paralympic sport to experiment with this system. This system demands that athletes be evaluated on what they can and cannot do in a particular sport.

Facilities

Facilities are gradually improving for disabled users, partly under the Safety at Sports Grounds Act 1975, and also through a growing desire to provide access. The programming of activities and the attitude of staff are also important considerations.

Outdoor facilities are increasing provision, for example, those run by the Calvert Trust and Scope. Several important sports centres exist, such as the Ludwig Guttman Sports Centre at Stoke Mandeville and the Midland Sports Centre for the Disabled in Coventry.

- **Make a checklist to see how a local leisure facility is designed to cater for the needs of the disabled people in your area.**
- **Once you have agreed a comprehensive list, visit a variety of facilities (ie, indoor, countryside, water) and review their effectiveness.**
- **Suggest effective modifications which could be made.**

Future Trends:
[adapted from de Pauw]

Sport for All

- Increasing numbers of individuals with disabilities will participate at all levels in the sport pyramid.
- Equity issues will continue to be addressed for groups who suffer the lowest levels of participation, particularly females and low income groups.
- Public awareness and acceptance of disability sport will increase.

Elite level

- Structured competitive programmes will operate from local, regional, national and international levels.
- Co-ordination between sport organisations concerned with disability sport with those that are more sport specific.
- Disabled athletes will continue to specialise in sport events, with classification and competitions becoming sport specific. This will result in improved standards of performance.
- Disabled people will participate more as coaches and officials especially as current athletes retire from competition.

Summary:
- Societal attitudes are changing towards wider participation and competition by athletes.
- The original rehabilitation purpose through sport has given way to sport for sports sake.
- The Olympic sport movement will continue to shape the future direction of disability sport.
- Classification, drug testing, advances in technology, improved training and coaching. techniques and sports medicine will further influence disability sport.

Sport for people aged 50 and over

Statistics show that over 50% of the adult population will be over 45 in the year 2000. This age group is increasingly affluent as personal pensions have improved during the twentieth century and people may have more disposable income. They are also generally more active and healthy than ever before, and an increase in physical activity can help to prevent the inevitable onset of ageing. Approximately three slightly strenuous sessions per week of 20 minutes duration are advised. Medical advice may need to be sought, particularly if the person has not participated in physical activity for some time. The important checks are cardiovascular, respiratory and orthopaedic.

In 1990 Allied Dunbar produced a survey on the physical capabilities of over 2,000 men and women; it was published in 1992. Research some of the findings. (This could link in with your Exercise Physiology unit.)

Social benefits of sport are also stressed, because this can be a time of dramatic change for many people. Some may become widowed; some may retire or be made redundant, and family obligations may change. Active lifestyles can help people overcome great social change. Thus, this group of people comprises a potentially rich market for sport.

Since the Sports Council's campaign, '50+ All to Play For' in 1983, more activities have been promoted for this age group. Here are some of the most popular ones:

1 Indoors – keep fit; aerobics; dance; carpet and short mat bowls; table tennis.
2 Outdoors – walking/rambling; cycling; jogging; archery; canoeing; golf; tennis; swimming; cricket; hockey; bowls.

Many other more adventurous activities are also enjoyed.

Select some of the activities mentioned and suggest why they are particularly suited to people over 50. Think about the physiological and social aspects of the activity.

Competitive days need not be over; many sports have veteran and 50+ sections. Other ways of getting involved are as sports leaders, such as coach, referee, club officials. Organisations which should be involved in developing this kind of activity are: local authority departments responsible for sport and recreation; sports centres and swimming pools; adult education classes; the national and regional sports councils; the governing bodies of sport.

Sport for young people

First of all we must recognise that not all young people share common lifestyles; they may have different socio-economic backgrounds, parental attitudes, social experiences and so on. Youth is often seen as a transition from school and childhood to work and adulthood. Individuals who struggle with this transition often become isolated from the main community and 'drop out', become deviant and when considered in larger numbers can form an underclass. This group will experience exclusion from society. Sport participation is mostly a result of early positive experiences in physical education curricula and recreational activities.

As early as 1960 the Wolfenden Report was concerned that the lack of provision for sport in the United Kingdom was poorer than in other European states and this led to the '**post school gap**' which results in a drop in participation on leaving school.
Some constraining factors are:

- the concentration in clubs on the talented youngsters
- the tradition of single sport clubs in the United Kingdom as opposed to more multi-sport clubs in Europe.

List other possible reasons why young people may 'drop out' of sport on leaving school and suggest ways in which to combat this.

Physical activities are promoted by a wide range of individuals and agencies, such as:

- the education system, in particular the physical education programme
- sports clubs and governing bodies
- play workers
- the youth service
- local authorities.

It is necessary for these agencies to co-ordinate their efforts. For example, national governing bodies and schools associations need to jointly plan programmes which will support a common youth sport policy.

In previous years, the Sports Council targeted the age band 13–24 years. However, recent research (General Household Survey) suggested that low participation was not the problem, but that young people do not play as many sports as children. However, young females still participate less than their male counterparts. On leaving school, more casual sports are enjoyed, alongside adventure sports and health related activities.

Consider the following groups of young people and suggest some of the advantages and disadvantages they face in terms of sports participation:

- **full time education**
- **full time employment**
- **unemployed**
- **young women**
- **young mothers**
- **young people in rural areas.**

National Junior Sports Programme

The National Junior Sports Programme was launched in February 1996 by the Sports Council, working alongside the Youth Sports Trust. Its aim is to encourage young children from the age of four to become involved in sport. It will provide kit, coaching and places to play, and the more talented performers can be identified from a wider base. It will be a rolling programme and many teachers will be trained. The advantage is that it can fit neatly into the current physical education system. There are four main elements:

- Top Play (4–9-year-olds)
- Top Sport (7–11-year-olds)
- Champion Coach
- Top Club (11 years+)
- Top Link

Due to a change of sponsor, Ecclesiastical Insurance, the Youth Sport Trust has expanded its TOP family to include the latest addition – Ecclesiastical Insurance TOP Link which will encourage secondary school pupils to develop sport festival days for their primary feeder schools. The main aim of this initiative is to develop vital links between primary and secondary schools.

Funding will come from the National Lottery, Sport England, Youth Sports Trust and business sponsorship (£14 million in total).

More recent initiatives have come from the Health Education Authority [1998] which targets girls aged 12–18 years, youth of low economic status and adolescents aged 16–18 including those from ethnic minorities, with disabilities, or clinical conditions like obesity, diabetes or depression.

Champion Coaching, initiated by the National Coaching Foundation, now Sports Coach UK, in association with governing bodies, developed programmes of taster courses for 11-14 year olds but although it has seen success the youngsters appear to emerge from the more privileged socio-economic groups.

Active Schools and Active Communities, the latest programmes of Sport England, require local authorities, schools and clubs to plan and work together.

- **active schools:**   forms the foundation
- **active communities:** looks at breaking down the barriers to participation and considers equity issues
- **active sports:**   links participation to excellence eg, millennium youth games
- **World Class England:** operates start, potential, performance, events.

They are intended to act as building blocks and are not necessarily linear. They complement the concept of the participation pyramid of foundation, participation, performance and excellence.

There have been growing calls for more 'inclusive' physical education programmes. These programmes need to cater for the diversity of students, their needs and the schools they attend. It is possible that the Government focus on competitive team sports, since the publication of 'Sport: Raising the Game' may not be successful as studies suggest these are not the sporting activities which attract this age group [Coalter 1999]. Sustaining the broader choice at school is likely to support lifelong participation.

In the New Opportunities Fund, Lottery fund money will be available for schemes that encourage the value of sport as character building and diversion such as summer play schemes, after school clubs and so on.

The National Junior Sport Programme is intended to support the National Curriculum as an additional resource for teachers.

Coaching for Teachers is a joint initiative funded by Sport England and co-ordinated by the National Coaching Foundation with support from BAALPE and PEA [Physical Education Association] to involve teachers in extra-curricular activities.

Youth and Delinquency

A large body of literature has developed worldwide on this issue suggesting increasing concern at governmental levels. The general consensus appears to be that sport:

- increases self esteem, mood and perception of competence and mastery, especially through outdoor recreation
- reduces self destructive behaviour [smoking, drug use' substance abuse, suicidal tendencies]
- improves socialisation both with peer group and adults
- improves scholastic attendance and performance.

Schemes:
Several schemes run to help this particular group but usually are not long enough and are participated in voluntarily suggesting those more hardened offenders will not benefit. An experience of a few days to a few weeks may in the short term be of benefit but if the individuals return to the same physical and social complex or deprivation the old values and behaviour patterns will re-emerge.

Sport therefore may not be the solution but may be part of the solution.

Socio-economic groups

The term 'social class' can refer to a person's income, status in society, family background and educational experiences. The development of sport in the nineteenth century was initially in the powerful and influential hands of the upper and middle classes. The working class male stamped his presence on the new mass spectator sports of football, boxing and horse racing, but administrative control was still in the hands of the middle classes. The working classes had to wait for the provision of recreational rights and public facilities.

Table. 9.7   PARTICIPATION IN SPORT BY SOCIO-ECONOMIC GROUP (GHS, 1998)

SOCIO-ECONOMIC GROUP	PERCENTAGE PARTICIPATING IN AT LEAST ONE SPORT IN LAST 4 WEEKS			
	1987	1990	1993	1996
Professional	65	65	64	63
Manager	52	53	53	52
Junior non-manual	45	49	49	47
Skilled manual	48	49	46	45
Semi-skilled	34	38	36	37
Unskilled	26	28	31	23
Total	**45**	**48**	**47**	**46**
Difference between professional and unskilled	39	37	33	40

Much research has concluded that lower socio-economic backgrounds do lead to a lower participation rate in sporting activities. This can be attributed to a variety of reasons:

- the cost of facilities
- the dominant middle class culture which operates in sport centres
- the lack of leadership roles
- a general lack of health
- the lower self esteem of low income groups (in particular the unemployed) which can encourage feelings of helplessness, inferiority, and isolation from major social institutions.

A working class 'sub culture' can operate where norms and values are different from the dominant group, and are passed down from one generation to the next. This has been termed the 'cycle of poverty' – where one form of deprivation tends to reinforce another. It is a very complex area which the sport initiatives need to address if they are to be successful in mobilising this section of the community.

Social exclusion does not just affect recreational participation: its effect is also felt at the élite level and its costly preparation training.

We have looked at categories of people within society and particularly at the participation base of the sports pyramid. Now it is time to discover how some people manage to extend beyond the recreational and performance end of the sports continuum, and onwards to sporting excellence.

1 **Summarise the main factors which result in the socially excluded groups having less opportunities to participate in physical recreation and sporting activities.**
2 **What 'action plans' could governing bodies and other relevant organisations put in place to improve this situation?**

Summary

- The broader the base of sport participation, the greater the talent pool from which to draw in order to increase the chances of sporting excellence.
- Unequal access to the 'sport for all' ideal will negatively affect the sports pyramid.
- Sport initiatives must take careful note of the complex nature of the various groups they seek to help.

Review questions

1 Draw the Sport Participation Pyramid or sport development continuum and briefly explain each stage.

2 What is meant by the term 'the dominant group' in society and how can this group affect sporting opportunities?

3 How can sport be an avenue of social mobility?

4 What does the term 'stacking' refer to in sporting situations?

5 Suggest four strategies organisations can implement in order to improve the participation of women in sporting and recreational activities.

6   Why is the 50+ age group a suitable target for sports organisations to target in order to increase their levels of participation in sporting and recreational activities?

7   What are the five main stages of the National Junior Sports Programme and which organisations in particular are involved?

8   What does the term 'Social Exclusion' mean and what measures can be taken to address the issues?

9   What is the significance of the emergence of the term 'Disability sport'?

10   What is the significance of the term 'Inclusiveness' when referring to disability and sporting participation?

The History of Sport

chapter 10

43-450AD	Roman Britain
450-613	Anglo Saxon invasion
613-1017	Division into Kingdoms
1017-1066	Danish Rule
1066	William I
1087	William II
1100	Henry I
1135	Stephen
1154	Henry II
1189	Richard I
1199	John
1216	Henry III
1272	Edward I
1307	Edward II
1327	Edward III
1377	Richard II
1399	Henry IV
1413	Henry V
1422	Henry VI
1461	Edward IV
1483	Edward V
1483	Richard III
1485	Henry VII
1509	Henry VIII
1547	Edward VI
1553	Mary I
1558	Elizabeth I
1603	James I
1625	Charles I
1649	Commonwealth
1660	Charles II
1685	James II
1689	William III & Mary
1702	Anne
1714	George I
1727	George II
1760	George III
1820	George IV
1830	William IV
1837	Victoria
1901	Edward VII
1910	George V
1936	Edward VIII
1936	George VI
1952	Elizabeth II

Fig. 10.1   HISTORICAL DATES

So far we have examined the present day situation regarding sport and physical education. We have occasionally referred to how the past has influenced the present. Now it needs a more in-depth analysis. In other words, how and why have we arrived at the present day situation?

We will:

- chart some social changes which have been influential to our everyday lives and see how recreational activities have been affected
- apply knowledge gained in order to analyse a variety of physical recreational and sporting activities.

Whatever we discover about sport must not be seen in isolation. The system of sport influences and is in turn influenced by the social system – economic, geographical, educational, social and political factors.

You will need to have a basic grasp of British history. It is not useful to refer to Regency or Victorian times if you have no idea of where they fall in the overall scheme. English Heritage has produced a useful ruler charting the different eras in chronological order – see fig 10.1. Looking at the origins of sports and pastimes, it is clear that they were initially *functional*, eg, for military and hunting purposes. When societies depended less on survival, many activities took on a recreational dimension, such as children's play and the feasts and festivals which often had religious associations, either pagan or Christian (see fig 10.2). Our main focus is from the Victorian era to the present day though it is useful to have an understanding of previous eras.

Fig. 10.2   FUNCTIONAL AND RECREATIONAL ORIGINS OF SPORT

Medieval England

The years between 1066 and 1485 are generally known as the Middle Ages. This period saw a change in fortunes for most people in England. The first half was prosperous allowing for the development of churches and universities. The bulk of the population were peasants in rural areas but there was an increase in the townsmen who were mainly merchants, lawyers and doctors. Their wealth increased as trade was made possible, due to fewer private wars between the different lords. The townsmen were above the serfs because they were free but below that of the lords, so they formed the beginnings of the middle class, who were to later grow even more powerful. They formed guilds which were special organisations to safeguard the rights of craftsmen and merchants to practice their trade within the town walls. As the

Fig. 10.3   Frontispiece to the Book of Falconrie, 1498

middle class grew richer the kings began to choose them as their lawyers and officials. Their sons would then study in order to be able to make their way in the world. The Church was responsible for the basic education available. Boys were taught to read and write in Latin. Bishops established cathedral schools. Much of this was to change after the Reformation.

Festivals and feasts played an important part of life in the Middle Ages. Much recreational pastimes took place at this time. The horse was a significant feature for the nobility, who used them for hunting and the tournaments (see above). Military activities were favoured over purely recreational ones and archery became a compulsory aspect of young men's lives. Some sports and games were banned as they were becoming so popular that it was feared they would interfere with men's archery practice, essential for the defence of the realm.

Festivals were held in honour of events that were important to people's daily lives; eg, the change of seasons, harvest, and the summer and winter solstices. As the pagan customs were taken over by the Church they were given new religious meanings. 'Holy days' were put aside for feasting, which is how the word 'holiday' originated. In many countries towns and villages had their own special festivals and saints' days which celebrated the death of a saint.

Easter is the most important feast of the Christian Church, and its date fixed the dates of the holy days connected to it – Lent, Shrove Tuesday, Ash Wednesday. Shrove Tuesday is the last day before the fasting of Lent, and was a time for feasting and fun. Recreations took place within a wide social pattern, and activities included mob football, wrestling, animal baiting, skittles and bowls. The minstrels provided entertainment, and were dancers, acrobats, composers and performers of music.

Summary: Activities were:

- occasional, due to limited time and energy
- simple in nature and orally passed down through the generations
- affected by prohibitions if considered unnecessary to the society by the ruling class
- functional first, particularly for hunting and defence
- participated in during feasts and festivals as outlets for leisure pursuits
- mainly local in nature due to lack of mobility and frequent wars.

The Tudor and Stuart era (1485–1714)

The Tudors   England changed rapidly under the Tudors. Religious disputes developed as people could not agree on how the Church should be run. Some wanted services similar to the old Catholic ways, while others wanted a 'purer' type of service. These people became known as Puritans; see below.

Under Henry VIII's rule, there was greater prosperity and more time for cultural pursuits like music, literature and the theatre. Henry was a great sports lover, and created one of the liveliest courts in Europe. He participated in all-day hunts and wrestling, and ordered his own real tennis court to be built at Hampton Court (it is still well worth a visit). Access to education, equipment and facilities enabled the upper classes the privilege of exclusive recreational activities.

Under Elizabeth, England was growing richer. Games and sports flourished at this time. This was the age of the Renaissance gentleman, who was knowledgeable, partook in the appropriate physical activities, and was appreciative of all art forms.

The mass of the population also enjoyed their traditional pastimes. Activities like mob football continued to develop, allowing for conjugal and territorial conflicts to be sorted out in an enjoyable manner. They were often disorderly and violent, allowing energies to be vented. Many activities were still regional, were played with a few simple rules (or none at all) and were passed down to future generations by word of mouth.

The baiting and killing of animals was also a great treat. People lived in harsh conditions, and held different attitudes about the treatment of animals compared with modern values. Activities like cock fighting, bull baiting, bull running were all popular. They originated in rural areas but were also enjoyed in the towns; there is an account of bull running in London as late as 1816. Again however, there were distinct social class divisions in physical activities.

Fig. 10.4   STAGHUNTING WAS A POPULAR
PASTIME DURING THE SIXTEENTH AND
SEVENTEENTH CENTURIES

The Stuarts   After the death of Elizabeth I, James VI of Scotland (the son of Mary Queen of Scots) became James I of England. He had been brought up a Protestant, and in 1617, issued a declaration known as the 'Book of Sports' which encouraged the notion of traditional pastimes, so long as they did not interfere with church attendance.

Following the civil war and execution of Charles I (James I's son) in 1646, Oliver Cromwell was made protector of Britain. He was intent on establishing Parliamentary rule allied with a Puritan lifestyle. Puritanism particularly objected to:

- practising sport on a Sunday
- inflicting cruelty on animals
- the idleness, drinking and profanity generally associated with sport and the public houses.

The effect of the Puritans on the development of sport was to be significant. They believed that people should concentrate on working hard and praying for salvation, and were opposed to recreational activities which they considered as sinful and a waste of time. As many of the traditional activities took place after church services on a Sunday, and many derived from pagan traditions, they came under fierce attack from the Puritans.

Cromwell failed to unite all the different factions, and Charles II returned as monarch in 1660. This period was known as the Restoration. Charles II was in favour of many sports. His Court enjoyed a lifestyle of ease, affluence and leisure; they occupied themselves lavishly on sporting pursuits, and there was an immediate revival of the 'courtly mould'. The Restoration helped to restore many of the previously banned popular activities, but never again to their past glories. The Cotswold Olympian games were revived by Robert Dover, who was both a supporter of the athleticism of the gentry but also longed for a return to 'merrie England', where all social classes had enjoyed recreations together. This was an annual sports event which was held with activities for the gentry and the peasantry. However, the influence of Puritan rule continued to be felt, and many recreational pursuits were slow to revive.

Summary:
- traditional sports and pastimes experienced confusing and changing conditions
- Tudor times allowed all classes to enjoy their recreation
- Puritanism greatly curtailed many activities establishing a new moral tone to society
- there was some regaining of pastimes but never again was the 'merrie England' concept to emerge.

The Hanoverian era (1714–1790)

The Industrial Revolution began in England in the middle of the 1700s and developed over a hundred years. It signified a dramatic movement of people from rural areas to the towns. Farming had become less important as small farms had been taken over by large landowners as a result of the enclosure system. The efficiency of the urban factories also put many people employed in the cottage industry out of work. Factory work required unskilled workers, who worked long hours in cramped, dirty conditions six days a week; young children were often employed in difficult and dangerous conditions.

Moving from rural areas to the new towns and cities had an enormous impact on people's lifestyles, not least on their recreational pursuits.

- Their previous games were increasingly difficult to accommodate, for example, mob football.
- Space was at a premium and so were facilities, so there was to be a shift in emphasis from a participation base to a more spectator based pursuits.
- The economic conditions of people had changed, and their long working hours also curbed their opportunities for recreation.

Some activities such as cricket, racing, rowing and pugilism (forerunner to boxing) had already begun their first phases of organisation. Rules developed in activities which began to occur more frequently, where the upper classes had control and when the moral climate within society began to change. Sports clubs and governing bodies developed to meet the recreation needs of 'Old Boys' who had left their public school and university and wanted to continue participating in sport. Evidence for this:

- the publication of the Racing Calendar from 1727
- the formation of the Jockey Club in 1752
- the rules for cricket, which were first drawn up in 1727.

In the eighteenth century, the Methodists continued the Puritan work ethic; they strengthened the attack on popular sports, believing that sport and drinking on a Sunday would lead to an after-life in hell. The violence associated with many of the pastimes, like wrestling, football and animal sports was believed to be the cause of social unrest; employees would use them as an excuse to miss work, at a time when eighteenth century employers required a more disciplined workforce in the mills.

Victorian Britain

Victoria became Queen in 1837. Her reign was a period of dramatic social change, which is reflected in the development of games and sport during the nineteenth century.

The working class Under Queen Victoria's reign, social reformers campaigned for improvements in the physical and mental health of workers in society.

Parliament passed many laws and reforms to address the problems of women and children being employed in factories under terrible conditions and for long working hours, eg, the Reform and Factory Act 1832, the Ten Hours Act 1847 and the Factory Act 1878. The custom of a half-day Saturday began early in her reign, followed by the movement for early closing for shop workers on Wednesdays.

Factory owners created factory sports facilities and sponsored work teams. The development of the railways enabled them to send their workers on recreational trips, such as to the seaside. Employers hoped to gain the goodwill of their workers, increase morale and encourage the moral benefits of participating in team games.

From the 1870s onwards, there was a move to encourage a healthy, moral and orderly workforce, illustrated by the provision of parks, museums, libraries and public baths. Sport developed into an important part of working life. The Municipal Reform Act 1835 led to the building of parks in the towns and cities; the general public were encouraged to use these parks for recreational use after 1870. The reasons for providing parks were:

- to improve the health of the population
- to discourage crime on the streets
- as part of the Temperance movement, to wean people away from the evils of alcohol and gambling
- to instil morality in workers by following the rules of rational, organised sport
- to demonstrate a sense of social justice.

The skilled workforce gradually shifted their attentions and interests away from the traditional popular sports, taking up pastimes such as reading and quieter exercise in the park:

The decline of traditional sports, especially those which involved fighting, was not simply a question of pressure from well-organised groups of evangelicals and businessmen; in addition to the agitation from abolitionists there was evidence of a gradual shift in public taste, especially amongst the literate and more highly skilled elite of working people themselves.
(R. Holt).

By 1900, working people were heavily involved in sporting activity. There was a continuity between the traditional and modern sports; bowls, darts, billiards, fishing, pigeon racing and dog racing provided sporting entertainment.

Sport for the upper classes

The upper classes were wealthy and powerful, possessed vast tracts of property and dominated Parliament well into the nineteenth century. They enjoyed a life of leisure, and were waited on by an army of servants. The aristocracy took part in local sports and affairs, usually in the form of patronage of prize fights (forerunner to boxing) and pedestrianism (road walking). A **patron** is a person who sponsors any kind of artist or athlete from their own private funds. Patronage tends to occur amongst a privileged class within a hierarchical society. Wealthy aristocrats who wanted to be associated with new styles and trends, would sometimes spend large amounts of money on sporting events and particular athletes. It was an age where some aristocrats could lead and others would follow. Examples are:

- the Duke of Cumberland's association with racing and prize fighting
- Lord Orford and coursing
- the Earl of Derby and cock fighting, and the hunt.

A group of patrons would join together and form an association, eg, the Pugilistic Club, which would then organise the sport. When patrons withdrew their funds, preferring to sponsor different, perhaps more elite, sports, the effect was similar to modern day commercial sponsors pulling out of sports events; it usually led to a decline in the activity. With regard to animal sports, on the one hand they supported the ban on cock fighting, while maintaining their own passion for fox hunting; another example of the powerful safeguarding their own interests?

Fig. 10.5   PRIZE FIGHTING, c.1840

The French Revolution had shown the possible results of a breakdown in relations between the aristocracy and the ordinary people. The English gentry were not now so confident of the complete acceptance of the respect shown them by the lower classes.

The new rich (or nouveau riche) who emerged from the Industrial Revolution, became a strong 'middle class' section of society. They wished to emulate the upper classes by buying old estates, educating their children in the established public schools, and establishing their own recreations which would separate them from the working classes. They also brought Christian morality to their recreation.

Inns and pubs

The inn had always been a social rural meeting place, and was used as a stopping place for the gentry on long journeys. A tradition of games developed, which was encouraged by the inn-keepers to increase their business; examples are fives, rackets, boxing, coursing, quoits. Many of the new sports' clubs met in pubs, and they formed mutually beneficial partnerships:

- The village cricket teams would often use the field next to the pub.
- The hunt would have their stirrup cup at the pub followed by dinner.
- Liquor tents would be provided by publicans at sporting events.
- Bowling greens and boxing rings were built on to pubs, and pubs often organised a football team.

Those associated with sports were often regulars at the inns, so it was in the interests of the publican to encourage sport.

The English alehouse had to adapt to the new urban recreational needs. The pub became a focal point for workers trying to maintain a sense of identity, which was being eradicated in the new urban culture. As early as 1879, there were strings of clubs in Blackburn which were the culmination of the formalising of street corner teams. Boxing took over from the previous animal baiting sports of cock fighting and ratting.

Religion

The Victorian era was a climate of suppressing vice and encouraging religion and virtue. Non-conformism and the Protestant ethic became more firmly entrenched. Sports became less brutal, gambling was driven underground and there was a decline in blood sports.

Muscular Christianity

Muscular Christianity was an evangelical movement, and Charles Kingsley was one of its most influential exponents. Kingsley helped to combine the Christian and the chivalric ideal of manliness. It was the return of the Platonic concept, the 'whole man'. It improved one's ability to be gentle and courteous, brave and enterprising, reverent and truthful, selfless and devoted.

Kingsley believed healthy bodies were needed alongside healthy minds. Neglect of health was as lazy as a neglected mind. He also led the hygienic movement which was to have a deep effect on the working conditions of the poor.

There was little or no support for sport for its own sake at this time; sport should increase physical health and military valour, and create Christian soldiers. It was a fusion of physical with moral training.

Evangelical developments were directly linked with two philosophies – the Muscular Christians were promoting what the non-conformists were sceptical of:

1 Muscular Christians regarded cricket, boating and football as positive recreation.
2 The Church was attempting to attract workers from the pubs by forming alternative social clubs, such as Hand in Hand clubs.

Eventually there was a strong link with the club development of working class sport, particularly football; eg,

- Barnsley: 1887, Rev Preedy appointed.
- QPR: 1881, Rev Young appointed.
- Aston Villa: 1874, a Wesleyan Chapel built.

In Birmingham approximately a quarter of football clubs were explicitly connected to religious organisations between 1870 and 1885.

The YMCA

The YMCA is a non-sectarian, non-political Christian lay movement. Its aims are to develop high standards of Christian character through group activities; improve the spiritual, social, recreational and physical life of young people. It began in London in 1844, led by George William, and initially concentrated on young men in the drapery and other trades. On the construction of the YMCA Gym at Liverpool in 1887, William claimed:

'The aim of the founders was not to furnish the public of Liverpool with increased facilities for athletic exercise, or intellectual development, important as these may be in themselves; but to multiply the number of Christ's true followers among the young men of our city, and to aid in strengthening their Christian character.'

'No sport on Sunday'

The proclamationists and muscular Christians were united by their desire to observe Sunday as a day of complete rest, without physical activity. This signified a slow development of working class sports, as workers were prevented from joining the elite sports, and parks were closed on Sundays. Wealthy people, who usually had private facilities, seemed to escape from the Sunday ban on sport; golf, tennis and croquet were regularly played on Sundays.

Alternative Sunday pastimes were encouraged by the muscular Christians, such as cycling, rambling and boating. The bicycle had revolutionised the English Sunday, and the clergy might with advantage arrange short services for cyclists passing through their parishes.

 **ACTIVITY 1**

What constituted the basis of Sabbatarianism, Evangelism and Protestantism and what influence did they have on working class leisure?

Youth and Religion

Major British youth movements admitted unlimited numbers of children, adolescents and young adults with the aim of promoting some sort of moral code of living. They also allowed for competitive activities and achieving awards and badges. The invention of adolescence as an age- defined social cohort segregated the young from adult status and created a social problem whose solution became the provision of adult supervised leisure pursuits. The middle classes were to use the combination of Evangelical Christianity, public school manliness, militarism and imperialism to instill normative values in the working classes.

The last decades of the nineteenth and beginning of the twentieth century saw the arrival of all the major British youth movements. This time was characterised by increasing economic and social unrest.

At home:

- Expanding influence of socialism
- Growing organisation of labour and the Labour Party
- Growing middle class fears of internal social change

Abroad:

- German naval developments
- Industrial competition from America and Germany

This led to a renewed cultural and social emphasis being placed by the ruling élite on the question of national unity. The gradual loss of control by the established church led to the middle classes organising the leisure of working class adolescents. Youth movements were seen as a way to curb increasing juvenile restlessness.

We will look at the Boys' Brigade, the Scout Movement and Girl Guides.

The Boys' Brigade

This movement successfully demonstrated that voluntary youth movements could reinforce the discipline of the schoolroom and work place. The movement began in Glasgow in 1883 founded by William Alexander Smith. It became a national organisation after 1885. His influences had been:

- involvement in the College free church
- the 1st Lanarkshire Rifle Volunteers and
- a need to discipline the rowdy working class boys attending his Sunday mission school.

It must also be stressed that the cultural superstructure provided by the Bible Classes and YMCA helped to make this movement possible.

One of the original members of Smith's first Glasgow company wrote:

"when we reached thirteen most of us felt we were too big for the Sunday School and there was a gap of a few years until we were able to join the YMCA at seventeen. To fill this gap Captain Smith formed the Boys' Brigade. During that gap period many working class boys ran wild, became hooligans and street corner loafers." Smith also felt that uniformed organisation would appeal to a sense of patriotism and martial spirit as well as being used primarily for a religious end. Boys were only admitted if they attended Sabbath School and punctuality and regular attendance were vital. The following table highlights the membership composition of the early movement. They were drawn mainly from the respectable working class section of Glasgow.

Table 10.1 1st GLASGOW ENROLMENT FIGURES, 1890–1895 (PARENTAL OCCUPATION)

	1890– 1891	1891– 1892	1892– 1893	1893– 1894	1894– 1895	TOTAL	%
Skilled manual*	17	2	5	6	6	36	72
Lower-middle+	4	2	6	2	–	14	27
Unskilled†	2	–	–	1	–	3	1
Total	**23**	**4**	**11**	**9**	**6**	**53**	**100**

* = joiners, cabinet-makers, engine-fitters, shoe-makers, masons, etc
+ = salesmen, clerks, travellers, insurances, insurance agents, drapers, grocers, etc
† = labourers, commissionaires

Source: Youth, Empire and Society

A weekly routine of drill, Bible classes and Club Room prevailed with an annual camp or the occasional field day to raise company funds. These activities would have been exciting for young adolescents confined to urban monotony.

TABLE 10.2   BOYS' BRIGADE UK MEMBERSHIP, 1884-1899

YEAR	ENGLAND & WALES		SCOTLAND		IRELAND		TOTALS	
	Cos.	Boys	Cos.	Boys	Cos.	Boys	Cos.	Boys
1884	1	30					1	30
1885	5	268					5	268
1886	4	191	40	1,808			44	1,999
1887	10	452	114	5,664			124	6,116
1888	37	1,516	183	8,872			220	10,388
1889	85	3,714	232	10,614	1	44	318	14,372
1890	122	5,023	260	11,109	12	520	394	16,752
1891	143	5,139	252	11,138	23	982	418	17,259
1892	212	9,248	245	10,293	33	1,461	490	21,002
1893	313	13,841	221	9,661	60	2,531	594	26,033
1894	371	16,718	239	10,552	64	2,579	674	29,849
1895	416	17,647	255	11,679	71	3,053	742	32,379
1896	435	18,711	264	11,522	64	2,629	783	32,862
1897	453	18,472	258	12,290	60	2,361	771	33,123
1898	468	18,823	259	12,858	59	2,528	786	34,209
1899	470	19,715	276	12,796	66	2,637	812	35,148

Source: Youth, Empire and Society

Other influences:

The Scout Movement set up by Baden-Powell in 1907-1908 and the attempts of the War Office to incorporate the Brigade into a national cadet force and Smith's death in 1914 all had to be countered.

The public mood of anti-militarism ensured support for Smith in his determination to steer the Brigade away from the Army Council's influence.

The success of the Boys' Brigade as a youth movement led other churches to consider imitating Smith's idea, recreating a similar blend of recreation and military training with the intention of binding the adolescent closer to religious influences.

Church Lads Brigade   1891
Jewish Lads Brigade   1895
Catholic Boys' Brigade   1896

They were all called upon to solve differing problems of social adjustment or racial accommodation in late Victorian England.

The Church Lads Brigade

This proved to be the most successful of all the rivals. The main founder was Walter Mallock Gee. He was particularly influential in combining it with the Temperance movement among the young, through the Church of England Temperance Society. It was consolidated as a military organisation in 1892 when the Governing Brigade Council was established. It was similar in that it drew its recruits from the artisans, or 'skilled workers', children. A deterrent to the lower sections of the working classes may have been the financial commitment required for membership.

1908   67 regiments
         118 battalions
         1300 companies
         70,000 boys enrolled

Values likely to appeal to the upwardly aspiring – sobriety, thrift, self-help, punctuality, obedience – were positively stressed in the Brigade handbook. They were unashamedly middle class values intended to counter the more working class street culture. It was almost the working class equivalent of public school *esprit de corps* and the norms of militarism and Christian manliness ethic.

They were more militaristic than the Scottish Boys Brigade evidenced by their acceptance in 1911 of the Army Council's recommendation to apply for local Territorial recognition as official cadets. Their initial religious objectives were weakened and they were to remain by far the largest national cadet force for 25 years. This militaristic approach, however, was to see a decline in numbers during the inter- war years due to the antimilitary view held by the public. By 1936 an attempt to de-militarise came too late and thus they could not rival the Boys' Brigade.

Temperance: Restraint or moderation especially abstinence from alcoholic drink

The Scout Movement

Baden-Powell, the founder of the Scout movement was born in 1857. The major influences in his early life became evident in the movement he was to establish:

* family competitiveness amongst his brothers
* Charterhouse public school [school clubs and societies, particularly the rifle corps]
* British Army [particularly military experiences in Africa and India]
* intellectual thinking [Social Darwinism; social imperialism; social reform].

The public school code of Charterhouse was to find its expression in Scout Law – honour, loyalty and duty. The public school ethos of 'muscular christianity' and athleticism was inherited by the Boy Scouts as a pastoral 'myth' of open air woodcraft, with the belief that Nature symbolised purity and encouraged class harmony. This was the opposite of the current trend towards capitalist, urban-industrial values.

The army life was to have an effect but Baden-Powell was not a supporter of unimaginative drill and instructed Scoutmasters not to pursue this type of activity. He also disliked bureaucracy. He was to achieve notoriety and become a national hero with the successful defence at the Siege of Mafeking. It came at a time when the British were suffering humiliating defeats in the Boer War and the public was ready to embrace news of a British success. This war revealed the military weakness of the British Empire and numerous Inquiries also pointed to the physical deterioration of the working classes and this was to become interchangeable with degeneracy and decadence.

Baden-Powell wanted to toughen up the next generation, creating a self-reliant, energetic manhood. Scouting was a response to the demand for organising British youth as efficiently as possible and he used the loss of the Roman Empire as an analogy to warn of the dangers of not holding on to the British colonies. He suggested inferior races were now in contention to win back their lands.

Social imperialism was a combination of patriotism and social reform that came above class distinctions. Raising an imperial race was seen as a necessity if the interests of the British Empire were to be realised.

Baden-Powell viewed scouting primarily as a form of physical and moral training to prevent national decadence. He sought the advice of William Smith, the founder of the Boys' Brigade to help convert his 'Aids to Scouting' to a format suitable for boys. The already established YMCA also provided a ready-made platform to circulate his ideas.

The first Boy Scout camp took place in the summer of 1907. He used the publicity campaign experience of Arthur Pearson, a publisher who sponsored the movement by publishing 'The Scout', a weekly penny magazine.

The book 'Scouting for Boys' came out in six fortnightly parts before being issued in hard covers. Its contents included ten chapters covering topics such as: camp fire yarns on scout craft, campaigning, camp life, tracking woodcraft, chivalry, life-saving and patriotism.

The result was the establishing of Scout troops by boys themselves. The training of leaders became urgent and local advisory committees, followed by County Scout Councils were set up. Scouting was run on what appeared to be democratic lines with a chain of command reaching down from the Chief Scout to the Governing Council's Executive Committee, from the County Scout Councils to local District Scout councils and to local committees with some representation of the ordinary Scoutmaster. However, none of the top positions was open to election so the rank and file could not openly influence policy or change of leadership. It was a patriarchal form of government, a compromise between democracy and bureaucracy with some autocracy.

The outbreak of the First World War allowed the Scout movement to show its contribution. They gave air raid warnings, helped with the flax harvest, acted as messengers, guarded reservoirs, and ran mobile canteens in munitions factories and performed numerous other duties on the Home Front.

A lesser-known contribution of Scouting to national defence was the formation of the Scouts Defence Corps. Its object was to 'form a trained force of young men who would be immediately available for the defence of the country should their services be required during the war'.

Throughout the 1920s Scouting retained its overwhelming position as a mass youth movement; increasing its total numbers in Britain alone from 232,000 in 1920 to 422,000 in 1930.

During the 1930s there was a decline, also felt by other youth movements. This can be accounted for by the economic depression, Baden-Powell's failing health and the proliferation of new leisure activities, particularly hiking and the Youth Hostel Association.

Fig. 10.6   MODERN DAY BOYS' BRIGADE

Fig. 10.7 MODERN DAY CUBSCOUTS
BUILDING A CAMPFIRE

Girls in Uniform

These movements were derived from the boys' movements.

The first to become established was the Girls' Guildry, forerunner of the Girls' Brigade, at the turn of the century. Its birthplace was also in Glasgow. It was a combination of a senior Sunday school class, friendly club and a female equivalent of the Boys' Brigade. It even adopted the marching and drill popular at the time of the Boer War. The aim of the Girls' Guildry was to develop 'girls' capacities of 'womanly helpfulness' given full rein during the

Table 10.3 U.K. COMPARATIVE
STRENGTHS OF VARIOUS YOUTH MOVEMENTS,
1900–1941

	Boy Scouts		Boys' Brigade		Church Lads' Brigade		Army Cadet Force	
Year	Groups	Totals*	Cos.	Totals†	Units	Totals (approx.)	Cos.	Totals (approx.)
1900			906	44,415	1,238			
1901			1,014	51,821	1,326			
1902			1,100	53,725	1,139			
1903			1,148	55,188	1,146			
1904			1,161	55,285	1,186			
1905			1,197	56,893	–			
1906			1,237	58,888	1,259	45,000		11,000
1907			1,267	60,648	–	–		–
1908			1,324	64,134	–	70,000		–
1909			1,396	69,472	–	–		–
1910	3,898	107,986	1,386	68,089	1,379	–		–
1911	–	123,904	1,326	63,126	1,363	36,000	251	14,399
1912	4,945	138,715	1,298	61,858	1,321		699	34,474

1913	5,345	152,333	1,282	65,852	1,430		846	41,108
1914	–	–	1,360	66,747	1,557		–	–
1915	–	–	1,369	70,127	1,730		1,411	64,314
1916	–	–	1,346	61,969	1,816		1,620	78,651
1917	6,717	196,930	1,184	53,809	1,869		–	–
1918	6,710	197,030	1,078	53,106	1,936		2,005	105,121
1919	7,434	218,318	991	51,701	2,167		–	–
1920	8,069	232,758	1,181	63,235	2,119		2,423	118,893
1921	–	237,075	1,199	65,455	1,999		2,318	119,706
1922	–	254,170	1,239	71,454	1,955		–	–
1923	–	270,110	1,267	73,648	1,848		–	–
1924	–	282,635	1,329	77,700	1,936		–	–
1925	–	298,819	1,380	84,406	1,994	18,189	953	49,841
1926	–	309,265	1,436	86,587	2,016	–	–	–
1927	–	326,068	2,075	113,663	2,070	–	–	–
1928	–	356,974	2,157	119,018	2,123	–	949	49,510
1929	–	383,497	2,209	123,791	–	–	–	–
1930	10,296	422,662	2,257	131,891	1,320	–	–	30,000
1931	10,741	440,043	2,326	138,774	–	20,000	–	23,953
1932	11,259	459,281	2,395	148,234	966	–	–	–
1933	11,505	461,740	2,510	157,292	1,021	–	–	–
1934	11,470	440,209	2,628	163,177	1,022	–	–	–
1935	11,372	427,911	2,673	155,838	1,040	–		
1936	11,072	422,994	2,717	154,599	1,051	–		
1937	10,771	421,804	2,734	154,779	1,083			
1938	10,719	438,713	2,756	158,006	1,097			
1939	–	–	2,821	161,976	1,073		–	20,000
1940	–	–	2,498	124,249	945			–
1941	8,521	300,024	2,150	103,144	951			

* Includes: Cubs, Sea Scouts, Scouts, Rovers, Scoutmasters, Warrant Officers.
† Includes: Boy Reserves/Life Boys, Officers and Boys' Brigade.

First World War in their work for the Red Cross.

By 1939 it had a total membership of 24,000. It arrived at a time when women were beginning to play a more conspicuous role in society but it was also considered an affront to those who felt the female sex should not be encouraged in unladylike behaviour. In the mid 1960s the various Girl Youth movements combined to form the Girls' Brigade bringing membership to 100,000.

Britain's largest youth association is the Girl Guide movement comprising Brownies, Guides and Rangers. They owe their origin to a group of 'Girl Scouts' who in 1909 demanded an inspection by Baden-Powell. He had not intended his movement to include girls but gave way to social pressure and wrote, 'Girl Guides: a suggestion for character training for girls,' followed in 1918 by 'Girl Guiding'. He was later to become Chairman of the Guides.

Comment on the similarities and differences between the Boys' Brigade and the Scout Movement.
What social conditions contributed to the growth in youth movements at the turn of the twentieth century?

Conclusion:

Youth movements helped to:

- smooth the way for upper working class and lower middle classes into the urban industrial order of British society
- instil religious, moral and militaristic values
- provide an opportunity for the working classes to experience something of the élite public school education and values
- provide a mass leisure outlet for working class adolescents controlled by middle class adults
- provide opportunities for outdoor activity
- acceptance by young of the social order.

The Romantic Movement

The work of Romantic poets such as Wordsworth and Coleridge had a considerable influence on recreation in the countryside; their poems made the countryside attractive to town and city folk. The excursions began as exclusive pastimes, as time and money were required. Rambling was regarded as recreational, while mountaineering was taken more seriously, with the Alps being a favourite location. Ramblers tended to be drawn from the liberal, educated professions, who approached the activity with educational aims: an appreciation of the topography and local knowledge, and an aesthetic appreciation of natural beauty. Excursion tickets on the rail networks later helped the lower social classes participate.

The transport revolution

The roads and canal systems in Britain were vastly improved during the eighteenth and ninteenth centuries. People, ideas, services and goods were mobile and could be transported around the country. Areas which had hardly been influenced by the outside world were now open to change. In terms of sport, inter-town fixtures could be held and spectators could travel to watch the spectacles. This tendency was to be transformed in the nineteenth century with the advent of the railways.

- Increased wealth and mobility enabled the sports of hare, stag and fox hunting to be more easily accessible to the middle classes. Animals could be transported with relative ease and comfort, and competitions changed from being on a local club level to national competitions between England, Ireland and Scotland.
- Ramblers, cyclists and mountaineers could access the countryside and more isolated areas.
- Fishing was revolutionised. In 1867 a book titled *The Rail and the Rod* was published; a guide to angling spots which could be reached within a 30 mile radius of London.

The major spectator sports of racing, cricket and football became national sports. Special excursion trains would carry spectators. William Clarke of Nottingham formed the first All England Cricket XI and transported them about the country, playing games against a variety of sides. The railways enabled them to play 30 or more matches a season, and allowed a high level of cricket to be enjoyed by those who would otherwise have been unable to experience such an event.

The game of soccer flourished, particularly in the newly industrial counties of Lancashire and Yorkshire. The teams and supporters travelled by rail. A team started by the Lancashire and Yorkshire Railway became Manchester United Football Club.

National sporting events then developed into international events, and foreign competition improved standards further. The re-birth of the Olympic Games in 1896 was only made possible by rail travel.

 **ACTIVITY 3**

Using a variety of sports, explain how the communications by water, road and rail influenced the development of different sports.

- **Consider the importance of rivers for sports and developments of towns.**
- **Consider the development of roads to the present day.**
- **Consider the railway for transport and animals, and for bridging the link between rural and urban areas.**

The British Empire

In the nineteenth century, British imperialists believed they had a duty to spread their forms of government, religion, and culture to those nations they considered less advanced or civilised. Some of the British colonies benefited by the growth of an infra-structure of roads, schools and hospitals, but the imposition of colonial rule permanently altered the cultures and traditions of the colonised countries.

The influence of the British Empire was felt across the world. Western culture (including sport and recreation) was spread via numerous groups of people – soldiers, administrators, missionaries, young men on the Grand Tour, engineers and businessmen. The public school ethos which viewed sport as a character-building vehicle was imposed on the colonies. British subjects imported and exported sports, usually modifying them to suit their own needs:

- Croquet came to England from Ireland, and was successfully transported to India.
- Polo was enjoyed by British soldiers in India, with the first polo match being played in England in 1871.
- Shooting was an experience which most of the gentry participated in, and their interest was fired up with the prospect of big game shooting in Africa, where they could collect and transport home their enormous trophies.
- Thoroughbred horses were exported to most of Britain's colonies, and with them the English style of racing.
- Football did not spread so easily within the Empire, perhaps because the colonial administrative staff preferred other activities.

Professionalism and amateurism

The concept of amateurism was thought to reflect the Ancient Olympian spirit, placing the ideals of fair play and team spirit high above any material objectives. In the 1850s Dr Penny Brookes founded the **Much Wenlock Olympic Games** and formed a National Olympic Association. He had a pure sense of amateurism, and encouraged the citizens of Much Wenlock to delight in the challenge of sport with no thought for a reward. The first Games were held in 1850, and included events such as football, cricket, quoits, a blindfold wheelbarrow race, and chasing a pig through the town. It had all the trappings of a rustic festival, and perhaps reinvented the Cotswold Games first started in 1612 in Chipping Camden. By 1870 the events included track and field athletics, such as the pentathlon and tilting at the ring (a version of the jousting tournament).

The public school influence established its own definition of amateurism, which superseded the Much Wenlock version. Much of the public school version of athleticism was Olympian in outlook: combining physical endeavour with moral integrity, where the struggle was fought for the honour of the house or school. Baron Pierre de Coubertin visited both Much Wenlock and Rugby School in 1890, in the years preceding the foundation of the modern Olympic Games. He looked forward to a time when anyone would be able to participate, regardless of social standing or race.

In England there were two distinct phases of amateurism:

1 Originally, amateurs were gentlemen of the middle and upper classes who played sports in the spirit of fair competition.
2 There was a shift in definition of an amateur, from a straightforward social distinction, to a monetary one. Originally there had been no problems perceived by earning money from amateur sport.

Fair play was the bedrock upon which amateurism was based. It was important to adhere to the rules of the game, but it was expected that a player would discipline himself rather than wait for a referee's decision. A situation was recorded that the Corinthian Casuals, founded in 1882, would withdraw their goalkeeper on the awarding of a penalty to the opposing side, on the principle that they should accept the consequences of a foul.

There were advantages and disadvantages to the amateur code. It promoted restraint in victory and graciousness in defeat; the acceptance of rules and consequent respect for decisions. However, it excluded the working classes which was a moral argument for its abolition. In 1894 the Rugby Football Union and the Northern Union split due to the refusal of the authorities to allow northern players to have enough leisure time to compete on the same basis as players in the south. Employers could not accept 'broken time payments' (compensation for loss of wages), and by so doing, excluded manual workers who needed time to train and travel for sport. Similar conflicts were felt in rowing and cricket [see Chapter 12].

 **ACTIVITY 12**

The role and status of amateurs and professionals have changed considerably during the nineteenth and twentieth centuries.

a Comment on this statement in relation to:
   i cricket
  ii rowing
  iii rugby football.
b Describe the characteristics of the gentleman amateur.

Rational Recreation

Concern over the amusements of the lower classes became a more pressing concern in the nineteenth century.

Sports, museums, libraries and baths were to play a large part in the way in which the ruling classes and new middle class reformers saw the development of the lower classes into a more orderly, disciplined and moral workforce.

The urban developments had left the Established Church with little influence – a religious census in 1851 revealed very little attendance at any sort of Church by a large section of the population.

Large groups of youth were regarded as potential social problems.

The Boys' Brigade founded 1883, the Church Lads' Brigade and the Young Men's Christian Association were all used to improve the appeal of organised religion by recruiting and also as a form of social discipline.

Aston Vlla, Everton, Fulham, Bolton – were all church-based Football Clubs.

Street football was banned and Military Drill in the Elementary Schools was tedious so adult workers usually had poor experiences of physical activity.

Philanthropy
"the practice of performing charitable or benevolent actions"

Quakers
members of a Society of Friends; reject formal ministry; hold meetings where any one can speak; promoted many causes for social reform".

Industrial influences

Industrial recreation programmes were not very widespread, although several individual projects were almost revolutionary in their social thinking.

West Ham Football Club developed from the philanthropic industrial policy of AF Hills, an old Harrovian. A range of activities was introduced as well as profit-sharing schemes. A sports stadium was built to cater for a variety of sports clubs.

The Cadbury family were Quakers who founded the model industrial community at Bournville, Birmingham. George Cadbury required women workers to learn to swim [for cleanliness] and men with heavy jobs to do weight lifting to protect themselves from industrial injury. Good sports facilities were provided as part of a company policy which 'rested on the importance of quick, well-executed work. Athletics and swimming, medical and dental care, proper breaks for meals and rest – all that helps to develop manual dexterity and visual awareness which are the commercial object'. The company was the first company in England to implement the half day Saturday.

Fig. 10.8   CANOEISTS (RECREATIONAL ACTIVITY)

Fig. 10.9   WINDSOR GREAT PARK (RECREATIONAL ACTIVITY)

Fig. 10.10   RECREATIONAL GROUNDS

Fig. 10.11   GIRLS IN SPA BATH (RECREATIONAL ACTIVITY)

Summary of the Victorian era

- The gentry detached themselves from the people as a result of social change and pressures.
- New wealth and ambitions from the urban areas were beginning to be felt in the country lifestyle.
- Despite legislation some activities persisted – traditional activities do not simply die out overnight.
- Reformers and abolitionists tried to discipline the industrialised workforce.
- The upper classes tried to remove themselves from the middle classes who in turn tried to disassociate themselves from the working classes.

Agenda for the Century

The Empire was at its height, famous for the phrase, 'the sun shall never set on the British Empire'. However, Queen Victoria died and dramatic social changes that would change the face of the world began.

The industrial urban working classes emerged as a significant numerical body and were starting to understand the power they could yield as a united force. The Labour Party with its trade union connections was to put this power into effect.

Transport was increasingly affordable, particularly the railways.

Sport became part of the fabric of working class culture and was budgeted for. International sport competitions were to become more organised, evident by the London Games 1908; World Series baseball was conceived in America; the first Grand Prix was held at Le Mans in 1906; the Tour de France was staged in 1903.

Spectator problems occurred, for example when a wooden stand collapsed at Ibrox in 1902 and in 1909 people were injured at a riot at Hampden.

Traditions started early in the century took hold so fast they can still be recognised today, particularly in football, cricket and rugby.

First World War 1914-1918

This war was fought mainly in Europe and the Middle East, in which the allies [France, Russia, Britain, Italy and the United States after 1915] defeated the central powers [Germany, Austria, Hungary and Turkey]. Millions were to die in static trench warfare. It also became known as the Great War.

Nationalism revealed itself in war and it was glorified like a football match and the football match between British and German troops at Christmas 1914 set the tone for how sport was to be used during war time. Football grounds were used extensively for recruiting though eventually the Football League bowed to pressure to stop fixtures for the duration of the war. Following the war there were hopes for a more equal society though this was not immediately realised.

Inter-War Years [1919-1939]

There were two social moods following the First World War:

- to build a 'new' country with values learned from the conflict
- to regain some sense of fun and frivolity.

The initial burst of lavish living by the upper classes was not to last. The General Strike of 1926 culminated in the economic depression, high unemployment and the rise of Hitler in the Thirties.

The upper classes had wild parties, attended their tennis, golf and cricket clubs and took holidays abroad.

The working classes participated in some sort of leisure activity mainly on a Saturday afternoon. Football saw enormous crowds; dog racing was first held on a track in 1926, at Belle Vue, Manchester. Bowls and darts were still popular pub games. It was still the exception to go on holiday apart from day trips or the Wakes Weeks when the mills and factories closed down. Only the wealthy went abroad at this stage and the middle classes tended to rely on the transport provided by the railways to go further afield.

Sport club membership provided problems as growing numbers applied for acceptance but their social standing left a little to be desired.

New interest in activities such as walking, bicycling and rambling was made possible by the growth in youth hostels.

County cricket was seeing a decline though club cricket was stronger than ever with southern businesses releasing players mid-week.

International Sport

The Test Series between England, Australia and South Africa was extended to include New Zealand, the West Indies and India. The Bodyline controversy occurred in the 1932-3 series.

Bodyline Tour

The defeat of England in 1930 by Australia, particularly as a result of Bradman's batting led the English to decide to use intimidatory bowling in the next series. Larwood and Jardine claimed it was a fair tactic and this is what caused the controversy. Bradman's batting slumped and England regained the Ashes. In the Third Test injuries resulted from Larwood's bowling and the Australian Cricket Board sent a telegram to MCC saying in their opinion it was 'unsportsmanlike'. This was undermining the ability of the English to play in good faith. Politicians in Whitehall and the Australian Prime Minister applied pressure to have the matter settled. However, the MCC stuck by the team for the duration of the Series but Larwood's and Jardine's careers were over.

The Olympic Games began again and regular competitions took place between nations in golf, tennis and motor racing.

The newspapers were reporting sport events on special pages and the BBC reported eyewitness accounts on the late evening news. The wireless [TV started in 1938] helped to capture people's imaginations and the cinema became a universal attraction. Consequently sportsmen became national heroes.

The women were keen to demonstrate their new freedom the war had given them and team games were a popular pastime - in particular cricket, tennis, hockey and lacrosse.

World War II 1939-45

The war (1939-45) in which the Allies, Britain and France, declared war on Germany as a result of the German invasion of Poland. After this war there was an extensive rebuilding programme following extensive bombing, and facilities were more sophisticated than ever before. The therapeutic effect of recreational activities was highlighted for the physical, mental and emotional benefits. The commando training during the war had developed the use of obstacle training and this was how the first apparatus began to appear in schools combining the *movement* approach and problem solving learning techniques. It was adopted in physical education lessons with the *Butler Education Act* (1944) reforming education in Britain. (See Chapter 12)

Post Second World War

Changes that occurred in recreational and sporting terms were dramatic:

- no distinction now between gentleman and players
- team games were giving way to more individual pursuits
- travel was now available to all classes, particularly hiking across different countries by the young
- the motor car enabled mobility for even the working classes
- air travel had become commonplace for sport teams which also resulted in an increase in competitions, particularly football on the continent
- stimulation and excitement took over from the pursuit of peace and quiet of the Romantic era
- entertainment outside the home became increasingly important
- television was to have a major impact on sports, creating interest in new heroes in sports otherwise unknown to millions. Also fees for professional sports people increased as well as the growth in spectating rather than participating.
- national and international standards rose at the expense of school performances
- local authorities were supplying more recreational facilities such as swimming baths, adventure playgrounds and so on
- the development of the National Parks opened up the countryside and encouraged outdoor activities
- recreation had come into its own for most of the population and had lost the 'should' or 'ought' philosophy. People were more free to choose their leisure pursuits than ever before.

The changing role of women

The role of women in society has undergone some radical changes. However, it is important to distinguish between the:–

- upper class
- middle class
- working class.

The involvement of women in football, since the late nineteenth century, highlights quite clearly that public interest in their competitive participation was high, until the Football Association banned them from playing on Football League grounds in 1921. Since then, the female game has made a slow recovery and is now beginning to attract media coverage at the higher levels. The USA female soccer team are household names and the Football Association and FIFA are taking positive steps to encourage the game.

WOMEN THROUGH THE CENTURIES		
CULTURE COLLISION		
Victorian female stereotype Health Medical Exercise Emotional Fair play Social limitations Games ethic. • Led to social sports – croquet; Tennis; Golf School sports – Lacrosse; Hockey; Netball. • Headmistresses had autonomy/games played in peace and privacy balance between emancipation and social respectability. • Distinctions made between the characteristics and capabilities of men and women/ladies did not have to compromise status as ladies' fashion signalled changes and used to maintain status quo.		
UPPER CLASS	MIDDLE CLASS	LOWER CLASS
18th Century • Cricket; Croquet; Riding **19th Century** • Pretentious education/social/leisure/ time/money/femininity/fashion • Rational sport • Copy boys' education • Athleticism modelled for women • Victoria – sport and refinement • Limited on medical grounds • Social mixing • Development of ladies' universities [Girton Hockey Team 1890]	• Aspire to Upper class lifestyle • Proprietary colleges • Own activities – Lawn tennis/cycling • Time and money not social breeding = restrictions • Professions e.g. teaching • Garden suburbs – Golf/Tennis • Sports clubs administrators • Cheltenham ladies' college/Roedean 1885 Miss Lawrence 1884 First ladies' singles Wimbledon	**Pre 19th Century** • Popular recreations/occasional/ festivals/rural **Post 19th Century** • Working/urban/industrial • Little time or money • Few sport opportunities • Education from 1870/ drill/ femininity/sport male domain • Improved work conditions gradual work outings/half day Saturday/ Bank holidays • Women's factory football teams 1921 FA Ban women

List some of the major differences between recreational pursuits after the First World War and postSecond World War.

Review Questions

1   What do the terms functional, recreational and religious mean in relation to the influence physical activities have within a particular culture? Give specific examples.

2   Write down in table form the summaries for the Medieval era and the Victorian era.

3   What was the significance of Shrove Tuesday in the recreational lives of people?

4   How did the constraints on free time and wages influence working class sport and how were conditions improved towards the end of the 19th Century?

5   The Municipal Reform Act of 1835 led to the provision of Public parks. What were the motives behind this provision?

6   What were the attitudes of the Protestant , Evangelist and Sabbatarian religions towards working class leisure?

7 Describe other factors which played their part in decreasing the leisure opportunities for the industrial working classes as they moved to the towns.

8 Explain the influence of a shorter working week on working class sport for men and women.

9 Why did some industrialists encourage young working class men to participate in sport and exercise?

10 What effect did the emergence of the middle classes have on recreational pursuits in Britain in the nineteenth century?

11 How did the inns and public houses cater for recreation?

12 Give some specific examples of how the railways affected recreation in the nineteenth century.

13 Why were youth movements considered a necessity in the nineteenth and early twentieth centuries?

14 What were the effects of the First World War on recreation in Britain?

15 What were the effects of the Second World War on recreation?

chapter 11

Historical Development of Physical Education

We have studied the current situation concerning Physical Education mentioning briefly some historical events.
We are now going to look in more detail at how we came to the present position. We will cover:

- Public Schools in the nineteenth century
- State School Education from 1870, linking up to the present day.

Although for ease of study we will deal with the State and Private sector separately, it is important to remember that the Private or Public schools which operated for the gentry or upper classes were already well established by the nineteenth century.

The State schools followed much later following the Forster Education Act 1870.

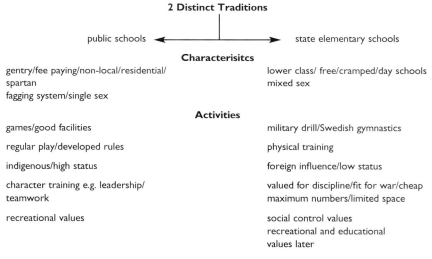

2 Distinct Traditions

public schools ← → state elementary schools

Characterisitcs

gentry/fee paying/non-local/residential/ spartan fagging system/single sex	lower class/ free/cramped/day schools mixed sex

Activities

games/good facilities	military drill/Swedish gymnastics
regular play/developed rules	physical training
indigenous/high status	foreign influence/low status
character training e.g. leadership/ teamwork	valued for discipline/fit for war/cheap maximum numbers/limited space
recreational values	social control values recreational and educational values later

Fig. 11.1 SCHOOL TRADITIONS   Gap between the two lessened as the 20th century progressed

The public schools

The sons of the gentry were educated at large, prestigious, fee-paying boarding schools. Separate schools for daughters were founded much later, and catered for very different needs; boys' schools were academic while girls' schools concentrated on social accomplishments like sewing and managing a household.

There were originally nine élite institutions, which were called 'Barbarian' schools as they maintained the gentry tradition: Eton, Harrow, Rugby, Shrewsbury, Charterhouse, Westminster, Winchester, St Paul's and Merchant Taylor's.

The emergence of the middle classes has already been mentioned as a major change in the social structure of nineteenth century Britain. When they acquired the necessary funds for their sons to attend these prestigious schools, they were unfairly rejected as the schools wished to remain exclusive, and so began to build their own proprietary colleges which were based on the élite schools. Examples of these 'Philistine' schools are Cheltenham College, Marlborough and Clifton.

The development of sport in the public schools radically changed previous concepts of sport. The boys brought to their schools their experiences of games like cricket and mob football and country pursuits such as fishing and coursing. Before the formalisation of team games, the boys would leave the school grounds, and participate in rowdy behaviour; this often involved poaching, fighting and trespassing, drinking alcohol and generally bringing the school's reputation into disrepute, causing conflict with local landowners and gamekeepers.

However, during this stage, they had began the process of organising their own activities and devising new ways of playing; these were often associated with individual architectural features of the different schools, eg, cloisters for fives, and the Eton wall game. This is an old form of football, and survives to this day. It developed from the unique architectural feature of a long red brick wall which separates the school playing fields from the Slough road. Ten players per side work the small ball along a narrow strip, 4–5 yards wide and 118 yards long. The players are assigned their playing position and specialised role according to their physique. The wall was built in 1717, but the game became popular in the nineteenth century.

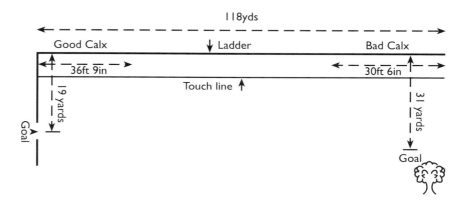

FIG. 11.2   THE ETON WALL GAME

 **Can you think of reasons why a game peculiar to this school should continue to be played?**

Thomas Arnold, the head of Rugby School encouraged the boys to develop activities which could be played on the school grounds and which would also highlight the more moral features of teamwork, such as self discipline, loyalty, courage; character-building qualities suitable for the prospective leaders of society.

The government was forced to intervene in public school education in 1861, when the Clarendon Commission was set up to 'inquire into the revenues and management of certain colleges and schools and the studies pursued and the instruction given there'. When the Clarendon Report was published in 1864, it strengthened the position of the headmasters by stressing the positive, educational features of team games as agents of training character. It did not place too much emphasis on skilled performance, but stressed moral qualities such as group loyalty. It also highlighted sports which were less useful, including hare and hounds, and gymnastics – both activities which focused on individual qualities. However, the report also revealed the extent to which games were becoming central to the school lives of the boys.

The Taunton Commission published in 1868 which examined other schools, also regarded gymnastics as inferior and less lively than the indigenous English games, which they recognised as having educational value. The headmasters rallied together at a conference in 1869 under the leadership of Edward Thring, and agreed that sport should encourage conformity in the boys' lives.

The Victorian public schools can be described as total institutions:

- The schools had institutional frameworks.
- The boys took part in regulated activities.
- The boys behaved in a way that was different to their role outside the school; eg, the fagging system placed younger boys in a subservient role to older boys. These were the sons of the gentry and would not normally be subservient to anyone.
- The boys were admitted and released on a termly basis.
- They had to assimilate the institutionalised values and rules in order to conform.

Can you think of any other social institutions which could match this type of analysis?

Cricket was already a fairly well established game in society and as such was considered suitable for the boys; mob football, on the other hand, was played by the lower classes in society and was not so acceptable, until the boys devised a more organised format. The game of rugby supposedly began at Rugby School, when William Webb Ellis picked up the ball during a game of football and ran with it.

The boys were in charge of organising the games, and senior bands of boys (normally called prefects) would be in control, reflecting the fagging system. Games committees were formed, eg, the Harrow Philathletic Club. The masters actively discouraged some activities (poaching and gambling) while others were allowed to exist on an informal recreational basis among the boys (fives and fighting). They actively encouraged the boys to organise team games.

Initially, inter-school fixtures were not feasible as no two schools had the same rules. However, by the mid nineteenth century, the headmaster and staff started to organise sports. Games were seen as a medium for achieving educational aims with a moral social sense; they could also help combat idleness and as such were a form of social control. Boys who excelled in games were admired by the other pupils.

Technical development of games:

- boys brought local variations to the schools from their villages
- played regularly in free time
- developed individual school rules/skills/boundaries etc
- played competitively ie, house matches
- self government meant boys organised activities initially
- later codified rules allowed inter-school fixtures
- development of games élite.

Athleticism

"physical endeavour with moral integrity"
The cult of athleticism stressed the physical and social benefits of sports:

- The physical benefits were seen to counteract the effects of sedentary lifestyles, and sport was viewed as therapeutic, invigorating and cathartic. It was also seen as a break from work.
- Sport would take place within a competitive situation which would help the boys learn how to cope with winning and losing all in a dignified manner. It helped to develop leadership qualities, and being Captain was a high status office to hold.

The House system was instrumental to the competitive sport events, in which the manner of the performance was considered more important than the result.

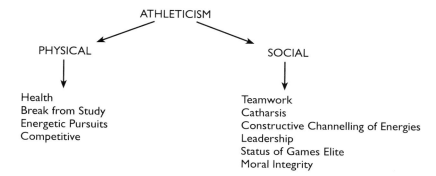

Fig. 11.3   THE BENEFITS OF ATHLETICISM

Athleticism also met middle class values of respectability and order, for example, values such as sportsmanship, leadership and abiding by rules. The middle classes were to become the organisers and administrators of society particularly highlighted in their role within governing bodies of sports clubs.

Consider the following areas and compare the situation in a state school today with a public school in the nineteenth century:

- **Physical education curriculum and the latest Government proposals**
- **Physical education exams**
- **Student lifestyles (part time work, increase in leisure activities, etc).**

There were also opponents of this emphasis on athleticism, with many people believing it was becoming more important than the boys' studies, and could lead to a regimentation of boys' thoughts and behaviour with a destruction of individuality. Old boys who returned as teachers after university were often employed for their games prowess as much as for their intellectual teaching contribution. They brought to the schools the new sports they had learnt at university, the fully codified versions of the games and also the philosophy to excel at their sport.

The public schools instituted the idea of the Sports Day, which operated as a public relations exercise to the old boys, parents and governors of the school. The funds of the school could benefit from generous donations and valuable publicity could be gained.

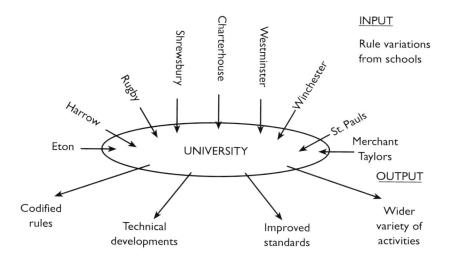

Fig. 11.4   THE INPUT AND OUTPUT OF
THE UNIVERSITIES

'The public schools were the first centres of excellence for sport and resembled modern day sports schools.' Discuss.

Thomas Arnold

Thomas Arnold became headmaster of Rugby School in 1828 where he directed a crusade against personal sin, eg, bullying, lying, swearing, cheating, running wild. They were to remain on the school grounds, he forbade shooting and beagling as these activities encouraged poaching, and fights should only occur within his presence and supervised by the prefects who enforced his authority.

Arnold is known for his contribution to Muscular Christianity, but he valued games only for what they could contribute towards the social control of the boys. The development of athleticism followed the cooperation of the boys in maintaining discipline and achieving Arnold's reforms.

Tom Brown's Schooldays by Thomas Hughes was published in 1860 and highlighted the Victorian ideal towards the physical side of the Christian gentleman. Hughes expanded the manliness ideals of Charles Kingsley – moral manliness became extrovert masculinity.

Fig. 11.5   The early days of rugby

Edward Thring of Uppingham

Uppingham rose from being an obscure grammar school to a famous public school in the nineteenth century under its headmaster, Edward Thring. From the start he encouraged the playing of games:

- He played fives and football with the boys.
- The school day began early and finished at midday to accommodate games.
- He was the first to open a gymnasium in 1859 and incorporated swimming and athletics as part of the physical education programme.

Other public schools tended to ignore Thring's innovations and continued with their diet of games. Thring did not place so much importance on the games élite, and believed that non-athletic boys could enjoy games. Thring had attended Eton as a boy which is where he developed his love for physical activity; he truly promoted sports for the love of it.

 ACTIVITY 5

Read the extract from *Tom Brown's Schooldays*, and consider the following questions:

1 **Comment on the level of technical development of the physical activity described.**
2 **Explain the different social relationships being identified.**
3 **Discuss the values being reinforced as part of a character-building process.**

> "Huzza, there's going to be a fight between Slogger Williams and Tom Brown!"
> The news ran like wildfire about, and many boys who were on their way to tea at their several houses turned back, and sought the back of the chapel, where the fights come off.
> "Just run and tell East to come and back me," said Tom to a small School-house boy, who was off like a rocket to Harrowell's, just stopping for a moment to poke his head into the School-house hall, where the lower boys were already at tea, and sing out, "Fight! Tom Brown and Slogger Williams."
> In another minute East and Martin tear through the quadrangle, carrying a sponge, and arrive at the scene of action just as the combatants are beginning to strip.
> Tom felt he had got his work cut out for him, as he stripped off his jacket, waistcoat, and braces. East tied his handkerchief round his waist, and rolled up his shirt-sleeves for him: "Now, old boy, don't you open your mouth to say a word, or try to help yourself a bit,—we'll do all that; you keep all your breath and strength for the Slogger." Martin meanwhile folded the clothes, and put them under the chapel rails; and now Tom, with East to handle him, and Martin to give him a knee, steps out on the turf, and is ready for all that may come: and here is the Slogger too, all stripped, and thirsting for the fray.
> It doesn't look a fair match at first glance: Williams is nearly two inches taller, and probably a long year older than his opponent, and he is very strongly made about the arms and shoulders,—"peels well," as the little knot of big fifth-form boys, the amateurs, say; who stand outside the ring of little boys, looking complacently on, but taking no active part in the proceedings. But down below he is not so good by any means; no spring from the loins, and feeblish, not to say shipwrecky about the knees. Tom, on the contrary, though not half so strong in the arms, is good all over, straight, hard, and springy, from neck to ankle, better perhaps in his legs than anywhere. Besides, you can see by the clear white of his eye, and fresh bright look of his skin, that he is in tip-top training, able to do all he knows; while the Slogger looks rather sodden, as if he didn't take much exercise and ate too much tuck. The time-keeper is chosen, a large ring made, and the two stand up opposite one another for a moment, giving us time just to make our little observations. The combatants, however, sit there quietly, tended by their seconds, while their adherents wrangle in the middle. East can't help shouting challenges to two or three of the other side, though he never leaves Tom for a moment, and plies the sponges as fast as ever.

Fig. 11.6 EXTRACT FROM *TOM BROWN'S SCHOOLDAYS*

Spread of athleticism nationally and world-wide

- Old Boys'/Girls' network
- Universities codified rules, developed activities technically, improved and devised new ways of playing
- Sports clubs and governing bodies became significant administrative features
- Officers in army and navy influential on troops

- Clergy influenced parishioners
- Teachers went back into schools
- Employers encouraged games in their workforce
- The empire enabled these developments to be spread worldwide.

Female education

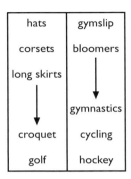

Fig. 11.7   AS SPORT FOR WOMEN DEVELOPED, SO DID THEIR CLOTHING

In the late 1800s the education of girls was very poor. It was pretentious and costly, with an emphasis on accomplishments for society rather than for the intellectual development of the girls. Music and dancing counted as the highest priorities, with writing and arithmetic being the lowest. 'Medical' reasons to limit women's sports participation were legitimised; it was believed that women who participated in strenuous physical activity would become muscle bound, which would be detrimental to childbearing. As physical activity and educational examinations incorporated a degree of competitiveness, this was not conducive to the social image of how women should behave.

In the Victorian era, constructive education for women was regarded as a threat to the norms for behaviour for that society. As the struggle for women's rights developed, their increased wealth in the nineteenth century enabled women even greater leisure time. The pioneers of female education had to overcome mountains of prejudice. These were hard-headed, common sense groups of middle class women, stirred by a sense of women's duties rather than their rights. Two of these pioneers were Frances Mary Buss and Dorothea Beale. The former founded the North London Collegiate School and Camden School for Girls, while the latter transformed the derelict Cheltenham Ladies College and turned it into a serious educational establishment for the upper and middle classes. They started the process of changing the Victorian ideals, and public day schools for girls were modelled on these schools.

Miss Beale wanted to teach the rudiments of science but had to call it 'physical geography' to escape condemnation. The introduction of physical education caused the most controversy. At this time girls were not supposed to exercise at all. Allowing girls to run and jump, and the removing of corsets was as culturally radical as the unbinding of Japanese women's feet.

The Schools Inquiry Commission 1868 was important for women's education, suggesting that girls' foundation schools would soon become a reality. By 1881, the universities recognised that girls had fulfilled the degree requirements of boys. By 1898, following the Endowed Schools Act, there were 80 endowed girls schools and by 1900 there were 36 girls' public day trust schools. The 1918 Act gave girls the same educational advantages as boys.

The improvement in general education was paralleled by the development of physical education for girls. There was a need for specialist physical education teacher training colleges; the first was established by Miss Bergman in 1885 at Broadhurst Gardens, using the Hampstead Gymnasium. She later moved to Dartford Heath in 1895, where physical education on a full-time specialist basis began. The object of the College was to teach gymnastics and swimming in girls' schools, to conduct outdoor games and to spread the knowledge of physiology and hygiene. Other training colleges soon followed:

- Anstey College, 1899.
- Chelsea College, 1898.
- I.M. Marsh College, 1899.

Miss Bergman was appointed Lady Superintendent of Physical Education in 1881 on the London School Board. The main emphasis came from Swedish gymnastics (See Page 246) with its focus on health rather than educational values. Miss Bergman modelled female education on that of the boys and was keen to implement some of the games available in schools. She wrote in the 'Teacher's Encyclopaedia' that the principal games represented in the English girls schools

Name. A.B.
Entered school, January, 1897.

			DATE	DATE
			January, 1897.	July, 1897.
Age	-		14	14 $\frac{1}{4}$
Height	-		4ft 9.5 in	4ft 9 $\frac{3}{4}$ in
Weight	-		6st 4.5 lbs	6st 7 $\frac{3}{4}$ lbs
Sight	-	Right	very good	Normal
		Left	very good	Normal
		Colours	–	–
		Glasses	–	–
Hearing	-	Right	Normal	Normal
		Left	Normal	Normal
Throat & c	-	-	Normal	Normal
Breathing	-		Normal	Normal
Lungs	-	-	Normal	Normal
Heart	-	-	Normal	Normal
Chest measure	-		27 $\frac{1}{2}$	28 $\frac{1}{2}$
Waist measure	-		23	23 $\frac{1}{2}$
Chest formation	-		Good	Good
Spine	-	-	Left curve (single) hollow back	Can stand perfectly straight
Muscles	-	-	Good	Good and equal
Arch in foot	-		Normal, slightly flat	Still slightly flat
Development	-		Limbs short and broadly built	Does not stand as straight as she can, is lazy. Walks badly.
Remarks	-	-	Rational corsets two inches too tight. Has never had backache.	
Advise	-	-	If possible, special private gymnastics for three months. To see me in three months.	No more treatment at present: possibly next year

Name. D.D.
Entered school, September, 1897.

			October 1, 1896	Nov 30, 1896	Sept 16, 1897
Age	-	-	10	-	-
Height	-		4ft 7 $\frac{1}{2}$ in	-	-
Weight	-		4st 9 lbs	-	-
Sight	-	Right	Normal	-	-
		Left	Normal	-	-
		Colours	Normal	-	-
		Glasses	-	-	-
Hearing	-	Right	Normal	-	-
		Left	Deaf from wax	-	-
Throat & c	-	-	Tonsils enormous	Tonsils have been	-
Breathing	-		Nasal, fairly free	cut. R. still large	-
Lungs	-	-	Normal	-	-
Heart	-	-	Normal	-	-
Chest measure	-		22 $\frac{1}{2}$	23 -	24 -
Waist measure	(over stays)		21	21	21.1 $\frac{1}{2}$

Fig. 11.8   SHEFFIELD HIGH SCHOOL:
PHYSICAL EDUCATION RECORD

were hockey, cricket, basketball and lacrosse. She also saw the benefit of tennis but felt her students were already reasonably proficient from their social backgrounds.

The Board of Education Syllabuses however paid scant attention to games, and of 11 publications issued between 1919 and 1927, only one was devoted to non-gymnastic activities. The games which were advocated were those where speed of eye, foot and hand combined with team play and cooperation.

Despite these restrictions, women athletes began to emerge in the last quarter of the nineteenth century, such as Lottie Dodd, Mary Outerbridge and Constance Applebee. They tended to shine in sports where they did not have to overcome heavy objects and where spatial barriers and rules prevent bodily contact with the opponent.

Thus, physical activities for girls developed much later than those for boys, and the gradual development was linked to sociological factors and the development of female education in general. When prejudicial attitudes began to change, girls began to participate in activities such as tennis, hockey, gymnastics and cricket. They then developed their activities along similar lines to the boys; they established clubs and entered competitions. There was a concentration on female sports developing a separately to boys, partly due to the single sex developments in schools, but social games like tennis allowed a mixing of the sexes.

 **ACTIVITY 6**

What characterised those activities deemed suitable for middle class females in their private schools?

Summary:

Nineteenth century Public Schools:

- provided an education for the social élite
- developed many traditional activities and games
- gave rise to the cult of athleticism parallel with the Muscular Christian movement
- games associated with character building qualities, for example, courage and loyalty
- female education developed later but was to be based on the boys' system
- female education helped in the growing liberation of women at the end and beginning of the twentieth century
- influenced the development of sport nationally and worldwide through their positions of leadership in society.

State education

Prior to 1870, the education of the masses had been the responsibility of the parish, and was very inconsistent. The Forster Education Act 1870 was a great milestone in social welfare, as it created a state system of education. There was a developing initiative to build more schools and the Act was the result of some radical changes in social thinking by philanthropists and social reformers.

Ever since the first Board Schools were built in 1870, teachers in the poorest districts were faced with the extreme poverty of many of its pupils. As many as three to four million children were living below the poverty line.

There were two main principles of state education:

1 There shall be efficient schools everywhere throughout the United Kingdom.
2 There would be compulsory provision of such schools if and where needed, but not unless proved to be needed.

The existing British schools, foreign schools, under the Foreign Schools Society 1808, and national schools, under the National Schools Society 1811, would continue to provide the bulk of the nation's education, provided they were good enough. The main points of the Education Act were as follows:

- England and Wales divided into 2,500 school districts.
- The Churches were to decide if they needed to build new schools.
- Failing this, a School Board had to be elected by local people, to finance schools from the rates.
- The children would pay a small fee, with an increase in government grants. The very poor could receive free education.
- The school age was not less than five years but no more than thirteen years. In London they were exempt at age 10 if they passed grade V and were needed to work for the family income.

Mundella's Education Act of 1880 made education compulsory for all children between the ages of five and ten, without exception. In 1893 the compulsory school leaving age was raised to eleven and in 1899 to twelve years.

1 **What faults could you find with the Education Act 1870?**
2 **What effect do you think the Education Acts had on poor children, teachers and parents?**
3 **Explain why there would have been a problem of non-payment of school fees.**

Characteristics of State Schools

Experiences of children at state schools were very different from those of their gentry counterparts. Small buildings with little space and no recreational facilities allied with a philosophy which denied any recreational rights to the working class, and placed its own constraints on the physical activities available to the state school system.

Gymnastics formed the bedrock of early state school physical exercise. Foreign influences, in the form of Swedish and German gymnastics, combined with the English style under Archibald Maclaren. Guts Muths from Germany wrote the first text which gained significant recognition, called *Gymnastik fur die Jugend* in 1793. This was to influence Per Henrik Ling in Sweden and together they can be called the 'fathers of modern gymnastics'. The Schools Boards tended to favour the Swedish system for its free flowing, free standing exercises possibly due to the employment of Swedish inspectors; whilst the strength based German gymnastics which utilised apparatus developed within the club structure.

Swedish Gymnastics

Suitable for state schools as it aimed to:

- suit the diverse objectives of physical exercise for the working classes
- promote health and fitness based on scientific principles gaining approval with the School Board
- encourage military preparedness
- improve industrial efficiency/work productivity
- foster social order/social control/discipline of large numbers of children
- promote the harmonious development of the whole body
- be safe and cheap
- be easy to learn and instruct.

The lack of fitness and discipline and the poor general health of the working classes had been noted in the Boer War (1899–1902) and blamed for the heavy loss of life suffered. Swedish gymnastics also came under threat as not being effective enough in improving the fitness of the working classes sufficiently for the hardships of war.

The Model Course

A policy of drill and physical training was initiated but had little recreational value. In 1902 the model course was instituted by Colonel Fox of the War Office. The main aim of the course was to

- improve the fitness of the working classes for military preparation
- increase their familiarity with combat and weapons
- improve discipline and obedience amongst the working classes.

Drill was characterised by commands issued by the teacher or NCOs (non commissioned officers) to the children who would be standing in uniform military style rows and obeying the commands in unison. Large numbers could be catered for in a small space, and as the movements were free-standing and required no apparatus, they were cheap. After 1873 boys and girls received drill.

The problems with this approach were that they were essentially adult exercises for children. They did not take children's needs and physical and mental development into account. There was no educative content and individualism was submerged within a group response. The use of NCOs also reduced the status of the subject as it did not use qualified teachers.

 **ACTIVITY 8**

1 **What qualities were required by the teacher and the pupils in military drill?**
2 **How do the pupil requirements compare with those being generated through team games within the public school system?**

Due to the problems and concerns over the model course, the Board of Education established a syllabus of physical training in 1904, 1909, 1919, 1927 and 1933. They stressed the physical and educative effect of sport:

1   The physical content would have been very much influenced by their primary concern for the medical and physiological base from which they approached the subject. As such the therapeutic effect, the correction of posture faults, and exercises to improve the circulatory systems would have been foremost in their aims.
2   The educational aims would try to develop alertness and decision making.

The 1919 Syllabus took into consideration the loss of life of the First World War, and the flu epidemic which hit the country shortly afterwards. Sir George Newman had recognised the beneficial effects of recreational activities in helping to rehabilitate injured soldiers. By 1933 there was more freedom of movement and a more decentralised lesson. This was a recognition of the increasing rights of the working classes and the educational value of group work.

First World War

The First World War, also known as the Great War, was fought from 1914 to 1918, mainly in Europe and the Middle East in which the allies [France, Russia, Britain, Italy and the United States after 1915] defeated the central powers[Germany, Austria, Hungary and Turkey]. Millions were to die in static trench warfare.

Nationalism revealed itself in war. Public schoolmen with their ideals of service were enthusiastic about the coming conflict. It was glorified like a football match and the football match between British and German soldiers at Christmas 1914 set the tone for how sport was to be used during war time. Football grounds were used extensively for recruiting and eventually the Football League bowed to moral pressure to stop fixtures for the duration of the war. Following the war there were hopes of a more equal society due to the massive loss of life sustained from all echelons of society.

Consider the 1904 and the 1933 syllabuses in fig 11.9 and trace the similarities and differences.

Post-Second World War developments

The Butler Education Act 1944 planned to reform education in Britain. It was a major social reform; it aimed to remove special privileges and ensure equality of opportunity for all. Its main provision were as follows:

• There were to be 146 local education authorities to replace the previous 300. They were required to provide recreational facilities to specific sizes.
• The school leaving age was to be raised to 15 from 1947.
• All education in state maintained grammar schools was to be free. To attend grammar schools children now needed to pass the eleven plus exam, rather than pay.
• All children would leave the elementary school at 11 and move to a secondary school – either grammar or secondary modern. This was a complete separation of the primary from secondary education, and meant that new schools had to be built.
• More mature forms of physical education were required to suit the higher ages of the children. The HMI (His Majesty's Inspectorate) for PE now reported to the Chief Inspector, not the Chief Medical Officer.
• The 1944 McNair Report gave PE teachers the same status as other teachers.

Effects of Second World War

- destruction of schools/deterioration of equipment
- evacuation of children to rural areas
- male physical education teachers enlisted
- work taken over by older men and women
- more mobile style of fighting
- apparatus for schools from commando training
- movement away from therapeutic and medical value of Physical Education
- more emphasis on heuristic/guidance style of teaching.

After the war there was an extensive rebuilding programme and facilities were more sophisticated than before. The therapeutic effect of recreational activities was again valued. The commando training during the war had developed the use of obstacle training, and this was how the first apparatus began to appear in schools – scramble nets, rope ladders, mats and frames, hoops, wooden tables and benches.

The 'movement' approach began in physical education lessons; children were required to use their initiative and learn by discovery. This also demanded new teaching methods and there was the development of a more heuristic style which placed the teacher in the role of *guiding* the children rather than being purely *instructional*.

The influence of Isadora Duncan and Laban with their form of dance using the body as an expressive medium, was taken up by women teachers. Modern Educational Dance 1948 gave 16 basic movement themes and rudiments of free dance technique and space orientation. The word 'Movement' came to reflect the 1940s and 1950s as 'posture' had reflected the 1930s.

I PLAY RUNNING OR MARCHING	Play or Running about. The children should, for a minute or two, be allowed to move about as they please.
II PRELIMINARY POSITIONS AND MOVEMENTS	Attention. Standing at Ease. Hips Firm. Feet Close. Neck Rest. Feet Astride. Foot Outward Place. Foot Forward Place. Stepping Sideways. Heels Raising. Right Turn and Right Half Turn. Left Turn and Left Half Turn.
III ARM FLEXIONS AND EXTENSIONS	Arms Downward Stretching. Arms Forward Stretching. Arms Sideways Stretching. Arms Upward Stretching.
IV BALANCE EXERCISES	Heels Raising. Knees Bending and Stretching. Preparation for Jumping. Heels Raising (Neck Rest). Heels Raising (Astride, Hips Firm). Heels Raising (Astride, Neck Rest). Head Turning in Knees Bend Position. Knees Bending and Stretching (Astride). Leg Sideways Raising with Arms Sideways Raising. Knee Raising.
V SHOULDER EXERCISES AND LUNGES	Arms Forward Raising. Arms Sideways Raising. Hands Turning. Arms Flinging. Arms Forward and Upward Raising. Arms Sideways and Upward Raising.
VI TRUNK FORWARD AND BACKWARD BENDING	Head Backward Bending. Trunk Forward Bending. Trunk Backward Bending. Trunk Forward Bending (Astride). Trunk Backward Bending (Astride).
VII TRUNK TURNING AND SIDEWAYS BENDING	Head Turning. Trunk Turning. Trunk Turning (Astride, Neck Rest). Trunk Turning (Feet Close, Neck Rest). Trunk Sideways Bending. Trunk Sideways Bending (Feet Close, Hips Firm). Trunk Sideways Bending (Feet Close, Neck Rest).
VIII MARCHING	Marking Time (From the Halt). Turnings while Marking Time. Quick March. Marking Time (From the March). Changing Direction.
IX JUMPING	Preparation for Jumping. *Note* Work from this Column should be omitted until above exercise has been taught under IV.
X BREATHING EXERCISES	Breathing Exercises without Arm Movements. With Deep Breathing, Arms Sideways Raising.

Note Exercises bracketed should be taken in succession.

Fig. 11.9   (a)

PART ONE

I

Introductory Activity 1. Free running, at signal, children run to 'homes' in teams. (Four or more marked homes in corners of playground.) All race round, passing outside all the homes, back to places and skip in team rings.

2. Free running, at signal all jump as high as possible and continue running. Brisk walking, finishing in open files, marking time with high knee raising.

3. Aeroplanes. (Following the leaders in teams.)

Rhythmic Jump 1. Skip jump on the spot, three low, three high (continuously) *(Low, 2, 3, high, 2, 3, etc.)*

2. Astride jump. *Astride jumping—begin! 1. 2. 1. 2. etc. stop!*

3. Skip jump, four on the spot, four turning round about (8 counts) and repeat turning the opposite way (8 counts)

2

1. (Astride [Long sitting]) Trunk bending downward to grasp ankles. Unroll. *(With a jump, feet astride—place! [with straight legs—sit.!] Grasp the ankles—down! With unrolling, trunk upward—stretch! With a jump, feet together—place!*

2. (Astride [Astride long sitting]) Trunk bending downward to touch one foot with opposite hand.

3. (Feet close [Cross-legged sitting].) Head dropping forward and stretching upward. *(Feet—close!) Head forward—drop! Head upward—stretch!* (Crouch) Knee stretching and bending. ('Angry Cats') *(Crouch position—down!) Knees— stretch! bend! up! down! etc. stand—up!*

3

1. As small as possible, as tall as possible. [(Crook sitting, Back to wall) Single arm swinging forward-upward to touch wall.] [(Crook sitting) Drumming with the feet, loud and soft.]

2. Single arm circling at a wall. (Run and stand with side to wall, nearest hand supported against wall about shoulder height. Circling with free arm. Turn about and repeat.)

4

1. Free running like a wooden man. Finish in open files in chain grasp. (One foot forward, heel level with the other toe). Knee full bending and stretching with knees forward. (Several times. Move the back foot forward and repeat.) (Lean standing) Hug the knee. [(Crook lying) Hug the knees. (Lower the feet quietly.)]

2. Running in twos, change to skipping, finish in a double ring facing partner holding hands. Knees full bend. Knee springing. Hands on ground and jump up. *Knees full bend! Knee springing—begin! 1, 2, 1, 2, etc. Stop! Placing the bands on the ground, with a jump stand—up!*

3. Form a ring. Gallop step left and right, at signal, run and stand with side to wall, nearest hand supported against wall (the other arm sideways). Kick the hand. (Turn about, or run to opposite wall and repeat several times with each leg.)

5

1. Brisk walking anywhere, change to walking on heels or toes, at signal run to open files facing partners. (Feet-close, Arms forward, Fists touching.) Trunk turning with single elbow bending. (Elbow raised and pulled back. 'Drawing the bow.') *(Feet—close! With fists touching, arms forward—raise!)* With the right arm, draw the bow— pull! Let go! With the left arm—pull! Let go! etc. Arms—lower!

2. Race to a wall and back to centre line and join right hand across with partner. Tug of war with one hand.

3. (Informal lunge with hand support.) Head and trunk turning with arm raising to point upward. *(Left (right) foot forward with knee bent and left (right) hand on knee (informal lunge)—ready!) With arm raising to point upward, head and trunk to the right, (left)—turn! With arm lowering, forward—turn. (Repeat several times.) With a jump, feet change!*

6

Class Activity

1. Running, jumping over a series of low ropes. (In ranks of six or eight in stream.)

2. Frog jump anywhere.

3. Free running or skipping, tossing up a ball and catching it. (A ball each. Who can make the greatest number of catches without missing.)

Group Practices

1. Running or galloping with a skipping rope. (A rope each.)

2. Running Circle Catch, with a player in the centre, throwing, or bouncing and catching a ball.

3. Sideways jumping over a low rope, partner helping. (Partner astride rope, performer holding partner's hands does several preparatory skip jumps on the spot and then a high jump over the rope landing with knees bent and standing up again.)

4. In twos, crawling or crouch jump through a hoop, held by partner.

Game

Odd Man.

Free Touch with 6 or 7 'He's.' ('He's' carry a coloured braid or bean bag as distinguishing mark.).

Tom Tiddler.

7

Free walking, practising good position, lead into school.

(b)

Fig 11.9 (A) 1904 SYLLABUS FOR PHYSICAL EDUCATION (B) 1933 SYLLABUS FOR PHYSICAL EDUCATION — EXCERPT

Moving and Growing, and Planning the Programme

These two publications were issued by the Ministry of Education in 1952 and 1953 respectively. They replaced the old syllabuses and were to be implemented in primary schools. They combined the two influences of:

- obstacle training from the army
- movement training from centres of dance.

Running parallel to these changes were:

1 Circuit training (devised by G T Adamson and R E Morgan at the University of Leeds)
2 Weight training – progressive resistance exercises
3 Outward Bound Schools promoting adventurous activities to develop the personality within the natural environment in challenging conditions.

These publications developed as a result of changes in educational thinking which was to make learning stem from a more child-centred approach. The physical education teacher was now more autonomous with personal control over the physical education syllabus. The activities included agility, playground and more major game skills, dance and movement to music, national dances and swimming. The key words which separate them from earlier forms of physical activity in state schools are:

- exploratory
- creative
- individual
- fun.

Educational gymnastics

During the 1950s to 70s, there was a significant rise in the uses of modern educational gymnastics. In this type of activity children were encouraged to respond with movement to a stimulus, or movement problem. For example, a teacher may set a task of finding as many different ways to travel across, along or over a bench. The child would be required to use a certain amount of imagination and creativity to answer the task.

However, there would be no right or wrong solution. The child was not forced too perform cartwheels but they could answer the task by responding with movements within their capabilities and therefore would develop confidence as they achieved a level of success.

This way very much a heuristic style of teaching as opposed to the more didactic and prescribed approach of the early twentieth century.

 **ACTIVITY 10**

Trace the involvement of government in education from 1870 to the present day. Concentrate on political aspects like centralisation policies, the intended aims of education and the use made of physical activities. Consider also the social factors operating at each stage.

Summary

- Physical activity in state schools at the end of the nineteenth century concentrated on Military Drill and Swedish gymnastics.
- Emphasis was placed on activities suitable for the poor conditions in state schools and discipline of the working classes.

Fig. 11.10 SYLLABUS DEVELOPMENT OF PHYSICAL EDUCATION IN THE UNITED KINGDOM

1870	Drill	centralised
1904-1933	Syllabuses of Physical Training	centralised
1933-1988	Physical Education teachers devise syllabus	decentralised
1988+	National Curriculum	more centralised

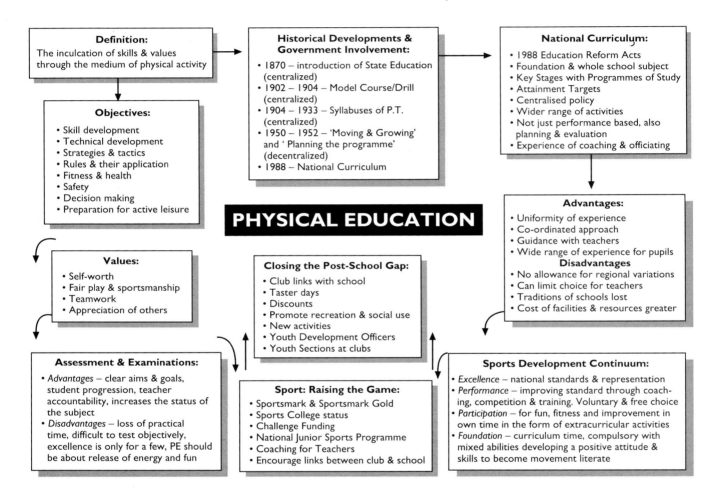

Definition:
The inculcation of skills & values through the medium of physical activity

Objectives:
• Skill development
• Technical development
• Strategies & tactics
• Rules & their application
• Fitness & health
• Safety
• Decision making
• Preparation for active leisure

Values:
• Self-worth
• Fair play & sportsmanship
• Teamwork
• Appreciation of others

Assessment & Examinations:
• *Advantages* – clear aims & goals, student progression, teacher accountability, increases the status of the subject
• *Disadvantages* – loss of practical time, difficult to test objectively, excellence is only for a few, PE should be about release of energy and fun

Historical Developments & Government Involvement:
• 1870 – introduction of State Education (centralized)
• 1902 – 1904 – Model Course/Drill (centralized)
• 1904 – 1933 – Syllabuses of P.T. (centralized)
• 1950 – 1952 – 'Moving & Growing' and ' Planning the programme' (decentralized)
• 1988 – National Curriculum

PHYSICAL EDUCATION

Closing the Post-School Gap:
• Club links with school
• Taster days
• Discounts
• Promote recreation & social use
• New activities
• Youth Development Officers
• Youth Sections at clubs

Sport: Raising the Game:
• Sportsmark & Sportsmark Gold
• Sports College status
• Challenge Funding
• National Junior Sports Programme
• Coaching for Teachers
• Encourage links between club & school

National Curriculum:
• 1988 Education Reform Acts
• Foundation & whole school subject
• Key Stages with Programmes of Study
• Attainment Targets
• Centralised policy
• Wider range of activities
• Not just performance based, also planning & evaluation
• Experience of coaching & officiating

Advantages:
• Uniformity of experience
• Co-ordinated approach
• Guidance with teachers
• Wide range of experience for pupils
Disadvantages
• No allowance for regional variations
• Can limit choice for teachers
• Traditions of schools lost
• Cost of facilities & resources greater

Sports Development Continuum:
• *Excellence* – national standards & representation
• *Performance* – improving standard through coaching, competition & training. Voluntary & free choice
• *Participation* – for fun, fitness and improvement in own time in the form of extracurricular activities
• *Foundation* – curriculum time, compulsory with mixed abilities developing a positive attitude & skills to become movement literate

Disenchantment with these systems led to:

• the Board of Education producing syllabuses in the first three decades of the twentieth century which schools were required to follow.
• the syllabuses laid out the content and style of teaching as a guideline for teachers to follow
• strong emphasis was placed on teacher authority.
• there was still very limited major games teaching.

Syllabuses became defunct with the improvements in teacher training.

• The publications of Planning the Programme and Moving and Growing reflected the change in emphasis from purely physical and organic developments to a focus on the development of the 'whole' child through the Movement approach.
• The use of different terms over the years[drill, physical training and then physical education] reflect the gradual development of certain ideas. Changes occurred in content as well as the relationship between the teacher and the class.

Review questions

History of Physical Education

1. What were the characteristics of the nineteenth century Public schools and the state schools?

2. Name the nine Barbarian schools.

3. What is the significance of the terms 'Barbarian' and 'Philistine' in relation to the nineteenth century Public schools?

4. Describe the process in the technical development of activities in the Public schools.

5. Define the term 'athleticism' and discuss its influence on society.

6. What influence did the Universities bring to bear in the development of sports?

7. Why was athleticism acceptable to the middle classes?

8. What is meant by the term 'self-government' in relation to the organisation of games in the nineteenth century Public schools? Give examples of how this system operated.

9. What influence did Miss Buss, Miss Beale and Madame Bergman Osterberg have on female education?

10. In what way was gymnastics used in state schools?

chapter 12

Physical Activities

The development of various physical activities within their overall social context should now make more sense. Always try and see the historical, political, economic, geographical, educational, and social and cultural aspects – as they will affect the pastimes and sports that we will study.

As well as learning about the history of specific sports it is also important that you can apply that knowledge and link it to present day developments. Other chapters will help you link the past to the present. Certain activities will be given where this ability can be tested. The activities will be:

- Lawn Tennis
- Cricket

It would be useful if you could apply similar logic to other activities.

Popular	Rational
• occasional	• regular
• few, simple rules	• complex, written rules
• limited structure and organisation	• highly structured
• participation sport	• spectator sport
• physical force	• refined skills
• lower class development	• upper class development
• local	• regional/national
• limited equipment and facilities	• sophisticated equipment and facilities

eg   MOB FOOTBALL   eg   REAL TENNIS

Fig. 12.1   DEFINITION OF POPULAR AND RATIONAL SPORTS

These are the generally accepted characteristics of Popular and Rational recreation. However, as with any other generalisation there are occasions when the general does not hold true. In this case there would have been **occasional discrepancies** evidenced by the following:

- Some athletes would have travelled to some festivals, games and race meetings.
- In the transition phase larger towns retained the rural pursuits such as mob games and bull baiting.
- Rules did not occur in all activities at the same time. Games such as cricket had early forms of rules and even mob games played to similar but limited rules year after year.
- There were approximately 46 holy days in the year allowing for animal sports, archery and so on.
- Not all activities were violent; for example archery, bathing.
- Festival occasions could also be smaller occasions.
- Many activities were lower class in their association but the gentry often had some control either in the form of land ownership or prize giving.
- Many activities were male based but women ran the smock race, played cricket early on.

Blood sports

Blood sports as entertainment were a part of British life up to the end of the nineteenth century. In a violent society where minor offences were punishable by hanging, little moral consideration was given for the suffering animals.

Characteristics of blood sports: physical violence; gambling was usually involved; vicarious interest in the infliction of pain; popular in rural and urban areas; involved all social classes.

Reasons for **popularity** of blood sports: excitement; limited entertainment available; to win money by gambling; accessible, easy to stage; ancient notion that animals exist merely as a resource for humans; to strengthen the mentality of soldiers before entering warfare.

In the nineteenth century, blood sports were banned because of:

- a new era of evangelical and humanitarian concern
- increase in concern over correct ways of behaviour; blood sports were not considered to be suitable in a civilised society
- the urban revolution stimulated new concepts of recreation
- complaints of breaches of the peace occasioned by the assembly of large, rowdy crowds
- employers discriminated against employees likely to suffer injuries due to violent pursuits.

Legislation included:

- 1822: to prevent ill treatment of horses and cattle (not including the bull)
- 1824: Royal Society for the Prevention of Cruelty to Animals established
- 1835: baiting sports banned, including the bull
- 1840: Cruelty to Animals Act (cockfighting now illegal).

Here are 2 examples of blood sports:

Bull and bear baiting

This sport was first recorded in the reign of Henry II. A bull or bear would be tied up and terriers would set at it, with the aim of hanging on without being dislodged; the dogs would fail if tossed away by the bull or bear. The dogs would eventually win, but betting took place on the performance of individual dogs. The bulldog was so-called because of its talent at this sport: with its thick set body, short legs and powerful jaws, it would cling to the bull and tear off chunks of flesh. It became a national symbol for British strength and determination.

Bear gardens were popular in the sixteenth century under the Tudors; there was one behind the Globe Theatre (where Shakespeare's plays were performed), and another in the Royal Palace. Four or five dogs would be let loose at the bear at the same time, and the fight ended when the supply of dogs ran out or the bear was too badly injured to carry on. Parliament tried to ban the practice in 1802, and was finally successful in 1835.

'Bull running' was a sport in which a bull was let loose in the streets of a town, and would be goaded by spectators with sticks; eg, at Tutbury and Stamford. The run usually ended on a bridge, and the bull would be spared if the crowd failed to toss it into the water. In rural areas, this sport was restricted to special festivals, but was more common in urban areas.

Cock fighting

This was the most popular blood sport which set animal against animal; it was thought that cocks' natural aggression made for a fair fight, and each had an equal chance of victory if well matched. Cocks were bred and trained to fight, and metal spurs were added to their feet during the seventeenth century. Breeds included Piles, Blackreds, Pollcats, Pirchin, Ducks, Gingers and Shropshire Reds.

This was a sport popular across all social classes in urban and rural areas, for its entertainment value and gambling potential. Large towns had cockpits where regular contest took place; in 1800, there were seven cockpits in Newcastle. Failure to pay bets could result in the offender being hauled up in a basket above the pit (as in the Royal Cockpit at Bird Cage Walk).

'Throwing at cocks' was a favourite sport for Shrove Tuesday. Birds would be tethered, and people paid to throw stones or sticks at them. The birds' legs would usually break, and they would be killed.

Aquatic activities

Spa towns

Britain's inland spa resorts became fashionable in the nineteenth century when it became popular for the upper classes to 'take the waters', and railways helped their mobility. Spa towns have their origin in Roman times where they developed from mineral springs or holy wells. The Tudors established taking the waters as a standard medical practice, which was a tradition continued by the Georgians towards the end of the eighteenth century.

They also offered rest and relaxation away from the growing industrial towns. Some of the notable towns are Bath with its Roman remains and impressive Georgian architecture, Buxton with thermal springs high up in Derbyshire, and Harrogate.

 **ACTIVITY 1**

Can you think of any modern practices which seem to try to recreate these kind of atmospheres?

Rowing

The art of propelling a boat is practised as a sport in most countries, but it began as a utilitarian activity when it provided power for war ships and transport in industrial towns.

The River Thames formed one of the main highways in medieval times; wealthy people had their own state barges and the professional watermen plied for trade. Watermanship refers to the skill of handling a boat. By the beginning of the eighteenth century, there were more than 40,000 licensed watermen. There were frequent contests between the watermen, and betting on the barges was common.

The earliest account of a regatta on the River Thames was in 1775. This occasion was derived from the Italian 'regata', originally boat races on the Grand Canal in Venice.

The standard of rowing increased in the nineteenth century due to an increasing professionalism. Rowing races attracted an enormous following and were widely reported in the press. Many rowers became coaches of amateur crews and eventually, due to the rapid and powerful rise of amateurism and the First World War, professional contests gradually died out.

In 1715 Dogget instituted what is now the oldest sculling race in the world. Crews race for an orange livery with a silver badge, hence the title 'Dogget's Coat and Badge'. (Broughton the prize fighter was an early winner.) Rowing clubs which emerged were mostly amateur; one of the most famous was Leander in 1818.

Bumping races were a traditional form of racing, especially in narrow stretches. Crews would attempt to touch or bump the crew in front and crews would change place according to the number of bumps scored. The crew finishing first would take the title 'Head of the River'. The public schools took to rowing, as it met their values of athleticism.

Leander Club is the oldest amateur rowing club in the world, believed to have been founded in 1818. Membership is a mark of distinction in the rowing world and a large proportion are former Oxford and Cambridge oarsmen. Leander's golden era came in the years between 1891 and 1914, during which they recorded 30 Henley wins (including 13 in the Grand Challenge Cup) and also won the Olympic eights in 1908 and 1912, and the Olympic pairs in 1908.

 **ACTIVITY 2**

What qualities of athleticism would be evident in a rowing fixture?

Fig. 12.2 SWIMMING AND ROWING ON THE RIVER THAMES

The need to win these fixtures led to the hiring of professional watermen, but due to the amateur ethos they reported that they were hired merely to provide competition! Rowing became competitive at Oxford and Cambridge Universities in the early years of the nineteenth century. The first University Boat Race took place at Henley in 1829; the Henley Regatta was established ten years later.

Henley Regatta

In 1839 James Nash established this event initially to drum up trade for tradespeople and hoteliers of the town.

This soon became a great traditional event, reflecting the Victorian love of combining sporting events with a grand social occasion.

- Initially, only amateurs could compete.
- Non-British competitors were briefly banned in 1908.
- The Manual Labour clause excluded anyone 'who by trade or employment is a mechanic, artisan or labourer'.

However, it became less exclusive; the Manual Labour clause was abolished in 1890, and the Leander Club began to compete against teams such as the Thames Tradesmen and the Metropolitan Police. The Amateur Rowing Association was formed in 1882, followed by the National Amateur Rowing Association in 1890. The NARA was formed to counter the unfair manual labour clause. Exclusion was to be a monetary distinction rather than a social one. Today Henley reflects the complex social class system. There are:

- Committee Lawn for Stewards and Guests
- Stewards Enclosure for Members and Guests
- Business and Club class
- Economy Class
- Public Banks.

Changes:
- 1946 women admitted to spectate but not to row
- training has become more scientific in terms of competitors' diet and technical developments in craft and coaching
- the event raises approximately £ $\frac{1}{3}$ million annual profit.

How do you think that Henley Regatta has reflected English society in the nineteenth and early twentieth century?

The seaside

The fashion for sea bathing began in the eighteenth century when it was regarded as serving medical purposes, rather than for fun. The seaside resort took over in popularity from the spa towns. Bathing became popular in the 1720s and the first bathing machines made their appearance in Scarborough in 1753. Bathing nude was not uncommon at this time and the bathing machine afforded some privacy when costumes were heavy and uncomfortable. These would be pulled by men or horses to the seaside. They would later be replaced by bathing tents at the turn of the twentieth century. Men and women would have separate bathing areas. Mixed bathing and the wearing of costumes came in the nineteenth century.

During the Victorian era, the railways and steamers with their cheap excursion fares made the seaside resorts accessible to large numbers of people. Thomas Cook established his travel company in 1841 and laid on excursion trains. This resulted in the exodus of the upper classes to more isolated areas like the west country resorts. The creation of Bank Holidays in 1871 resulted in even more people visiting the seaside, sometimes as day trippers.

Swimming

Swimming for recreation developed in the eighteenth century when rowing and yachting became popular:

- In 1734, the first open air swimming pool was built in London.
- Captain Webb swam the English Channel in 1875.
- Swimming was initially undertaken in Britain in natural facilities such as rivers and canals for recreation, hygiene and safety. The lower classes in particular used these facilities which made the middle and upper classes less ready to use them.
- Developments in swimming technique came particularly from the overseas influence, for example the front crawl came from the Indians and John Trudgeon learnt his stroke from the Bantu tribe in South Africa [that brought both arms over the water]. He introduced this to England in 1873.
- The first modern Olympics in 1896 at Athens included the 100, 500 and 1200 metres freestyle.
- An increase in public baths following the Public Baths and Washhouses Act in 1840.
- The success in swimming races in Britain from the mid-nineteenth century led to a proportional increase in prizes which were usually won by 'professional swimmers' who were swimming teachers involved in giving lessons in return for money.
- The Amateur Swimming Association was formed in 1886 followed by FINA, Fédération Internationale de Natation Amateur.
- Teachers of swimming in Great Britain were excluded from racing.
- Women's swimming was introduced at the 1912 Olympic Games in Stockholm.

- The nature of the sport places it in the category of an athletic activity. The keeping of records by 'racing against the clock' is an important element. Other factors have also played a part – social acceptability and regulation governed both the style and materials worn by male and female swimmers.

List some of the modern changes that have occurred in swimming. Consider types of swimming, facilities, access to participation and so on.

Racket sports

Real tennis

This game originated in France, as suggested by the terminology: 'dedans', 'tambour', 'grille'. It was an activity of the French Royal court, and was made popular in England by the Tudors. One of the most famous courts is still in use at Hampton Court. This was the sport of the noblemen and royalty and in 1536 there were restrictive acts which forbade servants and labourers to play. This helped to retain the privileged status of the élite. The game was originally played with the hand, 'le jeu de paume', until the sixteenth century when rackets were used.

This was a very sophisticated, exclusive game requiring expensive facilities, equipment and an understanding of the complex rules and social etiquette of the game. The emphasis was on the individual's skill and tactical and strategic awareness; as ever, wagering was evident. It was the epitome of rational sport.

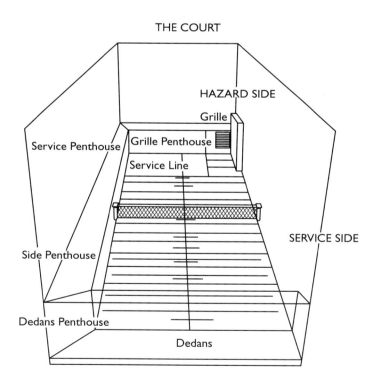

Fig. 12.3   A REAL TENNIS COURT

Rackets

This game began in fairly humble circumstances in England. Open courts existed in the back yards of taverns and inns, and in many towns. They were social meeting places and there was always a wall to be used. Equipment could also be hired from publicans wishing to make the

Fig. 12.4   An early version of tennis, taken from *Orbis Sensualium Pictus* by John Comenius, 1659

most of their business opportunities. They had all the requirements – willing opponents, alcohol and wagering.

The game was a test of strength and accuracy. In a four-handed match the players took alternate 'out' and 'in' games, which would lead to exciting rallies.

Rackets was taken up by the public schools for its simple qualities and the possibilities of using architectural features within the school grounds. It was a game which suited the cult of athleticism, containing rules, etiquette and sportsmanship.

Fives

Fives was played with the palm of the hand, wearing a glove, and the ball was hit against the wall. It was played in inns and other public places, and was a much more individual game than rackets. In the public schools it tended to be played more in the boys' recreation time and consequently did not establish well-known formal rules. As the game was not taken up at the universities, individual schools' variations continued. These qualities tended to make it a less favourable game than rackets as far as the staff were concerned.

Lawn tennis

Real or Royal tennis was an aristocratic pastime and was not conducive to the lives of the middle and lower classes. However, in the nineteenth century the middle classes with their increasing wealth and leisure time wanted to establish their own form of recreation which would set them apart from the lower classes. The game became enormously popular midway through Queen Victoria's reign.

Major Wingfield took most of the credit for the game's popularity. His invention, which he called Sphairistike, had an hour-glass shaped court. He provided a commercial product which could be bought in kit form making it attractive to the middle classes whose wealth was often determined by trade. The Marylebone Cricket Club (MCC) then took it one stage further, calling it lawn tennis and adopting an oblong shaped court.

It ousted croquet from the lawns of the middle classes, and proved to be an ideal game for large suburban gardens to be played by both social classes, in their increasingly leisured society. There were few recreational activities at this time that both sexes could enjoy together. The ladies were able to play privately away from the public gaze, and it was a game which helped to remove some of the stereotypes. They could run around becoming increasingly energetic and clothing began to be slightly less restrictive. Their schools also accepted the game as it was non-contact, had rules and was acceptable to the parents.

The middle classes also ensured its club development and the administrative structures. The lower classes had to wait until there was public provision, so their participation was delayed.

ACTIVITY 5

1 **Who invented the game which he called Sphairistike and what is the game called today?** **[2 marks]**
2 **How did the structure of Real Tennis differ from mob football and how did this reflect the class of people who played them?** **[4 marks]**
3 **It has been suggested that Lawn Tennis is the only game that was invented by the urban middle class.**
   a **Discuss this view and explain why there was a delay in working class participation** **[4 marks]**
   b **Why was Lawn Tennis suitable for professional class ladies to play?** **[4 marks]**
4 **Tennis has been a part of the school physical education curriculum for the latter half of the twentieth century though the skills of tennis are challenging for young children to master.**
   a **What strategies could you use to help children learn to adapt to the full game?** **[2 marks]**
   b **How could a physical education teacher keep some elements of play whilst maintaining the educational aims of the lesson?** **[3 marks]**
5 **The democratisation of tennis has become an important issue in the late twentieth century.**
   a **How has this been reflected in the approach of the Lawn Tennis Association towards the game?** **[4 marks]**
   b **Discuss the view that tennis has changed from a Victorian garden party game to a highly commercial enterprise.** **[5 marks]**

Cycling

This was an activity which reflected the technological advances and social changes in the nineteenth century.

- The **Hobby Horse** (1818) was the forerunner to the bicycle. It was propelled by the rider who sat astride and pushed alternate feet on the ground.
- The **Boneshaker** (1868) was invented by the Michaux brothers in Paris.
- The **Penny Farthing** (1870–1890) – The large front wheel was developed to obtain more speed for every turn of the pedals, so that the wheel covered more ground.
- The **National Royal Tricycle** (1884) was developed from the Penny Farthing to make a safer ride.
- The **Rover Safety** (1885) was the machine that set the fashion and was built with the first Diamond frame.

The bicycle was developing during the machine age, and could be produced in large numbers. It was an alternative mode of transport to the horse and cart, and consequently more appealing to the middle classes. The gentry initially retained their preference for the horse and were disdainful of 'new fangled' machine. The roads initially were poor, but improvements were gradually made.

(a)

(b)

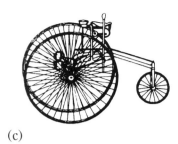

(c)

(d)

The gentry ladies however were keen to take on this new form of transport which gave them a sense of freedom from their claustrophobic lives which required that they were chaperoned everywhere and were expected to fulfil rigid social roles. Further encouragement was given by the Royal daughters' use of the bicycle.

The growing interest in the countryside also made the bicycle useful, as a route out to the country lanes. The railways offered Rover tickets which would take the cycle and the cyclists further afield. Club developments became hugely popular, particularly the touring branch. Bicycles were expensive however, and the majority of people had to wait for the second hand trade to develop.

(e)

Fig. 12.5   (A) THE BONESHAKER, 1868;
(B) THE HOBBY HORSE, 1818;
(C) THE NATIONAL ROYAL TRICYCLE, 1884;
(D) THE PENNY FARTHING, 1870;
(E) THE ROVER SAFETY, 1885

Football

Football began as a mob game. It lacked the organisational features of the modern game and was characterised by large numbers of players, exclusively male and from the lower classes, involved in a territorial struggle. The game tended to be played occasionally on annual holidays like the Wakes as the people had limited free time, and would cover distances between villages. Due to only being played a few times a year there were limited rules, and

Fig. 12.6   ENGLAND V SCOTLAND AT THE OVAL, 6 MARCH 1875

hence violence, injury and sometimes death, were common as the game was determined by force rather than skill. There was no division of labour; players had no particular roles, and there was a loose distinction between participating and spectating. This was originally a rural activity and reflected the harsh way of life lived by uneducated, rural people.

What changed the game out of all proportion to its original character? The gentry sons in the public schools began to play the game regularly on the school grounds. Though they started with variations in rules from school to school, they gradually began to develop them in the form of shape of goals, boundaries, limits on the size of the team and so on. A competitive structure emerged with inter-house and inter-school matches. Some variations remained and were distinctive to individual schools; the unique facility features like the Close at Rugby with soft turf and the Quad at Charterhouse, where the dribbling game emerged. There is also the Eton Wall game which still exists today.

University graduates further codified the game and established associations; the Football Association was established in 1863. When university graduates became employers they encouraged the game among the workers, partly to boost morale and loyalty, and also to instil middle class values and discipline. They also established their middle class sports clubs based on amateurism.

The roads and pavements were the playgrounds of working class children and they devised numerous types of street games. Football was one of them and most streets had a football team associated with a strong community feeling. The cramped living conditions and shortage of facilities led to a more spectator-based interest in the game. Developments in transport opened up the rest of the country for fixtures further afield.

There was therefore a curious development across the different social classes. The game began as a mob game by and for the lower classes. The public schools made it popular with the gentry in the south of England, who also incorporated middle class values within the game as it developed along strictly amateur lines – the southern amateurs. However, in the north of England it developed in the industrial towns, and professionalism soon crept in with clubs like Sheffield Wednesday being established, when Wednesday became early closing day. The Football League was established in 1885. When the two sides met there was a culture shock!

 **ACTIVITY 6**

Explain the major changes that occurred from the mob game to the game of Association Football.

Cricket

Cricket is one of the oldest established games and was played from the outset by both social classes; the aristocrats and the commoners played together. There were not many activities which both social classes played together, though they had particular roles within the game to signify their status. The game reflected the feudal structure of the village. The early clubs emerged from the rural village sides, with the gentry acting as patron. There were a variety of reasons for this: the game took place in the summer season when light was at its best allowing the workers time to participate, and because of its non violent nature, there were no threats to the gentry in playing with the peasants. The early rules and gentlemanly behaviour ensured a level of respectful behaviour.

Games would attract spectators in their thousands. The first written rules were drawn up by the Duke of Richmond in 1727 to help control country house games where sometimes

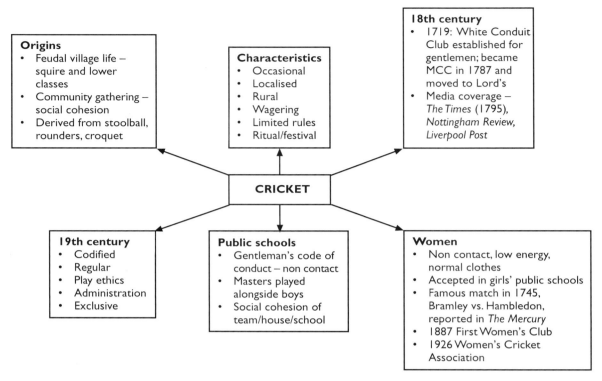

Fig. 12.7   The development of cricket

large sums of money would hinge on the outcome. The MCC emerged as an organisational feature comparatively early in the game's development. The terms 'gentlemen' and 'players' emerged to distinguish the amateurs from the professionals.

Though it was a game to appeal to all social classes, county cricket remained quite exclusive, holding matches mid-week. The suburban middle classes began to take out county membership and the large grounds began to take over from the smaller, more portable fixtures. This would detach it even more from the working classes. The Lancashire League was established similarly to the Football League, to cater for the needs of the working classes.

Cricket was immediately acceptable in the public schools as it matched all the criteria for social control for the masters and athleticism for the boys. The rules meant a code of behaviour by the boys who would be expected to behave within the spirit of the game. The fags, or younger boys, would help the older boys in practice and the assistant masters would also play. When fixtures became prestigious and important to win, professionals were employed to raise the standards of play amongst the team.

The first official women's cricket match is recorded as having taken place in 1745, between Bromley and Hambleden. It grew in popularity during the nineteenth century, as women's clothing began to adapt to sporting conditions. The Women's Cricket Association was formed in 1926.

1 The acceptability of cricket as a respectable game was such that 19th Century Public Schools adopted it as a vehicle for the development of Christian gentlemen.

The engraving by Rowlandsen called 'Rural Sports' captures the mood of a three-day county match between Hampshire and Surrey.

  a What technical features point to this being an 18th century match?
                                                          [3 marks]

  b The term 'Rural sports' was usually associated with popular recreation. What were the characteristics of this form of recreation, some of which may be evident in this engraving?
                                                          [3 marks]

  c What do you understand by the term 'gentlemen' and 'players' in relation to cricket?   **[1 mark]**

2 Cricket was a popular game for both sexes from the 17th century onwards, though women's cricket saw a decline in the early 19th century.

  a What aspects of nineteenth century cricket made it such an attractive activity in boys' Public Schools?   **[3 marks]**

  b Why was cricket an acceptable game for women to play by the end of the 19th century?   **[2 marks]**

3 The emergence of the West Indies in world standard Cricket was no coincidence.

  a What may have motivated an emerging country to specialise in such an activity?   **[3 marks]**

4 Games can be classified into certain categories – Invasion, Net and Innings.

  a What are the characteristics of innings games?   **[4 marks]**

5 Cricket is still as popular in these modern times but some elements of the game have changed.

  a Suggest what some of these changes have been and account for them.
                                                            [3 marks]

Athletics

Many athletic activities developed from functional activities like the throwing events, while others from agricultural pursuits like hunting and clearing obstacles. Pedestrianism was similar to race walking, and developed in Stuart and Georgian Society where young men were sent ahead of a coach to warn the inn keeper of their imminent arrival. Wagers were placed and the gentry acted as patrons. It developed into an endurance event covering long distances against the opponent or the clock. Can you see the similarities between the sculling races like the Doggett Coat and Badge and the Prize Ring? It involved a working class performer and a gentry patron, but it was often a corrupt activity. Pedestrianism was a commercial attraction, with notable characters like Deerfoot the American earning large sums of money.

Hurdling is said to have evolved from the boys at public schools improvising in their leisure time and re-enacting events they saw at home like the association between hunting and hare and hounds and hurdling with horse racing. Other events were included like high and standing broad jumps, and athletics meetings began. They developed athletics clubs, eg, the London Athletic Club.

In 1896 the revival of the modern Olympic Games heralded an international appeal for athletics. Specialisation was taking over from the traditional all-round English amateur sportsman; play had moved on to competition and winning.

Golf

The origins of golf are thought to derive from ancient activities played by the Patagonian Indians, from a game called *jeu de mal* in France and *het kolven* in Holland. However, the Scots claim that they were the first responsible for the game developing to its present form. It was banned in 1457 as it was feared that it interfered with people's archery practice.

The Stuarts made golf a Royal pursuit and Mary Queen of Scots was frowned upon for playing the game following her husband's death. The French Royal connection also brought the term 'caddy' which derived from the word cadets – the younger sons of the French aristocrats who came over to England as her pages. The Scots adopted this to mean loafers and scroungers! Many monarchs to follow were interested in the game.

The competition for the Silver Golf Club in 1744 was the first ever held in golf, and a Code of Rules was agreed.

However, golf originally seems to have been for the ordinary people, eg, the Fish Wives of Musselborough. From the seventeenth century onwards, equipment changes meant increased prices which effectively priced the fishermen and labourers out of golf. The first balls were made of turned boxwood followed by a feathery ball. Rubber balls wrapped in gutta-percha, in the nineteenth century, were much more expensive. The shafts were made from hickory which had to be imported from the USA. This led to the situation where the gentry played and the commoners carried the clubs as caddies. With the enclosure of land and the cost of laying out courses on expensive land near suburban areas, it soon became the exclusive preserve of a wealthy minority.

The proliferation of clubs meant an equal proliferation of local rules. By 1919 the matter of rules was passed to the Royal and Ancient Society. The clubs were governed by the upper and middle classes, and women were admitted on the understanding that a level of internal segregation was accepted. They could not vote or be shareholders.

Golf helped to foster a community life in the suburbs. Women from all social classes had played the game from its early days, and by 1898 there were 220 ladies' clubs. However, as the Victorian stereotype of female behaviour took hold of society, they met with problems.

They were considered physically inferior to men, which led to a miniature version of the course or from the forward tee on men's courses. They were advised to attempt no more than 70 yards for a drive.

 **ACTIVITY 8** **In order to carry out research on activities and games, referring to a checklist can help to organise the information in a manageable format. Table 12.1 shows the checklist applied to badminton; research some details about the development of hockey using this approach.**

Table 12.1   GATHERING INFORMATION ABOUT BADMINTON

PRINCIPLE	INFORMATION	REASON
origin	evolved about 1870 from ancient children's game of Battledore and Shuttlecock army officers exported/imported – India	British Empire
social event	derives its name from the seat (estate) of the Duke of Beaufort at Badminton, Gloucestershire played in Victorian salons by men and women	leisure activity, ie, upper class
social class	upper class	• leisure time • space and equipment
influences	• Duke of Beaufort • army	played game on estate imported/exported games
early game	• hour glass shaped court • doubles popular but 3, 4 and 5 a side usual	to accommodate doors of Victorian salon singles considered selfish
later game	1870 Poona 1st laws; 1893 Badminton Association 1899 All England Championships; 1901 court made rectangular	regulate court size and rules for competitions
sporting atmosphere	equipment (net; rackets; shuttle); court (boundaries); spectators; recreation in leisure time	
education	not initially popular in either public or state schools	• no team game values • lack of facilities
clothing	men – informal day wear women – formal restrictive long dresses	modesty
amateurism professionalism	originally amateur	developed by Victorians – amateur code
clubs	250 clubs were members of the Badminton Association by 1914	Victorians developed the club ethos; made competitions possible
other	1934 International Badminton Federation	

Summary

From this selection of activities, you can see how sport within society is a dynamic experience, constantly changing to adapt to new pressures and sometimes exerting its own influence on society.

- From brutal and blood sports to a system where legislation curtailed activities or caused modifications.
- The change in emphasis from rural to urban sport with a philosophy of participation was hindered by lack of facilities and space.
- From watching in small local groups to mass spectatorism; business enterprise; improved communications and a national interest in sport.
- From local rules to fully codified rules formulating governing bodies.
- Control passed from the aristocracy to the middle classes.
- Bribery, corruption and vice largely eliminated, and with it the old concept of professionalism.
- Recreation was no longer the privilege of the nobility. By the end of the nineteenth century, the working class had won the same right to recreation.
- With the spatial restrictions of urbanisation came the desire to escape to the country. The weekend exodus became a national characteristic.

Review questions

1   List four characteristics of popular and rational recreation.

2   What caused the rise and decline of fencing and boxing?

3   How did fox hunting reflect the social status of the social classes in the nineteenth century?

4   What were the two types of angling that developed?

5   Why were blood sports popular in the eighteenth and nineteenth centuries and why were they later banned?

6   What were the first professional rowers called?

7   What was the 'manual labour' clause and which sport did it affect in particular?

8   Explain why Real Tennis was for the upper classes whilst Lawn Tennis developed for the middle classes?

9   Why did Rackets meet the concept of athleticism whilst Fives did not?

10   What factors made cycling a popular activity?

11   Explain the influence of the various social classes on the development of football.

12   In what way was the development of cricket different to that of football?

13   What is the link between hurdling as an athletic activity and the development of the public school's hare and hounds?

14   How and why did golf shift from being accessible to all social classes to being an exclusive activity of the middle and upper classes?

15   From Table 12.1 suggest some of the major influences on the development of the game of badminton.

chapter 13

The Nature of Skilled Performance

T his chapter will give you a basic understanding of the terminology that is used by those involved in physical education and sport in relation to skill development and learning. You should be able to:

- understand the terminology of skill development and learning
- use it in the correct context
- relate it to practical examples.

Here is a list of the key terms to be covered in this chapter. It is important that you understand them and begin to use these in both your observation/analysis as well as your classroom discussions.

- Motor skill
- Perceptual skill
- Cognitive skill
- Simple skill
- Complex skill
- Ability
- Psychomotor ability
- Gross motor ability
- Perceptual ability

- Continuum
- Gross and fine skills
- Discrete, continuous, serial skills
- Self paced/externally paced skills
- Open/closed skills
- High/low cognitive skills
- Feedback
- Complex skill

Once you have read this chapter you should gain a working understanding of:

- the phrase **skilled performance**
- the phrase **acquisition of skill**
- the terms **skill** and **ability**.

What is skilled performance?

 **ACTIVITY 1**

In most occupations, sports, daily activities and in the development stages of young children the results of skill learning are evident.

1 Discuss with your fellow students what you think makes a human activity a skilled performance.
2 Try to come up with a short list of examples from various walks of life.

In discussion with your fellow students you will all have been able to suggest various examples of skilled performances, recognising perhaps that a:

- concert pianist may be said to be performing skillfully
- ballet dancer's coordination and timing are skillful
- perfect pass by a quarterback in American football is skillful
- long range three point score in basketball is skillful
- well executed off drive in cricket is skillful
- gymnast performing a vault in the Olympic Games is skillful
- pole vaulter completing a vault is skillful
- potter using a potting wheel is skillful.

In other words we can all recognise the outcome or the end product of a skillful performance. However, as students of physical education and sport you need to know:

- how does this end product come about?

What process underlies the acquisition of skill and control of movement? How is skill acquired? What factors influence its attainment and how is it retained? The following chapters will help you develop a better understanding of the underlying processes involved in acquiring skill.

As a student of physical education and sport you should then be able to:

1 Analyse movement situations.
2 Recognise good practice and performance.
3 Recognise any faults or problems.
4 Solve any problems of how to improve skill levels and overall performance.

As you read through these chapters you will realise that the study of the acquisition of skill is not an exact science. There are no one hundred per cent 'correct' or right ways of acquiring skill. Having been made aware of the various related theories, concepts, principles and methods you should be able to:

- use this information to support your understanding
- develop your own ideas
- think about the implications for teaching and coaching.

Using the term 'skill'

You may have noticed in the list of examples given or in your own discussions that the word 'skill' can be used in two slightly different ways. We can use the word to relate to skill as an **act** or **task** or use it as an indicator of **quality** of performance.

Skill as an act or task

The word in this context is used to denote an act or a task that has a specific aim or goal to achieve, for instance a gymnast performing a vault. Further examples are:

- taking a penalty flick in hockey
- shooting a free shot after a foul in basketball
- serving in tennis.

Fig. 13.1 A GYMNASTIC PERFORMANCE IS MEASURED AGAINST SET CRITERIA (ABSOLUTE)

Fig. 13.2 PERFORMANCE IN A RACE IS MEASURED IN RELATIVE TERMS

If we observed players carrying out any of the examples given above on a regular basis and they were achieving a high percentage success rate then we would consider them as being skillful players. The use of the word in this context refers to a physical movement, action or task, involving some or all of the body, that a person is trying to carry out in a technically correct manner. Thus skill can be seen as goal directed behaviour.

Skill as an indicator of quality of performance

The word in this context is probably a little more ambiguous than skill as an act or task. The word **well** added to the description of the skill infers a qualitative judgement of the skill being made by you as the observer, for instance you may remark on a well-executed off drive during a cricket match. Very often we make judgements between players comparing performances, looking at players' achievements in the context of the class or school team or against set criteria. Thus we measure or assess in either relative or absolute terms. What you have to understand however, is: What makes it a 'well' performed skill? After reading through the rest of this chapter you should be able to understand, explain and apply the main criteria that are used to judge whether a performer is skillful or not.

Defining different types of skill

Psychologists have considered *different types of skill*, trying to differentiate for instance between **motor skills** and **verbal skills**. Examples of three different types of skill are:

1 **Intellectual skills or cognitive skills**
   Skills which involve the use of a person's mental powers, eg, problem solving, verbal reasoning (verbal skill).
2 **Perceptive skills**
   Interpreting and making sense of information coming in via the senses.
3 **Motor skills**
   Smoothly executing physical movements and responses.

Consider two other activities in addition to fig 13.3. For each activity, make a list of the things the performer is having to consider and take into account.

Fig. 13.3 NATIONAL LEAGUE BASKETBALL PLAYER DRIBBLING

When National league basketball players are performing a 'skillful' dribble and 'driving' the basket they are not only showing technically good movements (ie, showing motor skill) but in carrying out the action the player has had to make many decisions including:

- whether to dribble or pass
- how to dribble
- position of opposition
- position of own team mates
- context of game
- situation in game – winning or losing?
- time in game (how long to go?)
- do we need to score or keep the ball?
- what are the odds of making the dribble, drive and possible shot?

Fig. 13.4 SKILLED PERFORMANCE IS A CONTINUOUS INTERPLAY BETWEEN TECHNICAL ABILITY, EMOTIONS, PERCEPTIONS, JUDGEMENTS, FITNESS AND PREPAREDNESS

This obviously involves a whole host of both **cognitive skills** and **perceptual skills**, as only after having taken into account all the various information (cues, signals, stimuli) being received from around them can a basketball player then carry out the necessary **motor skill** to any degree of proficiency. Therefore, as we can see, although many psychologists have tried to define the ways in which motor, cognitive and perceptual skills are independent of one another, from a physical educational and sporting point of view when we talk of skill we usually mean a combination of all three areas. Skill is therefore more than just technical excellence. In your further reading around this topic you will come across the phrase 'perceptual motor skills' or very often just 'motor skills' – the perceptual or cognitive involvement is usually implied.

Complex skills and simple skills

In your consideration and discussions for activity 2 you will have concluded that in carrying out movement we are rarely just 'doing'. Some level of thought and decision making has usually taken place. However, as you develop your understanding in this area you will come to realise that certain sporting activities and physical movements require *more* thought, conscious control and decision making than others. These are known as **complex skills** whereas those activities and movements requiring very little conscious thought or decision making and only basic movement patterns are called **simple skills** (refer to information processing).

Acquisition of skill

In the phrase 'acquisition of skill' the word 'acquisition' infers that skill is something that you can gain as opposed to something that you already have.

Skill is said to be gained through 'learning'. Skill is said to be 'learned behaviour'!
                                                                        (B. Knapp).

Definitions of skill

You will have a better understanding of the nature of skill if you consider a variety of definitions and see how those definitions have developed.

In your group either individually or in twos and threes select one of the following definitions and consider what it is trying to imply or say and then feedback your understanding of the definition to the rest of the class.

1 **Professor GP Meredith, *Information and Skill***

   'Excellence of performance – the successful integration of a hierarchy of abilities (all the abilities we have) appropriate to a given task under given conditions.'

2 **Oldfield, *The Analysis of Human Skill* – New Biology**

   'The behaviour which tends to eliminate the discrepancy between intention and performance.'

3 **Guthrie, from *Skills in Sport*: modified by B Knapp**

   'The learned ability to bring about pre-determined results with maximum certainty often with the minimum outlay of time, energy or both.'

4 Argyle and Kendon, *The Experimental Analysis of Social Performance*

'An organised, coordinated activity in relation to an object or a situation which involves a whole chain of sensory, central and motor mechanisms.'

5 M Robb, *The Dynamics of Skill Acquisition*

'While the task can be physical or mental, one generally thinks of a skill as some type of manipulative efficiency. A skilled movement is one in which a predetermined objective is accomplished with maximum efficiency and with a minimum outlay of energy. A skillful movement does not just happen. There must be a conscious effort on the part of the performer in order to execute a skill.'

6 R Magill, *Motor Learning: Concepts and Applications*

'An act or a task that has a goal to achieve and that requires voluntary body or limb movements to be properly performed.'

The definitions given above emphasise the following aspects of skill:

Definition 1

Skill involves:

- excellent performance (high quality)
- bringing together various abilities to a lesser or greater degree (dependent on which task) for a **specific** movement to be carried out.

Definition 2

Skill involves:

- the intention to do it, it is not just luck; there must be a conscious decision and effort.

Definition 3

Skill involves:

- learned ability – learning through practice and experience to use the appropriate innate abilities (See Abilities)
- pre-determined results – you have an aim to achieve
- maximum certainty – you are consistent in your achievement of success
- minimum outlay of time and energy – you are performing the actions efficiently, you are not wasting time or energy.

Definition 4

Skill involves:

- Sensory-mechanisms – taking on information via the various receptor systems, eg, senses – this links later to chapter on information processing
- Central-mechanisms – brain (interpretations and decision making)
- Motor-mechanisms – nerves and muscles system being used to create movement – but basically suggests that skills involve the use of the *senses* to detect and take in information, the *brain* to interpret the information and make decisions according to what you know about the situation, and the *nervous system* together with muscles to work the various parts of the body in order to carry out the action.

Definition 5

This definition basically combines several main aspects of the others.

Skill is a learned behaviour

From your discussions and feedback sessions relating to activity 3 you will have realised that the term 'skill' is a complex term to define. Any definition should, however, involve several important points. The better-known definitions which tend to be referred to are the ones by B Knapp (after Guthrie), R Magill, and M Robb.

Overall you can see that, according to these various definitions, skill involves **learning** via practice and experience. A skilled performer **learns** to be **effective** and efficient in:

- achieving a well-defined objective (goal directed)
- maximising – being **consistently** successful (can be repeated)
- minimising – maintaining the physical and mental energy demands of performance at an optimum level (aesthetically pleasing, coordinated, precise, decisions)
- minimising – taking only the minimum time required (well timed).

Thus a skillful performer has gone through some form of '**learning process**'. There is intention in their performance ie, it is not just luck. It is not enough just to say they are accurate and have good technique, the key word is that they are '**consistent**'. The performance is also carried out '**efficiently**' ie, not wasting time or energy.

 **Using an example from either the individual or game activities you have covered, work through the above definitions trying to give in depth practical examples of how they might apply to physical education and sport.**

Using the term 'ability'

It is important at this stage to consider another term which is very often synonymous with the word skill and is often used in definitions of skilled behaviour. The term is **ability**.

In your discussions of what constitutes skill, the term ability has probably often been used in the wrong context. Often in a variety of sports, players from abroad are referred to as having higher levels of ability than our 'home' developed players. When what we mean is that their skills in terms of technique are of a higher quality. It is the word 'ability' which is being used in the wrong context. We often talk of players as having 'lots of ability' when what we mean is they have developed high levels of skill.

Definitions and characteristics of ability

It is important that you understand the differences between skill and abilities. The study of abilities comes under the umbrella of 'differential psychology'.

'Motor abilities are relatively enduring traits which are generally stable qualities or factors that help a person carry out a particular act.' (E. Fleishman).

'Motor abilities are innate inherited traits that determine an individual's coordination, balance, ability and speed of reactions.' (R. Arnot and C. Gaines).

It is sufficient at this stage for you to realise that abilities are said to be stable and **enduring** capacities or qualities and characteristics that a person has within themselves. A person is therefore **born** with these qualities. Abilities are said to be innate, inherited traits, factors that help, for instance, a person's agility, coordination, balance and speed of reactions.

A person trying to carry out a sporting activity will *learn to use* and combine these underlying innate qualities or characteristics in an organised way in order to carry out coordinated movement.

Taxonomy of human perceptual motor abilities – Fleishman, 1972

The work of Fleishman (1972), which is one of the better-known pieces of research, developed a taxonomy of human perceptual motor abilities. He carried out extensive testing of over 200 tasks, the results of which led him to propose that there seemed to be 11 identifiable and measurable **perceptual motor abilities**. In addition he identified nine **physical proficiency abilities**. These differed from **perceptual motor abilities** in that they are more generally related to gross physical performance.

1 **Limb coordination** – the ability to coordinate the movement of a number of limbs simultaneously.
2 **Control precision** – the ability to make highly controlled and precise muscular adjustments where large muscle groups are involved.
3 **Response orientation** – the ability to select rapidly where a response should be made as in a choice reaction time situation.
4 **Reaction time** – the ability to respond rapidly to a stimulus when it appears.
5 **Speed of arm movement** – the ability to make a gross, rapid arm movement.
6 **Rate control** – the ability to change speed and direction of response with precise timing, as in following a continuously moving target.
7 **Manual dexterity** – the ability to make skilful, well directed arm hand movements, when manipulating objects under speed conditions.
8 **Finger dexterity** – the ability to perform skilful controlled manipulations of tiny objects involving primarily the fingers.
9 **Arm hand steadiness** – the ability to make precise arm, hand positioning movements where strength and speed are minimally involved.
10 **Wrist finger speed** – the ability to move the wrist and fingers rapidly, as in a tapping task.
11 **Aiming** – the ability to aim precisely at a small object in space.

Fleishman's proficiency abilities

Typically these more general athletic abilities could be considered physical fitness abilities.

1 **Static strength** – maximum force exerted against an external object.
2 **Dynamic strength** – muscular endurance in exerting force repeatedly, eg, pull ups.
3 **Explosive strength** – the ability to mobilise energy effectively for bursts of muscular effort, eg, high jump.
4 **Trunk strength** – strength of the trunk muscles.
5 **Extent flexibility** – the ability to flex or stretch the trunk and back muscles.
6 **Dynamic flexibility** – the ability to make repeated, rapid trunk flexing movements as in a series of stand and touch toes stretch and touch toes.
7 **Gross body coordination** – the ability to coordinate the action of several parts of the body while the body is in motion.
8 **Gross body equilibrium** – the ability to maintain balance without visual cues.
9 **Stamina** – the capacity to sustain maximum effort requiring cardiovascular effort, eg, a long distance run.

Additional further abilities which have not been included by Fleishman but identified later are such things as:

- **Static balance** – the ability to balance on a stable surface when no locomotor movement is required
- **Dynamic balance** – the ability to balance on a moving surface or to balance while involved in locomotion
- **Visual activity** – the ability to see clearly and precisely
- **Visual tracking** – the ability visually to follow a moving object
- **Eye–hand coordination** – the ability to perform skills requiring vision
- **Eye–foot coordination and the precise use of hands or feet.**

These and others are, however, equally acceptable abilities as they are measurable and quantifiable. In your additional background reading and task analysis you will probably come across many more. It is important to understand that all individuals possess all the above abilities identified, however we do not all possess them at equal or similar levels. If a person has not got the appropriate levels of specific abilities needed for a specific sport then the odds against them making it to the top in that sport may be high. But this does not mean that such a person has to give up all together. Practically no one is born with a package of superior abilities large enough to make for an overall athletic ability. Although researchers have tried to identify the possibilities of an 'all round general athletic ability' results have actually tended to support the view that *specific skills require specific abilities*.

However whilst we are born with certain levels of abilities they can be trained and improved in specific situations.

Ability is task specific

Certain skills may use different sets of abilities or they may use the same abilities put together in a different order. Also abilities are not necessarily linked or related; for example a person having high levels of trunk strength may not necessarily have high levels of explosive strength. If a person is good at throwing a cricket ball there is no guarantee that they will be good at throwing a basketball or a javelin. In other words the fact that a person does not have the level of abilities necessary to succeed at one activity does not mean that they do not have the potential to succeed in another activity requiring slightly different abilities or levels. Performers 'learn' to combine and use abilities in specific situations and for carrying out specific skills.

Fig. 13.5 EXPLOSIVE STRENGTH

Using the lists of abilities above:

1 **Individually make a list of the abilities required for the following activities:**
   - **Badminton**
   - **Hockey**
   - **Gymnastics**
   - **Table tennis**
   - **Weight lifting**
   - **Swimming**
   - **High jump**

2 **Compare your list with a partner and then try to decide on the ability-level needed in order to excel in these activities:**
   - **high level**
   - **reasonable level**
   - **basic level**

   Eg. High jumpers fig. 13.5 need high levels of explosive strength.

In your discussions you will have found that whilst there is a certain degree of overlap between the requirements of activities, for example strength, coordination and speed, when you came to analyse the level and type of abilities required they became much more specific to the sport being considered, eg, different types of strength. Dynamic strength is used in weight lifting but explosive strength in the high jump.

The implications for teaching and coaching

1 What we have to ensure that we *do not* assume from this is that two people cannot achieve similar standards of performance in a physical activity because of different levels of genetically determined abilities. If one person, possibly with lower levels of specific abilities, is given the opportunity at an early age to use their abilities (eg, parents take them to the local sports club) and they are prepared to work hard *learning* to use their abilities in an appropriate manner then they could achieve a level of proficiency similar to a person who has not had the opportunity or is unwilling to develop higher levels of innate abilities.

2 By analysing the types of abilities needed for specific sports teachers and coaches could ensure that their students experienced the appropriate types of practice necessary for these abilities to be developed more fully. Since balance is an essential ability, required for the successful completion of a wide variety of complex or difficult skills, it would appear relevant for a PE programme in infant and junior schools to provide the opportunity for children to develop their balance ability in a variety of situations.

3 Teachers and coaches should ensure that children who show a high inherited potential for sports are not disadvantaged from an early age as a possible result of their personality and social environment. Some young children appear to display natural athletic tendencies often as a result of being initially bigger and stronger. This can result in early success, greater motivation, higher teacher expectations and further development. However, without early success even children with higher levels of innate ability will avoid continued participation in sport, thus building up what has been termed a **skill deficit**. This has obvious sociocultural implications for a child's future interest in sport.

4 The role of ability identification as predictors of potential achievements in learners has to be considered carefully. Consider the implications, both good and bad, if we were able to measure a beginner's abilities and then 'channel' them into the appropriate sport. Prediction studies have shown, however, that abilities which are important at the early stages of learning (cognitive phase) are not necessarily the same as those which are important at the more advanced stages of learning (autonomous phase). For example, Fleishman's and Rich's 1963 work suggest that:
   * a greater number of abilities (more general to the task) contribute to learning a task in the early stages than do so later on.
   * different and fewer abilities (more specific to the task) contribute more and more to success with practice.

5 The ability to take in information and make sense of it, in other words 'perceptual ability' involving cue selection, concentration attention along with vision spatial orientation, are more important at the early stages of learning than later when learning is replaced more by kinaesthesis.

Verbal comprehension is also very important at the early stages of learning as a person is precluded if they cannot understand instructions or what is being asked of them.

It is therefore generally understood that whilst testing a person's abilities to assess future potential can be useful, testing of this kind is not accurate and should not be used in isolation.

There are many other factors psychological, physiological as well as sociocultural that can influence future performance levels.

Consider the following situation and answer the question.
   A coach has a large class for basketball. In order to achieve what they feel might be more effective teaching, they decide to divide the class up into smaller groups. The whole class is first asked to carry out various related tasks, eg, bouncing, catching, dribbling, shooting. As a result of observing the way people carried out these tasks the coach splits the class into groups according to each person's initial performance levels.
   What are the possible implications of this approach for the whole class's future success at basketball?

Classification of skills

Having worked your way through the chapter to this point you will be aware of:

- what constitutes a skill
- how specific skills are underpinned by the appropriate abilities.

This gives you a better understanding of the implications for teaching and coaching the acquisition of skills in the widest sense. You will have realised that different skills require different kinds and amounts of abilities and also possibly different patterns. In the same way in which we analyse skills to assess which different abilities are needed we can also analyse skills in relation to things they have in common. Looking at skills in terms of the characteristics that they have in common is called **classification of skill** and is part of the overall process of **task analysis**. By classifying skills that are involved in sporting activities:

- a teacher or coach is enabled to **generalise** across groups of skills and apply major concepts, theories and principles of learning to types of skills
- a teacher or coach will not necessarily have to consider each specific skill in a unique way
- a teacher or coach will be able to select the appropriate starting point for a learner
- the identification of the appropriate types of practice conditions required will be made easier, eg, whole, part, whole, massed or distributed (see page 357). Similar methods can be applied to skill within the same groupings
- the timing and types of instruction to be given is clarified, eg, verbal feedback, ongoing or terminal
- the detection and solving of any problems the learner may be facing is made easier
- a teacher or coach would probably not use the various classifications in isolation but move from one to another, or combine aspects of all of them at the appropriate time.

Classification systems

Several different ways of classifying or grouping skills have been developed in order to try and help our understanding of motor skills. In order to solve the problem of listing skills under certain headings which could lead to confusion over where to list skills made up of several different aspects, the use of a **continuum** was devised. A continuum is an imaginary line between two extremes. This enables you to analyse skills and place them between two given extremities according to how they match the analysis criteria being applied.

Criteria
A

Criteria
B

Gross and Fine classification

If you used the Gross–Fine classification given in table 13.1 in terms purely of *headings* for lists of skills the criteria for analysing the skills would derive from the 'degree of bodily involvement' or the precision of movement.

As you can see from table 13.1, some skills do not fall easily into specific categories nor can they be listed exclusively under exact headings.

Table 13.1   GROSS – FINE SKILL CLASSIFICATION

GROSS SKILLS	FINE SKILLS

• involve large muscle movements
• major bodily movements skills associated with:
  strength
  endurance
  power
• for instance
  walking
  running
  jumping
  kicking a football
	• involve small muscle movements
	• small bodily movements skills associated with:
	  speed
	  accuracy
	  efficiency
	• associated more with industrial motor skills:
	  writing
	  painting
	  sewing

?←—DARTS—→?	
?←—SPIN BOWLING—→?	
?←—BADMINTON—→?	

Darts, spin bowling and serving in a game of badminton all involve wrist finger speed and dexterity along with aiming accuracy which would suggest they should be taught as a fine skill. In addition however, in order for these small movements to be made larger movements – particularly in spin bowling – have also had to be made which would suggest they should be taught as a gross skill. Therefore the use of exact lists is not always possible when analysing what a skill is made up of. Hence the use of a continuum where the complex nature of motor skills can be taken into consideration; they can be placed on the continuum somewhere between the two extremes according to the degree of similarity they have to the various criteria being applied.

Now, using the same Gross–Fine classification (see table 13.1) place darts, spin bowling and badminton along a continuum according to how they match the criteria being applied.

Gross   **Fine**

The Discrete, Serial, Continuous continuum

This classification is made on the basis of how clearly defined the beginning and end of the skill is.

The use of this type of continuum has been popularised by researchers viewing performance from a human engineering perspective.

Continuous skills:

- practised as a whole (see section on Practice)
- difficult to break into subroutines
- may lose the flow of the movement if broken down
- kinesthetic awareness needed (see information processing).

Kinaesthetic awareness is linked to the 'feel' or intrinsic feedback provided as a result of movements being correct or incorrect. This is provided via proprioceptors

Table 13.2   THE DISCRETE, SERIAL CONTINUOUS CONTINUUM

DISCRETE skills	SERIAL skills	CONTINUOUS skills
CRITERIA	CRITERIA	CRITERIA
• well defined beginning and end • usually brief in nature a single specific skill • if skill is repeated have to start at beginning eg, ◇ a basketball free throw ◇ kicking a ball ◇ hitting, catching ◇ diving ◇ vaulting	• a number of discrete skills put together to make a sequence or series • the order the distinct elements are put together is very important • each movement is both a stimulus and response eg, ◇ gymnastic routine ◇ triple jump ◇ high jump	• poorly defined beginning and end • activity continues for an unspecified time – (ongoing) • The end of one movement is the beginning of the next eg, ◇ swimming ◇ running ◇ cycling

Using the information in Table 13.2 decide where the following activities fit on the continumm. Make sure you can justify your decision.

DISCRETE	SERIAL	CONTINUOUS
• Hockey pass • Long jump • Dance routine • 1500m run	• Serve in tennis • Throwing a javelin • Skiing • Trampoline routine	• Throw in at football • Penalty flick in hockey • Aerobics • Penalty corner routine in hockey

The pacing continuum

This classification is based on the degree of control that the performer has over the movement or skill being carried out. This classification is synonymous with the next classification open and closed.

Table 13.3   THE PACING CONTINUUM

SELF PACED/ INTERNAL PACED SKILLS	EXTERNALLY PACED SKILLS
• Performer controls the rate at which the activity is carried out • Performer decides when to initiate movement • Involves pro-action • more closed skill eg, ◇ shot put ◇ forward roll	• Action is determined by external sources • Involves the performer in reaction • more open skill eg, ◇ white water canoeing ◇ receiving a serve in tennis

DEFINITIONS

Open/externally paced skills:

'At every instant the motor activity must be regulated by and appropriate to the external situation.' (B. Knapp, 1972)

Closed/skills:

'Conformity to a prescribed standard sequence of motor acts is all important.' (H. Whiting, 1969)

The open/closed continuum

This is one of the better-known classifications and is based on the stability of the environment or situation in which the skill is being performed.

Table 13.4   THE OPEN/CLOSED CONTINUUM

CLOSED SKILLS	OPEN SKILLS
• not affected by the environment • stable fixed environment (space/time) • internally/self paced predominantly habitual stereotyped movements eg, ◇ headstand in gymnastics ◇ weight lifting	• very much affected by the unstable changing environment • externally paced environment • predominantly perceptual movement patterns require adjustment (adaptation) • very often rapid adjustments, variations of skill needed eg, ◇ passing/receiving in netball or basketball ◇ tackling rugby

Draw an open–closed continuum and place the following skills on it.

Free shot in basketball; serve in tennis; serve in badminton; dribbling within a game of football; rugby tackle; running 1500 m race; sailing; backhand defensive shot in table tennis; judo.

Select an open skill from one of the major game activities, for instance:

- **tackling in hockey or rugby**
- **fielding in cricket**
- **passing in netball**

Try to explain in detail all the aspects of the skill and situation that would have to be considered when carrying out the skill. Do not forget to apply all the criteria, showing why it would be classified as an open skill.

 **Using the skills/techniques listed in Activities 9 & 10 build up a classification profile for each by placing them on the continuum below and justify your placements.**

Gross		Fine
Discrete	Serial	Continuous
Externally paced		Internally paced
Open		Closed

More recently, with the emphasis moving towards information processing modules, classifications have been suggested that consider the degree of cognitive/perceptual involvement. Do skills have higher or lower levels?

Examples of high cognitive skills are:

- chess
- batting in cricket
- strategies/tactics, within any games.

Decision making is critical.

Examples of low cognitive/motor skills are:

- walking
- power lifting.

Primary determinant of success is the quality of movement.

Other researchers have considered the types and timing of feedback availability, for instance:

- intrinsic F.B. (high or low levels available)
- ongoing/concurrent
- terminal
- delayed / immediate.

Other research has considered the '*coherence*' of a skill. This looks at whether a skill can be broken down into parts (sub routines) or does it have to be taught as a whole. Eg.

Part	Whole/part	or	Whole

The implications for teaching and coaching – skills classification

Knowledge of skills classification could help in identifying the appropriate teaching and coaching strategies. The use of the Fine–Gross classification would have a practical use in rehabilitation and training programmes within special education and would also be useful in infant and primary education. In addition it would help in identifying the levels and types of fitness and preparation needed for certain skills and activities.

It has also been suggested that it is often easier to teach more open or complex activities, eg, netball or basketball to beginners by breaking the whole game down into a series of more closed skills where the beginner is not having to make lots of decisions (perceptual requirements) and adapt their skills before they have learnt the basics.

However, if for instance a skill is classified as an open skill it would be a very short-sighted teacher or coach who always demanded practice of the skill in isolation. Practice in a variety of realistic situations would be essential once the basic techniques have been learnt in isolation (see the sections on schema and types of practice).

Task analysis

Task analysis is the organised and systematic evaluation of an activity/task/game in order to find out the:

- constituent parts
- organisation
- relevant cues
- objectives/purpose.

It is important that the teacher or coach is aware of all the various demands being placed on a learner at any one time within either simple or complex skills.

It has been suggested that the major factors contributing to task difficulty are:

- the degree of perception necessary
- the degree of decision making involved
- the nature of the act itself (movement patterns)
- the feedback availability.

(J. Billing).

The effect of the above factors will depend on the relative level of the performer (see phases of learning and information processing). Therefore you can see that just labelling a task as difficult or easy is not enough. It is necessary to specify the degree and nature of the difficulty if appropriate and effective instructions and strategies are to be developed.

Figure 13.6 shows a task analysis for the tennis serve (executive programme) indicating the appropriate components (subroutines) and identifying some of the underlying perceptual motor abilities necessary for the plan of action to be completed.

Figure 13.7 shows how motor skills can be analysed according to the complexity of each subcomponent.

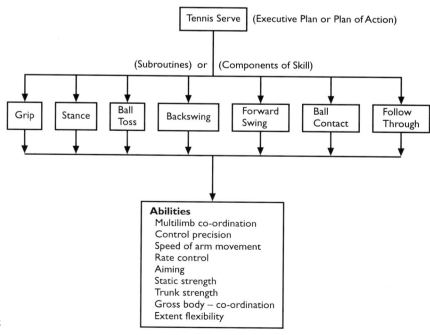

Fig. 13.6 A TASK ANALYSIS FOR THE TENNIS SERVE

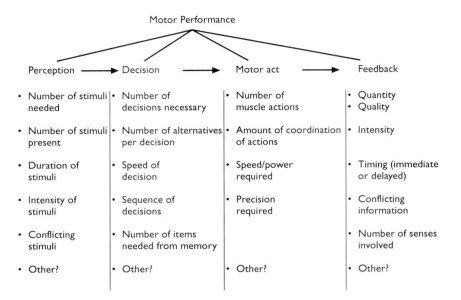

Fig. 13.7 ANALYSING MOTOR SKILLS
Source: Adapted from J Billing, 1980

Summary

Skills

1 Skill can be an act or task.
2 Skill can be used to indicate quality of performance.
3 Motor skills are essentially a combination of cognitive/perceptual and motor skills put together.
4 Skill is learned behaviour.
5 Skills have pre-determined objectives to achieve.
6 Skill involves being able to carry out the action consistently.
7 Skills are performed with an efficient use of time and energy.
8 Skills involve 'internal processing' in addition to physical actions.

Abilities

1 Abilities are innate, enduring qualities or capacities.
2 Abilities are task specific. Specific skills need different abilities.
3 Abilities underpin skill development.
4 The idea of one overall 'athletic ability' is largely a myth.
5 Many other factors contribute to all round athletic development.

Classifying skills

1 It is important to consider all aspects of the skill/task being taught.
2 Classification considers the common characteristics of skills.
3 A continuum is a more effective tool in classifying skills.
4 Teaching strategies are linked to the in-depth analysis of skills.

Review Questions

1   What is a motor skill and a perceptual skill?

2   What are cognitive skills?

3   What are complex skills and simple skills?

4   What is an ability? What is a psychomotor ability? What is gross motor ability?

5   Differentiate between gross and fine skills. Give examples.

6   What are discrete, continuous, serial skills? Give examples.

7   What are self paced and externally paced skills? Give examples.

8   What are high and low cognitive skills? Give examples.

9   What are open/closed skills? Give examples.

10   What is the purpose of a coach/teacher carrying out a task analysis?

11   Select a specific skill/technique and try to carry out an in-depth task analysis.

chapter 14

The Principles of Learning

L earning plays a central role in most of psychology and as such it is one of the most expansively researched and discussed areas in the whole of psychology. Learning is said to be a hypothetical construct, in that it can only be **inferred** from either:

- observing behaviour; or
- testing, measuring and evaluating performance.

All human beings have tremendous capabilities for learning. As a student of physical education and sport it is not enough just to recognise that learning has or has not taken place (the end result or outcome); you should have a more in-depth understanding of the theories and principles associated with the underlying learning process and be able to apply this understanding to the practical learning situation.

Here is a list of the terms to be covered in this chapter. It is important that you understand them.

- Learning definition
- Inference
- Practice observation
- Retention tests
- Transfer test
- Cognitive learning
- Affective learning
- Effective learning
- Cognitive phase

- Associative phase
- Autonomous phase
- Performance curves
- Linear
- Negative
- Positive
- Plateaus
- Learning variables

It would be very convenient to have a list of absolute truths about the learning and teaching of specific motor skills related to every possible sports performance. However, your own individual experiences should help you realise that there are no conclusive statements and guarantees cannot be given. This is because:

- learning is a complex process during which many physical and psychological changes are taking place
- there are many variables to be considered
- it is very difficult to consider the many variables and parts of the learning process in total isolation
- most of what we know about how and why people learn is based on the practical application of theories alongside educated reasoning (behavioural evidence).

Once you have read this chapter you should gain an understanding of:

- definitions of learning
- different types of learning
- stages/phases of learning
- performance/learning curves
- major factors that can affect learning
- key issues surrounding how people learn.

Definitions of learning

As we have discussed in the previous chapter, implicit in the understanding of the term skill is the notion that **learning** has taken place, that skill is **learned behaviour**. To become skilful involves a person's performance changing in line with certain criteria and characteristics associated with skill.

It is generally accepted that for learning to have taken place there has to be a recognisable **change** in behaviour and that this change in behaviour has to be **permanent**. Thus, the performance improves over time as a result of practice and/or experience becoming more consistent in terms of its:

- accuracy
- efficiency
- adaptability.

Learning has been defined as:

'the more or less permanent change in behaviour that is reflected in a change in performance.'
(B. Knapp).

'a change in the capability of the individual to perform a skill that must be inferred from a relatively permanent improvement in performance as a result of practice or experience.'
(R. Magill).

'a relatively permanent change in behaviour due to past experience.' (D. Coon).

'a set of processes associated with practice or experience leading to relatively permanent changes in the capability of skilled performance.'
(R. Schmidt).

 **ACTIVITY 1**

In discussion with other students in your group consider the four definitions given above and select the main aspects of the definitions.

In your discussion of the four definitions you should have concluded, and psychologists generally agree, that:

- learning is not a 'one-off' lucky effort/performance
- learning is *relatively* permanent
  (This does not mean, however, that the skill is performed one hundred per cent correctly each time. It does mean that a learner's capability to perform a particular skill consistently has increased.)
- learning is due to past experience and or practice.

How do we judge if a skill has been learned?

There are various methods of assessing a performance in order that more accurate inferences can be made about learning. The general methodology would be to:

1 **observe** – behaviour/performance
2 **measure/test** – behaviour/performance
3 **evaluate** – behaviour/performance
4 **translate** – the information gained into meaningful conclusion
5 **infer** – that learning has or has not taken place.

Fig. 14.1

Three common methods of measuring and testing which have been used to enable teachers and coaches to make more accurate inferences with regard to learning have been:

- practice observations
- retention tests
- transfer tests.

Measures are actual values indicating skill levels. **Tests** are the procedures used to obtain the scores.

Practice observation

This is when a teacher or coach records a learner's performance over a period of time in an accurate way in order to provide a quantitative means for evaluating progress: eg, results showing more accuracy or consistency in relation to time spent practising (see later section on performance curves).

Retention tests

This is when a teacher or coach tests a student's performance after practice and then re-tests again after a few days and then again in order to check whether the initial levels of performance have been maintained, persisted or improved after a period of little or no practice.

Transfer tests

This is when a teacher or coach determines how well a particular skill has been learned by seeing how well it can be performed in a different situation to that experienced by the student during practice: is the accuracy and consistency maintained from practice to game situation?

Each of the above methods and many more can be used in various ways and at different times according to the needs of the teacher, learner or situation. A teacher/coach who is interested in helping a learner/performer to improve should be able to evaluate whether improvement has been relatively permanent and not just a temporary change due to maturational or fitness changes for example.

Reasons for evaluation

- To give the learner/performer accurate/meaningful feedback.
- To assess whether goals/targets have been achieved.
- To assess the effectiveness of teaching/coaching strategies.
- To record progress/achievement over time.
- To assess performance potential.
- To carry out match/performance statistical analysis (eg, accuracy, technique, timing, errors, amount, frequency).

Evaluations can be:

- formative (ongoing – helps to provide feedback)
- summative (provides a summary over time).

Tests must be:

- valid – does it measure what it sets out to measure? (Sports skills tests usually lack validity.)
- reliable – is the measurement consistent?
- objective – can the same test be applied by different testers to gain the same measurement?

Measurements can be:

- qualitative – direct observation, usually of a subjective nature
- quantitative – precise/accurate monitoring of movement specifics, usually using technical equipment.

Learners and performers can be evaluated as follows:

- self-referencing – with reference to themselves
- norm-referencing – with reference to other people
- criterion referencing – with reference to external criteria.

Types of learning

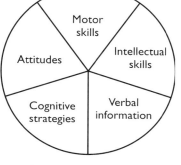

Fig. 14.2 THE CATEGORIES OF LEARNING

As you will have realised in your earlier discussions with regard to types of skill, in order to carry out motor skills at the highest levels more than just pure physical movement is involved. There is usually some cognitive and perceptual involvement to various degrees depending on the skill being carried out. In the same way therefore that motor skills involve more than purely the physical movement of muscles, limbs, etc, then learning can occur in more than just a physical way. There have been many different approaches to the analysis of what form learning can take in relation to the types of skills or situations being experienced.

Robert Gagné (1977) suggested that there are five main categories of human performance that may be developed by learning and that any learned capability whatever it is called, History, Geography, Physics, Football, Swimming, etc has characteristics from one or other of these categories.

1 **Intellectual skills**
   Dealing with the environment in a symbolic way, eg, reading, writing mathematical symbols, etc.
2 **Verbal information**
   Learning to state or tell ideas or information by using oral, written or body language, ie, communication.
3 **Cognitive strategies**
   Learning to manage one's own learning, ie, use of memory, thinking, problem solving and analysis.
4 **Attitudes**
   Acquiring mental states which influence choices of personal actions, eg, choosing badminton rather than hockey as a preferred recreation.
5 **Motor skills**
   Learning to execute movement in a number of organised ways, either as single skills or actions, eg, catching a ball, or more comprehensive activities, eg, playing netball or basketball.

1 **Individually select a game activity, eg, netball, hockey, badminton, tennis, football, etc.**
2 **Using Gagné's categories as a guide, write a list of all the aspects of the activity that you may learn about when being introduced to the game.**
3 **Feedback your list to your member of staff along with everyone else in the group.**

In carrying out activity 2 you will probably have come up with examples of learning under each heading.

For example:

1 Developing particular motor skills, eg, catching, throwing, kicking, hitting/striking etc, depending on the game.
2 Developing tactical awareness, defensive strategies and attacking strategies.
3 Learning the rules and regulations.
4 Learning the ethics/morals of the game, eg, sportsmanship.
5 Developing positive attitudes towards the game and sport in general.
6 Understanding training principles.
7 Learning how the body works and how to make it work more efficiently.
8 Learning how to analyse movement in order to recognise strengths and weaknesses in your own and others' game.
9 Communication skills, both verbal and non-verbal.
10 Learning to interpret information.

All these and probably many more examples will be on your lists. Whilst we are primarily concerned with learning associated with motor skills, it is obvious that in order to learn motor skills we also experience learning in many other ways. Although experimental psychologists have tried, it is difficult to separate learning in its widest sense from motor performance, since all contribute to the level of motor skill achieved.

A more simplistic view of learning experienced within physical education and sport is seen in table 14.1. When asked to comment on the types of learning experienced within Sport & PE Cognitive, Affective and Effective would be the three types you would need to refer to.

In dealing with motor learning, it is often difficult to separate the various aspects as all will contribute in some way at some time to the level of skill. It is therefore necessary to develop all areas in order to make the learning process more meaningful, eg, a sensitive teacher or coach may find that in order to develop a student's high jumping technique (effective learning) they may have to help the student understand the basic biomechanics of the movement and link this to their ability to analyse their own movement (cognitive learning). In addition positive attitudes may be needed with regard to specific physical training and psychological aspects, eg, confidence and focusing and having the moral belief that the use of drugs is cheating (affective learning).

Table 14.1   THE THREE TYPES OF LEARNING

Cognitive	Affective	Effective
to know	to feel	to do
• mental processes eg, ◇ tactical awareness ◇ strategies ◇ problem solving	• attitudes and values eg, ◇ ethics ◇ sportsmanship	• motor learning eg, ◇ physical ◇ catching ◇ passing
(inclusive of Gagné's categories 1, 2, 3)	(Gagné's category 4)	(Gagné's category 5)

Phases of motor skill learning

As there are different types of learning associated with the learning of motor skills there are also different stages or phases of the learning process.

In order to gain a clearer understanding of the learning process there have been many attempts to identify the various phases, or stages, that students go through when learning motor skills. It has been agreed that whatever the number and name of phases identified the phases are not separate or distinct, but that they gradually merge into each other as a person moves from being a novice to being proficient.

Having a better understanding of what is happening and what the learner is experiencing during each phase should help you in developing appropriate teaching and coaching strategies to ensure that the learning process is efficient and successful.

NB: Be careful not to confuse the three *types* of learning with the three *stages* of learning discussed below!

Three stage model

Paul Fitts and Michael Posner (1967) identified one of the better-known models which in its turn has been expanded upon by others.

The three phases identified are:

1 Cognitive
2 Associative
3 Autonomous.

Whilst each of these phases has certain characteristics associated with it, movement from one phase to the other is seen as developmental and gradual along a continuum. The rate at which a performer progresses through the phases is different for each individual.

| I Cognitive phase | 2 Associative phase | 3 Autonomous phase |
| BEGINNER | | HIGHLY SKILLED |

Cognitive phase

This is the initial phase in the learning process when, as a beginner faced with a new skill or set of skills to learn, you need to know, for example:

- what is required of you?
- what task is to be performed?
- what are the basic rules?
- how do I hold the stick?

The beginner is trying to 'get to grips' with the basics whilst dealing with lots of visual, verbal and kinaesthetic information in the form of:

- demonstrations from the teacher or fellow students (visual guidance)
- instructions and explanations (verbal guidance)
- initial trials/practice in the form of basic trial/error.

Fig. 14.3 THE COGNITIVE PHASE: BEGINNERS NEED TO BUILD UP A 'MENTAL IMAGE OF THE SKILL' BEFORE 'HAVING A GO' AND DEVELOPING A 'FEEL' FOR THE ACTION.

The emphasis in this phase is very much on early understanding or cognitive involvement (internalising information) in order that initial plans of action can be formulated. Beginners are directed towards important aspects of the new skill to pay attention to. These cues may be intensified in order to help concentration, eg, bigger or brighter bats and balls are often used, and any initial success is enthusiastically reinforced. The length of this phase varies according to the beginner and the strategies being used but it is generally a relatively short phase.

Problems linked to cognitive phase

- Beginner has difficulty deciding what to pay attention to (see selective attention).
- Beginner has difficulty processing information (potential overload).
- Gross errors made (often uncoordinated movements).

Children do not always understand adult words and descriptions. Explanations are not always comprehended by the learner. Teaching/guidance needs to be **simple, clear and concise**. Demonstrations (visual guidance) are generally seen as being more effective than lots of verbal input at this stage.

The associative phase

This intermediate or practice phase in the learning process is generally significantly longer than the cognitive phase, with the learner taking part in many hours of practice. The characteristics of this phase are that the fundamental basics of the skill required have generally been mastered and are becoming more consistent.

- the mental or early cognitive images of the skill have been associated with the relevant movements enabling the coordination of the various parts of the skill (subroutine) to become smoother and more in line with expectations
- motor programmes are being developed
- gross error detection and correction is practised
- the skills are practised and refined under a wide variety of conditions
- a gradual change to more subtle and detailed cue utilisation
- more detailed feedback is given and used
- greater use of internal/kinaesthetic feedback.

Whilst the skills are not yet automatic or consistently correct there is an obvious change in the performance characteristics.

The autonomous phase

After much practice and variety of experience the learner moves into what is considered the final phase in the learning process, the autonomous phase. The characteristics of this phase are that:

- the performance of the skill has become almost **automatic**
- the skill is performed relatively easily and **without stress**
- the skill is performed effectively with little if any conscious control: it is **habitual**
- the performance is consistent with highly skilled movement characteristics
- skills can be **adapted** to meet a variety of situations.

The performer is able to:

- process information easily, helping decision making
- concentrate on the relevant cues and signals from the environment
- concentrate on additional higher level strategies, tactics, and options available
- detect and correct errors without help.

Once a player has reached this phase of learning it does not mean that learning is over. Although the performer is very capable, small improvements can still be made in terms of style and form, and to the many other factors associated with psychological aspects of performance which can help develop learning even further eg:

- self evaluation of performance
- mental practice

- stress management
- personal motivation.

Some performers may never reach this stage, however once at this stage performers will be continually referring back to the Associative phase ie constant practice, in order to remain in the Autonomous phase.

Use the criteria for each phase given above to judge your own level of learning.
Place on the continuum where you would classify yourself in relation to your performance of the following skills. Be able to justify your placements.

Cognitive   Associative   Autonomous

Headstand, Throwing a cricket/rounders ball, Kicking a ball, Shooting a netball, Jogging, A backward roll in gymnastics, Indian dribbling in hockey.

The relationship between learning and performance

Fig. 14.4 IN THE AUTONOMOUS PHASE SKILLED SOCCER PLAYERS CAN DRIBBLE THE BALL HABITUALLY, ENABLING THEIR ATTENTIONAL CAPACITIES TO CONSIDER OTHER ASPECTS OF THE GAME AT THE SAME TIME, EG, MOVEMENTS OF OTHER PLAYERS AND OPTIONS AVAILABLE

As we have already stated, occasional good or 'one-off' performances are not a true indication of learning having taken place. There has to be a relatively permanent change in performance over time as a result of practice and or experience. One of the more traditional ways of gathering evidence in order to discover if learning has or has not taken place has been by comparing practice/performance observations. Performance levels over a certain length of time are recorded and the results are plotted on a graph, producing **performance curves**. Very often these curves of performance are inaccurately referred to as learning curves. This has been based on the assumption that changing levels of skill closely parallel performance scores. However, it is performance not learning that is being measured. By keeping records of skill performance over a period of time (eg, a lesson, one hour, a term, a season) an individual's, but more often a group's, progress can be plotted. This will provide a graphical representation of the specific aspect of performance being tested. Thus a picture of the relationship between practice and performance is presented from which inferences can be made. It has been suggested that the validity of performance curves as true representations of learning is problematical due to the many variables that may have an effect. However, as long as they are not used in total isolation, such curves do act as useful indicators of general trends in learning. Although they may be used to show changes in an individual's performance of a particular motor skill or skills, performance curves tend to be more widely used to represent composite or group performance.

A performance curve consists of three areas:

- The vertical y-axis of the graph showing the level of performance being measured.
- The horizontal x-axis of the graph indicating the amount of time over which the performance has been measured.
- The shape of the curve from which inferences can be made re – the amount of learning taking place.

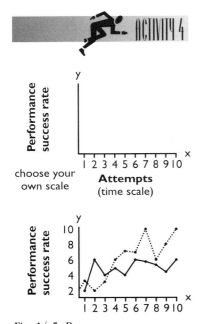

Fig. 14.5 PERFORMANCE SUCCESS RATE GRAPHS

You are going to undertake a learning experiment in one-handed ball juggling. No practice is allowed beforehand or in between attempts.
 1 Divide yourselves into pairs.
 2 Have two tennis balls per pair and a piece of graph paper.
 3 Have ten consecutive goes each at one-handed juggling.
 4 Count the number of successive throw-ups each person can manage in each of their ten goes.
 5 Log the results on a table as below.

Attempts	1	2	3	4	5	6	7	8	9	10
Success										

 6 Plot the performance of both yourself and your partner on a piece of graph paper and compare the graphs.
 7 Average out your two scores and draw another graph.
 8 Average out all the scores of the members of your group and draw a composite graph for the whole group.
 9 What inferences can be drawn from this final graph?
10 What variables may have affected the individual and group performances? How could you make this experiment scientifically more valid?
11 What did you notice with regard to the shape of the curves as you average out more by adding more results?
12 A further way to develop your performance curves would be to treat the ten attempts as a block of trials and average this out. Then, over a period of time, repeat the block of ten attempts on a regular basis. This could be done with various skills, eg, basketball free throws, serving in tennis, target shooting in hockey or football, shooting in netball, etc.

Types of performance curves

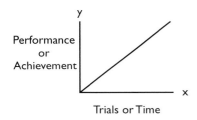

Fig. 14.6 LINEAR CURVE OF PERFORMANCE

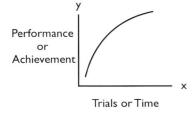

Fig. 14.7 NEGATIVELY ACCELERATED CURVE OF PERFORMANCE

When analysing performance curves it has been found that graphs are made up of several different shapes within the overall context of the general performance curve. The curves shown in figs 14.6–14.10 are termed smooth curves. However, as you will have noticed from your own individual graphs and further reading, curves found in research studies are usually erratic in nature.

Figure 14.6 indicates that performance improves directly in proportion to the amount of time or number of trials. In fig. 14.7, the curve of decreasing gain indicates that a large amount of improvement occurred early on in practice and then although improvement usually continues, it is very slight in relation to the continued amount of time or trials. The inverse curve of increasing gain in fig. 14.8 indicates small performance gains early on in practice followed by a substantial increase later in practice. Figure 14.9 is a combination of the previous types of curve. The plateaus in fig. 14.10 indicate that during certain periods of practice or from one particular trial to another there was no significant improvement in performance.

Plateaus

The levelling off in performance preceded and followed by performance gains has been called a plateau. A learning plateau occurs when no apparent improvements in performance appear to occur. Plateaus in performance and possibly learning have been the subject of considerable research. One of the earliest pieces of research to suggest that plateaus existed was by Bryan and Hunter (1897) when studying the performance of trainee telegraphers learning the morse code. Think of experiences you have had when trying to learn particular

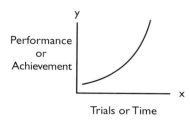

Fig. 14.8 POSITIVELY ACCELERATED CURVE OF PERFORMANCE

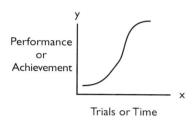

Fig. 14.9 OGIVE OR S-SHAPED CURVE OF PERFORMANCE

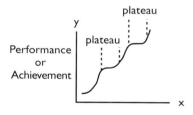

Fig. 14.10 PLATEAU IN PERFORMANCE

skills; there must have been times when initial success was followed by a period of time when, however hard you tried, no apparent improvement was achieved. Then, all of a sudden everything 'clicked' together and you cannot now remember what the problem was. Although such an experience is often described by individual learners and by performers at the highest level, performance curves generally relate to group or class results and therefore experimental evidence to support the existence of plateaus related to individual learning is hard to come by. Whilst we may experience plateaus in practice and performance it has been argued (FS Keller, 1958) that learning continues or at the very least plateaus do not necessarily mean that learning has also plateaued. In terms of learning development it is generally agreed that if plateaus do exist they are something that should be avoided as they can lead to a stagnation in performance and a possible loss of overall interest.

Possible causes of plateaus

It has been suggested that the following factors have to be considered as possible causes of plateaus.

1 Movement from learning lower order or simple skills to higher order or more complex skills may create a situation in which the learner needs to take time to assimilate more involved information and attend to correct cues and signals (transitional period).
2 Goals or targets are set too high or too low.
3 Fatigue/lack of physical preparation.
4 Lack of variety in practice.
5 Lack of motivation/interest due to problems associated with the above.
6 Lack of understanding of plateaus.
7 Physical unreadiness for new skill or next stage
8 Low level of aspiration
9 Lack of ability to adapt skills.

1 **Individually, consider the possible causes of plateaus given above and try to make some practical suggestions as to how a teacher or a coach might try to ensure that learners do not experience plateaus in their skill development.**
2 **Present your suggestions to the class and compile a full list of suggestions and strategies.**

Combating the performance plateau effect

A coach/teacher may have to consider the following strategies to reduce the effect of a plateau:

- breaking the practice into shorter/distributed periods
- re-setting goals with agreement of performer
- offering extrinsic rewards/encouragement
- using mental rehearsal in practice
- using appropriate feedback
- arranging relevant competition against realist opposition
- breaking serial skills into parts, eg, whole–part–whole practice (see later section)
- ensuring performer pays attention to appropriate cues
- emphasising role in team – enjoyment
- changing role/position/responsibility.

Fig. 14.11 EXAMPLE OF A BEGINNER COMPLETING A MASSED PRACTICE OF GIVEN SIMPLE, CLOSED SPORTS SKILLS

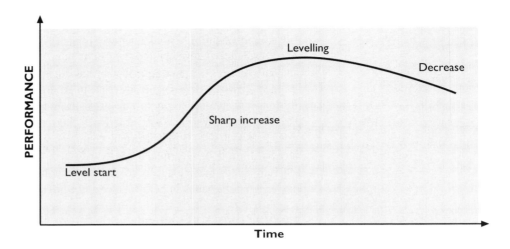

Fig 14.11 demonstrates the performance curve of a beginner.

- The graph starts at a low level because the beginner has a low skill level.
- Early practice produces a sharp increase in performance level.
- The upper level is achieved due to either optimum performance/decrease in motivation.
- Levelling out can also be caused by poor coaching/lack of information on how to improve skill level.
- The fall in performance is due to lack of motivation/boredom/fatigue/distraction/faulty technique.
- There is a build-up of reaction inhibition.

As you can see from your earlier experiment, discussions and reading there is no one curve of performance. The appearance of these curves is the function of a combination of variable factors. It is important that when you interpret the curves and make certain inferences you are aware of the many factors that can influence learning; if any of these are seen to be problems in the learning process, then the reasons or causes can be recognised, isolated and dealt with in the appropriate manner.

More recently research has been conducted using applied behavioural analysis in order to produce graphical evidence similar to performance curves. If gathered from correctly conducted experiments using control groups this evidence can help in determining, for instance, which instructional methods, types of motivation or reinforcement strategies are effective with certain groups or types of activities.

Considerations in motor learning

There are many different factors called **learning variables** that you have to be aware of, understand and consider; these can influence the effectiveness of the learning process.

There are four main categories of learning variables. In considering these categories you may come across unfamiliar terms, which are explained in later sections.

Category 1: variables associated with the learning process

The basic process that learners go through when faced with a new situation to which they have to respond is usually similar for all.

The learner will:

- observe the situation
- interpret the situation

- make decisions as to what they have to do
- decide on plans of action
- generate movement plans
- take in further information (feedback) as the result of actions becomes available in one form or another.

The learner can experience success or difficulty in any part of this process. Understanding it helps a teacher in the task of presenting useful information to the learner.

For a more detailed coverage of the information processing approach to learning see Chapter 15.

Category 2: *variables associated with individual differences*

A sensitive teacher or coach would try to develop a good knowledge of the individual differences listed below, and consider how they might affect the learner, in order to help the learning process.

- ability
- age (chronological and maturational)
- gender
- physiological characteristics, eg, physique (size, shape, weight linked to maturity, fitness)
- psychological, eg, motivation, attitudes, personality (see Chapters 19–20)
- previous experience
- sociological aspects.

Category 3: *variables associated with the task*

A teacher would need to consider:

- the complexity of the task, eg, simple or complex?
- the organisation of the task, eg, high or low?
- the classification of the task, eg, open/closed? fine/gross?
- the transfer possibilities.

An understanding of task analysis is essential (see the sections on task analysis) in order that the appropriate teaching strategies can be developed.

Category 4: *variables associated with the instructional conditions*

Teachers and coaches can manipulate the learning environment in a variety of ways:

- through styles of teaching
- through mode of presentation
- by using different forms of guidance
- by choosing appropriate types of practice.

All the above approaches will have a considerable affect on the learning experience of the individual or group. See later sections.

Summary

- Learning is relatively permanent.
- Learning is due to practice or experience.
- Learning is inferred.
- There are different types of learning (cognitive, affective, effective).

- There are different phases of learning (cognitive, associative, autonomous).
- Learning develops along a continuum.
- There are different types of performance curves.
- Plateaus are to be avoided.
- Learning is affected by many variables.

Review Questions

1   Explain the difference between performance and learning.

2   Why can we only infer learning has or hasn't taken place?

3   What are the characteristics associated with the three stages of Fitts and Posner's model of learning?

4   In what ways does a performer in the autonomous phase differ from a performer in the cognitive phase?

5   How is the notion of a continuum related to learning development?

6   Why is the term performance curve used rather than learning curve?

7   What is a plateau in a performance curve?

8   Should we infer that plateaus in performance mean learning is not taking place?

9   How might you learn from performing wrongly?

10   What factors may cause plateaus in performance?

11   What strategies can a coach use to try to stop plateaus occurring?

12   Consider an ogive-shaped curve of performance for a beginner and explain the reasons behind the shape.

chapter 15

Theories of Learning

We have already seen that learning is a relatively permanent change in behaviour. In order to help your understanding of how this relatively permanent change in behaviour comes about it is necessary to consider some of the more important theories and models of learning that have been proposed since the turn of the last century. Having an understanding of major theories, together with an historical perspective of their development, should enable you to see the relevance and practical application of teaching and instructional conditions associated with the methods and strategies which are prevalent in physical education and sport today.

Here is a list of the terms and theories to be covered in this chapter. It is important that you understand them.

Theories of learning

- Stimulus
- Response
- Bonding
- Classical conditioning
- Operant conditioning
- Behaviour operants
- Law of readiness
- Law of exercise
- Law of effect

- Trial error learning
- Reinforcement – positive and negative
- Punishment – tangible and intangible
- Drives
- Drive reduction
- Cognitive theory
- Gestaltism
- Insight learning
- Socialisation
- Social learning
- Observational learning (modelling)

Conditioning theories

In the early twentieth century **behaviourism** was thought to provide a scientific base for the explanation of human behaviour. This approach placed the emphasis on the learning environment where behaviour in response to specific stimuli could be observed and used to make predictions about future behaviour in relation to similar situations or stimuli. The early behaviouristic approach was based on what became known as **stimulus-response theories** or **theories of association** where the 'outcome' or 'product' was more important than the process. It has been referred to as a very mechanistic and generalised approach implying that all learners can have their behaviour shaped or conditioned through regular association (ie, practice) and manipulation of the learning practice environment by the teacher or coach. The performer learns to associate certain behaviour (response) with certain stimuli from within the environment. Once this connection or bonding together of a particular stimulus and response occurs then the performer's behaviour becomes habitual enabling predictions to be made about that person's future responses to the same or similar stimuli. Although dating from before the last century **Stimulus (S)** and **Response (R) theories** as we know them owe much to the work carried out by Pavlov, Thorndike and Skinner. Although both Pavlov (classical or respondent conditioning) and Skinner (operant conditioning) both represent the behaviouristic S–R approach to learning there are some important distinctions that need to be considered.

Classical conditioning (Pavlov 1849–1936)

During his experiments Pavlov noticed that the dogs being used would salivate (unconditioned response) very often before their actual food (unconditional stimulus) would arrive in response to the noise of food being prepared, clanking of buckets, sight of the food, etc. Thus the dogs were learning to associate these other stimuli within their environment with the taste of the food. Pavlov conducted various experiments to see if he could produce the same behaviour but with an alternative stimuli.

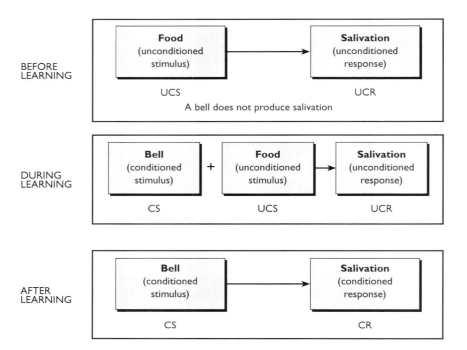

BEFORE LEARNING

Food (unconditioned stimulus) → Salivation (unconditioned response)

UCS   UCR

A bell does not produce salivation

DURING LEARNING

Bell (conditioned stimulus) + Food (unconditioned stimulus) → Salivation (unconditioned response)

CS   UCS   UCR

AFTER LEARNING

Bell (conditioned stimulus) → Salivation (conditioned response)

CS   CR

Fig. 15.1 PAVLOV'S EXPERIMENT TO PRODUCE CONDITIONAL RESPONSE WITH CONDITIONED STIMULUS

Fig. 15.2 EARLY CHILDHOOD EXPERIENCES GOOD OR BAD COULD LEAD TO 'STIMULUS GENERALISATION' BOTH POSITIVE AND NEGATIVE EG: WHERE A CHILD MAY BE PUT OFF SPORT THROUGH EARLY FAILURE OR INJURY

In his later experiments Pavlov found that by pairing specific stimuli, ie, a bell, lights, shapes (conditioned stimulus) with the food (unconditioned stimulus) over a period of time he could produce the same salivation (unconditional response).

He found that although ringing a bell (stimulus) would not normally produce the salivation, by this continual pairing or association of food and bell he could eventually produce the salivation in the dogs by merely ringing the bell independently, thus creating a conditional response (CR) to a conditioned stimulus (CS).

You may ask what has an experiment involving dogs and food got to do with learning in Sport and physical education. It is the principles associated with the theory that are important: Pavlov showed that a certain conditioned response and behaviour could be developed by association with a certain conditioned stimulus. If applied into a learning environment within physical education the teacher or coach can, through repetitive practice, get a beginner to associate a particular type of action or movement with a particular stimulus. It was felt that this approach could be generalised across all learners, with all students being treated the same, experiencing the same repetitive practice and being expected to behave in the same way. The traditional 'drill' technique, whereby all students in a class respond to the same stimulus or cue (almost reflex behaviour) with the students having no real choice, has developed from these basic S–R principles.

Think of your time back in junior school. What happened when 'playtime' was over? Generally a teacher would come out into the playground and ring a bell or blow a whistle and all pupils would line up before being given permission to return to their classrooms. This is pure behaviourism, stimulus and reponse theory.

This approach relies very much on the teacher manipulating situations within the learning environment (gymnasium, hockey pitch, etc.) in order to create habitual responses. A criticism of classical conditioning is that although behaviour or response may be triggered automatically and may be correct, it is not necessarily linked to understanding – which may be needed if further or more complex skills and strategies are to be developed.

It also does not really explain what happens when teaching a novel skill ie: what would be the unconditional stimulus?

This theory is concerned with the following:

- learning is dictated mainly by specific stimuli from the learner's situation/environment
- existing SR (stimulus–response) connections are replaced with new bonds
- the response remains the same but the stimulus changes
- classical conditioning techniques can be used by sports psychologists to help performers control anxiety eg: relaxation or meditation techniques can rely on controlled breathing exercises using repetition of a calming phrase or repetition in drill training.

The use of well timed commands (stimuli) to stimulate action is a very effective technique that is still used today. It can be applied to many sports.

Operant conditioning (Skinner 1904–1990)

In his later work on instrumental or operant conditioning, Skinner drew heavily on Thorndike's (1874–1949) three laws of learning. He did not totally reject the work done on classical conditioning by Pavlov but suggested that this view of how behaviour could be created was too simplistic. He saw the learner as being more involved in the learning process. Behaviour was not seen as being reflex or inevitable with the learner having no choice or alternative, as in classical conditioning. For Skinner, the learner's behaviour in the present situation was very much as a result of consequences of their previous actions. The learner associates the consequences of their previous actions with the current situation (stimulus) and responds accordingly taking into account whether those previous consequences were satisfactory, pleasing and successful or unsatisfactory, unpleasant and unsuccessful. These consequences would either serve to strengthen the bond between certain stimulus and response or weaken it. Skinner suggested also that these bonds could be further strengthened or weakened by the use of appropriate reinforcement, thus increasing or decreasing the probability of that behaviour happening again in the future. Both **Positive** and **Negative reinforcement** could be used to increase the probability of a certain behaviour happening again and punishment could serve to weaken the bond and thus reduce the probability of certain unwanted behaviour or performance happening again.

Thorndike's laws of learning

Skinner's studies in operant conditioning developed out of considerable early research by Thorndike who, in developing his own research on 'trial and error learning' linked to S–R bond theory, proposed many laws of learning, the most famous of which are as follows.

Law of readiness

In order for learning to be really effective the performer has to be in the right frame of mind psychologically as well as being physically prepared and capable of completing the task, ie, appropriate maturational development, motivation and prerequisite learning.

Law of exercise

In order for the bond between the stimulus and response to be strengthened it is necessary for regular practice to take place under favourable conditions. Repetition of the correct technique is important, sometimes referred to as 'the law of use'. However, he suggests that failure to practise on a regular basis could also result in 'the law of disuse' when the bond is weakened. Appropriate or favourable conditions could be created by the use of reinforcement.

Law of effect

The law of effect is central to understanding the essential differences between classical and operant conditioning. Thorndike concluded that:

1 What happens as a result of behaviour will influence that behaviour in the future.
2 Responses that bring satisfaction or pleasure are likely to be repeated again.
3 Responses that bring discomfort are not likely to be repeated again.

This is not the same as classical conditioning where the stimulus always produces the same response whether it is good or bad. However, his basic premise was that:

- behaviour is shaped and maintained by its consequences.

Shaping is the gradual procedure/process for developing difficult/complex behaviour patterns in small stages.

For example, if a badminton player receives a return which is only half court and not too high he will 'smash'. If this proves to be successful and therefore pleasurable it will serve to strengthen the connection between the stimulus (half court return) and the response (smash) and thus make it more likely that this behaviour will be repeated the next time the same situation occurs. However, a problem sometimes associated with trial and error learning is that a beginner may learn a poor or wrong technique (R) which may be effective in a limited way. This may result in having to re-learn at a later date in order to weaken the S–R bond which they have developed.

Skinner went on to suggest that certain additional reinforcement or motivational techniques such as praise or rewards could serve to support even further his view of the law of effect.

The consequences of operants or behaviour, ie, performance can be:

1 positive reinforcement ⎫
2 negative reinforcement ⎬ strengthen behaviour
   or
3 punishment – weaken behaviour

The above reinforcements or punishments can come in various guises.

Definition of reinforcement

Any event or action or phenomenon that by strengthening the S–R bond increases the probability of a response occurring again. In other words it is the system or process that is used to shape behaviour in the future.

Positive reinforcement usually follows *after* a learner has demonstrated a desirable performance, eg, the basketball player has developed the correct 'set shot' technique and receives praise from the coach. This will hopefully motivate and encourage the performer to repeat the correct set shot technique and try to improve.

In discussion with a partner try and think of other types of positive reinforcements that may increase the probability of a response being repeated.

Negative reinforcement again serves to increase the probability of a certain desirable behaviour happening again but it is by the withdrawing of a possible aversive stimulus, eg, a teacher or coach constantly shouting at their team from the sideline suddenly stops shouting. The team or players would assume that they were behaving or performing in the correct way and thus try and repeat the same actions or skills again.

You must ensure that you do not confuse negative reinforcement with negative feedback or punishment.

Definition of punishment

An event or action, usually an aversive stimulus, to try and reduce or eliminate undesirable behaviour, eg, a penalty is given in football for a foul within the penalty area or a red card is given to a player who repeatedly infringes the laws of the game. Punishment can be effective but may result in frustration and bitterness and is seen by many as a negative approach.

When and how to use reinforcers

Fig. 15.3 PUNISHMENT IS USED TO ELIMINATE UNDESIRABLE BEHAVIOUR. IT TELLS US WHAT NOT TO DO, NOT WHAT TO DO!

In using reinforcement techniques a teacher or coach needs to be aware of the effect that different reinforcers may have and how and when to use them effectively to ensure the appropriate learning and performance of motor skills. Within operant conditioning once the teacher or coach has decided what the desired level of performance or skill level is they will use reinforcers knowledgeably to condition the learner's behaviour in the appropriate way. It may be that the teacher plans the lessons in order that success is gained quite easily in the first part of the session. Success itself can act as the reinforcer. As the skills become more demanding praise for achieving aspects of the desired response may be given. The teacher or coach must ensure that the praise is given soon after the correct behaviour is performed in order that the beginner can link it to their actions (temporal association) and has no doubt what it is for (see the section on feedback). In using reinforcers a teacher or coach needs to consider the following.

1 How often to use them (too much or too little, partial or complete).
2 Ratio of positive to negative.
3 How soon after response.
4 What type to use.
5 Size and/or value of reinforcer.

All the above will be affected by the teacher's and beginner's interpretation and perception of the reinforcers used.

In discussion with a partner make a list using the table below of both tangible and intangible reinforcers and punishments that could be used with a learner in the associative phase of learning.

Reinforcers		Punishments	
Tangible	**Intangible**	**Tangible**	**Intangible**

Complete the same table for a professional sports performer. Discuss the differences.

**Summary –
Practical
application of
operant
conditioning**

- Concerned with responses rather than stimuli.
- Not concerned with associations between stimuli and responses but with the association between responses and consequences.
- Reinforcement is a key factor of this conditioning.
- Reinforcement increases the probability of a behaviour occurring, eg give praise when a successful performance occurs.

Skills can be taught using the operant method by:

- simplifying complex actions
- using a target area on wall/floor
- demonstration of correct style
- use of trial and error learning ('have a go' in the Cognitive/Associative phase of learning).

When the skill/performance (response) achieved relates closely to the desired action (response) the teacher can:

- give knowledge of results
- give praise/positive feedback/positive reinforcement

This will strengthen the S–R bond and promote success.

If the required skill/performance is not produced the teacher can weaken the bond between the stimulus and the inappropriate response (S–R) by:

- giving negative feedback
- using punishment.

In order to be more positive, and to decrease the probability of the poor performance re-occurring, the coach could teach other strategies to promote success as opposed to failure.

Drive reduction theory (C L Hull 1943)

Whilst drive reduction theory is primarily linked to motivation it has strong links to learning and our understanding of S–R bonding; see Arousal. Hull's theory suggested that continual repetition on its own may not serve to increase the strength of the S–R bond and thus shape the required performance. The strength of the S–R bond (learned behaviour) is affected by the:

- level of motivation or drive
- intensity of the stimulus/problem
- level of incentive or reward
- amount of practice/reinforcements.

Hull believed that learning could only take place if drive reduction (acting as reinforcement) occurred and that all behaviour (learned performance) derived from a performer's need to satisfy their drives.

There have been many criticisms of Hull's work but in relating it to physical education and sport we can see that once the S–R bond is strengthened and performance of the task has become a habit (drive reduction) then in order to develop skills learning or performance levels further and prevent '**inhibition**' or lack of drive a teacher or coach must set further goals or more complex tasks to ensure that drive is maintained. Practices must be organised (see distributed practice) in order that the learner is constantly motivated, preventing '**inhibition**' occurring.

It is also important that the teacher or coach ensures that only correct technique or good performance leads to the drive reduction as it is *this* S–R bond that will be reinforced. Bad technique or habits must not be allowed to achieve drive reduction.

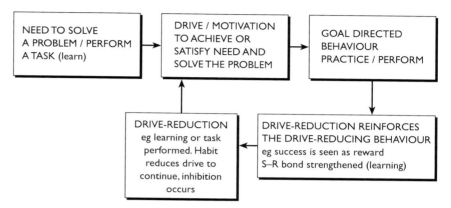

Fig. 15.4 HULL'S DRIVE REDUCTION THEORY

Simplistic summary of drive theory

- We are all motivated or have desires to achieve or solve problems – these are known as **drives**.
- When faced with learning a new skill we generally have a **drive** to achieve competent performance.
- Once we have practiced and achieved this skill our drive naturally reduces as we have accomplished what we wanted to do.
- This reduction in our drive acts as a form of reinforcement and strengthens the S–R bond.
- If we continue to just do the same thing 'inhibition' occurs.
- At this point more/new goals need to be set.

Cognitive theories

As research of human behaviour and performance developed further, many psychologists began to move away from the traditional behaviouristic approaches. Cognitive theorists saw the individual as being central to the process of learning, not merely reacting in a reflex manner (response) to outside influences (stimulus). **Understanding** of the total relationship between the many stimuli within the environment at any one time, and indeed their link to previous and future stimuli, was an essential part of cognitive theory.

Relationships between stimuli and certain responses were not learned in isolation but were part of the learner's awareness of a 'whole' variety of inter-related variables and experiences. It was argued that this would involve a whole host of cognitive processes such as use of senses, perception/interpretation, problem solving and being able to relate the present situation to previous similar experiences, thus involving memory.

The main early supporters of this approach, whose views have become synonymous with the cognitive approach, were known as 'gestaltists'. They believed that 'the whole is greater than the sum of its parts'. Gestaltists such as M Wertheimer (1880–1943), K Koffka (1886–1941) and W Köhler (1887–1967) argued that in the learning situation a beginner will continually organise and reorganise mentally in relation to previous experiences the various aspects that they are faced with in order to solve a problem in the present situation ie, they would 'figure it out'. The time scale involved together with the strategies and methods used was seen as being different for each individual.

This view of learning is known as 'insight learning': a learner suddenly discovers the relationship between the many stimuli they have been faced with and 'it all comes together!' (for instance a learner suddenly gets the timing of a serve correct). Insight learning often results in the performer progressing very quickly after periods of apparently little progress in the early stages. It is then important that further questions, problems or goals are set in order to motivate the learner to develop their performance further. The association of S–R by 'trial and error learning' (or chance which is then reinforced when correct thus gradually strengthening the bond) has no role to play in the cognitive perspective. Learning is not seen as a random process. What is learned within insight learning is therefore not a set of specific conditioned associations but a real understanding (cognitive) of the relationship between the process and means of achieving the end result. For instance, a defending hockey player who has the reasons explained to them why, when they are the last person in defence, they should not commit themselves, but 'jockey' their opponent, keeping goal-side, as this will enable other players to get back to help or put pressure on the attacker possibly forcing a mistake, is more likely to understand when and why to carry out the coach's instructions in future situations and also see the relevance of their role.

This, it is argued, is better in the long run than simply being told what to do or possibly punished if they do 'dive in' and commit without thinking. In practice, following the cognitive approach it would be important that the teacher or coach had an in-depth understanding and knowledge of both the individual learner and the various coaching strategies relevant to the skills being taught. It seems that a variety of experiences are essential for learners to develop their 'insight' of the present task or problem using knowledge gained from previous situations. There is evidence to suggest that **insight** in the learner can be further developed by the teacher giving helpful hints or cues. This is particularly useful when considering transfers from previous learned activities or skills (see transfer of learning). Gestaltists would suggest that a learner experiences the 'whole' skill or activity, learning individually to develop his/her own map of understanding rather than 'part' or 'whole', step to step, association.

'The whole is greater than the sum of its parts.'

This whole learning approach allows learners to develop their own strategies and routes of understanding alongside general principles thus enabling the quicker learners to progress at their own rate: this has obvious links to the promoting of motivation and the developing of an individual's full potential.

Socialisation

In global terms socialisation is seen as the life-long process of transmitting a culture by teaching and learning behaviours appropriate to the accepted norms, values and expectations of a society.

Socialisation, particularly within a sporting setting, is a dynamic process linked to the way in which people are influenced to conform to expected appropriate behaviour. Socialisation plays an important role in social integration.

General socialisation is heavily influenced by **prime socialising agents**. These are seen as:

- parents/family
- teacher/school
- peers/friendships
- coach/club
- media
- role models.

Although the parents and family are seen as the most important agents of socialisation all the others can exert a great influence in helping to create role models, real or imagined, that can be imitated. While socialisation can be considered in the global or national context of

---

DEFINITIONS

Norms are patterns of accepted behaviour within a particular society or sports group.

Expectations are commonly accepted positions and roles within a particular society or sports group which are actively promoted.

Status is the position in societies' or sports groups' social structure.

Role is the expected behaviour of a person related to their status within a particular society or sports group.

learning the **norms**, **values** and **expectations** of society, it can also be viewed in the more specific context of how:

- sport can act as an agent of socialisation for society in general
- performers are socialised into specific sports/teams or groups norms, values and expectations.

Sport as an agent of socialisation

Socialisation into sport
- **A process which results in adoption of the sport culture/norms/values.**
- **Occurs with reference to player/coach/referee/ spectator roles.**
- **Adopting sport behaviour appropriate to acceptable sport role models.**
- **Agents e.g. parents/peers/school/ coaches/clubs/families/ media play a large role.**

Sport in its widest sense is seen by many as an important aspect of life in most societies, and therefore a fundamental component of the socialisation process experienced by the vast majority of young people. Research in this area, although often criticised, argues that performers, particularly young children, who take part in sport are being taught skills both physical (motor) and cognitive that will enable them to participate fully and effectively within society as a whole (social learning).

The focus of this research has been on personality, moral behaviour, leadership roles, character building, cooperation, social roles and so on. It has been claimed that games teach young performers to develop appropriate attitudes and values by providing specific learning experiences. It has been shown, however, that not all learning in these situations is positive. The specific type of experience is important and has to be taken into account. The increasing 'professionalisation' of sport can serve to promote the 'win at all costs' attitude, thus leading young performers possibly to imitate deviant behaviour, eg, cheating and aggression. It has also been suggested that the traditional values and roles portrayed by sport and performers have heavily influenced gender stereotyping both in sport (eg, female activities, weaker, less suited to sport) and outside sport. This influence is coming under increasing criticism from within society at present. It is felt that sport and physical education should be doing much more to influence the image of women positively, together with that of other equally under-represented groups in both sport and society in general.

Socialisation through sport
- **Values learnt through involvement with sport eg, unselfishness/loyalty /cooperation/fairplay etc.**
- **Negative values may also be socialised eg, foul-play /racism/gender/stereo- typing/win at all costs attitude.**
- **Values influenced by agencies within sport eg, coach/captain/teacher/ Governing Bodies.**

Social learning

Social learning theory came about as an important alternative explanation to conditioning. It was Bandura who, in the 1960s and 70s, carried out more extensive research in this area. Although he viewed learning and behaviour as being linked to reinforcements (as had conditioning theories), he viewed the reinforcements as being more related to **vicarious reinforcement**. He saw this vicarious reinforcement as being the result of two elements, **observation** and **imitation**, particularly when related to the acquisition of social and moral behaviour. In introducing certain cognitive factors which can only be implied from a person's social behaviour, social learning theorists, and Bandura in particular, emphasise the notion of learning through observation.

In the previous section we discussed the concept of socialisation through sport; the social learning perspective has been the traditional theme behind this notion. Learning is seen as taking place within a social setting in the presence of others with the learner and the socialising agent being involved in a two way (reciprocal) interaction. A person, therefore, observes other people's behaviour in various ways not necessarily through direct interaction. The behaviour is taken in, the consequences assimilated and then copied in the appropriate situation at the appropriate time.

Observational learning

In identifying observational learning, social learning theorists have emphasised a type of learning distinct from conditioning. New behaviour and attitudes are acquired by a performer in a sporting situation through watching and imitating the behaviour of others. The person who is being observed is referred to as the model and 'modelling' is a term used synonymously with observational learning. Within physical education and sport, demonstrations are often

Fig. 15.5 TOP SPORTS PERFORMERS CAN ACT AS POSITIVE ROLE MODELS FOR BEGINNERS

used by teachers and coaches to give beginners a good technical model to work to. Very often this also serves to help a learner's specific confidence (see self efficacy). The degree of this effect will be enhanced if the person doing the demonstration is of similar ability (team mate) (similarity) and/or is of a high status (professional performer). In addition to showing a current technical model observational learning or 'modelling' can also influence a performer's attitudes and moral behaviour by inhibiting or encouraging certain behaviour/performance (see persuasive communication/attitudes and aggression in A2).

Teachers and coaches often hope that the consequences of disciplining a certain team member for unacceptable behaviour, e.g. substituting a player for fighting or arguing, will not only have an effect on the specific player substituted but will also affect the behaviour of other team members who are watching. The other players will internalise the consequences of the team mate's behaviour and are thus warned against copying it.

Modelling is not always carried out either by the observer or the model at a conscious or intentional level. Very often the model does not intend their behaviour to be copied and is usually unaware that their behaviour is acting as a model for others. The behaviour of top professional sports performers can therefore, have either positive or negative repercussions for the behaviour of beginners. Although role models are an important factor within observational learning they do not always have to be real or in direct contact. Remote sports stars, cartoon characters or fictional media related models can prove equally influential. By identifying with the model the performer will not only replicate existing behaviour but may also reproduce certain behaviour in novel situations.

People of influence in physical education and sport have to be aware that unacceptable models of behaviour or attitudes are often being presented and possibly influencing the behaviour of others eg, gender stereotyping and aggression.

Although for most learners and beginners the model is known directly by the observer and is usually a significant other, eg, parent, teacher, coach, team mate or professional sports person, the degree of the effect or endurance of observational behaviour will depend on several factors (see social learning and aggression).

Bandura's often quoted 'Bobo doll' experiments in relation to children learning aggressive behaviour through the observation of others, led him to suggest that imitation is more than just copying a model's behaviour and depends very much on how **appropriate**, **relevant**, **similar**, **nurturant**, **reinforced**, **powerful** and **consistent** the behaviour is. Further research has also shown that the learner not only has to imitate the behaviour but also identify with the role model.

Important characteristics of models

Appropriateness

If the behaviour of the model being observed is perceived by the observer as being appropriate in relation to accepted norms and values then it will increase the probability of it being imitated. For instance in our society male aggressive behaviour appears more acceptable than female aggressive behaviour (accepted norm) and therefore young beginners/learners are more likely to copy male aggressive behaviour than female. This has obvious repercussions for male/female stereotyping in western culture.

Relevance

Again, in relation to the young performer's perceptions of the model is how relevant is the behaviour? Young males are more likely to imitate male models of aggression than are girls as they have in general been socialised into seeing this as part of the accepted male role in society. The behaviour should also be realistic ie, a live performance is more likely to have an effect than a video.

Similarity

By as young as three years of age youngsters are beginning to identify with their 'gender roles' and will identify more readily with similar models.

Nurturant

Whether the model is warm and friendly will have an effect on the likelihood of their behaviour, attitudes and morals being imitated. A teacher presenting an activity in a friendly unthreatening way is more likely to be taken notice of and is thus nurturing the appropriate behaviour (see styles of leadership).

Reinforced

If a model's behaviour is reinforced or rewarded in any way then it is more likely to be imitated. Again this has repercussions for the media who very often directly or indirectly draw attention to certain behaviour thus reinforcing it in the eyes of the beginner. The imitation of gender appropriate behaviour is often reinforced by parents (significant others).

Powerful

The more powerful model is seen to have a more significant effect than a less powerful one ie, more likely to be copied if highly skilled.

Consistency

The more consistent the model's behaviour is the more likely it is to be imitated. Research has shown, however, that sometimes a role model's inconsistent behaviour can inadvertently have an effect on young performers' behaviour.

A performer will take into account the above factors and evaluate them in relation to the consequences of the behaviour. These consequences can be viewed in two ways, the second more crucial than the first.

1 What were the consequences of the model's behaviour?
2 What are the perceived consequences of modelling the same behaviour for the observer (learner/beginner)?

The consequences may either be immediate or appear at a later stage.

If observers can imitate a certain behaviour at a later appropriate stage, then they are said to have socially learned it. In physical education and sport more long term learning can also occur when young performers begin to 'think', 'feel' and 'act' as if they were the role model rather than consciously copying technical motor skills. Over a longer period young performers can assimilate the attitudes, values, views, philosophy and levels of motivation demonstrated by significant others (teacher or coach) to ensure that they become a 'model' professional themselves.

Bandura's four stage process model of observational learning

While social learning theory (and others) takes into account the effect of reinforcement, Bandura's original model referred to learning without any direct rewards or reinforcement. He argued that beginners/performers learn and behave by observing other performers or events (vicarious experience), not merely from the direct consequences of their own behaviour.

The practical application of Bandura's research into observational learning can be related to the four stages of the modelling process identified in fig 15.6. This will help teachers and coaches to ensure that learners are focused and maintain their attention in order to produce a learned competent performance.

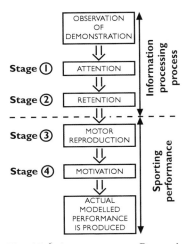

Fig. 15.6 ADAPTED MODEL OF BANDURA'S OBSERVATIONAL LEARNING PROCESS

Stage 1 – Attention

In order to ensure that a performer learns through observing it is very important that they give careful and specific attention to the model. The level of attention paid to a model will depend on the level of respect that the learner has for the perceived status and attractiveness of the model. A beginner, for instance, is much more likely to take notice of and try to emulate a highly skilled professional or a coach who has significant knowledge of the activity.

Attention is gained by models that are:

- attractive
- successful
- powerful

or those whose behaviour is

- functional.

Teachers and coaches must also be aware of the beginners/learners stage of learner in order to ensure that they don't overload them with too much information. A good coach will ensure that a beginner focuses on the main points and that their attention is not distracted in any way from the task. It is important that the demonstration:

- can be seen and heard
- is accurate
- focuses attention on specific details and cues
- maintains the level of motivation.

Stage 2 – Retention

In order that modelling is effective the beginner must be able to retain the skill in their memory and recall it when appropriate. One way of achieving this is to use mental rehearsal. Another way is to ensure that the demonstration/practice is meaningful, relevant or realistic. By using symbolic coding in some form a coach can help the performer retain the mental image of the skill. Thus retention often involves cognitive skills.

Stage 3 – Motor production

While a performer can pay attention and retain a clear picture of what is required of them they will in general need time to practice the modelled technique if they are to be able to carry out the skill themselves. It is important therefore, that the 'model' is appropriate to the capability level of the learner/observer: the observer must be able to act out the task. Therefore if complex tasks are being developed then the methodology of teaching and practice must allow for general progression and provide opportunity for staged success.

Stage 4 – Motivation

If performance of the model is successful then this will provide the motivation for the learner to try to reproduce it again at the appropriate time.

Without motivation a learner will not carry out the previous three stages, i.e. pay attention, remember and practice the task.

According to Bandura, the level of motivation is dependent on:

- the level of external reinforcement (praise, appropriate feedback)
- the level of vicarious reinforcement
- the level of self reinforcement (sense of pride or achievement)
- the perceived status of the model
- the perceived importance of the task.

Practical application of Bandura's model

In order to make demonstrations more effective a teacher or coach should:

- make sure the learner is aware of the importance and relevance of the skill to the final performance
- refer to a high status model
- get someone of similar ability to demonstrate to help self efficacy
- make sure the performer can see and hear well
- show complex skills from various angles and at different speeds
- highlight the main aspects of technique
- focus attention on a few points particularly for beginners and children
- not have too long a delay between instruction and demonstration
- allow time for mental rehearsal
- not allow too long a delay between demonstration and mental rehearsal
- repeat the demonstration if necessary
- reinforce successful performance.

Summary

Learning theories

1 The key components of the behaviouristic perspective are stimulus (S) and response (R). The S–R theory is based on the concept that learning involves the development of connections or bonds between specific stimuli and responses.
2 In classical conditioning, drill and habit are very important elements of every lesson.
3 In operant conditioning, reinforcement is central to shaping behaviour.
4 The teacher or coach must try to produce feelings of satisfaction to give strong reinforcements (law of effect).
5 Hull's drive theory links motivation to the strengthening of the S–R bond.
6 Cognitive theories suggest that performers must be able to understand events. The concept of 'insight' is a major aspect of cognitive theories.

Socialisation

1 Most behaviour in sport takes place within a social setting.
2 Socialisation is the general continuous process of transmitting a culture to people and teaching them behaviour appropriate to the accepted norms, values and expectations of society.
3 As a member of a sports group/team a performer can be socialised into the 'modelled' norms of that sub-culture. These can be carried over and influence behaviour outside the sporting situation.
4 The family is the most important 'prime' socialising agent. However, teachers, coaches and high status models and peers can also heavily influence a performer's behaviour.

Social learning and observational learning

1 Social learning theory advocates that we learn and acquire new behaviours and attitudes, both acceptable and unacceptable, as a result of vicarious reinforcement through observation and imitation.
2 The person being observed is the model.

3   The effect of observational learning is dependent upon the model having certain characteristics.

4   Observational learning can take place without intention.

5   The effect and level of social learning through observation is increased if the model is of a high status and their behaviour is reinforced.

6   Demonstrations are an important aspect of observational learning.

7   The process of observational learning involves 4 stages: attention, retention, motor production and motivation.

Review Questions

1   What is a theory of association?

2   Explain the S–R bond.

3   What is a major criticism of classical conditioning?

4   In what ways does operant conditioning differ from classical conditioning?

5   What does reinforcement mean?

6   How does positive and negative reinforcement affect the probability of behaviour happening?

7   How does punishment affect behaviour?

8   What is the law of effect?

9   Give a practical example to show your understanding of how behaviour is shaped and maintained by its consequences.

10   How does a teacher or coach prevent 'inhibition' developing?

11   What does 'insight learning' mean?

12   Why is the cognitive approach to learning thought to be more effective?

13   What do social psychologists mean by socialisation?

14   What part can sport play in this process?

15   What are socialising agents?

16   Why is observational learning important to social learning theory?

17   According to Bandura what are the main characteristics of a model that influence the likelihood of imitation taking place?

18   Explain Bandura's four stages of observational learning.

chapter 16

Information Processing

Information processing is a key topic and is central to your understanding of many other areas within this book. A sports performer uses information from the current situation, previous experience and their memory systems in order to reduce uncertainty and help them to decide how to act. Information processing is an approach which sees the development of human motor behaviour (motor learning) as a *process* rather than a specific stimulus and response relationship. It has developed under the umbrella of cognitive psychology.

Here is a list of terms to be covered in this chapter. It is important that you understand them and can apply the principles involved to practical situations within Sport and Physical Education:

Information processing

- Display
- Cues/signals/stimulus
- Proprioceptors
- Exteroceptors
- Introceptors
- Kinesthesis
- Selective attention
- Short-term sensory store
- Short-term memory
- Long-term memory
- Reaction time

- Hicks Law
- Psychological refractory period
- Channel capacity
- Feedback
- Knowledge of results (KR)
- Knowledge of performance (KP)
- Intrinsic feedback
- Extrinsic feedback

WHAT IS INFORMATION?

Information:

- reduces uncertainty
- allows players to make decisions on actions
- comes from previous relevant experience
- comes from current experience/game/situation.

Information processing models

Much of the terminology used in the various models is reflective of the post war computer age in which it developed. The models appear to make comparisons between the ways in which machines function and process information and the ways in which humans 'achieve, retain and transform knowledge' (Jerome Bruner, 1972). Although research and the many models produced tend to suggest that the process learners go through is basically the same the information processing approach recognises the individuality of the learner. Individuals are studied as active beings using knowledge in ways personal to themselves. This involves a whole host of processes. In breaking down what is seen as a very complicated process into manageable proportions individuals will be involved in:

- information reception
- information translation
- information transmission
- information reduction
- information collation
- information storage
- information retrieval.

The information processing approach has been traditionally based on two assumptions.

1 That the processing of information can be broken down into various sub-processes or components/stages.
2 That each of these components has limitations in terms of capacity or duration which affect the amount of information that can be processed.

Information processing emphasises that:

- perception
- attention
- memory
- decision making and
- feedback

play an important part in the overall learning process.

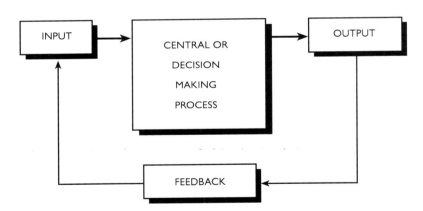

Fig. 16.1 SIMPLISTIC INFORMATION PROCESSING MODEL

Various psychologists have put forward graphical representations of how they see the various parts of the cognitive process relating together. These models are intended to aid understanding by helping teachers/coaches in their task analysis. The learning process is, however, a changing, complex, multi-dimensional process and such models must be seen as hypothetical and flexible. Two of the better-known models which are generally referred to are Welford's (1976) and Whiting's (1970), in figs 16.2 and 16.3.

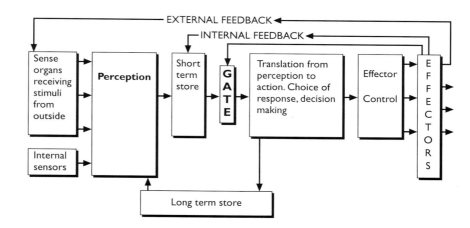

Fig. 16.2 WELFORD'S INFORMATION
PROCESSING MODEL.
Adapted from A.T. Welford, 1976

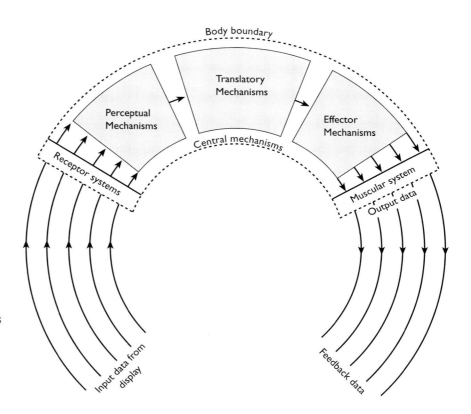

Fig. 16.3 WHITING'S MODEL (1969) IS
A WELL-KNOWN ILLUSTRATION OF THE
INFORMATION PROCESSING THEORY.
Adapted from H.T.A. Whiting, 1970

Both models reflect basically the same process:

- stimulus identification stage/input stage
- response identification/selection stage/central stage
- response programming stage/the output stage

although they use slightly different terminology.

Stimulus identification stage (INPUT)

This stage is mainly a sensory stage where the stimulus (eg, a ball) is detected along with speed, size, colour, direction of movement, etc.

Fig. 16.4 A PLAYER HEARS HER TEAM-MATES CALL, SEES THE BALL, FEELS HER GRIP ON THE STICK AND BRACES HER LEGS IN READY POSITION TO RECEIVE THE BALL

The display
This is the physical environment in which the learner is performing. The display for the player shown in fig 16.4 would be her own team mates, opposition, the pitch, ball, goal posts, the crowd and whatever else is going on in the vicinity of the game, whether important or not.

Stimuli and cues
These are specific aspects of the display that are being registered by the learner's sense organs (eg, a ball being passed to them or players calling for the ball).

Sense organs, sensory systems and receptors

These are the receptors which take in the sensory information. There are three types or categories of receptors.

1   Exteroceptors – **extrinsic** information from outside the body (from the display):

 • visual
 • audition
 • touch
 • smell
 • taste.

2   Proprioceptors – nerve receptors within the body in muscles, joints, etc. providing **intrinsic** information regarding what class of movement is occurring. Kinesthetic information is also provides about the feel or sense of movement. The inner ear also helps to provide proprioceptive information. eg – Are you unbalanced.

3   Introceptors – information from the internal organs of the body, heart, lungs, digestive system, etc. This information is passed to the central mechanism of the brain via the body's sensory nervous system. eg – How fast heart is beating, register fatigue etc.

Perception
This process involves the interpretation of the sensory input, along with discrimination, selection and coding of important information that may be relevant to the decision making process. The process of selective attention and use of memory are important at this stage (see later sections).

Response selection stage (central/decision making stage)

Having identified information from the display, this stage involves deciding on the necessary movement in the context of the present situation, eg, does the hockey player receive the ball and pass, change direction and dribble, or hold the ball?

Translatory/decision making mechanism
This involves an individual having to use the coded information received to recognise what is happening around them in order to decide on and select the appropriate motor programme to deal with the situation.

Response programming stage (OUTPUT)

In this final stage the motor systems are organised in order to deliver the chosen plan of action.

Effector mechanisms/effector control
Motor programmes or schemas (plans of action – see later section) are selected and developed. These plans, in the form of coded impulses, are sent via the body's *effector* or motor nerves to the appropriate muscles telling them what action to carry out.

Muscular system/effectors

The muscles receive the relevant 'motor programme' or plan of action in the form of coded impulses, initiate the movement and the action is performed.

Feedback

As a result of whatever action has been carried out the receptor systems receive information in various forms. There are many different types of feedback but it can be either extrinsic from outside the body or intrinsic from within the body.

It can be seen that the body's control system (brain) through a series of receptors and effectors, controls our physical movements by evaluating the need for action and then executing it when and where it deems necessary. How effective this processing of information is depends on many variable factors which will be discussed over the following pages.

Memory

The memory is seen as a critical part of the overall learning process. It is central to our ability to receive the relevant information, interpret it, use it to make decisions and then pass out the appropriate information via the body's effector systems.

There has been much debate about the structure, organisation and capacity of the memory process with many modifications being suggested to the basic 'two-dimensional process' or 'multi-store' model of memory as described by Atkinson and Shiffrin (1968). It is generally suggested however, that there are two main aspects of memory: short-term memory (STM) and long-term memory (LTM). These two parts of memory are in some way preceded by a third area known as the sensory system or short-term sensory store (STSS) which involves a selection and attention process.

The STSS receives all sensory information provided by sensory receptors. It can hold large amounts of information (it is virtually limitless). Information usually lasts in the STSS for a fraction of a second (maximum 1 second). Unless it is reinforced or rehearsed it will be lost – scanning is a way of reinforcing information.

Selective attention

Due to the apparent limited neurological capacity of the short-term memory suggested by many single channel models (eg, Broadbent 1958, Norman 1969, 1976) it is acknowledged that there is some form of selection system in order to prioritise information, although there are disagreements about the positioning of this filtering system (see Welford's model fig. 16.2, the gating process).

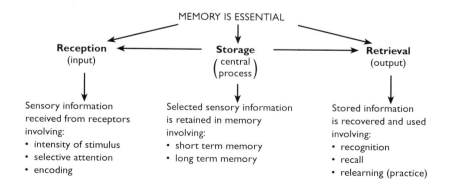

Fig. 16.5 MEMORY IS ESSENTIAL

The process of selective attention is responsible for selecting relevant from irrelevant information from the display. This allows the tennis player, for example, to focus on the specific cues being presented by their opponent when receiving serve (the grip, throw up of the ball, angle of racket, position in relation to service court, etc.) and ignore other aspects of the environment (display) which may distract them (eg, crowd, noise from the next court, ball boys, etc.) thus helping to prevent potential information overload.

The efficiency of the short-term sensory store and the selective attention process is influenced by several factors.

- **experience** – know what to look for – an experienced tennis player will know what to look for when facing an opponent
- **arousal** – the more alert you are the more likely you are to choose the appropriate cues. In cricket, a batsman who is alert is able to pick up on spin, speed and direction of the ball
- **quality of instruction** – as a beginner you don't always know what to respond to. The coach or teacher can direct your attention verbally, visually, mechanically
- **intensity of stimulus** – the effectiveness of the senses (eg, short sighted, poor hearing) when detecting, eg, speed, noise, size/shape and colour.

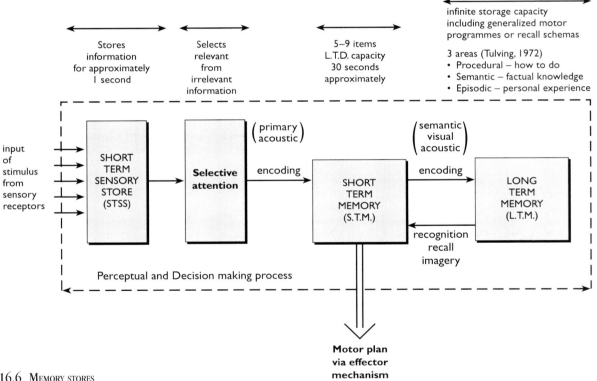

Fig. 16.6 MEMORY STORES

Selective attention can be improved by:

- lots of relevant practice
- increasing intensity of the stimulus
- use of language associated with or appropriate to the performer in order to motivate and arouse
- use of past experience/transfer to help explanations
- direct attention.

Short-term memory

Because the short-term memory appears to function between the STSS and the long-term memory receiving and integrating relevant coded information from both areas and passing on decisions via the body's effector systems (processing and storing information) it is often referred to as the 'working memory' or 'work space' (Atkinson and Shilfrin, 1971). The information in our STM at any one time is said to be our 'consciousness'.

Capacity of STM

Compared with the two other aspects of memory the STM has very limited capacity hence the need for the process of selective attention (when only relevant information is encoded and passed to STM). Seven plus or minus two items (7 ± 2) appears to be the maximum amount of information 'chunks' that any one person can hold. It has been suggested, however (Miller, 1956) that by practising a process called 'chunking' or grouping together of many items of information, a person can remember several 'chunks' of information rather than just seven individual items. Thus a games player with practice will possibly be able to remember at least seven different tactical moves or options happening around them rather than the seven aspects of a specific skill or strategy. In addition, a performer, by linking various aspects of a particular skill together, eg, a tennis serve, will see it as a whole, once learned, rather than as all the various parts of sub-routines of the service, grip, stance, throw up, preparation of racket, point of contact, follow through and recovery.

Duration of STM

It is generally accepted that unless the 7 ± 2 item of information within the STM are reinforced in some way by practice, repetition or rehearsal then they will only remain in the short-term memory for a relatively short period of time: approximately 30 seconds. If 'attention' is directed away from the information being held in the short-term memory then it tends to be forgotten. In order to keep information 'circulating' within the STM, research has suggested that it is more effective for a person to repeat it verbally. Visual imagery, although slower, can also be used. Important areas of information are passed on to the long-term memory for retrieval and use at a later date.

Long-term memory

The long-term memory is what is generally thought of as someone's 'memory'. Information about past experiences is stored, including learned knowledge, perceptual skills, motor skills, etc. In short, all classes of information associated with learning and experience are retained in the LTM.

Capacity of LTM

The long-term memory is thought to have unlimited capacity. It enables a performer to deal with present situations or tasks by using information that has been specifically learned (either behavioural or factual) or information gained from general past experiences.

Duration of LTM

Information, once learned and stored in the long-term memory, is thought to be there indefinitely, perhaps permanently. The main problem with information stored in the long-term memory is one of retrieval. Once information has been rehearsed, reinforced and linked together in the appropriate manner within the STM (coding) it is passed to the LTM for storage. It is generally thought that once learned and stored in the LTM motor skills in particular are protected from loss. There is evidence to suggest that retrieval is more effective with skills that have been 'overlearned' (practised continually) and become autonomous. Skills that are linked or associated together in a more continuous way (cycling, swimming) rather than individual discrete skills (handstand, headstand) can also be retrieved more effectively.

Retrieval of information

Retrieval of information that has been stored in the LTM for future use can take several different forms. The more common forms are recognition, recall, re-learning.

- **Recognition:** when a tennis player sees something familiar with regard to a style of serve by their opponent or a defender in soccer sees several things happening in front of them and they have to make their mind up which one is the most dangerous and adapt their own movement to it having 'recognised' certain cues or signals (retrieval cues).
- **Recall:** when a performer has to actively search their memory stores for certain previously learned skills or information that may help solve a problem in the present.
- **Re-learning:** if something has previously been learned but then forgotten it will possibly be easier to learn a second time round.
- **Imagery:** when a performer is able to 'hook' their present cognitive or motor situation onto some form of visual image of previously well-performed situation, skill or strategy (see mental rehearsal). Movement memory is aided by **verbal labels** which can produce a **mental image** of the correct movements.

To ensure important information stays in the long term memory a teacher/coach/performer will need to:

- rehearse/reinforce/repeat regularly
- link or associate information with familiar information
- make information meaningful/relevant/enjoyable
- make stimuli more recognisable/intense
- group or 'chunk' information together
- use imagery.

Decision making

In adopting an information processing approach to analysing how a performer uses present information in the form of cues and signals from the environment (display), in conjunction with previously learned or experienced information or movement skills in order to carry out some form of response (decision making), you should now have realised that this process takes time. Being able to select the correct plan of action (make a decision) quickly, is obviously critical in many sports, particularly those classified as using open skills, where adapting to continually changing situations is important, eg, tennis, basketball, hockey. It therefore follows that the quicker a performer can go through the whole process the greater advantage this should have for the motor action being carried out: anticipation becomes possible.

Reaction time

Reaction time is seen as an important performance measure helping researchers to find out exactly what happens prior to a response being made (response preparation time) and what factors can affect the speed and effectiveness of the response.

- **Reaction time** is defined as:

'the time between the onset of a signal to respond (stimulus) and the initiation of that response.'
(R. A. Magill).

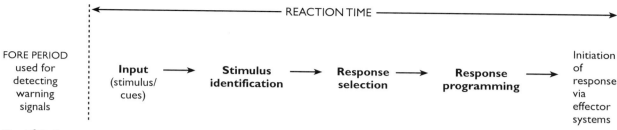

Fig. 16.7 REACTION TIME

This is different to two other time zones very often associated and sometimes confused with reaction time, namely 'movement time' and 'response time'.

- **Movement time** is defined as 'the time from the initiation of the first movement to the completion of that movement'
- **Response time** is defined as the time from the onset of a signal to respond (stimulus) to the final completion of the response or action, ie, reaction time + movement time.

 **With reference to figure 16.7 and the following diagram complete the missing labels in the list below.**

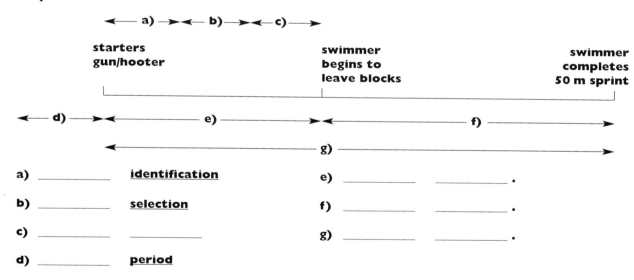

a) _____ **identification**   e) _____ _____ .

b) _____ **selection**   f) _____ _____ .

c) _____ _____   g) _____ _____ .

d) _____ **period**

Individuals differ considerably in their speed of reactions (reaction time – RT) or what has been termed 'response preparation time'. There are many important factors that can affect a performer's reaction time, usually associated with either the

- stimulus (type or amount)
- individual performer
- requirements of the task.

Response preparation time (decision making) can be affected by various factors associated with the amount of information and the number of decisions that have to be made.

Simple reaction time

This is a specific reaction to a specific stimulus (one stimulus – one response), eg, reacting to a starter at the beginning of a race.

Choice reaction time

Fig. 16.8 DARREN GOUGH

This is when there are a number of alternatives: either a performer has to respond correctly when faced with several stimuli all requiring a different response or a performer has to respond correctly to a specific stimulus from a choice of several stimuli. Generally, the more choices a performer has to face with regard to either number of stimuli to deal with, or, more importantly, the number of optional responses, the more information they have to process and the longer or slower the reaction time is. This general 'rule of thumb' is based on Hick's Law (1952).

Hick's Law states that: 'Reaction time will increase logarithmically as the number of stimulus response choices increase.'

The linear relationship implies that reaction time increases at a constant rate every time the number of response choices is doubled. This has obvious implications for a performer when trying to outwit an opponent. A bowler in cricket is better placed to dismiss a batsman if they have more types of delivery at their disposal and can use them at various times to create a feeling of uncertainty in the batsman's mind – RT can be increased by over 50%.

Stimulus–response compatibility

The compatibility of a stimulus and response (S–R) is related to how 'naturally' connected the two are. If a certain stimulus happens, what usual response does it cause? The more 'natural' or usual the response the quicker the reaction time.

The converse obviously applies, eg, in hockey, a player's natural response to a ball played down their left-hand side is to reach over with the stick in the left hand and lay the stick down taking the ball on the reverse (stimulus–response compatibility). However, if the coach wants a player to move across and take the ball on the open stick in order to be 'strong on the ball' after receiving, this, for most beginners, is S–R incompatibility (unnatural), therefore RT would be increased considerably.

Experienced sailors can reduce their reaction time to almost zero as they move the tiller of the boat in relation to wind changes (S–R compatibility). It appears almost natural.

Predictability of stimulus occurring

The more predictable a stimulus is the more effective the response can be in terms of time and accuracy. If a performer can predict in advance what is going to happen by being able to pick up on various cues and signals or advanced information, then RT can be reduced dramatically. This pre-cueing technique, as it is sometimes called, has the similar but reverse relationship caused by Hick's Law regarding choice reactions.

A player's reaction time however, can only be reduced if they pick up on the correct cues and predict the correct stimulus.

In discussion with a partner, consider a badminton or tennis situation. What pre-cueing information might you be looking for when facing a serve? What might this enable you to do?

Previous experience/ practice

The more experienced a performer is and the more practice they have had of making choices, and relating the compatibility and probability of certain responses to certain stimuli, then the more likely it is that their RT will be faster. The effect is obviously greater where choice RT rather than simple RT is involved. Hence the experienced badminton player, when placing the shuttle in various parts of the court, knows, through a good deal of appropriate practice, that only certain types of shot can be played by their opponent from this position. This will allow them almost to pre-select plans of action (see motor programmes), ie, anticipate, thus reducing their reaction times and response times to what appears to be almost instant processing.

Anticipation

Anticipation is linked very closely to experience. Anticipation, where a performer is able to initiate movement programmes or actions with 'perfect timing' relies very much on a performer using signals and cues and recognising certain stimuli early, thus predicting what is going to happen. The defender in hockey or football who always appears in the right place at the right time to make the tackle or intercept the attacking pass is using their previous experience.

An experienced tennis player receiving a second serve would have picked up on their opponent's angle of racket and subtle positioning of feet, etc., to recognise that a top-spin serve, causing the ball to 'kick' up high and wide to the forehand, was probably coming over the net. He or she then prepares accordingly, thus processing has begun earlier. An inexperienced beginner on the other hand would not understand what a top spin serve can do to the ball or be able to recognise the warning signals/cues (selective attention). Thus they would be totally unprepared for the high bouncing ball when it arrived. Beginners need more processing time in order to organise, prepare and initiate a response.

Types of anticipation

Two types of anticipation have been recognised: **spatial anticipation** and **temporal anticipation**.

1 Spatial or event anticipation is when a performer can judge or predict what is actually going to happen and therefore prepares his/her appropriate actions accordingly, enabling the response to be initiated almost immediately the actual shot occurs, eg, blocking in volleyball.
2 Temporal anticipation is when a performer knows what is going to happen but is unsure of when it will happen.

While temporal anticipation is useful, having *both* temporal and spartial anticipation is much more effective. The fact that many sports performers, particularly in 'open type' activities involving rapid changes in actions, rely heavily on anticipation means that as well as using anticipation to their own advantage they can also use the principles behind it to disadvantage opponents (see PRP below).

Factors affecting anticipation are:

- predictability of stimulus
- speed of stimulus
- time stimulus is in view
- complexity of response
- practice
- age.

Psychological refractory period (PRP)

A performer using previous experience in order to help them anticipate certain moves or actions depends heavily on making the correct predictions in order to reduce the time needed to prepare a response. One way a performer can try to increase the RT of their opponent is by presenting certain false information, a certain stance or movement of the racket in tennis or stick in hockey which implies to the opponent that a certain shot or movement will occur (predicting). The opponent then processes this information in order to prepare and initiate a response. As the opponent's response to the first 'dummy' or fake action is initiated, the player changes the move or shot causing the opponent to re-evaluate the situation and react to the second set of stimuli. The processing of the new information, for instance a drop shot in badminton rather than the anticipated overhead clear, takes time, creating a slight time delay. This delay in being able to respond to the second of two closely spaced stimuli is termed the **psychological refractory period** (PRP). In practice, if timed correctly, the opponent in tennis or badminton or defenders in hockey or basketball, are made to look foolish as, by the time they have reorganised their movement to deal with the second stimulus, the point has been won or they have been beaten by the attack.

Theoretically the delay is created by the increased processing time caused by a hold-up or 'bottleneck effect' within the response programming stage. Within this stage it is suggested that the brain can only deal with the initiation of one action or response when presented with two closely following stimuli. This is known as the single-channel hypothesis. A PRP will only occur however, if the 'fake' or 'dummy' move or action is significant enough to cause the opponent to think it is actually going to happen.

There must also be no lengthy delay in carrying out the second stimulus or 'real' action as this may negate the whole significance of the PRP.

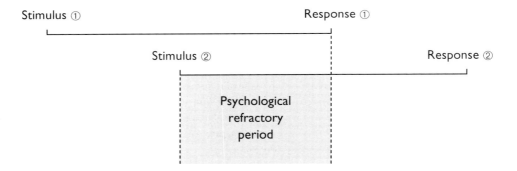

Stimulus ①   Response ①

Stimulus ②   Response ②

Psychological refractory period

How to make use of 'deception' in sport

- Deception makes use of the psychological refractory period.
- The response to one stimulus must be completed before the response to a second stimulus can begin.
- Therefore by introducing a second stimulus before the response to the first stimulus is completed the performer playing the dummy gains time.
- For example when setting a dummy in team ball games the ball player pretends to pass/run one way/direction then when the opponent responds to that movement the ball player changes direction/passes the other way.
- More time is gained because the opponent must finish the first movement before reacting and re-adjusting to the second stimulus.
- Deception creates uncertainty/insecurity.

Strategies to deceive opponents

- Delay movements as long as possible.
- Disguise relevant cues.
- Emphasise non-important cues.
- Present false information eg, fast early action then soft contact – 'selling a dummy' →
  This will create uncertainty → the opponent will slow down if alternatives are presented →
  should s/he tackle/try to intercept a pass etc → attention of opponent will be distracted by
  the uncertainty → reactions of opponent will be delayed by the second movements.

Intensity of stimulus

There is evidence to support the view that as intensity of stimulus increases, reaction time
decreases, eg, larger, brighter implements (rackets or balls) for beginners in particular.

Age

It is generally accepted whilst being relatively limited in early childhood RT improves rapidly
through the developing years up until the optimum level which is thought to be the late
teens/early twenties. After this it levels off only to slow down considerably as old age
approaches. Lack of experience on which to base quick and effective decisions has been
suggested to explain children's limited RT.

Gender

Research has tended to support the view that males have shorter reaction times although
female reaction times deteriorate less with age. The factors already discussed, however, have
much more of an influence than gender.

Strategies to improve response/ reaction time

- Mental rehearsal – going over responses in your mind.
- Concentration/ignoring irrelevant signals.
- Practice reacting to specific stimuli/signals/cues (groove the response).
- Improve physical fitness.
- Anticipate.
- Concentrate on warning signals and early movements.

Arousal, attention and alertness

Here are the three As of information processing.

Arousal

The level of arousal of a performer is seen as a significant influencing factor upon their ability to
make decisions quickly (response preparation time). We will consider various arousal theories
and their links to motivation and performance in much greater detail within the A2 psychology
of sport specification. As an introduction to the concept, arousal can be viewed as the energy or
excitement levels of the individual generated at the time the performance is taking place. These
levels can vary from extremely high, almost agitated behaviour to the lowest level, sleep. Both
these extreme states are not recommended for the performer in sport as they do not create the
'optimum' state of mental readiness for effective decisions to be made.

Attention

Over-arousal creates 'states of anxiety', causing lack of concentration and lack of attention to important coaching points.

Performing under high arousal conditions has been shown to reduce a performer's ability to pay attention to all the important and relevant aspects from the displays, possibly creating an inadequate response particularly if something unexpected happens. This phenomenon is known as **perceptual** or **attentional narrowing**. (See Arousal, Chapter 20).

Alertness

Linked to the concept of optimum arousal and levels of attention is the term alertness. Being continually prepared (alert) to pick up on specific changing cues/signals and thus make correct decisions has been, in the main, linked to the performer's ability to maintain arousal levels or state of readiness. For instance, when a goalkeeper in hockey or football is seen 'prowling' the 'D' or penalty area watching the game, keeping on their toes, they are working on maintaining 'alertness'. While it is relatively easy to maintain optimum levels of arousal and thus attention for very short periods, particularly if you are involved in the game continually, it is sometimes difficult to maintain alertness over longer periods, such as in a full game situation or in repetitive practice situations.

Feedback

The final part in the information processing system is feedback (FB). Strictly speaking feedback is a processing term referring to information coming from within the system rather than information coming from the outside world. Feedback is now generally referred to as all the information in its various forms that a performer receives as a result of movement (response produced information). When a performer is taking part in physical activity in any shape or form information is fed back into the system either during the activity or after the activity. This information can come from within the performer or from outside relating to the adequacy of their performance. This information is used to either detect and correct errors during the activity or to make changes/improvements the next time the skill is performed. As well as changing performance, feedback can also be used to reinforce learning and motivate the performer. It has been argued that without FB learning cannot occur. Evidence to support this view is provided by research conducted by Bilodeau and Bilodeau (1959, 1961) and G Stelmach (1970). The nature of the feedback will alter depending on the performers' stage of learning, but it is vital that all information is accurate, limited to key points and relevant. Feedback in the early stages should be as frequent as possible – reducing as learning progresses in order to reduce the possibility of feedback dependency.

 **ACTIVITY 3**

1 **In discussion with a partner and using practical examples, try and create a list of as many different kinds of feedback that a performer may receive when taking part in sporting activities.**

Activity	Type of feedback	Example from sport

2 **Try to think of possible methods or classifications that you might use to group together the different types of feedback you have thought of.**

Types and forms of feedback (FB)

Intrinsic feedback

Sometimes referred to as internal or inherent feedback, this type of FB comes from within the performer from the propriceptors. When a golfer swings at the ball they can feel the timing of the arm movement and the hip movement in conjunction with a perfect strike of the ball. This is also referred to as kinesthetic FB. The golfer can see and hear their club swing, and hear the ball being struck, which serves to back up the proprioceptive information being received. All this information is inherent to the task. The more experienced and skilled a performer is, the more effective their use of intrinsic FB will be.

Extrinsic feedback

Sometimes referred to as external or augmented FB, this type of FB is information received from outside the performer about the performance and is given and used to enhance (augment) the already received intrinsic FB. This is the type of FB that is generally referred to in teaching and coaching. It can however, be received from team mates within the context of a game. Performers usually receive this type of FB by visual or auditory means; for instance the coach or teacher tells or shows a performer the reasons why success or failure has occurred.

This form of information is used extensively during the cognitive and associative phases of learning. A less experienced performer will rely on guidance from the coach/teacher concerning their performance, as they have not yet developed their kineasthetic awareness fully and can not yet interpret feedback arising intrinsically.

Extrinsic FB can obviously be made up of a mixture of several different types and forms:

- Continuous
- Terminal
- Knowledge of results (KR)
- Knowledge of performance (KP)
- Positive
- Negative

Continuous feedback

Sometimes referred to as ongoing or concurrent FB, this type of FB is being received *during* the activity. It is most frequently received as proprioceptive or kinesthetic information, eg, a tennis player can 'feel' the ball hitting the 'sweet spot' of the racket when playing strokes during a rally.

Terminal feedback

This is FB received by the performer *after* they have completed the skill or task. It can either be given immediately after the relevant performance or be delayed and given some time later.`

Positive feedback

This type of feedback occurs when the performance of a task was correct or successful. It can be used to reinforce learning, increasing the probability of the successful performance being repeated, eg, a coach or teacher praising a beginner when they catch a ball successfully.

Although positive FB is thought to facilitate perceived competence and help intrinsic motivation, it is important that a teacher doesn't give too much positive FB thereby distorting a performer's perceptions of their own performance and possibly affecting motivation.

Negative feedback

This type of FB occurs when the performance of a task was incorrect, eg, a basketball player will receive negative FB in various forms if they miss a set shot: they see the ball has missed, friends comment, they realise they did not put enough power behind the ball and the teacher or coach may indicate faults and suggest correction. All this should help to ensure that further shots are more successful.

Knowledge of results and knowledge of performance

Knowledge of results (KR) is an essential feature of skill learning. Without knowing what the results of our actions have been we will be unable to modify them in order to produce the precise movements needed for the correct performance of a skill. One of the more important roles of a teacher or coach is to provide this type of information. Knowledge of results is usually given verbally, eg, a netball coach saying 'You missed the net by 10 cm' or an athletics coach shouting out lap times during training. This type of FB about goal or task achievement is thought to be very useful in the early phases of learning when beginners like to have some measure of their successful performance. An eight-year-old child will see her performance in terms of 'I scored a goal today' or 'Our team won all the games', not in terms of the quality of her own performance.

Once KR has been given it is then usually necessary for the teacher or coach to give information as to why or how the result came about. A hockey coach, when trying to develop passing, may give KR as in 'Your pass was far too wide'. They may support this by adding 'The reason it was so wide was because your left shoulder was not pointing towards your partner, your feet were not in the right position and your stick did not follow through in the direction the ball was meant to go'. This gives the performer additional (augmented) extrinsic information in order to help them know not only the result of the action (KR) but also know why the result was incorrect and how to correct the performance. This type of FB about the actual movement pattern is more like the FB given by a teacher and is known as 'knowledge of performance' (KP). Although most of the traditional research has been carried out with regard to KR, due to its ease of measurement, there has been a definite shift in emphasis towards researching KP particularly with the increased availability of more modern computer and video technology allowing greater mechanical analysis of technique and performance.

Knowledge of results (KR) as used in most psychology or coaching texts is referred to as:

'Information provided to an individual after the completion of a response that is related to either the outcome of the response or the performance characteristics that produced that outcome.'

(R. Magill).

The use of feedback

Feedback can be used to help with:

- the correction of errors
- reinforcement
- motivation.

Fig. 16.9 How feedback moves the performer through the three stage model

There are numerous studies to support the importance of feedback (KR) in the learning process. In referring back to Fitts' and Posner's phases of learning, feedback can be used to move the performer through the three phases of the learning process.

Once in the autonomous phase the performer should be less reliant on KR and should, through their knowledge and understanding of the activity, be able to detect their own errors and, in conjunction with kinesthetic FB, be able to make corrections to their own performance.

Although skills can be learned without FB it is generally accepted that FB makes the learning process more efficient by improving error correction and developing better performance. Relating this to the section on motor programmes, we can see that if a performer receives additional information the quality of his or her generalised patterns of movement (schemas which help initiate and control movement) can be effectively enhanced, particularly in the early phases of learning. When considering the use of FB the teacher or coach needs to be aware of the following:

- current skill levels of the performer (phase of learning)
- nature of the skill (complexity/organisation/classification) and its transferability.

In relation to the above points, the coach or teacher has to decide on the following aspects of FB:

- general or specific
- amount (too much or too little)
- how to present it (visual/verbal)
- frequency, eg, after every attempt, or summary after several attempts (performer must not become dependent on extrinsic FB).
- time available for practice/processing.

Although the quantity, distribution and whether it is positive or negative are important considerations, the most crucial aspects of feedback are *quality* and *appropriateness*.

KR must not provide too much information otherwise the performer will not know what to pay attention to or how to use the FB to help future attempts. Attention must be directed to specific or major errors particularly with beginners. If major errors are left then this could lead to the performer assuming them to be correct, strengthening the incorrect S–R bond and making it much more difficult to deal with later. As well as telling the beginner what the problem is a teacher or coach must provide information on how the performer can correct the error.

Feedback (KR) must be meaningful and relevant to the phase of learning. Beginners might need general information whereas experienced performers may need more specific information. Sometimes however, beginners may need much more specific information: a more experienced badminton player would understand 'Your positioning is not right' and probably rectify the fault immediately. The same statement made to a beginner would be of little value as they need much more specific FB with regard to the position of feet, angle of upper body or preparation of racket prior to the shot, etc. in order for them to make the necessary corrections. It is important that the FB given is useful to the performer and not just repetition of what is already obvious to them. Such repetition is called **redundant** FB.

Researchers have found that time intervals after the performance have a bearing on how KR should be used. A teacher needs to be aware that once KR has been given the performer has to have time to assimilate the information and put the KR into action. However, too long a delay could allow the performer to forget what has happened or to lose understanding of the relevance of the KR being given.

Feedback can also be used as reinforcement. Reinforcement, as you already know, increases the probability of certain behaviour being repeated. Using FB to strengthen the bond between stimulus and response is useful.

Positive FB has a great role to play in reinforcement. Both KR or KP can be useful in motivating a performer, maintaining interest and effort (direction and intensity). Seeing performance improve, eg, an athlete improving their personal best or a tennis player increasing the accuracy and percentage of successful first serves, should ensure that performers keep on practising. It is very helpful if this is carried out in a formal way with statistical evidence being logged by the teacher or coach. This information can be used both for the evaluation of current performance (error detection) and for future target setting. In this way, feedback can be used as an incentive. Using feedback in conjunction with goal setting has been recognised as being very effective in the learning process.

Consider the three stages of learning. For each stage make a list of the most appropriate and effective types of feedback (with egs.) that a coach should use.

Summary

Information processing

1 The human motor system can be viewed as a processor of information with sensory information passing through various stages.
2 The performer is involved in gathering data, processing the relevant stimuli to form a decision, which is then executed by the muscular system.
3 The process consists of three basic stages:
   - Stimulus identification (input)
   - Response selection (decision making)
   - Response programming (output).
4 The effectiveness with which a performer processes various forms of sensory information often affects overall performance.
5 Reaction time is an important measure of information processing speed, and is affected by many factors.
6 In order to assess the effectiveness of the decision and completed actions, feedback is obtained from a variety of sources either internally or externally.
7 Feedback provides information about errors to help make corrections and improve performance. It can act as reinforcement for correct actions and help to develop motivation.
8 The quality of feedback information is important to ensure learning is effective.
9 Performers at different stages of learning will use various forms of FB in different ways.

Review Questions

1 What is meant by information processing?

2 **(a)** Draw a simple model of information processing.
   (b) Give practical examples from tennis or badminton for each of the parts of your simple model.

3 What are receptors? Explain the different types.

4 What happens within the three stages of Stimulus identification, Response selection and Response programming?.

5 Draw and label Whiting's model of information processing and explain the terms.

6 What are various parts of the memory process?

7 Draw a simple model to show your understanding of how the parts of memory link together.

8 What is the process of selective attention?

9 What is response preparation time better known as?

10 How does 'Hicks Law' relate to this response preparation time?

11 What other factors affect a performer's speed of reactions?

12 What is anticipation?

13 What are the possible good and bad effects of anticipating?

14 What does PRP stand for? Explain a situation in a game where it could be used to benefit performance.

15 What are KR and KP?

16 When using feedback what does a teacher or coach need to be aware of?

17 In what ways can extrinsic feedback be used to modify performance?

chapter 17

Control of Movement, Motor Programmes and Schemas

During discussions of information processing models' as a way of explaining how the sports performer uses informatioon to carry out certain actions in order to solve problems, we have often mentioned the notion of 'plans of action' or 'motor programmes' being selected from the long-term memory. These coded motor programmes are said to pass out by the short-term memory via the body's effector systems. The view that motor programmes exist is not a new one; it has been around since the turn of the 20th century. After many years of research and argument the concept of motor programmes now appears to be generally accepted. However, the question of what a motor programme is exactly, and how it works to control movement is still under discussion.

Here is a list of terms to be covered in this chapter. It is important that you understand them and can apply them to help you appreciate how human beings initiate, control, adapt and develop movement patterns within sporting situations.

- motor programmes
- executive programme
- sub-routines
- open loop control
- closed loop control
- memory trace
- perception trace

- schema
- recall schema
- recognition schema

Motor programmes and control of movement

The traditional view of a motor programme was that it was a centrally organised pre-planned set of very specific muscle commands that, when initiated, allowed the entire sequence of movement to be carried out without reference to additional feedback. This view helped to explain how performers sometimes appear able to carry out very fast actions that have been well learned (particularly closed skills) without really thinking about the action, almost like a computer. In other words, they use very little conscious control. This has obvious links to Fitts' and Posner's autonomous stages of learning, which was covered in an earlier chapter.

In relating this notion of automatic movement to information processing you can appreciate that the limited capacities of the memory process would easily be overloaded, and take considerable time, if every part of every action had to pass via the STM. The notion of a motor programme being decided upon and initiated from the short-term memory appears to solve the overload problem where, in relatively stable situations, movement can be carried out without the need for modification. This type of control of movement is called 'open loop control', without feedback. Two areas of research which support this view are:

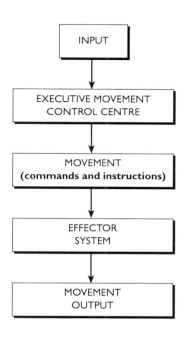

Fig. 17.1 SIMPLIFIED MODEL OF OPEN LOOP CONTROL

1 Reaction time has been found to be longer in actions which involve more complex movements. A tennis serve, for example, has many component parts. This suggests that the action is carried out following a pre-planned organisation.

2 In animal experiments involving **deafferention** where the **afferent** nerve bundles are severed near the spinal cord, it has been shown that even though the brain cannot receive sensory information via the central nervous system (no feedback) the animals are still capable of carrying out movement. This suggests that movement is centrally organised and that feedback is not critical in certain movements.

Open loop control

Motor programmes or pre-learned mastered movements initiated on command are thought to be developed through practice. A series of movements is built up, starting with very simple movements, until certain actions are stored as complete movements. These complete movements or motor programmes can be stored in the long-term memory and retrieved at will; the whole movement to be carried out can then be initiated by one complete command. It is suggested that such skills are built up in a hierarchical or schematic way (see task analysis and sub-routines).

Closed loop control

Within the closed loop model the loop is completed by information from the various sensory receptors feeding back information to the central mechanism or executive.

While it is accepted that there are many types of feedback, in this view of feedback control the feedback is internal (kinesthetic) allowing the performer to compare what is actually happening during the movement with the point of reference, namely the correct or currently learned and stored motor performance. This evaluation of the movement currently being undertaken means errors, if any, can be detected and acted upon. As you can see from fig 17.4, all feedback goes back through the processing system, which means that the process of detecting and correcting errors is relatively slow.

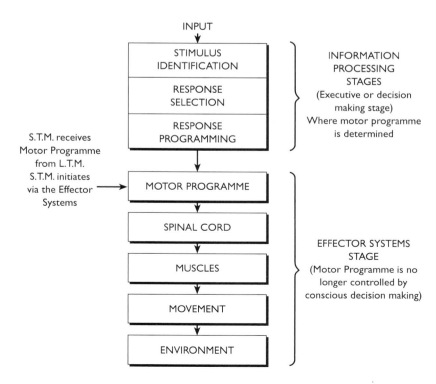

Fig. 17.2 EXPANDED MODEL OF OPEN LOOP CONTROL

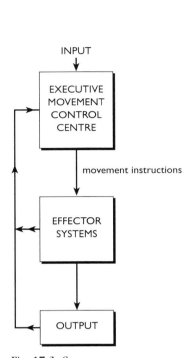

Fig. 17.3 SIMPLIFIED MODEL OF CLOSED LOOP CONTROL

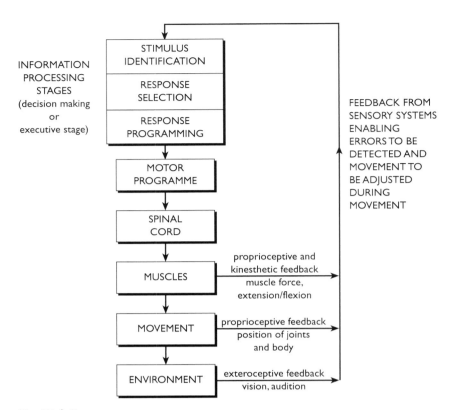

Fig. 17.4 EXPANDED MODEL OF CLOSED LOOP CONTROL

Research has shown that the closed loop system of movement control generally works more effectively with movements taking place over longer periods of time (continuous skills, eg, running) or with skills requiring slower limb movements (headstand or handstand). Closed loop models are not thought to be effective for controlling quick discrete-type movements; in this case open-loop control of movement appears to be a better explanation for what happens.

In practice, while in certain actions one specific mode of control may dominate, the fact is that most sporting activities involve both fast, slow, simple and complex movements in a whole variety of coordinated ways. This suggests that performers are continually moving between open loop and closed loop control, with all systems of control being involved in controlling the performers' actions.

Schema theory

It was stated earlier that motor programmes were traditionally considered to be a specific set of pre-organised muscle commands that control the full movement. This suggests that specific motor programmes for all possible types of action are stored in the long-term memory awaiting selection and initiation. If we accept that motor programmes operate via continuously changing closed and open loop control (with or without the use of feedback), it is the stored motor programme which either directs all movements or is used as the point of reference for a movement to be compared against.

Although the question of how these motor programmes are structured and stored has been considered since the 20th century, it was not really until Jack Adams presented his closed loop theory specifically related to motor skills in 1971 that more up-to-date research began in earnest.

For Adams the motor programme was made up of two areas of stored information.

1 **The memory trace** – used for selecting and initiating movement, operating as an open loop system of control prior to the perceptual trace. It does not control movement.
2 **The perceptual trace** – used as the point of reference (memory of past movements) and also to determine the extent of movement in progress. Thus the perceptual trace is operating as a closed loop system of control making the ongoing necessary adjustment where/when needed.

The quality or strength of all these traces is built up and developed through practice with the performer using both intrinsic and extrinsic feedback, particularly knowledge of results (KR), which in the early cognitive stages is very often provided by the teacher or coach. Once the perceptual trace in particular is strong and well developed the performer is able to carry out his/her own error detection and correction. (Performer moves from associative phase to autonomous phase and learning).

Schmidt presented his well-known **schema theory** as a way of dealing with the limitations, as he saw them, of Adams' closed loop theory. Schmidt proposed that schemas, rather than the memory and perceptual traces suggested by Adams, explained recall of movement patterns. Instead of there being very specific traces for all learned or experienced movement, schemas as Schmidt saw them were 'a rule or set of rules that serve to provide the basis for a decision'.

These generalised patterns or rules of movement solved the following dilemma:

- how do we store possibly thousands, if not millions, of specific programmes of movement?
- how do we initiate and control fast and more complex movements?

In addition, if we can only initiate movement via memory traces, developed through practice:

- how do we initiate movement in totally new situations that we have never faced before and have no memory trace of, or programme of movement for?

Schmidt suggested that we learn and control movements by developing generalised patterns of movement around certain types of movement experience, eg, catching, throwing. A performer does not store all the many specific but different types of catching and throwing; rather they collate together various items of information every time they experience either catching or throwing. This helps in building up their knowledge of catching or throwing in general. Performers thus construct schemas which enable them at some future time to successfully carry out a variety of movements.

A schema for throwing can be adapted to:

- returning a cricket ball to wicket keeper
- a long pass in basketball/netball
- a goalkeeper in football setting up an attack
- throwing a javelin
- playing darts.

By collating as much movement information as possible with regard to throwing we can adapt to new situations because we know the general rules associated with throwing long, short, high, low, etc. Variety of practice is essential. In order for schemas to be constructed and developed, the performer has to collate information from four areas of the movement: see table 17.1.

Table 17.1   RECALL AND RECOGNITION SCHEMAS

recall schemas information is stored about determining and producing the desired movement (similar to memory trace)	1 initial conditions (where we are)	• knowledge of environment • position of body • position of limbs
	2 response specification (what we have to do)	• specific demands of the situation • direction • speed • force
recognition schema information is stored enabling evaluation of movement	3 sensory consequences (what movement feels like)	• information based on sensory feedback • during and after movement • involves all sensory systems
	4 response outcomes (what has happened)	comparisons are made between • actual outcome • intended outcome • KR is important

Whenever a performer takes part in an activity he or she will collate together these four areas of information to form schemas of movement and store them in the long-term memory. The fact that these are abstract rules of response will enable the performer to cope in unfamiliar surroundings. In order to increase the possibility of the performer making the correct decision and being able to carry it out effectively, variety of practice is essential! It is important that the teacher or coach not only ensures repetition, but that practice is organised in order to take into account the various demands that the skill places on the performer in the 'real life' situation.

Strategies/methods to enable schema to develop

- varied practice conditions
- avoid blocked or massed practice
- practice relevant to the game, eg – opposition
- include plenty of feedback – continuous and terminal
- realistic practice
- tasks should be challenging/gradually more difficult
- slow motion practice
- include transferable elements.

Summary

1   Motor programmes are pre-planned sets of muscular movements, stored in the memory, which can be used without feedback.

2   Organised in a hierarchical structure with sub-routines making up executive programmes.

3   Sub-routines eg:

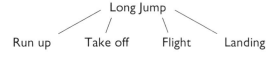

4   Sub-routines are short fixed sequences which when fully learned, can be run off automatically without conscious control.

5   'Open loop' explains how we perform fast movements without having to think about them (subconsciously).

6   Pre-learned mastery of motor programmes is essential for open loop control, feedback is not integral in motor control.

7   Feedback and kinesthesis are imperative in closed loop control.

8   Schema are seen as generalised sets of movement patterns stored in the long term memory, allowing performers to tailor movements to the specific demands of the situation they are faced with.

9   Schema are built up through practice and experience.

10 Schema theory works on the basis that there are four sources of information that are used stored in order to modify the programme of movement.

11 Variability of practice helps to develop schemas by the performers experiencing different situations.

12 Schema theory suggests that every variation of a particular task/skill does not require the learning of a new motor programme.

13 The principle of 'transfer' between tasks/skills is supported by schema theory. (See transfer of learning, next Chapter).

Review Questions

1   What are motor programmes?

2   What are the sub-routines of a tennis serve?

3   Explain open loop and closed loop control of movement.

4   What are the two types of schema? Explain their funtion.

5   What four sources of information are used to modify schemas?

6   Why is variability of practice important for the development of schemas?

7   What are the main strategies a coach can adopt in order to develop quality schemas?

chapter 18

Turning Theory into Practice

In previous Chapters, we have considered the nature of skilled performance, principles of learning and theories associated with learning. In general it is accepted that having a better understanding of the principles and theories associated with perceptual motor skill learning helps a teacher or coach prepare and deliver more effective teaching and coaching strategies. In order to create an effective learning environment a teacher or coach needs to consider many variables which can be categorised into several main areas. Here is a list of the terms to be covered in this chapter. It is important that you understand them.

- Complex skills
- Simple skills
- Organised skills
- High/low skills
- Sub-routines
- Interrelated skills
- Independent skills
- Transfer
- Positive transfer
- Negative transfer
- Retro-active transfer
- Pro-active transfer
- Bi-lateral transfer
- Near/far transfer
- Inter-task
- Intra-task
- Zero transfer
- Identical elements
- Similarity

- Transfer appropriate processing
- Visual guidance
- Verbal guidance
- Manual/mechanical guidance
- Forced response
- Physical restriction
- Massed practice
- Distributed practice
- Mental practice
- Whole method
- Part method
- Progressive part method
- Variations in teaching styles
- Command style
- Reciprocal style
- Discovery
- Guided discovery
- Problem solving

Once you have read this chapter you should gain an understanding of the considerations related to:

- the learning and performance process
- the learner/individual differences
- the task
- the instructional/practice conditions.

Considerations linked to the learning and performance process

In considering the learning and performance process we have already stated that there is no definitive approach guaranteed to succeed. A teacher or coach needs to be aware of the positive and negative aspects of the many theories and models associated with effective learning. They then need to be able to use and adapt them where appropriate according to the individual needs of the learner and the demands of the situation.

Considerations linked to learner/individual differences

Considerations related to the individual can be identified and researched in isolation but usually they are variables that are interlinked and difficult to separate in real life situations. They include:

- age – chronological age; maturational age (physical and mental)
- gender
- abilities – perceptual and motor
- psychological – motivation, interests, attitude, personality
- physiological – size, shape, weight, fitness components
- sociological
- previous experience – links to transfer, information processing, perception, motor programmes and schemas
- stage of learning
- any personal limitations – sensory, physical, learning problems
- future expectations of performer/learner.

It is essential that a teacher/coach is aware that the above differences exist and is also aware of their possible effects on the learning process.

Considerations linked to the task

When considering the task a teacher or coach would carry out a Task Analysis and would ask themselves:

- is it a simple or complex task?
- is it an organised or unorganised task?
- what is the classification?
- is transfer possible?

Complex or simple tasks

When deciding on the degree of complexity of a skill/task a teacher or coach will consider the difficulties it could present to the beginner. These difficulties are generally associated with the amount of information that the performer has to cope with when trying to complete the skill/task (cognitive involvement).

Complex tasks have a high degree of cognitive involvement and require a great deal of 'attention' to the skill. Simple tasks have a low level of cognitive involvement and require a lower level of attention. By being aware of the information processing and memory demands placed on a learner a teacher or coach can try to structure practices in order to reduce the complexity of skills.

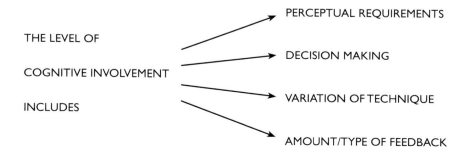

Fig. 18.1 COPING WITH INFORMATION — COGNITIVE INVOLVEMENT

One way of achieving this is for the teacher or coach to break down the main skill/task into various parts thus reducing the amount of information (cognitive involvement) the performer is having to cope with (see presentation and organisation practice). As the performer moves through the various stages of learning (see earlier Chapter) the amount of information they have to deal with can be increased.

Organisation of a skill/task

Fig. 18.2 A CARTWHEEL IS HIGHLY ORGANISED: THE COMPONENTS ARE INTERRELATED. OFTEN MECHANICAL GUIDANCE HAS TO BE GIVEN WITH HIGHLY ORGANISED SKILLS IN ORDER TO KEEP LEARNING IN THE COGNITIVE/ASSOCIATIVE STAGES OF LEARNING

Having suggested that complex skills can be broken down into their constituent parts to simplify them, some skills/tasks by their very nature are very difficult to break down into sub-routines and therefore have to be taught as a 'whole' movement. Skills or tasks that are difficult to break down are said to be highly organised: there is a very strong relationship between the components of the skill.

If a skill/task is said to be **low in organisation** this means that it can be broken down easily into sub-routines. These sub-routines can be practised in isolation as they are relatively independent of each other.

High in organisation

Low in organisation

Skills/tasks can be placed along the continuum according to their degree of organisation

Fig. 18.3 HIGH TO LOW ORGANISATION CONTINUUM

Transfer

Having considered the complexity, organisation and classification of a skill/task a teacher needs to consider structuring the learning environment in order to take into account the concept of **transfer**. The instructional approaches used to introduce and teach skills/tasks to performers very often depend on the relationship between various skills that have either been taught previously or are going to be taught in the future. The transfer of performance and learning from one situation to another has been an essential element of organisational and instructional approaches for many years.

Transfer of learning is seen as being the influence or effect of performing or practising one skill/task on the learning of another skill/task. There is evidence to support the following general points.

1 That different types of transfer possibilities exist.
2 That certain practice conditions can either help or hinder the actual effect or degree of transfer.
3 That the amount and direction of transfer can be affected by many factors.
4 That teachers need to be aware of the principles associated with transfer.
5 That teachers need to be able to apply these principles in order to structure effective teaching or coaching situations.

Types of transfer

The following are types of transfer:

- pro-active
- retro-active
- positive

- negative
- bi-lateral
- near

- far
- inter-task
- intra-task

Pro-active transfer

When a skill/task presently being learned has an effect on future skills/tasks this effect is said to be pro-active. This common form of transfer concept works forward in time. A teacher ultimately aiming to teach basketball may start off by introducing beginners to throwing, catching, passing, moving, dribbling, thus building up skills to be transferred into the future game situation. Simplified forms of more complex activities are introduced.

Retro-active

When a skill/task presently being learned has an effect on previously learned skills/tasks this effect is said to be retro-active. Thus transfer is seen as working backwards in time.

Positive transfer

Positive transfer, as the term suggests, is when skills/tasks that have been learned/experienced help or facilitate the learning of other skills. This can be positive retro-active or positive pro-active. Similarities in both skill components and information processing characteristics will help increase the possibilities of positive transfer. If these similarities are pointed out, particularly to beginners in the associative phase of learning, the effect of transfer can be enhanced further.

Important early work in this area was carried out by E L Thorndike who developed his identical elements theory in 1914. In this work he suggested that transfer possibilities are greater between tasks that have common elements. If the S–R bond expected in one task were the same as earlier learned S–R bonds then the effect of transfer would be greater. Thorndike's work was based on mental processes, but a practical application example related to motor skill learning is as follows.

A diver wishing to improve his co-ordination of turning and twisting may take part in trampolining practice in order to develop more control and possibly understanding of rotation and twisting. The components in the practice situation (trampolining) are very similar, and realistic to the main task, thus improving the likelihood of positive transfer occurring.

It is important, therefore, if we accept this basic principle, that a teacher or coach must ensure that practice situations are as realistic as possible. Research on similarities between the stimulus and response has shown that maximum positive transfer can be produced when the stimulus and response characteristics of the new skill are identical to those of the old skill. Other theories have supported the idea that it is general principles of understanding and movement that are transferred as well as the specific elements of a skill. Thus it is when the information processing requirements (cognitive components) are similar that the effect of transfer is greater.

A player involved in team games, such as either football or hockey, would be able to transfer their spatial awareness, tactical understanding of passing, moving and tackling from one game to another. Having learned to throw a cricket ball the basic principles of the movement can be transferred to throwing a javelin (see the schema theory). This view of positive transfer being more likely between activities having similar cognitive elements (information processing conditions) has been termed **transfer appropriate processing**.

Negative transfer

When one skill/task hinders or inhibits the learning or performance of another skill/task this is known as negative transfer. Sports performers and coaches tend to believe that this happens on a regular basis. Thankfully the effects of negative transfer are thought to be limited and certainly temporary; it is thought to happen when a performer is required to produce a new response in a well-known situation (familiar stimulus). Stimuli are identical or similar but the response requirements are different. Initial confusion is thought to be created more as a result of the performer having to re-adjust their cognitive processes rather than problems associated with the motor control of the movement. The familiar example of tennis having a negative effect on badminton is often quoted, but although the two games have similar aspects, tactics, use of space, court, net, racket, hand eye coordination, etc., the wrist and arm action are very different.

When a basketball or hockey coach changes tactics at set plays any initial negative transfer is thought to be as a result of the players having to re-adjust cognitive processes rather than inability to complete the movement task being asked of them. In order to overcome or limit the effects of negative transfer teachers and coaches should be aware of areas that may cause initial confusion. Practices need to be planned accordingly, ensuring that the players are aware (direct attention) of possible difficulties they may experience. At the same time the teacher or coach needs to be aware of possible positive effects and try to ensure that these outweigh the negative possibilities. In addition the psychological habits of positive attitude, sustained motivation and a conscientious approach to training and practice can also be transferred positively in order to limit any negative effect, as can an understanding of how to deal with new problems.

Bi-lateral transfer

In the earlier discussion of transfer we have considered transfer from one skill/task to another. Bi-lateral transfer, however, occurs when learning is transferred from limb to limb, ie, from the right leg to the left leg, etc. When a basketball coach tries to develop their player's weaker dribbling hand by relating it to earlier learned skills with the strong hand they are involved in bi-lateral transfer. This involves the player in transferring both motor proficiency and levels of cognitive involvement. The performer is thought to adjust and transfer the parameters of stored motor programmes linked to one limb action to the other.

Thus, with appropriate practice, the levels of learning developed with the performers stronger or 'preferred' hand or side can be transferred to the weaker hand or side.

Zero transfer

When one skill/task has no effect on the performance of another skill, eg, swimming on horse riding, zero transfer is said to occur.

 **Consider why it is important for a learner to have reached a sound level of performance in one skill before trying to learn a new skill involving some aspects of the old skill/technique.**

Research into transfer

Inter-task

The effect of a skill/task on a different or new skill/task is called inter-task transfer. Typical experiments would relate to the amount of time saved in learning, for instance, the lay up shot in the game by using a particular type of drill in basketball practice.

Intra-task

Intra-task transfer occurs when the relationship between two different types of practice or conditions of practice are considered. Comparisons can be made to show how different types of practice conditions might influence the learning of a specific skill/task.

Near transfer

When a coach develops specific practices/skills which are very realistic and relevant to the 'real game' situation in order to try and help players in future games this is referred to as near transfer.

Far transfer

Far transfer is when a teacher or coach tries to develop general skills and understanding which may be used in the future to transfer to more specific games or activities. A teacher working with primary children on developing their coordination, spatial awareness or general throwing and catching skills for future use in basketball or netball is working on far transfer.

Strategies a coach/teacher could employ to promote positive transfer

- Ensure that the movement and cognitive requirements of the skills are similar.
- Ensure that the performer understands the principles of transfer.
- Ensure that the performer is involved in the analysis of the skills.
- Ensure that the original skill is well learned before starting the new skill.
- Ensure that the performer practices in a closed situation before trying it in a game.
- Ensure that practice is realistic.

Links to complexity and organisation

- If a task is **complex** but **low** in organisation, transfer is promoted by practising an easy version of the task first before moving on to a more difficult version.
- If a task is **simple** but **high** in organisation more difficult practices can be introduced.

Considerations linked with instructional/practice conditions

Finally, a teacher or coach has to consider possible variables associated with themselves and the situation when deciding on curriculum methods and strategies. These considerations can again be categorised into several main areas. When a teacher or coach is aware of all the previously discussed considerations to do with the learning process, the learner and the task, they can then ask themselves, in order to be effective:

1 What types of guidance shall I use?
2 What types of practice/presentation shall I use?
3 What style of teaching shall I use?

Types of guidance

Guidance is information given to the learner or performer in order to help them limit possible mistakes (incorrect movement) thus ensuring that the correct movement patterns are carried off more effectively. While guidance or instructions are usually given to beginners when skills/tasks are unfamiliar, it is obviously used continually in various forms at all stages of learning and performance (see section on feedback and knowledge of results). The form of guidance given, together with its effectiveness, will depend on several aspects:

- the learner – motivation; stage of performer's experience/learning linked to their information processing capacities and capabilities

- the type/nature of the skill/task
- the environment or situation.

In order to facilitate the acquisition of skill formal guidance can take several forms:

- visual guidance
- verbal guidance
- manual/mechanical guidance.

If formal guidance does not serve to improve performance through the long-term retention of learning then it cannot be called guidance.

Visual guidance

Visual guidance can be given in many different ways in order to facilitate the acquisition of skill:

- demonstration
- video/film/TV/slow motion
- posters/charts
- OHTs/slides
- modify the display

Visual modes of receiving information are valuable at all levels. Visual guidance is however particularly useful in the early stages of learning (cognitive phase) by helping the learner establish an overall image or framework of what has to be performed. This modelling of the elements involved in skills is an important aspect of skill acquisition. (See section on observational learning).

When presenting the learner, particularly beginners, with effective visual guidance it is important that:

- accurate/correct models of demonstration are used/given (usually provided by the teacher or an experienced performer)
- attention be directed in order that major aspects of the skill are emphasised/reinforced (refer to selective attention)
- demonstrations/models should not be too complex/lengthy (usually whole skill first then parts later)
- demonstrations/models should be realistic/appropriate
- demonstrations must be repeated or referred back to
- can be combined with verbal guidance to highlight key points.

There are considerable differences of opinion with regard to the long-term effectiveness of visual guidance. However, for the more advanced performer, specific and complex information can generally be provided more readily by modern technology.

Visual guidance can also be used to highlight certain cues or signals from the display helping the selective attention processes of beginners in particular. Equipment in infant and junior schools is often brighter or bigger in order to help performers 'see things' more clearly.

The teacher or coach can **modify the display** more specifically by highlighting areas of the court or pitch that shots should be played into or by making target areas bigger. Routes of movement can also be indicated by markers, etc.

It is very difficult in reality to consider visual guidance in isolation as verbal explanations very often have to accompany the demonstration or visual image being presented.

Verbal guidance

Verbal guidance is again a common form of guidance used by teachers or coaches and can be either very **general** or **specific**. A teacher may talk through a particular strategy in team games in order to give players a general picture of what is required before putting the move into practice. This **priming** helps to reduce the stimulus uncertainty (see decision making and reaction times). It is also useful to draw learners' attention to specific details of certain movements by giving verbal cues alongside visual demonstrations. **Verbal labelling** of specific aspects of a movement by a performer is also thought to facilitate learning. A teacher may help the beginner link their visual image of the task to certain verbal cues.

It is important that the learner does not become too heavily reliant on verbal guidance thus reducing their own ability to pay attention to aspects of performance, process information, make decisions and solve their own problems when guidance is removed. Verbal guidance is thought to be more effective with advanced performers who, because of increased experience and wider movement vocabulary, are able to transfer or transpose verbal comments into visual images more readily. Teachers or coaches may therefore find difficulty in simply describing certain movements to beginners particularly those involving more complex or highly organised skills. They will have to use a combination of both visual and verbal guidance in order to help the learner to internalise the information being presented.

In discussion with a partner try to think of ways you could verbally guide a performer through the pole vault.

When considering verbal guidance, it is important that it is: **clear/precise**, **relatively short** (not too lengthy), **appropriate** to the level of the learner, and **not overdone**.

Do not overload. Only a few important points will be taken in during the first few attempts. Children have very short attention spans (see information processing).

It is also useful to note that when giving verbal guidance:

- everybody should be able to hear
- the pitch and tone of the voice should be varied in order to encourage or emphasise a specific point
- a sense of humour is a great help.

Manual/mechanical guidance

This type of guidance involves trying to reduce errors by in some way physically moving (called forced response) or restricting/supporting (called physical restriction) a performer's movements. This form of guidance is particularly useful in potentially dangerous situations. A performer may initially need physical or mechanical support in order to develop the confidence to 'have a go' themselves. In trampolining a coach may stand on the bed and physically support the beginner through the stages of a somersault (manual/physical guidance). With more advanced performers they may also use a twisting belt which would provide mechanical guidance by physically restricting the performer. A performer may have their response or actions **forced** by the coach or teacher. In taking a performer through an action they will very often take hold of the racket arm in tennis forcing the performer to carry out certain movements, eg, a backswing for early preparation.

While in the initial stages of learning, the use of mechanical aids, such as floats and armbands in swimming, serve a very useful purpose, it is important that beginners do not become over reliant on them and lose their own 'kinesthetic feel' for the movement. There has to come a time, in gymnastics for example, where support for the learner has to be gradually removed once the teacher or coach is sure that the performer is 'safe'.

By producing his or her own movements and not relying on what has been termed 'a crutch' the performer can develop their own kinaesthetic awareness. This will help in reducing possible bad habits (negative transfer) and by increasing confidence should serve to develop the performer's motivation (refer to self efficacy A2).

Disadvantages of verbal visual and manual guidance

Visual guidance

- depends on coach's ability to demonstrate the correct model
- can be dependent on expensive equipment, eg video
- limited value to group coaching situation regarding technical skill
- dependent on coach's ability to demonstrate problems within skills
- some skills may be too complex to be absorbed by the performer
- some information presented may not be relevant
- some images may be rather 'static' and therefore give little information about movement patterns
- difficault to use in isolation.

Verbal guidance

- heavily dependent on the coach's ability to express the necessary information
- less effective in early stages of learning
- dependent on the performer's ability to relate the verbal instruction/information to the skill under practice
- some techniques are very difficult to verbally describe
- verbal guidance can become boring if too lengthy.

Mechanical guidance

- limited use in group situations
- limited use in fast/complex movement
- the 'feel' of the movement is not experienced by the performer to the same extent as an unaided movement
- kineasthetic awareness limited
- performer may become reliant on the 'support'
- possible implied sexual harassment.

Choose one type of guidance and in relation to a particular activity, discuss how you might adapt the guidance given when it is offered to a beginner (Cognitive phase) and someone more experienced (Associative/Autonomous phase)

Types, structure and presentation of practice

What types of practice shall I use? In deciding how to use their allotted time to benefit learners effectively, teachers or coaches need to make decisions about when to practice, and how often. In making these decisions they should consider whether practice is better all at once (massed), or whether breaks are required (distributed). Within these blocks of practice they will consider whether the skill should be taught as a whole, in parts or various combinations. The question of mental practice or rehearsal also needs to be considered.

As ever, there are no easy answers. Decisions made regarding questions of which type of practice would be more effective will depend on the:

- individuals stage of learning
- nature of the task
- nature of specific situation
- time available

Massed and distributed practice

For the purposes of this text, **massed practice** is seen as being almost continuous practice with very little or no rest at all between attempts or blocks of trials.

Distributed practice is seen as practice with relatively long breaks or rest periods between each attempt or block of attempts.

Practice and the learner

Although massed practice may appear to save time as the teacher or coach does not have to spend time after long breaks either re-introducing the performer to the task or reducing psychological barriers (fear, anxiety, etc.), this may be a short-sighted policy as distributed practice for beginners is seen as being a more effective learning process. The length of the practice session should be appropriate to both the physical and psychological maturity (state of readiness) of the performer. Beginners are more likely to be affected by lack of attention/concentration and lack of appropriate physical and mental fitness to sustain long periods of practice. Distributed practice with beginners, allowing for greater variation of practice, is seen as essential as it not only allows for better schema developments and transfer possibilities but also helps maintain motivation. Random practice is seen as being more effective than ordered.

Table 18.1 Practice and the individual

MASSED PRACTICE	DISTRIBUTED PRACTICE
Better when the individual is: • experienced • older • fitter • more motivated	**Better when the individual is:** • beginner • less experienced • limited preparation (physical/mental) • less motivated

Interestingly, research suggests that the learners and performers themselves are not always the best judges of structure and time allocation, generally preferring to rush through things superficially. There is evidence to support the view that for the more experienced/older/fitter performer massed practice is more effective.

Practice and the task

Practice sessions need to be long enough to allow for improvement but should not be overly long. Whilst the effect of fatigue in relatively dangerous situations (gymnastics, outdoor pursuits) could be potentially serious, the effect of fatigue in massed practice can hinder performance in the short term although not necessarily skill learning in the long term. Alternatively, distributed practice for discrete skills may lead to lack of motivation due to the performer's frustration at having delays between attempts. Group or team activities can be practised for longer than individual tasks as players can have rests in between thus lessening fatigue and frustration. At the same time groups should not be so big that rest intervals or waiting times become over long thus de-motivating learners or allowing opportunities for ill-discipline.

The use of rest periods or intervals needs to be considered within distributed practice. They can be used for the following:

- to reduce fatigue
- to reduce short-term inhibition
- to give feedback (KR and KP)
- to offer an alternative activity/novelty game (must ensure no negative transfer)
- to develop positive transfer
- to re-motivate
- to offer mental practice/rehearsal (see section below).

Table 18.2   PRACTICE AND THE TASK

MASSED PRACTICE	DISTRIBUTED PRACTICE

Better when the task is:
• Discrete
  brief in nature
  e.g., hitting a golf ball,
  shooting baskets
• Simple
	Better when the task is:
	• Continuous
	  requiring repetition
	  of **gross skills**
	  e.g., swimming, cycling, running
	• Complex – precision orientated
	• Dangerous

Variability of practice

Repetition of skills is important in order to reinforce the correct movement patterns, particularly at the early stages of learning and with closed skills. However, as already discussed in the sections on 'open skills' and 'schema' development variability of practice is also essential.

VARIABLE PRACTICE
• skills practiced in new/different situations   • useful for open skills   • helps development of schema   • helps performer successfully adapt to meet the demands of the situation   • practice should be similar to 'real game' situation   • practice should be meaningful   • variety of massed and distributed practice   • will maintain motivation

Mental practice

The definition of mental practice is: the mental or cognitive rehearsal of a skill without actual physical movement.

When looking at the various types of practice available for a teacher or coach to use mental practice or mental rehearsal is an area often overlooked. We have mentioned above that time intervals or rest periods between practice can be used for mental practice.

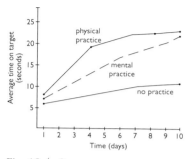

Fig. 18.4 COMPARISON OF EFFECTS OF
MENTAL AND PHYSICAL PRACTICE ON
PERFORMANCE
Source: Rawlings, Rawlings and Chew Yilk
(1972) *Psychonomic Science* 26 page 71.
Copyright 1972 by Psychonomic Society Inc.
Source: Rawlings, Rawlings and Chew Yilk
(1972) *Psychonomic Science* 26 page 71.
Copyright 1972 by Psychonomic Society Inc.

Mental practice or rehearsal is seen as being very beneficial. In the early stages of learning (cognitive phase) mental rehearsal is initially seen as the learner going through a skill/task and building up a mental picture of the expected performance in their mind (a cognitive process). This may involve a performer in deciding how to hold a hockey stick or a gymnast going over a simple vault in their mind. More advanced performers can use mental practice to rehearse possible alternative strategies or complex actions/sequences, thus almost pre-programming their effector systems and possibly helping with response preparation, reactions and anticipation. Mental practice can be a powerful tool in the preparation of the highly-skilled performer. Top class skiers regularly use it to rehearse turns, imagine the approach to gates and certain aspects of terrain. A traditionally-held view has been that through mental practice a performer could slightly stimulate (below optimum threshold) the neuromuscular systems involved in activities and thus simulate (practice) the movement. In addition, mental practice is used regularly by more experienced performers in learning to control their emotional states. Optimum levels of arousal can be reached and maintained for effective performance. Wider developments in sports psychology have meant that mental rehearsal is being increasingly used to reduce anxiety and increase confidence, by getting the performer to focus their attention on winning, or performing successfully.

Although mental rehearsal is now seen as an important element of practice (better than no practice at all), it is not seen as a substitute to be used exclusively; rather it is much more effective when used in conjunction with physical practice.

The use of mental practice prior to performance

The performer needs to be advised to seek out a relatively quiet situation where they can focus mentally on the task. This will probably involve moving away from the competitive or performance situation.

The learner or performer needs to:

- go somewhere quiet
- focus on the task
- build a clear picture in their mind
- sequence the action
- imagine success
- avoid images of failure
- practice regularly.

The use of mental practice between practices

When used in between physical practice a performer must try and re-create the kinaesthetic feeling and mental image they recently successfully experienced (remembering what was good). Equally so when a performer makes a mistake, stopping for a few seconds to reason why and then rehearse a good performance may have a positive effect on future performances.

This reviewing mentally of good and bad practice both during and after performance will help in building up good positive images. A golfer, when playing a practice swing, is very often mentally rehearsing the positive feel for the shot, imagining distance, angles of trajectory and power needed.

The uses of mental rehearsal in sport and physical education

- Mental rehearsal creates a mental picture of what needs to be done.
- Mental rehearsal evaluates possible movements and can mentally experience their outcomes (success/failure).

- Mental rehearsal can build self-confidence.
- Mental rehearsal can be used as a mechanism to focus attention.
- It has been proved that mental rehearsal actually produces small muscle contractions simulating actual practice.
- Performers at the cognitive stage of learning can use mental rehearsal to focus on the basis of a skill/the whole movement.
- Performers in the autonomous stage of learning can use mental rehearsal to control arousal level/to focus attention to immediate goals.
- Mental rehearsal provides mental warm-up.
- Mental rehearsal must be regularly practised if it is to be useful.
- Mental rehearsal can be used before competition and in rest periods during competition.
- Mental rehearsal must be as realistic as possible to be effective.
- The performer can use all the different senses during mental rehearsal.
- The performer can use mental rehearsal to envisage images of both success and failure.
- May be used during rest periods during distributed practice.
- May prevent physical 'wear and tear' eg triple jumpers use mental rehearsal to save joints.

Whole or part method of practice

Performers differ in their response to whole or part practice. The **whole method** of learning is when the activity or skill is presented in total and practised as a full/entire skilled movement or activity. The **part method** of learning is when the activity or skill is broken down into its various components or sub-routines and each sub-routine is practised individually.

Additional variations have been developed whereby whole-part, part-whole or progressive part methods have been used.

Whether it is effective to teach a skill as a whole or whether it is more effective to break it down into its various sub-routines depends very much on the answers to several questions.

1 Can the skill/task be broken down into its sub-routines without destroying or changing it beyond all recognition? (see complexity and organisation).
2 What is the degree of transfer from practising the parts (sub-routines) back to the main skill or activity (see transfer).
3 What is the performers' level of experience (stage of learning).

Whole approach

It is argued that if a whole approach is used then a learner is able to develop their kinaesthetic awareness or total feel for the activity. The learner is usually given a demonstration or explanation of what is required, builds up a cognitive picture and then becomes acquainted through practice with the total skill; they are then able to positively transfer the actions/skills more readily to the competitive or 'real' situation. By being able to link together the essential spatial and temporal elements of the skill the activity/skill quickly becomes meaningful to the performer. This approach is seen as a more effective use of time and should be used whenever possible particularly when skills have low levels of complexity and high levels of organisation, eg, a bench press in weight training. Skills which are very rapid (discrete or ballistic in nature) are also usually better practised as a whole. Although they could possibly be broken down, the parts are usually very much interrelated and therefore if broken down the skill would be changed out of all recognition – with possible negative effects on transfer, eg, hitting a softball.

When a skill is complex, highly organised and thus difficult to break down, very often an easier way to present it to beginners has to be found. Simplifying the activity/task enables the performer to experience the whole activity but with less information and decision making to deal with. Equipment is very often made lighter or bigger/smaller and less technical rules are imposed, or fewer physical demands and dangers, eg, uni hoc, mini hockey, short tennis. In general experienced performers will benefit more from the whole approach as they are better prepared to deal with skills that cannot be broken down or are very complex.

Part approach

Fig. 18.5 SERIAL SKILLS SUCH AS THE LONG JUMP, WHERE THE SKILLS ARE SEQUENTIALLY ORDERED, LEND THEMSELVES MORE TO A PART METHOD OF LEARNING

Skills which are very complex but low in organisation lend themselves to being practised and learned more effectively by the parts method. An additional consideration is again how interrelated or independent the various sub-routines are. Just because sub-routines are easily separated does not mean, however, that they have to be practised by themselves. The part method, while allowing teachers and coaches to work on areas of the skill that a beginner finds difficult, also tends to be more time consuming.

Activities such as front crawl in swimming which are not too complex but low in organisation lend themselves to being taught by the part method. The arm action, leg action, breathing pattern and body position can all be analysed and taught individually. While each can be and usually are practised independently, allowing the performer to experience success and thus gain confidence, it is important that the performer is able to practice synchronising the various sub-routines together. If the beginner does not experience the whole stroke there is a possibility that the kinesthetic feel for the whole action could be lost eg, the timing of breathing in co-ordination with the arm action. In breaststroke, where the kick, glide and pull have to be exactly synchronised, this is even more important. When teaching the skills of passing in major team games, eg, soccer, rugby, hockey, it is essential that they are not taught in isolation. The beginner needs time for the interrelated units or sub-routines to be practised together in order that they can make the natural link between the parts. This, therefore, becomes a more progressive part method with combinations of the whole.

The progressive part method

The progressive part method or gradual metamorphosis is where earlier independent actions change their form to become something totally different. A learner being taught complex skills by the progressive part method benefits from the positive aspects of both part and whole methods. A gymnastic coach trying to develop a gymnast's routine would often follow this progressive part method. All the relatively complex but independent parts of the routine, eg, handstand, cartwheel, handspring, somersault, etc. are learned and practised in isolation, but then linked together into small units in order that the gymnast can experience and learn how to fluently link (sequence) the individual skills together. These units or blocks of skills are then linked again until eventually all the various parts of the action have been built up (the chain is completed) into the whole routine. These methods often rely on the operant method of learning discussed earlier. The teacher or coach endeavours to shape the complex performance by reinforcing good aspects of technique. The performer is rewarded in some way for successful achievement and gradually develops their movement repertoire along with their understanding of how the various aspects of the skill are interrelated.

Whole-part – Whole-method

A variation on the 'whole' or 'part' method that is often used with performers in the Cognitive/Associative stages is the 'whole-part-whole practice'. The teacher/coach introduces the complete skill, highlighting the important elements. The performer then attempts to carry out the skill. As a result of any problems or faults observed the teacher then breaks the whole skill down into various sub-routines in order to allow the learner to practice appropriate areas of difficulty. The isolation of the difficult elements may differ for individuals. Once the teacher is satisfied that the problem areas have been mastered the parts are then intergrated back into the whole skill.

 **ACTIVITY 4**   **Consider a golf stroke being carried out and decide how you would teach it taking into account not only its moderate levels of both complexity and organisation, but also the fact that it is a discrete skill. Should you use the whole? part? or progressive part method of practice?**

Teaching by any specific method is not guaranteed to work and the better teachers and coaches are generally flexible, using various combinations of the three basic methods discussed at different times. Many teachers begin an activity by allowing the beginner to

Table 18.3   SUMMARY OF METHODS OF PRACTICE

WHOLE METHOD	PART METHOD	PROGRESSIVE PART METHOD
• Low level of complexity/simple task • High levels of organisation • Interrelated sub-routines • Discrete skills • Short duration/rapid ballistic • Lacks meaning in parts • Allows co-ordination of important spatial/temporal components	• High levels of complexity • Low levels of organisation • Independent sub-routines • Serial tasks • Slow tasks • Lengthy or long duration • Dangerous skills	• Complex task • Helps 'chaining' of complex skills learned independently • Allows for attention demands to be limited • Allows for co-ordination of spatial/temporal components to be experienced • Helps with transfer to whole
Performer is: • experienced • high levels of attention • in the later stages of learning • older • highly motivated • using distributed practice	**Performer is:** • a beginner • someone with a limited attention span • in the early stages of learning • having problems with a specific aspect of skill • someone with limited motivation • using massed practice	

Table 18.4   ADVANTAGES OF WHOLE AND PART METHOD

WHOLE METHOD	PART METHOD
• Wastes no time in assembling parts. (quick) • Useful for quick discrete skills where a single complete action is required • Better for time synchronised tasks if the learner can cope with the level of the skill eg, swimming stroke • The learner can appreciate the end product • The movement retains a feeling of flow/kinaesthetic sense. (fluent) • The movement can be more easily understood/the relationship between sub-routines. • The learner can develop their own schema/motor programme through trial and error learning • Transfer to **real** situations from practice is likely to be positive. (meaningful)	• Allows serial tasks to be broken down and learned in components eg gymnastic movement • This reduces the demand on the learner when attempting complex skills • Allows confidence and understanding to grow quickly or gradually built up with more complex skills • Helps to provide motivation to continue if progress can be seen to be being made • This is especially important with skills which can be seen as being potentially dangerous eg, some gymnastic skills • Can reduce fatigue in physically demanding skills • Allows the teacher to focus on a particular element and remedy any specific problems • Provides stages of success • Good for low organisational tasks which can be easily broken down

Table 18.5   DISADVANTAGES OF WHOLE AND PART METHOD

WHOLE METHOD	PART METHOD
• Ineffective with complex tasks • Not appropriate in tasks with an element of danger • Not always appropriate if group/performer of very low experience • May overwhelm a performer and produce little success at first • Could lead to learner losing confidence	• Transfer from part to whole may be ineffective • Highly organised skills are difficult to break down in parts • Loss of awareness of end product • Loss of continuity/feel of flow • Loss of kinaesthetic sense • Can have a de-motivating effect when not doing full movement • Can be time consuming

experience the sequencing of the whole movement. They will then analyse strengths and weaknesses enabling them to develop a part method to deal with any problem areas. Then a progressive part process may develop where chunks or units of actions are practised together in a simplified task or small sided games. The performer is then allowed to return to the whole movement again. Small problem areas may continue to be practised in isolation in order to refine technique. Complete adherence to one or other method is not advisable or useful.

In analysing the tennis serve to determine its components you could arrive at the seven sub-routines given in fig 18.6.

I   Where on a continuum would you put the serve?

High   complexity   Low   High or low?

2   Are any of the sub-routines more interrelated than others? (Difficulty in practising in isolation.)
3   Are there more independent sub-routines than others? (Easier to practise in isolation.)
4   Would you practise as a whole? If so, why?
5   Would you practise in parts? If so, why?

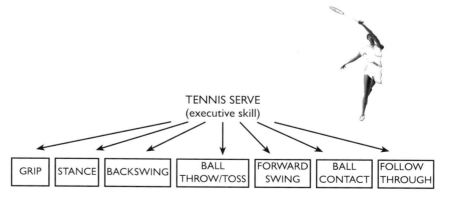

TENNIS SERVE
(executive skill)

| GRIP | STANCE | BACKSWING | BALL THROW/TOSS | FORWARD SWING | BALL CONTACT | FOLLOW THROUGH |

Fig. 18.6   THE TENNIS SERVE — AN EXECUTIVE SKILL

6   Would you practise via a combination or modified part method? If so, why?
7   Discuss your ideas with the rest of the class.
8   Choose another skill or activity that you have experience of and carry out the same type of analysis to decide which teaching method or methods would be more effective.

Teaching styles

What style of teaching should you use? It is important that you are aware that the style of teaching adopted by a teacher or coach can considerably affect the learning environment. In planning strategies using the various methods already discussed a teacher or coach is trying to create a favourable learning environment. An effective style of teaching aims to present information and thus develop effective learning by promoting achievement, satisfaction and motivation. Teachers invariably adopt different styles in various situations. A teacher's or coach's style of teaching is developed as a result of many factors. These are shown in table 18.6.

Table 18.6   Factors affecting teaching style

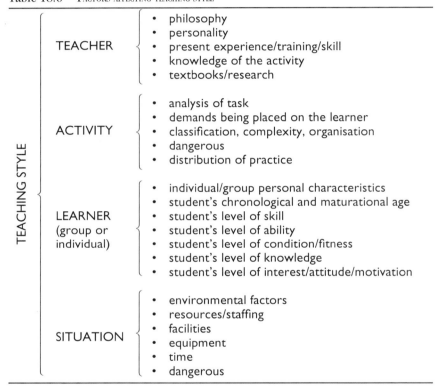

TEACHING STYLE	TEACHER	• philosophy • personality • present experience/training/skill • knowledge of the activity • textbooks/research
	ACTIVITY	• analysis of task • demands being placed on the learner • classification, complexity, organisation • dangerous • distribution of practice
	LEARNER (group or individual)	• individual/group personal characteristics • student's chronological and maturational age • student's level of skill • student's level of ability • student's level of condition/fitness • student's level of knowledge • student's level of interest/attitude/motivation
	SITUATION	• environmental factors • resources/staffing • facilities • equipment • time • dangerous

Fig. 18.7 Continuum of styles

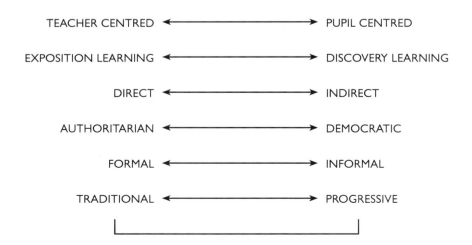

TEACHER CENTRED	←→	PUPIL CENTRED
EXPOSITION LEARNING	←→	DISCOVERY LEARNING
DIRECT	←→	INDIRECT
AUTHORITARIAN	←→	DEMOCRATIC
FORMAL	←→	INFORMAL
TRADITIONAL	←→	PROGRESSIVE

Mosston and Ashworth spectrum

In looking at the decisions to be made over what, when and how to teach and learn, Mosston and Ashworth (1986) developed their spectrum of teaching styles.

The more teacher orientated position, 'A', is referred to as the **command style**. The other end of the spectrum, where the learner makes more of the decisions, is referred to as **discovery learning**. There are obviously variations between the two extremes.

Fig. 18.8 SPECTRUM OF TEACHING STYLES
Source: Mosston and Ashworth (1986)

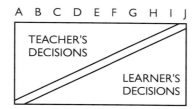

A B C D E F G H I J

TEACHER'S DECISIONS

LEARNER'S DECISIONS

Command style (A)

Fig. 18.9 MANY AEROBIC CLASSES ARE TAUGHT BY A COMMAND STYLE OF TEACHING

This style tends to see the teacher adopting a very authoritarian style! Within this rather behaviouristic approach there is little consideration given to the individual with all learners being treated in generally the same way. This style is thought to inhibit cognitive learning as thinking and questioning are not encouraged by the teacher. The teacher makes all the decisions. The learner is not allowed to develop responsibility for their own learning and is in danger of becoming a clone of the teacher by following movements, decisions and strategies dictated by the teacher. It can also lead to poor self discipline. This type of learning has limitations for developing open skills as open skills require the performer to be able to adapt.

In addition, due to the formality of the situation there is little opportunity for any social interaction. This traditional approach helps to establish: pupil control, clear objectives/models for pupils, routine/organisation/rules, and safety procedures. It is useful when working with beginners, large groups and in dangerous and limited time situations. It is often adopted in the early stages of learning as a starting point from which other styles develop.

Reciprocal style (C/D)

Developing further along the spectrum than command style this approach is based more on cognitive theories. Although what is to be taught or covered is still decided by the teacher, it allows learners to take slightly more responsibility and become more involved in the decision making process. The sessions are structured in order that the objectives are clearly stated to the learners. The learners work in pairs taking alternative goes at being observer and performer. Although there is regular general and specific input from the teacher, the situation lends itself to more social interaction than the command style. Learners are encouraged to give feedback as a result of their analysis and evaluation of the performer's progress. In analysing and evaluating their partner's performance the learner is developing a greater understanding of the movement and passing this on to the partner. They should also be able to transfer this to their own performance when their partner has to reciprocate, giving additional individual feedback.

This style of teaching is useful in developing a learner's:

- self image
- confidence
- communication skills (encourage interaction)
- cognitive strategies (encourages decision making).

The teacher does, however, need to monitor the process carefully and interject regularly to ensure that incorrect techniques are not being developed and reinforced. It is also important that the learners are at the appropriate maturational level of development and can cope with both giving and receiving constructive criticism from their peers and not merely focus on the negative or destructive aspects.

Discovery learning/guided discovery

This much more individualistic style of teaching is rather time consuming and is usually developed into guided discovery learning. In guided discovery the teacher generally has to lead the performer by providing the appropriate information, cues and questions in order to get the learner to 'discover' effective and correct movement skills or the understanding associated with certain techniques. The teacher needs to have an in-depth knowledge of each pupil and be constantly evaluating progress. Due to inevitable time limitation, learning will not be uniform for all. Students will progress at different rates, creating extra demands on the teacher.

By using progressive question and answer techniques in association with reinforcement, teachers can guide a learner's greater understanding. In developing greater understanding in one area the performer will also learn to adapt decision making and reasoning processes from previous or correct skills (pro-active positive transfer) to future learning situations. In being more involved with their own learning the learner is thought to gain greater personal satisfaction together with a more positive self image which in turn will help to develop even greater motivation.

Problem solving approach

Very often associated with the guided discovery method discussed above, the problem solving approach encourages students to be creative and develop their individual cognitive and performance processes. According to their different sizes, shapes, abilities and capabilities learners can approach problems set by the teacher individually.

Table 18.7   ADVANTAGES & DISADVANTAGES OF THE PROBLEM SOLVING APPROACH

ADVANTAGES	DISADVANTAGES
• Gives a sense of responsibility for one's own learning • Improves self-confidence • Encourages creativity • Aids self-fulfilment/self actualisation • Allows for group interaction and therefore promotes cohesiveness (if in a group) • Allows future strategies to be developed through a trial and error process • Good for high level performer	• Not as good for early stage of learning as performers do not have enough knowledge to work with

These more 'cognitive perspective' approaches are believed to have long-term benefits as learners are encouraged to think about, understand and adapt performers according to a variety of situations. Variety of practice is therefore important, particularly if the effects of positive transfer are to be developed. The development of *schemas* relies heavily on variety of practice and are a more cognitive explanation of how learners deal with new or novel situations.

Consider the styles discussed above and decide which style of teaching would be best suited to the following situations:
- **abseiling on an adventure trip**
- **a group of well motivated students with sound technical knowledge of the skills**
- **a teacher coaching 4 students per session**
- **a teacher of dance developing creativity.**

Summary

1 Teachers must be able to adopt and adapt many theories associated with teaching and learning in order to develop a learning environment appropriate to the needs of the learner.
2 Transfer refers to the influence of one activity/skill upon another. There are a variety of types of transfer and transfer can be effective forwards or backwards in time.
3 Transfer between tasks that are very similar is greater than transfer between dissimilar skills.
4 The relationships between skills/concepts and cognitive processes need to be pointed out and explained to learners in order to increase the probability of positive transfer taking place.
5 Teachers should try to minimise the possibility of negative transfer occuring.
6 When deciding on whole or part practice the complexity and organisation of a skill/task needs to be analysed in relation to the individual needs of the learner and the situation.
7 Practice over an extended period with short practice periods and limited rest periods is generally found to be more effective.
8 Teachers or coaches can adapt a variety of guidance techniques appropriate to the individual needs of the learner. Visual, verbal, mechanical/physical are the main types of guidance.
9 The effectiveness of massed or distributed practice depends on the type of task, level of the learner and the situation.
10 Sticking rigidly to one method of either whole or part practice is not generally advised. A combination is often more effective.
11 Research studies have shown that learners can benefit greatly from mental practice. The effectiveness of mental practice is increased considerably if used in conjunction with, rather than instead of, physical practice.
12 It is important that learners are taught how to use mental practice effectively.
13 There are a variety of teaching styles that can be adopted and it is important that teachers are flexible in their approach to teaching and coaching styles.

Review Questions

1 What are the four categories of variable factors that need to be considered by a teacher before they can develop an effective learning environment?

2 What are the main variables associated with the individual learner?

3 Using examples, explain complex and simple tasks.

4 What is meant by the organisation of a skill/task?

5 What type of task can be broken down into sub-routines?

6 What is meant when sub-routines are said to be interrelated?

7 What is meant by Transfer of Learning?

8 What are the main types of transfer?

9 In what ways can a teacher structure practices towards helping positive transfer?

10 Why is variety of practice important for a learner?

11 What use might simulators, eg, tennis ball machines, be in the learning of skills?

12 What might be the positive and negative effects of using a 'soft ball' for developing Shot-putt?

13 In what ways can a teacher try and reduce the effect of negative transfer?

14 Give two practical examples of negative transfer.

15 What are the various types of guidance a teacher can give to a learner?

16 What are the advantages and disadvantages of using visual aids?

17 What problems may be caused by a lengthy set of instructions prior to practice?

18 When a demonstration is given, what important factors must a teacher consider?

19 Why is distributed practice more appropriate for a beginner?

20 What type of practice might suit a more advanced performer and why?

21 Choose two specific skills from an individual and a game activity and explain why you might use whole or part practice.

22 Is it possible to learn a skill by mental practice? Support your answer.

23 In what ways can a teacher help a learner use mental practice more effectively?

24 How an why would an experienced performer possibly use mental practice?

25 Why is it better for a teacher or coach to be flexible in their structuring of practice sessions?

26 What are the main reasons for a teacher adopting teaching style 'A' on Mosston's and Ashworth's spectrum of teaching styles?

27 What are the advantages of adopting a more discovery learning or problem solving style of teaching?

chapter 19

Individual Differences

Similarities and differences between individuals involved in sport are often obvious, eg, size, shape and gender to mention but a few. Similarities and differences in terms of a performer's physiological behaviour can also be easy to recognise, but the reason why a person *behaves* in a certain way is often not so easy to define. Research into the personal and individual factors that can influence learning and behaviour in sport has been widespread. Trying to gain a better understanding of the psychological make-up of performers in a learning and sporting setting, ie, 'what makes them tick?', has traditionally involved research into personality.

Here is a list of the terms to be covered in this chapter. It is important that you understand them.

Personality
- Credulous
- Sceptical
- Traits
- Great maw theory
- Social learning theory
- Interactionist perspective
- Reliability
- Validity
- Iceberg profile
- Mood states

Personality

The proliferation of research in this area supports the view held by many that personality is a major factor in creating sporting behaviour. The research has traditionally been directed towards the relationship between individual performance and personality variables. Among the questions raised are the following:

- do the personalities of top class performers, moderate performers and non participants differ?
- can sporting success be predicted as a result of a performer's personality type?
- are the personalities of performers in various sports different or similar?

The early research of the 1960s and 70s failed to produce many useful conclusions with regard to the relationship between personality and performance in sport. This was mainly as a result of problems with validity and research methodology.

The fact, however, that people began to predict how their captain, team mate, friend or even opponent was going to behave on the basis of what they believed them to be like (ie, stereotyping), means that personality is a concept that has real meaning in the context of sporting inter-personal behaviour. In presenting this 'credulous' viewpoint (Morgan, 1980) where personality is seen as a significant causal factor of behaviour we must however, be aware that it is questioned by the 'sceptical' viewpoint, which argues that sporting success is not related to personality. What we must therefore do is take an overview and accept that we need to be aware of all the major theories of personality and how they relate to performance in sport. The word personality is a term which everybody uses to describe different things. However, psychologists have given a special, precise meaning to it. Personality is seen as a hypothetical construct in that it cannot be directly observed but only inferred from behaviour. It makes no sense therefore, to talk in general terms suggesting that someone has 'lots of personality' which will help them play sport. It is suggested that personality in the context of sport is not a thing that someone has or has not, but is more to do with how a person relates to another whilst taking part in physical activity and how they deal with the demands of a situation.

Consider, for example, the behaviour of people you know well, the captain of your sports team or your closest friend. It would appear that, in the main, their behaviour is hardly ever random or unpredictable. Usually they are consistent in the way they react or approach certain situations, eg, always aggressive and argumentative or stable and reliable. In addition, there are also consistent differences between people we know. Some people are outgoing, easy going, whilst others are quiet, withdrawn and lacking confidence. It is these factors that contribute to both the behavioural differences between people and the behavioural consistency within people that are referred to as their personality.

Definitions of personality
Nature or nurture?

Due to the many different approaches and theories with regard to personality it is almost impossible to present a definition acceptable to all. However, in 1992 Richard Gross put forward a common sense definition which enables us to leave the starting blocks:

'Those relatively stable and enduring aspects of individuals which distinguish them from other people, making them unique but at the same time permit a comparison between individuals.'
(R. Gross).

Lazarus and Mowat (1979) gave an earlier definition:

'Personality is the underlying relatively stable psychological structures and processes that organise human experience and shape a person's actions and reactions to the environment.'
(Lazarus and Mowat).

Both definitions highlight certain questions that are central to the study of personality and sport.

1 Is personality made up of certain permanent or enduring characteristics?
2 Do these enduring characteristics affect how a person perceives a situation and therefore how they behave towards it?
3 If they are enduring characteristics, can they be identified?
4 Can they be measured?
5 Are they innate? (Nature)
6 Can these characteristics be influenced or changed? (Nurture)

The trait approach

The trait or dispositional approach dominated the early study of personality but has been criticised for not taking into account how a particular situation might also influence an individual's behaviour in different environments. Thus it emphasises the person as opposed to the situation. Traits can be seen as being **relatively stable** and **enduring** characteristics which could be used to predict an individual's behaviour in a variety of situations.

Trait theorists believed that these personal characteristics or traits could be identified, were consistent and could be generalised across the population as a whole. Thus an extreme trait approach would suggest that if a person was assessed as being aggressive and as competitive then these characteristics would be displayed in all aspects of the person's behaviour (stable) at all times (enduring) and therefore it would be possible to predict this behaviour in all future situations. Two of the better-documented trait/type theories have been associated with Eysenck and Catell. Although both theories have distinct similarities in that they both propose neurological models, their structures of personality were derived quite differently.

Eysenck's type theory

Eysenck regarded personality as largely resulting from inherited (innate) tendencies (Nature). He attempted to measure these inherited characteristics through a Personality Inventory (EPI, 1964) and Personality Questionnaire (1975). Those tested were expected to give a yes or no answer to a variety of test questions. Using a statistical technique known as factor analysis to identify general trends in his research evidence Eysenck identified two major personality dimensions which can be viewed more readily as a continuum:

Fig. 19.1 MAJOR PERSONALITY
DIMENSIONS VIEWED ON A CONTINUUM

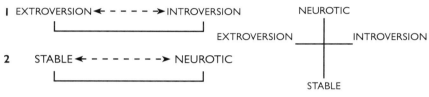

A third dimension of psychotism |_____| intelligence relating to how far a person was prepared to conform to society's rules and conventions was added later, in 1976

Fig. 19.2 EYSENCK'S PERSONALITY
DIMENSIONS LINKED TO PERSONALITY
CHARACTERISTICS (TRAITS) GENERALLY
DISPLAYED. MOST PEOPLE ARE NOT FOUND AT
THE EXTREMES OF THE TWO DIMENSIONS BUT
TEND TO COME SOMEWHERE IN THE MIDDLE

The better known extroversion/introversion dimension linked to a person's Reticular Activating System (RAS) related to how social or unsocial people appeared to be. The stable neurotic dimension linked to a person's autonomic nervous system referred to the levels of nervousness and anxiety that a person was susceptible to.

The RAS, which Eysenck argued affected the levels of introversion/extroversion, is part of the central cortex of the brain. It acts to either inhibit or excite brain activity in order to maintain optimum levels of alertness or arousal. He suggested that extroverts had an RAS which was biased towards inhibiting or reducing the affects of incoming sensory information therefore creating a severe state of under-arousal. According to Eysenck, extroverts therefore need increased levels of stimulation to maintain optimum levels of attention and brain functioning. They could become bored very easily and would tend to seek out and be happier in new and challenging situations, particularly those involving other people, thus creating higher levels of stimulation to balance their naturally low levels of arousal. Extroverts, for example, were said to achieve optimum performance at higher levels of arousal preferably in team orientated activities or those involving gross motor skills. Activities of a more continuous nature (cross-country and marathon running) could be demotivating to such personalities.

Introverts on the other hand had high levels of excitation naturally occurring within them (highly over-aroused). They therefore tended not to need external or additional stimulation or excitement in order to function at an optimum level. Introverts, for example, were said to achieve optimum performance at lower levels of arousal preferably in individual activities requiring more precision (shooting, archery, etc.). Many spurious claims have been made with regard to extroverts and introverts and tenuous links have been made with sporting performance (see the Evaluation of Trait theory, below). It was claimed that extroverts were more likely to take part in sport and be more successful, that they prefer team games and that:

- extroverts cope better in competitive and highly charged stressful situations
- extroverts cope better in the presence of distracting stimuli (eg, audience/noise)
- extroverts can cope with pain more easily than introverts.

Cattell's theory (1965)

Cattell also adopted a trait approach to personality, but argued that more than just two or three dimensions were needed in order to create a full picture of a person's personality. He proposed that personality could be reduced to and measured in terms of sixteen personality factors, hence his 16 PF Questionnaire. He argued that measuring these factors via his test would give an appropriate personality profile. In identifying certain common traits (possessed by all) and unique traits (possessed by some) he recognised that personality was more dynamic than Eysenck suggested and could fluctuate according to the situation.

By defining a wider personality profile Cattell's model was seen as providing a more accurate description of personality than Eysenck's thus enabling deviations from the norm to be more easily observed and assessed.

Evaluation of trait theory

These two traditional theories received wide criticism and as a result of further research both Eysenck and Cattell continued to update their questionnaires. There has been much discussion as to the validity of the dispositional trait approach but it certainly provided a framework from which future personality research could develop. The trait approach:

- was seen as a rather simplistic or limited view of personality
- failed, according to cognitive theorists, to recognise that individuals are actively involved in subjectively constructing their own personalities
- failed, according to situational theorists, to recognise the specific effects of different environmental situations
- failed to recognise that individuals do change.

Traits are seen as poor predictors of behaviour or at best predict a limited proportion of behaviour. The view of personality traits as rigid and enduring characteristics is questioned in terms of the validity and long-term reliability of the scales used. It is argued that although people may have certain core tendencies, or are disposed to act in certain ways, these behaviours are not general but specific to certain situations. Thus a more interactionist perspective is suggested. The generalisation of specific traits across the population as a whole in order to predict behaviour is also questioned.

The self report tests themselves have been widely criticised in terms of:

- accuracy
- a participant's honesty
- a participant's desire to create a favourable impression
- a participant's possible lack of objectivity
- the fact that neurotics were seen as possibly over emphasising certain traits
- inappropriate or ambiguous questions.

Answers could also be influenced by:

- the personality of the tester
- time of day
- a participant's previous experience of tests
- a participant's mood swings.

Finally, the concept of personality is seen as far too complex to be measured by a mere yes or no answer.

Table 19.1 CATTELL'S 16 POINT PERSONALITY TRAITS

FACTOR	LOW SCORE DESCRIPTION	STANDARD TEN SCORE (STEN) 1 2 3 4 5 6 7 8 9 10	HIGH SCORE DESCRIPTION
A	RESERVED, DETACHED, CRITICAL, ALOOF (sizothymia)	•	OUTGOING, WARMHEARTED, EASY-GOING, PARTICIPATING (affectothymia, formerly cyclothymia)
B	LESS INTELLIGENT, CONCRETE-THINKING (lower scholastic mental capacity)	•	MORE INTELLIGENT, ABSTRACT-THINKING, BRIGHT (higher scholastic mental capacity)
C	AFFECTED BY FEELINGS, EMOTIONALLY LESS STABLE, EASILY UPSET (lower ego strength)	•	EMOTIONALLY STABLE, FACES REALITY, CALM, MATURE (higher ego strength)
E	HUMBLE, MILD, ACCOMMODATING CONFORMING (submissiveness)	•	ASSERTIVE, AGGRESSIVE, STUBBORN, COMPETITIVE (dominance)
F	SOBER, PRUDENT, SERIOUS, TACITURN (desurgency)	•	HAPPY-GO-LUCKY, IMPULSIVELY LIVELY, GAY, ENTHUSIASTIC (surgency)
G	EXPEDIENT, DISREGARDS RULES FEELS FEW OBLIGATIONS (weaker superego strength)	•	CONSCIENTIOUS, PERSEVERING, STAID, MORALISTIC (stronger superego strength)
H	SHY, RESTRAINED, TIMID, THREAT-SENSITIVE (threctia)	•	VENTURESOME, SOCIALLY BOLD, UNINHIBITED, SPONTANEOUS (parmia)
I	TOUGH-MINDED, SELF-RELIANT, REALISTIC, NO-NONSENSE (harria)	•	TENDER-MINDED, CLINGING, OVER-PROTECTED, SENSITIVE (premsia)
L	TRUSTING, ADAPTABLE, FREE OF JEALOUSY, EASY TO GET ALONG WITH (alaxia)	•	SUSPICIOUS, SELF-OPINIONATED, HARD TO FOOL (protension)
M	PRACTICAL, CAREFUL, CONVENTIONAL, REGULATED BY EXTERNAL REALITIES, PROPER (praxemia)	•	IMAGINATIVE, WRAPPED UP IN INNER URGENCIES, CARELESS OF PRACTICAL MATTERS, BOHEMIAN (autia)
N	FORTHRIGHT, NATURAL, ARTLESS, UNPRETENTIOUS (artlessness)	•	SHREWD, CALCULATING, WORLDLY, PENETRATING (shrewdness)
O	SELF-ASSURED, CONFIDENT, SERENE (untroubled adequacy)	•	APPREHENSIVE, SELF-REPROACHING, WORRYING, TROUBLED (guilt proneness)
Q₁	CONSERVATIVE, RESPECTING ESTABLISHED IDEAS, TOLERANT OF TRADITIONAL DIFFICULTIES (conservatism)	•	EXPERIMENTING, LIBERAL, ANALYTICAL, FREE-THINKING (radicalism)
Q₂	GROUP-DEPENDENT, A 'JOINER' AND RESOURCEFUL SOUND FOLLOWER (group adherence)	•	SELF-SUFFICIENT, PREFERS OWN DECISIONS, (self-sufficiency)
Q₃	UNDISCIPLINED SELF-CONFLICT, FOLLOWS OWN URGES, CARELESS OF PROTOCOL (low integration)	•	CONTROLLED, SOCIALLY PRECISE, FOLLOWING SELF-IMAGE (high self-concept control)
q₄	RELAXED, TRANQUIL, UNFRUSTRATED (low ergic tension)	•	TENSE, FRUSTRATED, DRIVEN, OVERWROUGHT (high ergic tension)

a score of 1 2 3 4 5 6 7 8 9 10 is obtained

by about 2.3% 4.4% 9.2% 15.0% 19.1% 19.1% 15.0% 9.2% 4.4% 2.3% of adults

Fig. 19.3 THE FEATURES OF AN EFFECTIVE PERSONALITY TEST

Personality tests are examples of psychometric testing: a good test should have the following features.

Discriminating power
To be useful a wide distribution of scores should be produced. The 'ceiling' and 'floor' effects should be avoided.

Standardisation
Either norm referencing (Eysenck's EPQ/EPI and Cattell's 16 PF are both examples of normative tests) or criterion referencing can be used. Comparisons using mean/standard deviations are needed and standardised instructions are necessary to avoid possible bias on the part of the tester.

Reliability
All tests should be consistent and be capable of reproduction both **internally** and **externally**: that is, all test items should test something and the test should produce the same results when repeated.

Validity
The test should measure what it claims to measure; in other words, it should have **internal validity**. This is ensured by asking:

- are the questions appropriate?
- does the test content cover the representative sample of behaviour it is intended to cover?

It should also have **external validity**. Is there a high correlation between test scores and the independent variable and can these scores be generalised to the population as a whole? Personality tests therefore, whilst being useful tools to generate impressions of performers, should not be used in isolation or as a means of selecting or assessing performers for teams or events. Care should also be taken in attaching labels to certain individuals or groups (see stereotyping, A2).

Situational perspective of personality

The situational perspective is based around theories of social learning. The situational approach suggests that personality is constructed and shaped as a result of strong environmental influences and indirect reinforcement factors which can override the individual's personality traits. A person learns to behave in specific situations due to what has been observed and reinforced socially. A performer may appear confident in a specific situation, eg, on the pitch or within the context of a game where assertive behaviour is demanded by the coach and the situation. Outside or away from the situation the same assertive performer may behave in a very quiet, unassuming manner. Thus personality is seen as being relatively enduring but only in learned specific situations. Whilst many such as Mischel (1968) supported this perspective, many psychologists viewed the approach with a degree of scepticism. It was felt that in trying to solve the limitations associated with the trait approach the situational perspective had taken up rather too extreme a stance. It also was seen as being insufficient to predict behaviour accurately.

Interactionist approach to personality

In deciding between the relative strengths of the person versus situation debate, many psychologists recognised that each, although being limited, represented a degree of 'truth' in explaining the nature of personality. Performers were seen as having certain core elements of personality which pre-disposed them to behave in certain ways, but at the same time were capable of being strongly influenced by changing environmental considerations. This compromise position is one which is taken at present by the great majority of sports psychologists: behaviour is explained as the result of a reciprocal interaction between both the individual's consistent psychological traits (core) and the situational factors present.

This **interactionist approach** suggests therefore that if we wish to try to understand and predict an individual performer's behaviour we need to consider in depth both the individual person and the specific situation. In doing so, a much more complete picture and explanation of a person's behaviour can be developed. An early equation formula suggested by Lewin represents this relationship very simply. $B = f(P.E.)$ where:

- **Personality traits**
- **Cognitive variables**
- **Physiological variables**
- **Psychological variables**
- **Sociological variables**

Fig. 19.4 THE VARIABLES CONSIDERED BY SPORTS PSYCHOLOGISTS

B = behaviour
f = function
P = personality traits
E = environment

This is seen as a much more individualistic approach as it recognises that performers in similar sports do not necessarily exhibit the same behaviour. Just because some top class marathon runners appear more introverted in their behaviour does not mean that you have to be the same to get to the top. All rugby players are not extroverts all the time: it is not a pre-requisite for success.

Coaches have to develop an in-depth knowledge of each 'unique' performer. This becomes therefore a much more dynamic approach. In addition to being aware of their physical, physiological, intellectual and learning capabilities a coach needs to know about a performer's arousal and anxiety levels, confidence, levels of attention, attributions, achievement motivation, attitudes etc (A2 topics). All these need to be considered in relation to the specific situations performers find themselves in. In addition what has been shown to influence behaviour further is the performer's perception (interpretation) of the situation.

Type A and Type B personalities

In reviewing tthe effects of taking part in sport and fitness programmes on personality researchers have considered two personality dispositions, Type A and Type B personality (Girdano D.A. et al 1990).

In looking at very specific areas of personality and its effect on coping with stress, a narrow band theory of personality associated with how people deal with stress was developed by Friedman and Rosenman (1959).

Type A personalities

These people tend to:

- have a very strong competitive drive/need to succeed
- exhibit high levels of agitation/alertness and a tendency to be easily aroused
- generally to work at a fast pace, are hasty or have strong sense of urgency
- find it hard to delegate, are intolerant or easily become hostile/angry
- need to be in control of the situation
- experience high levels of stress.

Type B personalities

These people tend to:

- be more relaxed
- delegate easily
- be less competitive
- be less concerned to get everything done immediately
- be tolerant and methodical and are calm in dealing with problems
- experience low levels of stress.

Although both types were seen as being equally productive, their differences were defined as to do with cognitive emotional aspects linked to the concept of self. The tendency (disposition) towards anger/hostility is thought to increase the likelihood of stress related disease. The development of these specific tendencies has been related not to specific recent situations (now) but to earlier sociocultural effects usually in terms of high expectations of performance due to early pressures. Fitness and exercise programmes have been shown to have a positive effect on the reduction of Type A behaviour, patterns which could lead to reducing the risk of cardiovascular disease.

The many types of research carried out have revealed a great deal of information on which to draw when trying to understand someone's behaviour.

Further problems associated with assessment and research into personality

As we have already seen, early research such as Eysenck's EPQ and EPI and Cattell's 16 PF have been criticised for their lack of sophistication and have problems of validity, methodology and interpretation of statistical data. Much of the more up to date research has been dogged by similar problems. The ethics of using personality tests has also been raised. Criticism of such tests as the Athletic Motivation Inventory (AMI) devised by Ogilvie and Tutko (1966) seemed to heighten sensitivity over the use and application of such research.

---

1 Participants should know the purpose and use of the test.
2 Tests should only be carried out and interpreted by qualified/experienced people.
3 Personality test results should not be used in isolation to predict behaviour.
4 Other information taken should include a person's life history, interview, observations, performance assessments.
5 Sport specific tests should be used.
6 Both trait and state measures should be used.
7 Feedback should be given to participants.
8 Personality tests should not be used for selection purposes and/or to discriminate for places on teams.

Fig. 19.5 GUIDELINES FOR PERSONALITY TESTING — AS SUGGESTED BY THE AMERICAN PSYCHOLOGICAL ASSOCIATION 1974 IN ORDER TO ENSURE TESTS USED ARE APPROPRIATE AND ETHICAL

Most sports psychologists however, still rely heavily on such sport specific objective inventory tests due to their ease of application and analysis. The Sport Competition Anxiety Test (SCAT) (Martens, 1990) is a popular example. Guidelines for the use of such tests have been drawn up to ensure both the validity and the ethical nature of testing.

Modern sport psychologists such as Martens (1975) R.S. Weinberg (1995) see Hollanders' (1967) model of personality as providing a more systematic and comprehensive framework for understanding the concept of personality (fig 19.6).

This model in encompassing both a trait and social environment perspective encourages a multi-method approach to the study of personality.

Fig. 19.6 ADAPTED FROM EDWIN
HOLLANDERS MODEL OF PERSONALITY 1967
(PRINCIPLES & METHODS OF SOCIAL
PSYCHOLOGY, OXFORD UNIVERSITY PRESS)

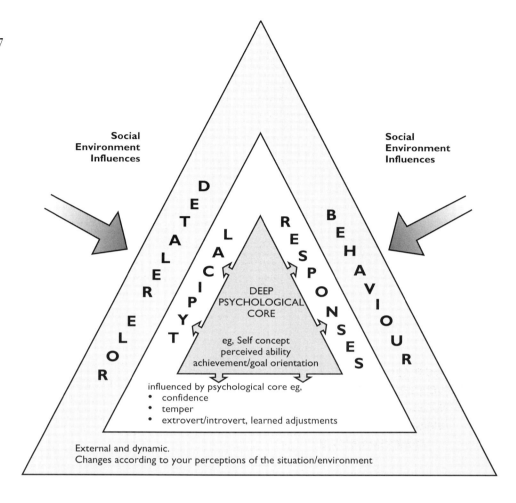

Personality is viewed as being in three different levels or layers with the outer layers being more changeable or readily influenced by situation demands and environmental factors.

Personality and sporting performance

Returning to the questions posed earlier, research attempting to clarify these has been found to be very contradictory. However, the general findings of more up to date research indicate that:

1   No obvious sporting personality-type distinguishes those involved in sport and
    non participants.
2   No obvious consistent personality characteristics have been found to distinguish between
    different types of sports performers – for instance performers participating in both team
    or individual sports are not disposed to certain specific types of personality behaviour.
3   Few personality differences have been found between male and female sports performers,
    particularly at the élite level. There is some evidence to suggest that there is a more
    marked difference between successful and unsuccessful female performers then in men.
    However, it has been suggested that this is linked more to socio-cultural effects.

4   To be successful in sport a person needs to demonstrate: positive mental health (iceberg profile fig 19.7); positive self perceptions (self confidence); positive/productive cognitive strategies. The Iceberg Profile (Morgan, 1978) has been related to characteristics associated with élite sports performers; they tend to be more vigorous and have low levels of tension, depression, anger, confusion and fatigue.

5   Mood states have been found to differ in successful and less successful performers. Successful performers generally display more positive mood profiles. Whether this more positive profile of mood state (POMS) helps to create better performance or whether it is itself caused by the success in sport is inconclusive. D. Gill argues that less than desirable mood profiles are negatively associated with success in most achievement situations.

Fig. 19.7 THE ICEBERG PROFILE.
Source: Morgan, W.P. etal., 1987, Psycholigical monitoring of overtraining and staleness, British Journal of Sports Medicine

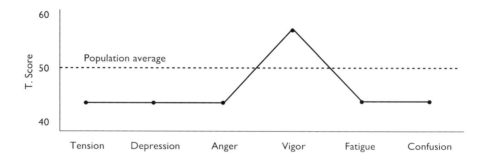

On Profile of Mood States (POMS) scores successful athletes were above the **waterline** (population norm) on vigor, but below the surface on the more negative moods, hence an 'iceberg' shape to the graph.

6   Successful performers have been found to be able to internalise – that is use cognitive (mental) strategies such as mental rehearsal, imagery or positive self talk for coping with anxiety more effectively than unsuccessful performers (see strategies for dealing with stress, A2). However, these cognitive strategies have not been found to change personality traits.

7   The claim that sport can influence or develop certain positive or socially desirable characteristics or attributes has not been supported by research evidence. The philosophical statements often made by physical educationalists and activity centres that certain sports can develop character and socially desirable types of behaviour are therefore quite considerably undermined. There is even some evidence to suggest that taking part in competitive sport can actually have a detrimental effect on social life, by increasing anti-social behaviour and rivalry (see socio-culture section).

8   The effect of taking part in sport and fitness work has been shown to have an immediate effect on mood states in the specific situation, and also help with a performer's concept of 'self'. The long-term or global influence on our individual personality traits is seen however, to be of little effect.

Summary

- Personality refers to those relatively stable and enduring aspects of an individuals' behaviour.
- There are several theoretical perspectives.
- The study of personality has tended to consider is it as a result of 'nature' or 'nurture'.
- *Trait theories* see personality as being innate and stable predispositions, enabling behaviour patterns to be predicted in all situations.

- *Social learning theories* see personality being formed as a result of the environment influencing individual learning experiences. Thus it can change in different situations.
- *Interactionist theories* see personality as being a combination between traits and the environment. B = F(PE)
- A variety of methods can be used to test personality. The most common being questionnaires, observation and interviews.
- Personality tests should not be used in isolation as there are question marks over their validity.
- No definite findings concerning the different personalities of successful to unsuccessful performers. Team to individual performers. Male to female performers.
- The closest we can get to predicting the behaviour of an individual is through 'mood states' which link to the suggested 'iceberg' profile.
- For success in sport each individual must be viewed differently by the coach according to the 3 levels of personality. Made up of psychological core, typical response and role related behaviour.

Review Questions

1   What do we mean by personality?

2   Explain the credulous and sceptical viewpoints of personality research?

3   What is the trait perspective view of personality?

4   What is the RAS? How did Eysenck relate this to personality characteristics?

5   How many personality characteristics did Cattell identify? How did these help?

6   What are the limitations of the trait perspective?

7   What are the main criticisms of personality tests?

8   Why is it important that research is valid and reliable?

9   What is the situational perspective of personality?

10   How does the interactionist approach differ from the trait approach?

11   Explain the equation B = F(PE)

12   What is meant by a personality core? Give an example.

13   What is meant by role related behaviour?

14   What is the iceberg profile? How does it relate to sports performers 'mood stages'?

chapter 20

Motivation in Physical Education and Sport

Motivation is a key area of sport psychology. It is recognised as an essential feature in both the learning of skills and the development of performance. In addition it plays an important role in a learner's preference for and selection of activities.

In evaluating the research we find that unfortunately there are, once again, no simple answers. What becomes obvious is that in order to gain an understanding of this complex and multi-functional concept we need to consider a wide variety of research. By taking an integrated approach to analysing motivation we will try to bring together the main aspects of various psychological perspectives. Motivation is the global term for a very complex process. Within this chapter we will introduce you to the basic concept of motivation and consider the following:

- what do sports psychologists mean by motivation?
- what are the different types of motivation?
- what are the effects of these different types on learning and performance?
- what are the main theories associated with motivation and achievement motivation?
- what different motivational techniques can be used in order to facilitate motivation?
- what are the related and interdependent factors that can influence motivational behaviour?

In considering these areas you should develop a clearer understanding of the underlying processes involved in how and why motivation can differ from person to person.

Here is a list of the terms to be covered in this chapter. It is important that you understand them.

- Intrinsic motivation
- Extrinsic motivation
- Arousal
- Drive theory
- The inverted 'U' hypothesis
- Catastrophe theory
- Reticular activating system
- Optimum arousal
- Perceptive narrowing
- Cue utilisation

In the second year you will take a more in depth approach to motivation and the elite performer.

Defining motivation

Answering the question 'What do we mean by motivation?' has been one of the fundamental difficulties faced by psychologists and explanations differ according to the psychological perspective adopted. The term 'motivate' comes from the Latin for move and motives are seen as a special kind of cause of behaviour that **energise**, **direct** and **sustain** a person's behaviour (Ruben and McNeil, 1983).

Fig. 20.1 MASLOW'S 1954 HIERARCHY OF NEEDS

It has been suggested that human beings have both primary motives (survival and function, etc) physiological needs and secondary motives which are acquired or learned such as the **need for achievement** and self actualisation which are complex, higher order cognitive behaviours. Motivation was historically linked with the concept of homeostasis, ie, maintaining the body's physiological balance. In order for a person's body to function correctly it requires certain essential elements: food, water, heat and rest (primary needs). If these basic elements are not available or lacking in anyway the body needs to obtain them. Maslow highlighted the basic needs of a person as being a mixture of the physiological and psychological. If the body has developed a need then it will eventually strive to meet the need – the body will be driven psychologically to meet its needs. As well as being psychological, the desire to overcome physiological deprivation implies a motivational state.

Maslow (1954) produced a psycho-social model referring to a human being's hierarchy of needs. Maslow's model suggests that our motives change, as one motive is achieved another is desired.

Definition

Motivation is: 'the internal mechanisms and external stimuli which arouse and direct our behaviour'. ***(G.H. Sage, 1974)***

Defining motivation in this generalised way can have certain disadvantages. Learners and performers may misunderstand the term when advised to '**be more motivated**', inferring certain character problems associated with themselves. It can also cause potential problems when motivational strategies are employed.

Seeing motivation as the direction and intensity of one's effort is regarded by more recent psychologists as too simplistic (M Weiss, 1992) (Weinberg, 1995). However, for the purposes of this book we will accept Sage's definition as a useful starting point.

In analysing the definition we can see that it involves four main aspects:

1 **Internal mechanisms** – motivation is linked to and affected by a person's inner drives.
2 **External mechanisms:** motivation is linked to and affected by external factors that we can experience within our learning/performing situations.

3 Arouse behaviour: motivation is linked to a person's state of arousal that energises and drives our behaviour. The strength of the energised state will determine the degree of intensity of effort used to achieve the goal-related behaviour.

4 Direct behaviour: motivation in its various forms can affect our goals or selection of activities as well as our maintenance of behaviour in activities (Richard Gross sees motivation as 'goal directed purposeful behaviour').

Motivation refers therefore to a general **energised state** which prepares a person to act or behave in some way. Motives relate to the direction that the behaviour will take or the goal which is set.

Interactional view of motivation

In recognising that motivation (the intensity and direction of behaviour) is formed as a result of both 'internal and external mechanisms' we are said to be taking an **interactionist perspective** on motivation.

To develop optimum motivation a teacher or coach must not only analyse and respond individually to each of the aspects listed in fig 20.2 but also to how the factors interact together. Very rarely can blame for poor motivation be placed on any one factor alone.

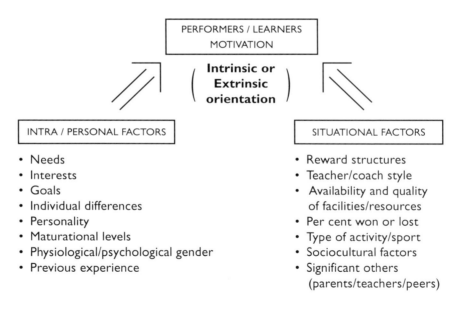

Fig. 20.2 The interactionist view of motivation

Why do performers take part in physical activities?

- The wish/desire/drive to participate in/perform well at a sport.
- Goal directed behaviour.
- Desire is associated with the expectation that the outcomes will be positive.
- The drive to achieve/will to win.

Types of motivation

A person's behaviour is affected by many different kinds of motives coming from both internal and external mechanisms.

Intrinsic motivation

The study of intrinsic motivation has been linked to cognitive theories. Intrinsic motivation is used to explain how learners/performers strive inwardly, being self determined in trying to develop competence or excellence of performance. They are said to have mastery orientation. A person who is intrinsically motivated will want to take part in the activity for its own sake, for pure love of the sport. They will focus on the enjoyment and fun of competition, try to develop their skills to the highest possible level (pursuit of excellence) and enjoy the action and excitement of seeking out new challenges and affiliations in doing so. A performer pushing themselves hard in difficult circumstances and feeling a sense of control and pride at achieving a high level of personal skill is said to be intrinsically motivated. Intrinsic motivation is greatest when learners/performers feel competent and self determining in dealing with their environment. Sports performers sometimes experience a situation when the timing of movements and actions appears perfect. They seem unable to do wrong. Everything they try works! It's one of those perfect days. They are said to be experiencing the ultimate intrinsic experience. Csikszentmihalyi (1975) describes this as the *'flow experience'*; in his research he identified the common characteristics of it as:

- complete absorption in the activity
- action and awareness are merged
- apparent loss of consciousness
- an almost subconscious feeling of self control
- no extrinsic motivation (goals, rewards, etc)
- effortless movement.

Such a peak experience, during which performers are able to lose themselves in the highly skilled performance of their sport, has been likened to Maslow's 'self actualisation' commented upon earlier in this chapter. Although it cannot be consciously planned for, the development of 'flow' has been linked to the following factors:

- positive mental attitude (confidence, positive thinking)
- being relaxed, controlling anxiety, and enjoying optimum arousal
- focusing on appropriate specific aspects of performance
- physical readiness (training and preparation at the highest level).

Obviously limitations in any of the above factors can result in 'disrupted flow'.

Extrinsic motivation

Extrinsic motivation is related to Sage's external mechanisms.

If used appropriately extrinsic types of motivation (contingencies) can serve a very useful purpose in effectively developing certain required behaviours (learning) or levels of sporting performance. The behaviouristic view of learning discussed in earlier chapters is founded on the principles of reinforcement (rewards for success) and punishment. The systematic use of rewards, or 'Effective Contingency Management' as it is often referred to, is recognised as playing an important role in modifying and shaping learning and performance (see operant conditioning). Rewards can expedite learning and achievement, serve to ensure that a good performance is repeated or form an attraction to persuade a person to take part in certain activities (incentive).

While extrinsic motivation is most obviously seen in terms of tangible or materialistic rewards, it can also be intangible.

When using extrinsic rewards and reinforcements to enhance motivation a teacher or coach needs to be aware of how often they are used (frequency). Should reward or reinforcement be used at every good or successful attempt or every so many times (ratio)?

TANGIBLE	INTANGIBLE
• Trophies	• Social reinforcers
• Medals	• Praise from teacher
• Badges	/coach/peers
• Certificates	• Smile
• Money	• Pat on the back
	• Publicity/national
	recognition
	• Winning/glory
	• Social status
	• Approval

Fig. 20.3 TANGIBLE AND INTANGIBLE EXTRINSIC MOTIVATION

How quickly after the event should reinforcement be used (interval)? What is the most effective type of reinforcement to use? (see fig 20.3). The value or quantity of the reward is also important (magnitude). In being aware of the above factors a teacher or coach clearly needs an in-depth knowledge of the likes and dislikes of the people being taught. The use of rewards is therefore closely linked to our earlier discussion of reinforcement of learning.

Research into the use of reinforcement principles has produced the following recommendations when considering extrinsic motivation:

- positive reinforcement is 80 to 90 per cent more effective
- avoid the use of punishment apart from when behaviour is intolerable or unwanted
- in order to be effective, extrinsic feedback and reinforcement must meet the needs of the recipient (they must be important to or desired by the individual)
- continuous reinforcement is desirable in the early stages of learning
- intermittent reinforcement is more effective with more advanced performers
- immediate reinforcement is generally more effective, particularly with beginners
- reward appropriate behaviour (cannot reward all behaviour)
  - (i) reward successful approximations, particularly by beginners (shaping) – performance will not always be perfect (trial and error)
  - (ii) reward performance – do not just focus on the outcome, ie, winning
  - (iii) reward effort
  - (iv) reward emotional and social skills
- provide knowledge of results (information re-accuracy and success of movement (see feedback)
- the use of punishment should be restricted or avoided as although it can be effective in eliminating undesirable behaviour it can also lead to bitterness, resentment, frustration and hostility. It can arouse a performer's fear of failure and thus hinder the learning of skills.

Look at the list of strategies for the use of extrinsic rewards. Try to give practical examples of how a teacher or coach might implement them in real life.

Consider top level sports performers such as Lindsay Davenport in fig 20.4. In discussion with a partner, try to suggest what motivates them to carry on once they have reached the top.

Combining intrinsic and extrinsic rewards

Both intrinsic and extrinsic motivation obviously play important roles in the development of skilled performance and behavioural change (learning). Extrinsic rewards are used extensively in sporting situations. Most major sports have achievement performance incentives linked to some form of tangible reward system. At first glance it would appear that the 'additive effect' of extrinsic rewards – money, cups and medals – and the high level of intrinsic motivation should result in performers showing a much greater level of overall motivation.

Although early research in this area supported this additive viewpoint, later research, for example by Deci (1971, 1972) and Lepper and Green (1975) began to suggest that under certain conditions (when intrinsic motivation is already high (Orlick and Mosher, 1978)) extrinsic motivation may actually decrease intrinsic motivation. This lead to many practitioners discouraging the use of extrinsic rewards in an educational setting. Further research with regard to the reduction in intrinsic motivation linked this effect more to the person's perception of the original extrinsic reward. To further explain this potential positive or negative effect of extrinsic rewards Deci (1985) developed his cognitive evaluation theory.

What happens when there are no further badges or trophies to obtain? How might a coach try to ensure levels of motivation are maintained?

Fig. 20.4 Lindsay Davenport collecting her trophy at the Australian Open 2000

Intrinsic motivation can be affected by extrinsic rewards in two ways. The performer may perceive the reward as an attempt to **control** or manipulate their behaviour (the fun aspect becomes work). The performer may also perceive the reward as providing information about their level of performance. A reward could be perceived by a performer as increasing the individual importance of a particular achievement. In receiving the reward that certain level of achievement is perceived as high. If they do achieve and gain the reward (positive information) then this sign of high ability can help intrinsic motivation. If, however, they fail to achieve the reward (negative information) then they may perceive this as being a sign of incompetence or low ability, thus lowering future intrinsic motivation.

If a person perceives extrinsic rewards as controlling their behaviour or providing information that they are competent then intrinsic motivation will be reduced. To increase intrinsic motivation the reward should provide information and positive feedback with regard to the performer's level of competence in performance.

Teachers and coaches should therefore try to involve the performer in decision making and planning with regard to their training programmes and performance goals. By becoming involved the performer will feel a shared responsibility for any success or achievement thus increasing their intrinsic motivation because they feel in control and competent. The now obvious link between competitive success and increased intrinsic motivation was shown by Weinberg (1978).

As success and failure in competitive situations provide high levels of information with regard to a person's level of competence or incompetence it is important that a teacher or coach ensures that intrinsic motivation is not lost by a person who experiences defeat. This is done by emphasising performance or task goals and concentrating on more subjective outcomes, eg, an action performed well. For instance: although you lost the tennis match it was to a better player; your number of successful serves increased and your tactical use of certain ground strokes also improved. By focusing on the subjective evaluation of success or performance outcomes (winning is not everything) teachers, coaches and parents can improve the performer's positive perceptions of themselves (self image, self confidence) and thus dramatically increase intrinsic motivation.

In conclusion then, intrinsic motivation is highly satisfying because it gives the performer a sense of personal control over the situation in which they are performing. Being intrinsically motivated will ensure that an individual will train and practise enthusiastically thus hopefully developing their acquisition of skill (learning) and overall performance.

Extrinsic rewards however, do not inherently undermine intrinsic motivation. It is essential that physical education teachers and coaches use them in addition to other strategies effectively. They must increase a learner's/performer's perceptions of success in order to develop intrinsic motivation within the overall educational and performance environment.

Successful strategies for the use of rewards to help develop intrinsic motivation should include:

1 Manipulation of the environment to provide for successful and enjoyable experience.
2 Ensuring that rewards are contingent on performance development (not outcome goals).
3 Emphasising praise (verbal – non verbal).
4 Providing variety in learning and practice situations.
5 Allowing learners to participate in decision making.
6 Setting realistic performance goals based on the learner's ability and present skill levels.

Look at the list of reward strategies on page 385. How many more can you think of? Now think of a sport or physical activity that you have taken part in or are still taking part in. Make a list of all the reasons or factors that influenced you to take part in that activity. Consider the following questions:

- **why did you start?**
- **why did you stop?**
- **why are you still taking part?**
- **are the reasons and motives that prompt you to continue taking part the same as the reasons and motives that originally prompted you to start?**
- **was your motivation more to do with intrinsic or extrinsic factors?**
- **did situational factors have an influence on your level of motivation?**

Compare and discuss your findings with the rest of the group.

Fig. 20.5 ANDRE AGASSI

Arousal

Any discussion of motivation is closely linked to theories of arousal. In the everyday use of the terms it is not always easy to distinguish between motivation and arousal. They are also closely related to the notion of stress and anxiety (A2 units, Optimising Performance). In our earlier consideration of Sage's definition of motivation it was stated that motivation was affected by both intrinsic and extrinsic factors that served to energise and direct behaviour. Arousal is linked therefore to the 'energised' state that drives a person to learn or perform and is therefore associated with the intensity dimension of motivation. Evidence suggests, however, that arousal is not just an internal state.

Definition of arousal

Arousal can be defined as being a general mixture of both the physiological and psychological levels of activity that a performer experiences; these levels vary on a continuum from deep sleep to intense excitement.

Highly energised states can be caused by an individual or team competing in an important competition. Arousal is not to be seen as good or bad, positive or negative, as it appears to represent the level of energy or effort that a learner/performer develops and applies to any sporting or learning situation. A sports performer can be highly aroused as a result of both winning and losing a competition or even looking forward to a competition (apprehension or excitement).

Placing the body under any form of physical (physiological) or mental (psychological) stress produces levels of arousal which can affect both information processing and final performance. If activities require a great deal of decision making to be done quickly and accurately then the effects of arousal are even more marked. Traditionally arousal has been linked to and measured by its physiological effects.

Arousal theories

Arousal theories suggest that our bodies need to be in a state of homeostasis (physiological and psychological balance). If the body is deprived or affected (put under stress – perceived or actual) in any way physiologically or mentally then arousal levels in the body are increased and we are motivated to behave in such a way as to reduce these levels back to the optimum level of arousal. Typical physiological reactions that are associated with increased arousal levels can be measured by heart rate, blood pressure, electronical activity, electromyograph, galvanic skin responses and biomechanical indicators such as adrenaline and epinephrine.

If an athlete is preparing for a big race (highly active) they need to be in a highly alert state (arousal). The body needs to ensure that it can meet all the physiological demands that may be placed on it. Muscles need to be supplied with blood sugars and oxygen, etc. The sympathetic system of the **autonomous nervous system** (ANS), ie, the glands, hormonal and endocrine systems also help to maintain and prepare the body for action. The **parasympathetic system** of the ANS, on the other hand, will work to restore the body's resources for future use.

The **reticular activating system** (RAS), which is part of the ascending structure of the spinal cord's link to the fore brain, is responsible for maintaining the general level of arousal or alertness within the body. It plays a part in our selective attention processes and serves either to inhibit or excite incoming sensory information to help our attention processes (see earlier Chapter for a discussion of Eysenck's work on personality and arousal levels linked to the effect of the RAS). The psychologists' interest in arousal has tended to focus on the links between the physiological aroused state and the experience of associated emotions. Just as periods of high intense exercise (eg, playing football or netball) are associated with all the symptoms of a highly aroused state, eg, high levels of adrenaline, increased HR, breathing rates, etc, aroused states can be equally associated with the emotional states of fear, anger, apprehension, tension, worry and anxiety. Some evidence suggests that these emotional states are reciprocal with one affecting the other and vice versa. They are closely linked to the physiological state. Within this chapter we are mainly interested in the psychological effects of arousal.

The various emotional states mentioned above are easily developed and often experienced particularly when exploring the unfamiliar (meeting something new or being asked to do something important or perform at a new high level of competition) and in the learning or acquiring of motor skills as well as the ultimate performance. Research has shown that levels of arousal can affect levels of perception, attention and movement control, all of which are obviously important in the learning and performance of motor skills.

As a learner's/performer's levels of arousal are important it must be equally important that they have the **appropriate** levels of arousal in order to promote effective concentration, attention and decision making levels to produce optimum performance. Teachers and coaches have been aware for a long time of the need for performers to be mentally prepared and alert; this is commonly referred to as a sports performer being 'psyched up' (readiness to respond). The intensity of arousal levels is often a crucial factor in both competitive sport and learning situations. If arousal gets too high a learner/performer can become anxious and equally if it is too low then they may become bored and demotivated, both states resulting in a negative effect on learning and performance.

Drive theory

Early research carried out by Hull in 1943 and later modified by J Spence and K Spence in 1966 suggests that the relationship between arousal and performance is a linear one. All performance was originally thought to improve directly in proportion to increases in arousal (see fig 20.6).

In other words, the more a sports performer was aroused the better they would perform. Further research by Spence and Spence adapted this view slightly. This relationship has been expressed in the equation

$$\mathbf{P} = \mathbf{H} \times \mathbf{D}$$
Performance = habit strength × drive

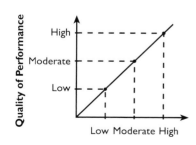

Fig. 20.6 ORIGINAL DRIVE THEORIES' VIEW OF THE AROUSAL/PERFORMANCE RELATIONSHIP

Hull saw drive as being synonymous with arousal. Habit strength was seen as the learned response or performance behaviour; essentially, it is a theory related to learning – Hull saw the likelihood of learned behaviour (dominant response) occurring as being greater as drive (arousal) levels increased. This theory has very close links with Zajonc's theory of social

Fig. 20.7 EVEN HIGHLY TALENTED SPORTS PERFORMERS HAVE 'CHOKED' IN HIGHLY CHARGED SITUATIONS

facilitation (A2). However, learned habitual behaviour may not always be the correct behaviour. The theory goes on to suggest that if the performer is a beginner trying to carry out newly acquired skills then increased drive (arousal) for whatever reason may cause the performer to rely on previously learned skills, thus the dominant response may be an incorrect response. A good example would be a beginner learning to serve in tennis. They have just been taught correctly how to serve, practised several times, appear to understand and carry out a reasonable serve. However, in a following competitive match their first serve hits the net and because of the increased pressure (drive/arousal) to get the second serve in they subconsciously revert back to their previously error-ridden learned serve, a little tap over the net in order to get the ball in play. Thus in the early stages of learning the effects of increased arousal on skill acquisition could lead to the dominant response being an incorrect one. In the latter stages of learning (autonomous) increased drive (arousal) levels would have a positive effect, as the dominant response would be the well learnt (habitual) and generally correct one. This is often called a 'grooved skill'. The many criticisms of this theory as a result of further research, together with observations of 'real life' situations in which even top class performers with highly developed habitual skill levels have been seen to fail in high arousal situations, has meant that this approach has generally lost credibility.

The inverted 'U' hypothesis

This explanation of the relationship between arousal and performance originated as a result of work carried out as early as 1908 when the Yerkes and Dodson Law first suggested that complex tasks are performed better when one's level of drive (arousal) is low, while simple tasks are performed better when drive/arousal is high. It recognises that there are different degrees of arousal, over or under arousal, and that different people can be affected in

Fig. 20.8 THE INVERTED 'U' PRINCIPLE STATES THAT INCREASED AROUSAL IMPROVES PERFORMANCE ONLY TO A CERTAIN POINT AFTER WHICH FURTHER INCREASED LEVELS OF AROUSAL WILL HAVE AN ADVERSE EFFECT

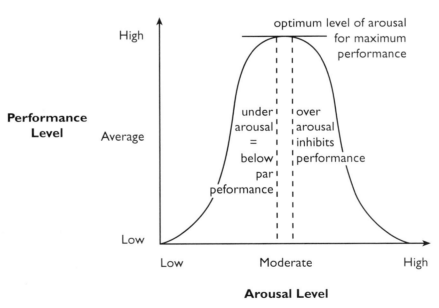

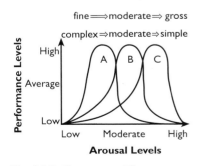

Fig. 20.9 THE INVERTED 'U' PRINCIPLE FOR DIFFERENT TASKS: OPTIMUM AROUSAL IS HIGHER FOR MORE SIMPLE TASKS WITH MORE GROSS-MOTOR CONTROL

different ways depending on the type of tasks they are faced with. Most sports performers and coaches can relate to the principles of the inverted 'U' hypothesis as most of them have experienced performances when both under and over arousal have inhibited their performance. They have also experienced times when their preparation has been exactly right, decisions have been made correctly and effectively and an excellent performance has resulted. This view contends that the relationship between arousal and performance is curvilinear, hence the inverted 'U' shape of the graph (see fig 20.8 above). Performance is said to improve up to a certain point of arousal; if arousal continues to increase beyond the optimal state then the performance will begin to decline.

It has been argued, however, that as a general principle, optimum levels of arousal are not the same for all activities or for all performers. The idea that optimum levels of arousal are variable according to the type and complexity of the task in relation to the individual performer has meant that the basic principles can be generalised and used by teachers and coaches to explain and predict behaviour in a whole host of situations. Teachers and coaches began to realise that the usual all-rousing pre-event pep talk was not necessarily the answer for all performers.

Using fig 20.9, try to place the following list of activities to one of the three curves A, B or C in relation to the level of arousal you would think might be appropriate to carry out the skill effectively:

- **free throw in basketball**
- **rugby prop**
- **a gymnastic routine**
- **boxing**
- **putting in golf**
- **tennis**
- **archery**
- **rifle shooting**

- **figure skating**
- **shot put**
- **power lifting**
- **swimming 100 m sprint**
- **running a marathon**
- **taking a penalty kick in football**
- **slip fielder in cricket.**

Consider a game or activity that you take part in regularly. In conjunction with a partner think of the levels of appropriate arousal you might need at various stages in the game and with certain types of skills.

Fig. 20.10 ARCHERY/RIFLE SHOOTING REQUIRES FINE MUSCULAR CONTROL AND HIGH LEVELS OF CONCENTRATION AND AS SUCH OPTIMUM LEVELS OF AROUSAL WOULD BE LOWER THAN THOSE OF THE POWER LIFTER

It has been found that motor skills generally need an above average level of arousal. If the skills or activity involve mainly gross movements and relatively simple skills using strength, endurance and speed, requiring little decision making, then higher levels of arousal will be found more effective. Activities involving very fine, accurate muscle actions or complex tasks requiring higher levels of perception, decision making, concentration and attention will be carried out more effectively if the point of optimum arousal is slightly lower.

It is therefore very important that a teacher or coach assesses the appropriate levels of arousal for each task in order to ensure that the optimum level is achieved. Even within teams the different requirements of each particular role or position may require different levels of arousal at various times, eg, batting and bowling in cricket, where loss of concentration and coordination could be disastrous, require different levels of arousal to those of a general fielder. Adjusting arousal levels to suit both task and situation could involve the coach in trying to increase or decrease a performer's arousal levels. Levels of excitement and anxiety caused by high arousal may need to be controlled by various stress management techniques (A2 units). As you can appreciate, many sports or tasks involve combinations of both fine and gross skills along with varying levels of information processing linked to complexity. Even within the context of a game different players will need different levels of arousal and at different times. Past experience, amount of practice and stage of learning will also have an effect on the choice of appropriate level of arousal.

Beginners need different levels of arousal to those of a professional sports person. In addition the level of complexity is relative to the stage of learning and/or experience. What for an experienced performer is a relatively easy task may be very difficult and involve a great deal of information processing for a beginner (see earlier Chapter). Even at moderate levels of arousal a beginner may 'go to pieces' and be unable to cope with what is required of them; an even lower level of arousal may be more appropriate.

The inability of a performer, particularly a beginner, to process the relevant information effectively has been linked to what has been called **perceptual narrowing** and **cue-utilisation theory**. These concepts help us to understand that as arousal levels increase a performer tries to pay more attention to those stimuli, cues and signals that are more likely and relevant in order to help them carry out the task (cue-utilisation). They focus their attention (perceptual narrowing). However, a performer's ability to focus their attention is severely hampered if arousal levels continue to increase. Perceptual narrowing continues which may cause a performer to miss important cues and signals (ineffective cue-utilisation) which could have a detrimental effect on performance.

This effect is even more noticeable if the cues and signals are not what was expected. Extreme levels of arousal can cause such acute levels of perceptual narrowing that a person is not able to concentrate or make decisions effectively, and can even hinder the smooth control of physical movements. This state of 'hyper vigilance' is commonly known as 'blind panic'. Perceptual narrowing is therefore an important aspect of both learning and performance where, in a state of high arousal, reactions to expected stimuli can be enhanced and reactions to inappropriate or unexpected cues and signals can be inhibited.

In discussion with your group try to recount a specific situation in which you have experienced 'panic' and been unable to concentrate on making the correct decisions. What sort of things 'triggered' these feelings? How did perceptual narrowing affect your cue-utilisation?

It would be more appropriate, therefore, when dealing with inexperienced performers or beginners in a learning situation to ensure that levels of arousal are initially very low. Audiences, evaluation and competitive situations are best avoided.

Teachers and coaches need to get to know the learner/performer and be aware of the effects that the situation can have on them.

Catastrophe theory

Several modifications to the inverted 'U' hypothesis have been put forward. One of the more interesting is that suggested by Hardy and Frazey (1987). The catastrophe theory is similar to the inverted 'U' hypothesis in that both argue that if arousal increases it will have a positive effect on performance up to a certain optimal level. Hardy and Frazey suggest however, that any further increase in arousal will not result in a gradual fall-off in performance as seen in the symmetrical shape of the inverted 'U' graph; this shape can be altered by a slight reduction in arousal. Slight reductions of arousal return the performer to the previous optimum level and effective performance, eg, in a game of squash/tennis a player becomes argumentative and angry over a call causing his/her game to deteriorate, but calming words from the coach restore a balanced performance. Hardy and Frazey then argue that in highly competitive and important matches, where both high physiological arousal combines with high

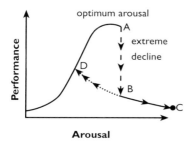

Fig. 20.11 CATASTROPHE THEORY
Source: adapted from 'A catastrophe for sport psychology', by L. Hardy and J. Frazey, in Bass Monograph No. 1 (p 21), (British Association of Sports Science N.C.F., Leeds, 1988)

cognitive anxiety, if a squash player for example becomes upset enough (over aroused) for it to have a detrimental effect on his/her game, the deterioration is much more extreme and cannot be arrested merely by calming the player down a little. 'Going over the top' in this situation will have a dramatic effect on the ability to concentrate, make decisions and play shots effectively. In other words a catastrophe. Recovery from this catastrophe can be very difficult; extreme 'mental toughness' will be required if they are to work their way gradually back to optimum arousal and peak performance.

Figure 20.11 illustrates the different shape and effect (catastrophe predictions) of arousal on performance:

- at point A cognitive anxiety (worrying) and physiological arousal (somatic) are high – reaching this threshold creates a catastrophic effect
- at point B the performer either continues with their extreme over arousal causing performance to decline further to C or
- they get to grips with their problem, taking serious steps to calm down and re-focus – performance will gradually improve to point D when arousal levels can return to the optimum levels: performance may once again reach the maximum effective level.

Summary

Motivation

1 Motivation is seen as energised, goal-directed purposeful behaviour.
2 Motivation is closely linked to inner drives and arousal.
3 Motivation can affect the direction and intensity of behaviour.
4 Extrinsic motivation is behaviour motivated by external rewards, tangible and intangible, or punishment.
5 Intrinsic motivation develops as a result of internal drives to achieve feelings of personal satisfaction and fulfilment (the flow experience).
6 Rewards should be monitored carefully and linked to giving information regarding a performer's level of competence.
7 Performers and coaches should have a shared responsibility in the planning and setting of achievable targets.
8 Current thinking supports the interactionist view.

Arousal

1 The concept of arousal is very closely linked to motivation.
2 Drive theory states that there is a linear relationship between arousal and performance (the more the better!).
3 Inverted 'U' hypothesis suggests that the relationship is curvi-linear. Increased arousal improves performance up to a certain point. Increases in arousal beyond this optimum level will have a detrimental effect on performance.
4 Levels of optimum arousal will be different according to the complexity and nature of the specific task in relation to the individual's characteristics and the specific situation.

Revision Questions

1 What is meant by the term motivation?

2 How is arousal linked to motivation?

3 Outline the differences between drive theory and the inverted 'U' hypothesis in relation to arousal and performance.

4 What does a curvi-linear shaped graph infer?

5 In what ways can arousal levels affect learning and performance?

6 Explain the different types of extrinsic and intrinsic motivation and give examples.

7 Why is intrinsic motivation thought to be more effective than extrinsic?

8 What factors should a teacher or coach be aware of when using extrinsic rewards?

9 Identify 3 disadvantages of extrinsic motivation.

10 If a performer is intrinsically motivated will the introduction of extrinsic reward enhance motivation? Discuss whether you agree or disagree.

11 Explain three ways to develop intrinsic motivation.

12 What is meant by an interactionist view of motivation?

chapter 21

Requirements and Assessment of the Individual Project at AS

The following chapters give details about the optional project component of the Assessment and Qualifications Alliance (AQA) Sport and Physical Education course. Although this section is specifically aimed at the AQA examination, the principles applied could be adopted for a variety of extended pieces of work where similar criteria are required. For example, the project course work component of Edexcel's Physical Education course.

This chapter gives a brief overview of the requirements for the project at AS and information about the method of assessment. The remaining chapters deal in more general terms with aspects of good practice regarding development of an extended piece of research. Guidance is also given for addressing the assessment criteria effectively.

The individual project – a general overview

If you choose this course work option from the AQA specification, you will be given the opportunity to complete a sport related project investigation linked to any area of the Sport and Physical Education specification. You will be expected to observe a sports performer of your choice and analyse their strengths and weaknesses, (two activities at AS). Based on your observations and evaluation you will be expected to devise a method to improve the performance for one of the activities you observed. In so doing you will complete 30% of your course at AS. Provided you are motivated and work within the guidelines given this course work should go a long way to helping you achieve a good overall grade, and giving you some confidence before taking the final two papers. It is not therefore, something which you should attempt to 'rush off' in a week (especially as your staff will be marking your planning!).

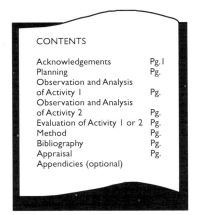

CONTENTS

Fig. 21.1   Specified format for the
project at AS level

AS Project requirements

The project should be at least 1,000 words in length (7 – 8 sides of A4). AQA have specified a format which should be adopted. This is dealt with in the following chapters, but the headings are given in fig 21.1.

Your completed work is assessed by your teachers. A representative sample of the work carried out in your school or college is then sent to an external moderator, who compares this work from other centres and hopefully confirms the marks awarded by your teachers.

Your teachers will base their assessment on specific criteria laid down by AQA. You should ask them for an up-to-date version of these criteria. At the time of writing (2002), there are 23 criteria, arranged into 7 groups at AS, and the marks available for each group will depend on the number of criteria within it. It would be a good idea to become familiar with these groupings before starting work, so that you gain an overall impression of the requirements. It will also be necessary to refer back to these pages as you progress.

The AS criteria groups are:

1 Planning
2 Observation (2 activities)
3 Analysis (2 activities)
4 Evaluation (1 activity)
5 Method
6 Bibliography
7 Communication

The remainder of this chapter explains the criteria group headings in more detail.

Planning

You will be awarded marks for evidence of your planning throughout the development of your project, so this needs to be demonstrated. This may be achieved in part through discussion with your tutor, but something more tangible will be required. At AS this means you will have to plan a timetable to complete all of the project tasks (see table 29.1). In addition you will need to prepare some data collection sheets to use during your observation of the two different activities. The planning stage of the project development will greatly affect the outcome. In addition to outlining what you hope to achieve, and how you intend to achieve it, you should also show that you are prepared to modify your initial plans in the light of subsequent developments.

Project brief

Although a project brief is not a compulsory requirement of the course work it will help you to formulate your ideas, and gives you something concrete to discuss with staff. A project brief is a summary of your intended project, giving information on the title, anticipated outline, subject for observation etc.

Table 20.1   Project
Development Plan (AS)

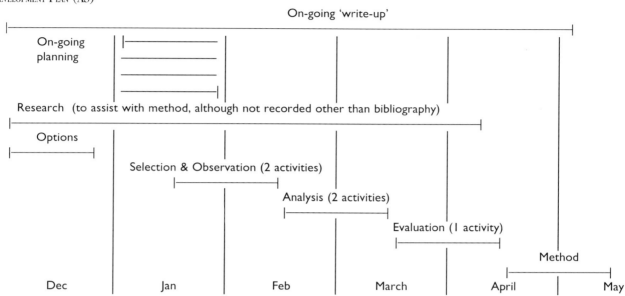

Observation and analysis

Once you have decided who to observe and planned the session to ensure you get a clear indication of the performer's strengths and weaknesses, you run or organise the session. In this section marks are awarded for using appropriate data collection sheets, for accurately recording your observations and for making an appropriate analysis of the performer's major strengths and faults.

Evaluation

You need to evaluate the quality of the performance you observed and give a brief discussion of some of the factors that may be responsible for the level of performance. You also need to select an area of weakness to improve and justify its selection.

Reporting of method

You should access appropriate books, journals etc to help you develop a method to improve the weaknesses you identified in your evaluation. You must then write up your method to improve performance. You should take care to give a precise account of the method employed, so that someone else could replicate the procedure if they wished.

References/ Bibliography

This section should contain a record of the publications used. There are several recognised ways in which to record sources used:

For a text book:
Author/s (Year) *Title*, where published: publisher.
Coolican, H. (1990) *Research Methods and Statistics in Psychology*, London: Hodder & Stoughton.

For a journal:
Author/s (Year) Title of article. *Journal*, Volume No, Pages.
Biddle, S. Mitchell, J. Armstrong, N. (1991) The assessment of physical activity in children. *British Journal of Physical Education, Research Supplement*, 10, 4–8.

Before adopting an approach check with your tutor in case a specific method is required.
    The important point about this section is that:

- it should be accurate, ie, you have actually used the articles/books that you list
- it should be possible to obtain the referenced material from the information given
- it should be in alphabetical order (on author's name).

Communication

To score highly on this section you will need to ensure that your project:

- is well written
- is clearly presented – neatly written or word processed

If word processed, the text should:

- be well spaced (1.5 line spacing)
- have a reasonable sized font (point 12, Times New Roman)
- be spell checked and proofread.

In addition the report will need to be well organised. If you follow the guidelines contained in this section, including the headings given this should satisfy the criteria. Examiners/ moderators also normally appreciate inclusion of appropriate diagrams, sketches, graphs, charts, tables, etc; but they must enhance and support the report, rather than merely adding bulk.

    In addition you will be expected to demonstrate orally your understanding of the work you have undertaken. At various points through the completion of your project, you will probably be involved in individual interviews with your tutor. During these sessions, it is important that you convince your tutor that you are knowledgeable about the work you are undertaking, have been actively researching information and understand the concepts involved.

    Further detail on each of the groupings may be found in the following chapters.

chapter 22

Planning

This chapter discusses the planning aspects of developing a research project. Planning is obviously vital at the start of any activity, but it should be remembered that the whole of the project development should be considered, and plans modified when necessary.

There are many approved methods of carrying out empirical research, and while they are not all identical, there appears to be a common consensus about the overall stages that should be employed. Before planning can really begin, an understanding of the task ahead is essential so that it can be broken down into manageable stages. The basic steps that should be followed are outlined in fig 22.1.

Identifying the research problem

The first stage as indicated in fig 22.1 is to identify the research problem. In other words you know that you have to carry out some research, but on what? What do you want to do the project on? One of the most difficult aspects regarding the project is deciding what to study; what at first seems to be a straightforward task, becomes complex. Faced with the problem of becoming committed to a specific idea, it is easy to put off the inevitable in the hope that inspiration will come, but unfortunately you could have a long wait! While it is good that you are not restricted in your choice of study (other than to the specification), this does present you with a vast choice and makes your decision harder.

In an attempt to get started, it is often helpful to break this first stage down into smaller tasks as shown in fig 22.2. A good starting point is to identify the areas of the course that are of specific interest to you. In order to do this:

- read through the specification and your course work notes to date and 'grade' each of the sections and subsections (don't forget the areas of the specification still to be covered);
- extend table 22.1, listing in rank order, your 'top ten' in terms of areas of interest from the specification.

The area of study is obviously important, as you could be working on your project over a 6 month period for AS, (see table 21.1 for a suggested timetable). You should choose something that you will be interested in, and not something that someone else thinks will be a good idea.

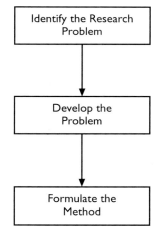

Fig. 22.1   Tasks associated with identifying the research problem

Specification Area	Topic	Rank Order	Taught By
eg Module I Physiological factors affecting performance	Body types, physique and involvement in sport	I	JS
Module I Psychological factors affecting performance	Personality & relationship to performance in sport	2	CP
Module 3 Analysis & evaluation of the factors which improve performance	Principles of training	3	JS

Table 22.1   Syllabus 'Top Ten'

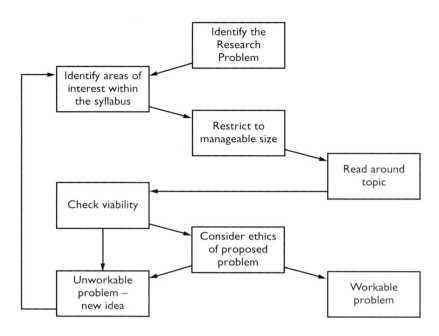

Fig. 22.2   REFINING THE TOPIC

Scale refers to the size of the problem to be addressed. You should try to limit your investigation to a specific question. For example, rather than the effects of fatigue on performance in tennis, this can be scaled down to the effects of fatigue on accuracy of the tennis serve.

Developing the research problem

Having established some areas of the syllabus of interest, you need to consider each in turn in order to determine whether they can be applied to the research problem; in other words would this topic allow you to address the assessment criteria? Reconsider table 30.1: would any of the three topics be appropriate? Hopefully you will have discounted topics 1 and 2 due to the difficulty of implementing a method based on them. For example, under topic 1 you might decide to observe a year 9 shot putter. Your observation of his or her performance might reveal that their poor distance is due to their ectomorphic somatotype. A method to alter their body type and thus improve performance is likely to be impossible, and unethical, therefore this topic is clearly unmanageable. Similarly with topic 2 you might decide that someone needs a complete change of personality to be successful and however desirable this might be it presents the same problems as the previous topic!

Topic 3 however would be manageable if you felt the performance was poor due to lack of fitness. A training programme could be developed and followed, applying appropriate training principles.

Re-examine your areas of interest and check that they could be applied correctly to the course work problem. You should also bear in mind that at AS there is no need to implement your method.

Don't be afraid to start – write down your general ideas as they arise: however vague or confused these are, they can be refined or discarded later on. If you try to create the perfect sentence to describe your ideas, you are unlikely to write anything at all. Once you have something written down, it can be shown to staff or discussed with other students. In this way your initial ideas can be sorted and refined.

When you have established the area of the specification to work within, it will now need refinement. Although the project must ultimately be your own work, the more discussion you have with others at this stage the better. Therefore try to address the following questions with someone else as you will benefit from hearing their ideas and points of view.

Is the scale of the project appropriate? (If the scale or scope is too broad the study will be too large to research in depth.) Look at table 22.3. Which research areas are appropriate or inappropriate in terms of scale?

Table 22.2 DEVELOPMENT OF SPECIFICATION AREA OF INTEREST

RANK ORDER FROM TABLE 22.1	APPLICATION
3 Training Principles	Devise training programme to improve fitness, and as a direct result, performance.

Table 22.3 SCALE OF TOPICS

• factors affecting performance in a gymnastic routine	[appropriate/inappropriate]
• organisation of training sessions to improve performance	[appropriate/inappropriate]
• use of extrinsic motivation in football to improve performance	[appropriate/inappropriate]
• use of training programmes to improve all-round performance	[appropriate/inappropriate]

Fig. 22.3 REFINING THE TOPIC

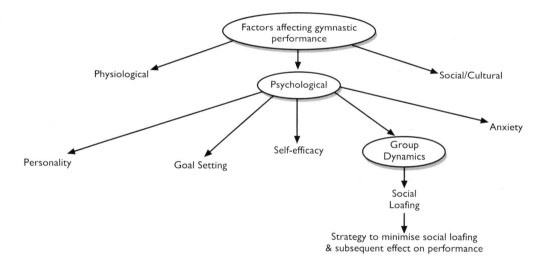

Although all of the examples given in table 22.3 could be used as the basis of a study, none could be used as they stand at the moment; some obviously need more work than others in order to arrive at a manageable area to research.

Refining the initial topic can be difficult; you could try to create levels and increase the focus of the topic at each level for the topics shown in table 22.3 (the first is done for you in fig 22.3). Apply this method to refine the topic you ranked at number 1 in table 22.2 so that the final level focuses on a particular question or issue that reflects what you would like to investigate.

Experimental design is the method you devise to test your hypothesis; ie, the situation you set up so that you can collect data to support your initial prediction.

Formulating the hypothesis

Your next step is to establish whether your idea is viable. To help you check this you need to form a draft hypothesis and experimental design. These are dealt with in more detail in the following chapter; all you need at present is an idea of the question you want to ask (the research problem), your predicted outcome to the question (hypothesis) and the experimental design you will use to test your prediction. An example is given in table 22.4. Extend this table with the information relating to your topic.

Although you will probably alter your hypothesis and design in the light of further research, this is an important part of the process. Failure to establish that your idea asks a valid question and is measurable at this stage could result in a waste of your time.

TABLE 22.4   RESEARCH QUESTION, HYPOTHESIS & DESIGN

RESEARCH PROBLEM	PREDICTED OUTCOME (DRAFT HYPOTHESIS)	DESIGN OUTLINE
Effects of extrinsic motivation on optimising performance	A series of rewards from a significant other will have a positive effect on performance	devise 'measure' of performance ; devise graded programme of rewards with performer, reward desired performance behaviour over time; re-evaluate performance

Although you obviously do not want to decide exactly what you are going to work on to improve a performance before you have even seen it, you will at least have some ideas about what might affect performance, and whether it is within your scope to investigate further. Information of this kind at your finger tips will be invaluable to you, and not wasted effort, as it can be put to good use in the synoptic course work (A2) where you have to apply a number of the specification areas to a performance.

You should consider the following before progressing further:

- Is there available literature on the topic? Your staff, school/college or local library staff might know where to look. You could browse through references and recommended reading books.
- Are there likely to be any organisations you could approach for information? You will need to be careful here though as many organisations (especially the Football Association) receive so many requests for information that they are usually unable to respond.
- Can you get the information you need from media sources (eg, newspapers, radio, television)?
- Who do you know who can help? If you are involved with a good standard sports club, are there people with the expertise you require (especially in terms of 'volunteers' for observation)?

To summarise:

1 What data/information do you need to collect?
2 Can it be collected?
3 How will you collect it?

If your response to these questions relies solely on someone else, or you cannot answer some of the questions, you should probably reconsider your topic and select another option from table 22.2. If however you feel your idea is still viable, the final task relating to this first stage is to ensure your project does not pose an ethical problem.

Ethical considerations

When conducting research, you need to be aware of a variety of ethical issues. The most relevant ethical areas for you to avoid are:

- plagiarism
- fabrication and falsification of data and information
- selective use of data
- inappropriate use of subjects.

The first three areas will be dealt with in turn at a later stage. At this point of the development process however, the fourth area should be considered in more detail. Most projects will involve the use of volunteers, who will place a large amount of trust in you to treat them fairly, psychologically as well as physically. The following titles are all related to the syllabus, but would be rejected on the grounds that they are potentially unethical. Why do you think they are considered unethical?

- Use of alcohol to reduce pre-match tension
- Use of an intensive weight training programme to increase leg strength of 11 year-old male sprinters
- Use of caffeine tablets to enhance performance
- Use of creatine to aid strength development
- Use of maximum heart rate to calculate training intensity for 0–50s squash team
- Use of an abusive audience in training to prepare for playing 'away'
- Sole use of negative feedback to improve performance.

See table 30.5 for reasons for rejection. In addition to the points emphasised from the above examples, you should also ensure:

- that you comply with any guidelines given by your school/college
- that where a physical session is taking place, there is a properly qualified coach taking the session or close at hand
- that any practice is safe, especially when in a potentially dangerous situation or if using potentially dangerous equipment: eg, diving or martial arts sessions, cycling road races, use of gymnastic apparatus, use of trampolines, use of javelin, etc.
- that the title does not imply racial or sexual discrimination.

Once satisfied that your project is ethical you should be in a position to begin your work on developing the research problem (stage 2, fig 22.1). If you are still experiencing difficulty in choosing a project, some suggested titles from the specification areas are given in Appendix 1A.

TABLE 22.5   ETHICAL PROBLEMS POSED BY TITLES

Use of alcohol to reduce pre-match tension	involves administration of drugs
Use of an intensive weight training programme to increase leg strength of 11 year-old male sprinters	subject/s still physically developing, therefore strength training should be avoided as it could lead to physical damage/injury
Use of caffeine tablets to enhance performance	involves administering drugs
Use of creatine to aid strength development	involves administering drugs
Use of maximum heart rate to calculate training intensity for the 0–50's squash team	not appropriate to inflict high intensity exercise on 'older' groups from a safety point of view
Use of an abusive audience in training to prepare for playing 'away'	could be psychologically damaging for subject/s
Sole use of negative feedback to improve performance	very discouraging for the subject/s – may totally de-motivate them

You should now have some idea of:

- what interests you
- what is feasible in terms of the course work problem.

You now need to find an appropriate performance to work with! Ideally you would observe any performance, establish the weaknesses of that performer and then set about devising a means to strengthen their performance. In reality however, you might be more successful if you decide on your areas of strength (in terms of the specification theory) and then match this with the appropriate subject!

chapter 23

Observation, Analysis and Evaluation

This chapter discusses how to select your performer/s and activity/activities for observation. Possible methods of analysis are given, before considering the evaluation.

Observation and Analysis

Lesson plans and pre-test proformas, as mentioned in the planning section, should be prepared before attempting this aspect of the project.

As previously mentioned your first problem is to decide who to observe. It might be helpful to consider the following points before making this decision:

- **What activities am I interested in?**
  Choose an activity that is of interest to you. You might be very knowledgeable about squash, for example, but no longer be interested in playing it, therefore you would probably be better off selecting another activity that you enjoy more.

- **What activities do I coach, play, or do I know anything about?**
  You will need to analyse a performer's strengths and weaknesses. This is obviously much easier if you are already familiar with the required techniques/tactics of a particular activity. If you are not already involved in coaching, volunteer, your powers of observation and analysis will improve with practice.

- **What performers could I get access to?**
  Do you play in a club? Do any of your friends/family play an activity you could observe? It is better to use someone other than class mates as they will have their own studies to complete and may not have the time available to help you

- **What link am I hoping to make with the specification?**
  You might have already decided that you want to investigate effects of fitness on performance, therefore to make the project more feasible you should really select a subject who you know lacks fitness (from earlier observations).

Use your responses to these points to complete Table 23.1

Table 23.1 YOUR POTENTIAL SUBJECTS

What sports/activities am I interested in?	
Delete any activity from this list that you: intend to study at A2 belongs to the same category as the activity you intend to study at A2	
Which of the remaining activities do you coach/feel confident you could coach?	
Who do you know who plays these sports/activities?	
Who from this list would be a reliable subject?	
Which of these performers are you most likely to be able to help?	

You now have your subjects!

Once you have established their willingness to help and explained the possible commitment required from them, you should prepare for the session/s you wish to observe. Initially you should observe a match/training session to establish the performers' strengths and weaknesses. It is vital that you have some way of objectively measuring **performance**. This will help in your evaluation.

There are many different ways of conducting an analysis of performance. Think about the activities below, and how they are analysed by 'experts' on television.

TENNIS
Aspects used for analysis:

FOOTBALL
Aspects used for analysis:

BASKETBALL
Aspects used for analysis:

Hopefully you will have identified typical match statistics as:

- number of aces
- points won on first serve
- unforced errors and so on for tennis
- percentage of possession
- number of corners etc in football
- fouls
- free throws
- offensive and defensive moves etc in basketball.

Your analysis is likely to focus on one performer, and be more in-depth than the examples given above. You might decide to use a video so that you can repeatedly review the performance. This is a good idea if you are only focusing on one skill, but might be time-consuming if the performance is extended. Whether live or recorded you are trying to establish:

- what the performer can do
- what the performer has difficulty in doing
- what the performer omits
- what effects the above have on performance.

Example match analysis sheets can be found in appendix 2A.

In addition to completing your analysis of the technical/tactical aspects of the performance, it is also a good idea to consider some of the physiological, psychological and sociological factors which may affect the quality of the performance so that you can record your observations on these areas as well. For example, a tennis player may not play the most appropriate shot for any of the following reasons:

- they are technically unable to do so
- they lack the necessary confidence
- they lack the fitness to get into position to play the shot
- they lack the necessary motivation to make the effort, etc.

By making brief notes on these aspects at the time of the observation you can refer to them, if appropriate, during your evaluation.

In your analysis you should list the major strengths and weaknesses and explain why they are considered as such within a performance situation. E.g. a badminton player may lack power making it difficult for them to return shots effectively from the back of the court. Once the performance has been analysed it can be evaluated.

Evaluation

Having completed the observation and analysis, **one** of the activities needs to be evaluated. This involves six tasks:

1 placing the performance in the context of other performers
2 discussing the variety of factors which may account for the quality of the performance
3 rank ordering the faults of the performance
4 justifying why certain aspects of the performance should be worked on before others
5 research appropriate sources of information to assist with devising method to improve performance
6 devise a method to improve performance.

1 Placing the performance in the context of other performers

This aspect of the project serves two purposes. It provides the examiners and moderators who will look at your work, the opportunity to assess the relevance of your fault correction. In addition, by discussing the quality of other performances you can lead into a discussion of your performer. For example, by discussing the technical/tactical ability of a performer who has achieved a better standard than your performer you can use this to outline your performer's weaknesses and conversely you can discuss your performer's strengths by comparing higher performance to a weaker performer.

To achieve this you should give some background information about the performer, for example, a paragraph about:

- the level they play at, recreational, club, county etc
- how often they play
- their 'history' of representation.

Thus you are attempting to give an idea of where your performer will 'fit' in the broader picture.

Fig. 23.1

Once you have identified where you think they will fit, a brief explanation of why you have placed them in this position should complete the requirements for this aspect of the assessment.

2 Discussing the variety of factors which may account for the quality of the performance

This is where you demonstrate your ability to apply the theory work you have been covering to a practical situation. You should take each section of the specification and look for possible reasons to explain the quality of the performance. Some examples are given in Table 23.2. Read through these and then try to extend the table for each of the areas, in relation to the performer you are observing. Access to a copy of the specification would be helpful to complete this task. (NB. AS students should only consider modules 1, 2 and 3.)

As mentioned previously it is a good idea to broaden your observation to look out for some of these additional factors that may affect performance. You should identify as many as possible from across the AS specification, but you do not need to discuss them in any great depth at this stage.

3 Rank ordering the faults of the performance

You need to consider all the weaknesses you recorded during your observation and place them in order of importance, ie, the faults causing the most problem should be at the top of the list, whereas those factors having little or no effect on performance should appear last.

Table 23.2   FACTORS AFFECTING PERFORMANCE

MODULE AREA	POSSIBLE FACTORS AFFECTING PERFORMANCE	POSSIBLE FACTORS AFFECTING PERFORMANCE: BASED ON OBSERVED PERFORMER
1. Physiological and psychological factors which improve performance	• lack of fitness (this can be broken down to the appropriate components of fitness) • learning plateau • stage of learning • inappropriate structure of training sessions	
2. Socio-cultural and historical effects on participation in physical activity and their influence on performance	• type of school • PE curriculum • socio-economic group • race • gender	
3. Analysis and evaluation of the factors which improve performance	• type of training • amount of training • methods of training	
4. Physiological, biomechanical and psychological factors which optimise performance	• gender • arousal levels • anxiety • self-efficacy • learned helplessness • poor biomechanical technique • attitudes	
5. Factors affecting the nature and development of élite performance	• financial pressure • cultural influences • levels of aggression • sponsorship • organisation of sport • country	
6. Analysis and critical evaluation of the factors which optimise performance	• stress • stress management techniques • goal setting	

4 Justifying why certain aspects of the performance should be worked on before others

Once you have rank ordered the recorded faults from the observation you need to explain why you have placed them in the order you have. For example, you may have observed a squash player. He or she may have many faults with his/her technique and be lacking in motivation and fitness. You might feel that if you could improve the technique so he/she was more successful that this would help with motivation. Once motivated you might feel that the player would then engage in some appropriate training. Thus you would consider the technical side of the performance first, and work on that before addressing issues of motivation and fitness levels. You would then consider the technical faults and establish which were having the greatest effect. For example you may have noticed that the player fails to play a straight forehand drive due to poor body position and that, although effective, his/her drop shot is technically poor. Rather than work on the drop shot, which is effective, your priority would be to work on the body position for the drive.

5 Research appropriate sources of information to assist with devising method to improve performance.

It is very important that you base your method to improve performance on relevant theory. In other words through completing the project you are demonstrating your in-depth understanding of an area of the specification. To acquire this in-depth knowledge you will need to consult appropriate texts, journals, the internet and so on.

6 Devise a method to improve performance.

Once you have carried out some research you should be able to put together a plan to improve the quality of the performance you observed. You will be marked on the appropriateness of your method. It is very important that you evidence your research through a bibliography and that this research uses a selection of resource material, ie. text books, internet, journals etc.

TASK	COMPLETED ✔	STILL TO DO ✘
Selected performer		
Planned session for analysis		
Prepared analysis sheets		
Considered factors which may affect performance		
Evaluated performance		
Research associated with identified faults/weaknesses		
Devised method to enhance performance		

Table 23.3 PROGRESS REPORT

chapter 24

Method

A lthough it is only at A2 that the method is implemented, you do need to be aware of some of the different experimental designs that can be employed, as students at AS will still need to record an appropriate method and design, even if it is not implemented. It is likely therefore that you will need to adopt a repeated measures design.

Experimental Group

Carry out Pre-test

Pre-test data

Conduct experiment

Carry out Post-test

Post-test data

Comparison of results from both tests. (As the subjects are the same, providing irrelevant variables are controlled, changes in score could be attributed to the effect of the independent variable).

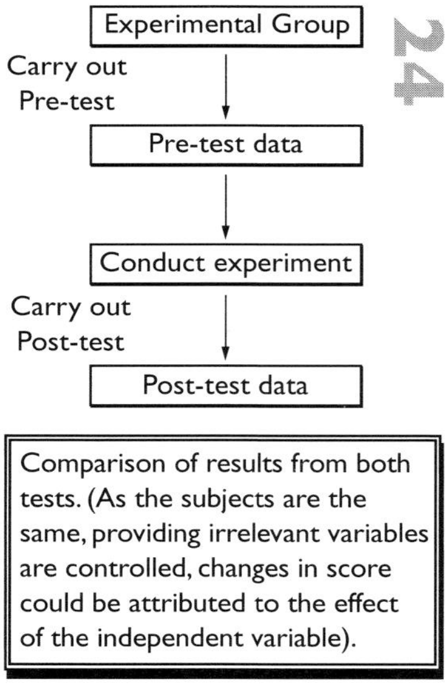

Fig. 24.1 REPEATED MEASURES DESIGN

Experimental designs

These may be categorised into related or unrelated designs, which refer to the subjects used:

- **Related designs** – when the same subjects are used for the whole of the experiment (repeated measures); when this isn't appropriate, 'doubles' are used. Subjects are matched with another using relevant criteria – one completing one part of the experiment while their double completes the other (matched pairs).
- **Unrelated designs** – when no attempt is made to match subjects. They might involve just one subject (single subject design), or groups who have not been matched (independent samples).

Each design type has its own advantages and disadvantages. You need to select the most appropriate for your experiment to ensure you obtain data relevant to your hypothesis.

Repeated measures

In this type of design the experimental group are tested before and after the experimental treatment (see fig 24.1). For example, if investigating the possible effect of a stress management programme on performance of set shots during match situations, performance will be tested before starting the programme and then again once the programme has been completed. Data is collected from the same group twice in the form of a pre- and post-test.

The main disadvantage of this test is that the subjects may improve their performance due to practice. This is potentially overcome by counterbalancing: one of the possible ways of achieving this is shown in fig 24.2. (Although in the example given counterbalancing would not be an option.)

Matched pairs

This method has the advantage that different subjects are used in each condition, therefore the data obtained will not be affected by practice. It does present other problems though: you must ensure that each member of group A is matched with a subject in group B. Careful selection of subjects is therefore required, plus an understanding of the important variables for the experiment.

An example of the design is shown in fig 24.3. A possible experimental hypothesis for this type of design would be that distributive practice will be more effective than massed practice

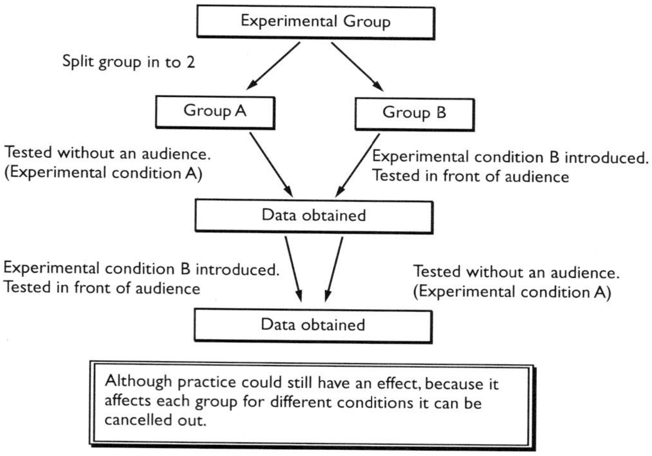

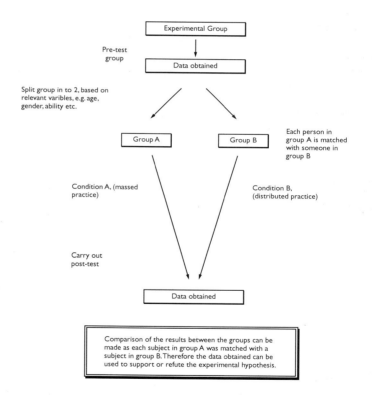

Fig. 24.2 REPEATED MEASURES DESIGN USING COUNTERBALANCING. ALTHOUGH PRACTICE COULD STILL HAVE AN EFFECT, IT CAN BE CANCELLED OUT BECAUSE IT AFFECTS EACH GROUP FOR DIFFERENT CONDITIONS

in improving the success rate of basketball lay-ups. In other words, it provides the opportunity to measure the effects of more than one condition.

Fig. 24.3 MATCHED PAIRS. COMPARISON OF THE RESULTS BETWEEN THE GROUPS CAN BE MADE AS EACH SUBJECT IN GROUP A WAS MATCHED WITH A SUBJECT IN GROUP B. THEREFORE THE DATA OBTAINED CAN BE USED TO SUPPORT OR REFUTE THE EXPERIMENTAL HYPOTHESIS

Independent samples

This design involves the use of two different groups of subjects who have not been specifically matched. The advantages here are that it saves time trying to find 'like pairs' of subjects, and means there will be no practice or order effect. The obvious disadvantage is that the data obtained may be due to the independent variable or due to the differences in the individuals between the groups. One way of attempting to overcome this problem would be to allocate subjects at random to each of the groups, although this might still be ineffective.

Writing up the method section

At first this might appear to be a less significant part of the project, and consequently one which does not require as much attention. This is not the case! Writing up your method provides the reader with information about your design and an explanation of the design decisions that you have made. Thus not only will you be gathering marks for your write up in this section, but also for your choice of method, ie, the means by which you attempted to gain the necessary data to support your hypothesis.

The method section can be presented in continuous format, or broken down into separate sub-headings. Whichever format you prefer you should ensure that it contains the following information:

Operational definitions

These are not always necessary, but it is a good idea to look at the dependent variable (the area of weakness) in your research/experiment hypothesis and decide if it requires defining in this way. For example one person's evaluation of the following terms would be different to another's:

- a quality shot in Tennis
- inappropriate level of fitness
- poor attitude towards performance.

Therefore definitions are given to increase understanding. The independent variable (aspect you are trying to improve to bring about an improvement in performance) does not normally require an operational definition as a greater explanation of it is automatically given when writing up the method section.

An outline of the design adopted

You need to state the nature of the experimental design. Why did you select this particular research method and what were the conditions that the research was carried out under? What are the independent and dependent variables? What irrelevant variables have you managed to control? (If you want to measure the effect of the independent variable, remove the potential irrelevant variables; you need therefore to identify them and then control their effects by keeping them out of the project where possible.) What irrelevant variables could not be controlled? (There will be some beyond your control. If you are aware of them, their possible effects can be examined in the discussion section of the project.)

Irrelevant Variable

These are variables which are irrelevant to the investigation, but which might have an effect. For example the weather would be irrelevant to a study concerned with the effectiveness of types of practice and distance thrown in the javelin. However although irrelevant it could affect the results of the study if the pre-test session was held on a calm day, and the post-test session on a very windy day. This irrelevant variable would need to be controlled, possibly by carrying out the tests at the same time, or by moving the tests inside.

Try to remember that this section should not give details about how the data was collected, but why it was collected in the manner it was. It should outline the design decisions that you made so that you could collect data appropriate to your hypothesis. Even though you do not implement the method at AS you should include this type of detail. You are demonstrating your knowledge of the process you should adopt.

Outlining equipment, materials and resources

You need to include sufficient detail so that the investigation could be replicated; leave out unnecessary detail which states the obvious. For example, detail regarding the number of basketballs required would be useful, but information about the pencil the researcher uses to record the scores would not! Specifications of specific equipment should be given and if commercial items are used the source of such items should be listed (eg, Multi-Stage Fitness Test, Loughborough University). If conducting an experiment, a diagram or photograph of the lay-out might also be useful.

A precise and full account of the procedure adopted

The procedure should be described with sufficient clarity that the experiment could be duplicated accurately by the reader. Try to describe exactly what should happen from the start of the experiment to the finish. The most common problem here is lack of relevant detail. Include any standardised instructions, ie, any instructions to be given to each participant, or those participants within a specific group. For example, if teaching a lay-up shot in basketball using massed and distributed practice, what common coaching points would be given to the performers? Exactly what format would the practice sessions take? Would all performers be present at the same time? If not, where would they be? You must ensure the reader is left in no doubt about the procedure that should be adopted.

The bulk of the information for this part of the project should already be available to you from the planning stages. It might be necessary however, to alter some of your initial plans in the light of research you carried out whilst compiling the literature review. For example you might have decided to investigate the effects of an audience on an accuracy task, believing that your subject would perform better if trained in front of a large audience. Further research as a result of compiling the review may have thrown some doubts on your original beliefs. As a consequence you may decide to alter your design, selecting a small supportive audience to begin with before progressing onto a larger, unknown audience, now that you have a greater awareness of the variables that can influence your results. This is to be expected so don't worry if your design has changed since the planning stage.

The experimental design and procedure should be written in standard academic prose – in the third person and past tense. For example, rather than writing:

I instructed the player to hit the twenty golf balls to get the ball to stop as close to the marker as possible. Then I measured the distance of each ball from the marker.

a more acceptable format would be:

The subject was instructed to hit 20 golf balls using his normal swing, so that the ball came to rest as close to the marker as possible. The distance of each ball from the marker was then measured.

Explain why the method would bring about desired outcomes.

The final section should be devoted to an explanation of why you think the method you have devised would result in an improvement in the areas of weakness you identified in your evaluation. For example, if you identified lack of strength resulting in poor overhead clears (badminton), you may have devised a strength training programme. The final section of your project should then explain how the method would result in increased strength, and how this would improve performance.

 **ACTIVITY 1** **Check your progress, by filling in table 33.1**

Table 24.1 PROGRESS REPORT

Task	Completed ✓	Still To Do ✗
stated research hypothesis arising from research		
considered irrelevant variables		
recorded main items of equipment/resources required		
written up the procedure to improve performance IN DETAIL		
explained why the method would bring about the desired outcome		

chapter 25

The Final Stages

Bibliography

This should be recorded after your method section. Details regarding the format of the bibliography are given on page 395.

Project completion

Before handing in the final version of your work make a couple of final checks:

- It is neat – even if it is word processed this does not necessarily mean the work is neat. Check you have used the same font size and spacing throughout, and that you have not added any hand written labels where you could have used a computer package.
- It is well written – flowing text, and no typing or spelling errors.
- It is well organised – a good idea is to follow the order of the assessment criteria, or the order given in this book.
- It has a variety of appropriate illustrations throughout – for example, you might include photographs of aspects of the observation of performance, diagrams or photographs of the method to be implemented.

Once you are satisfied, it is time to hand the work in (and probably start your revision!).

Further reading

H Coolican, *Research Methods and Statistics in Psychology* (Hodder & Stoughton, 1990)
MD Gall, WR Borg, JP Gall, *Educational Research, An Introduction* 6th edition (Longman, 1996)
JR Thomas, JC Nelson, *Research Methods in Physical Activity* 3rd edition (Human Kinetics, 1996)

Suggested Project Titles

Module I
- The effects of plyometric training on the performance of a line out in rugby
- Use of plyometric training to improve jumping ability of volleyball players
- Reduction in unforced errors in a game of badminton due to training
- Use of aerobic training to increase VO_2 max in cyclists
- Improvement in mid-field play due to increased aerobic fitness

- Use of feedback to improve performance of a complex skill
- Use of visual and verbal guidance to improve technique
- Use of distributed practice to teach the high serve to a novice player
- Use of massed practice to optimise performance
- Consideration of changing the organisation of training sessions to improve performance
- Increasing confidence to optimise performance.

Module 2
- Opportunity to participate and its effect on performance
- Positive discrimination and its effect on performance
- Provision and its effects on performance

NB: Module 2 titles are best studied at AS level where it is not necessary to implement your intended 'method' to improve performance.

Module 3
- Planning an exercise programme to improve performance
- Use of interval training to improve speed
- Use of circuit training to improve games play
- Use of mobility training to improve performance in gymnastics

Appendix 1B

Example match analysis sheets for squash

1 Analysis of basic shots

Every shot played by the performer is recorded during each rally. + equals a good shot, − equals a poor shot.

BASIC SHOT	FOREHAND	BACKHAND
Service		
Straight drive		
Cross-court drive		
Boast		
Volley		
Drop shot		

This type of analysis gives information on the 'quality' of the shots played, and the frequency of their use, thus you can establish if the performer is avoiding playing a particular shot, or overuses a shot.

2 Analysis of winning shots

In addition to recording the score the winning shot is also recorded.

PLAYER 1	PLAYER 2	EXPLANATION
OR	(FH)	Player 1 starts the game and serves from the right hand side of the court. Player 2 wins the rally
	OR (FHB)	Player 2 wins the rally with a forehand boast
	1L (FHX)	Player 2 wins the rally with a forehand cross-court drive
(BHD)	2R	Player 1 wins the rally with a backhand drive
OR	(FHB)	Player 2 wins the rally with a forehand boast
	2R (FHV)	Player 1 wins the rally with a forehand volley
	3L (FHV)	Player 1 wins the rally with a forehand volley
	4R	....

Player 2 wins a lot of the initial rallies on the forehand side of the court. If this were to continue throughout the game Player 1 would be advised to keep the ball on his/her opponent's backhand side, thus playing on their opponent's weaker side. If you were coaching Player 2, although pleased at their victory, you might use this information to suggest a weakness on their backhand side and work on this in subsequent sessions.

This type of analysis can be extended by recording the shots of the player being analysed, whether they win the rally or not. If analysing Player 1 for example the table would record his/her final losing shot, rather than Player 2's winning shot:

Player 1	Player 2	Explanation
OR (–FHD)		Player 1 starts the game and serves from the right hand side of the court. Player 1 plays a loose forehand drop, allowing Player 2 to play a winning shot
(–FH)	OR	Player 2 serves, Player 1 plays a poor length forehand drive, allowing Player 2 to play a winning shot
(–BHX)	1L	Player 2 serves, Player 1 plays a poor width backhand cross-court drive, allowing Player 2 to play a winning shot
(+BHX)	2R	Player 2 serves, Player 1 plays a good length backhand drive to win the rally
OR (–BHX)		Player 1 serves, Player 1 plays a poor length backhand cross-court drive, allowing Player 2 to play a winning shot
(–FHD)	2R	Player 2 serves, Player 1 plays a loose forehand drop, allowing player 2 to play a winning shot
(–BHX)	3L	Player 2 serves, Player 2 plays a poor width backhand cross-court drive, allowing Player 2 to play a winning shot
	4R	Player 2 serves, ...

NB: The explanation given above is there to explain the example, it would not be necessary to record this information during the game.

3. Style of play

You could record whether the player plays in an attacking or defensive manner. Attacking play in squash can be measured by recording the number of attacking shots played from the front of the court, (winning kills, dropshots or angled shots), whereas defensive play can be measured by recording shots played at the back of the court (lengths, widths, boasts and lobs). This can easily be applied to other activities once you have identified the appropriate attacking and defensive plays.

Fitness Test Ratings

The following tables gives test ratings for fitness tests described in Chapter 7.

Table A2.1 GRIP STRENGTH NORMS

CLASSIFICATION	NON-DOMINANT (KG)	DOMINANT (KG)
Women		
Excellent	>37	>41
Good	34–36	38–40
Average	22–33	25–37
Poor	18–21	22–24
Very poor	<18	<22
Men		
Excellent	>68	>70
Good	56–67	62–69
Average	43–55	48–61
Poor	39–42	41–47
Very Poor	<39	<41

For persons over 50yrs of age, reduce scores by 10%

Source: Data from Corbin, Lindsay and Tolson (1978) Concepts in Physical Education

Table A2.2 30M SPRINT TEST

TIME (SECS) MALE	TIME (SECS) FEMALE	RATING
<4.0	<4.5	excellent
4.2–4.0	4.6–4.5	good
4.4–4.3	4.8–4.7	average
4.6–4.5	5.0–4.9	fair
>4.6	>5.0	poor

Table A2.3   CLASSIFICATION OF AEROBIC FITNESS ($\dot{V}O_2$ MAX IN ML KG^1 MCN^1)

AGE YRS	LOW	FAIR	AVERAGE	GOOD	HIGH
Women					
20–29	<24	24–30	31–37	38–48	49+
30–39	<20	20–27	28–33	34–44	45+
40–49	<17	17–23	24–30	31–41	42+
50–59	<15	15–20	21–27	28–37	38+
60–69	<13	13–17	18–23	24–34	35+
Men					
20–29	<25	25–33	34–42	43–52	53+
30–39	<23	23–30	31–38	39–48	49+
40–49	<20	20–26	27–35	36–44	45+
50–59	<18	18–24	25–33	34–42	43+
60–69	<16	16–22	23–30	31–40	41+

Source: Data from American Heart Association (1972)

Table A2.4   NORMATIVE SCORES FOR THE ABDOMINAL CURL CONDITIONING TEST

STAGE	NUMBER OF SIT UPS	STANDARD	
	CUMULATIVE	MALE	FEMALE
1	20	poor	poor
2	42	poor	fair
3	64	fair	fair
4	89	fair	good
5	116	good	good
6	146	good	very good
7	180	excellent	excellent
8	217	excellent	excellent

Table A2.5   SIT AND REACH TEST RATINGS

MALE	FEMALE	RATING
>35	>39	excellent
31–34	33–38	good
27–30	29–32	fair
<27	<29	poor

Table A2.6   ILLINOIS AGILITY RUN TEST

TIME IN SECONDS		RATING
MALE	FEMALE	
<15.2	<17.0	excellent
16.1–15.2	17.9–17.0	good
18.1–16.2	21.7–18.0	average
18.3–18.2	23.0–21.8	fair
>18.3	>23	poor

Table A2.7 STICK DROP TEST

REACTION TIME	RATING
>42.5	excellent
37.1–42.5	good
29.6–37.0	average
22.0–29.5	fair
<22	poor

Table A2.8 VERTICAL JUMP TEST SCORES

DISTANCE (CMS) MALE	DISTANCE (CMS) FEMALE	RATING
>60	>47	excellent
51–59	36–46	good
41–50	29–35	average
27–40	25–34	poor
<26	<24	very poor

Index